The Ground You Stand Upon

Life of a Skytrooper in Vietnam

Joshua E. Bowe and Wilbur E. Bowe

Copyright © 2018 Joshua E. Bowe

Full-Color Hardcover ISBN: 978-0-692-14139-7 published June 2018, 2nd Edition ISBN: 978-0-578-54106-8 published July 2019, 3rd Edition published November 2019

Black & White Paperback ISBN: 978-1-717-99437-0 published July 2018, 2nd Edition ISBN: 978-1-079-02638-2 published July 2019, 3rd Edition published November 2019

E-Book ISBN: 978-0-692-11189-5, Kindle ASIN: B07DCJNN8X published May 2018, 2nd Edition published June 2019, 3rd Edition published November 2019

Audiobook ASIN: B07KFQ5W25, published November 2018

All rights reserved. No part of this book may be reproduced in any form or by any means, electronic, mechanical, photocopying, recording, or otherwise, without the written permission of the author, except for a reviewer, who may quote a brief passage in a review.

The author does not claim copyright to the photos included in this work as they were obtained from various sources, but requests that, if used, proper credit be given to the original owner as noted in caption. Unless otherwise noted in caption, all photos may be assumed to have been contributed by Wilbur Bowe or the subject of the photo.

Every effort has been made to trace copyright holders and to obtain their permission for use of copyright material. The author apologizes for any errors or omissions and would be grateful if notified of any corrections that should be incorporated into future editions of this book.

The following permissions have been obtained:

"Letter by Richard Cantale", from *DEAR AMERICA: Letters Home From Vietnam*, edited by Bernard Edelman. Copyright © 1985 by The Vietnam Veterans Memorial Commission. Used by permission of W.W. Norton & Company, Inc.

ASSOCIATED PRESS Photo 670211176, Catherine Leroy, photographer (photo of soldiers climbing down rope ladder from CH-47, Chapter 14)

Several articles from the 1st Air Cavalry Division's *Cavalair* newspaper appear reprinted in this book. The United States Army does not claim copyright on any of its material, but does request that proper credit be attributed to all Army photos and articles.

To request permission to use any part of this work, email the publisher at: joshbowe@hotmail.com.

Contents

5/7th Cavalry Areas of Operation 1966-1967 7

Prologue 12

1. The Letter 22
2. Army Life 27
3. Airmobile 53
4. Seasick 73
5. Sorry About That 81
6. Into the Jungle (Operation Roadrunner) 98
7. Air Assault (Operation Golden Bee) 119
8. The First to Fall (Operation Irving) 150
9. Deliver Us From Evil 170
10. Life and Death in the Jungle (Operation Thayer II) 187
11. Thanksgiving 215
12. The Best Day 228
13. The Outpost 245
14. Rumors (Operation Pershing) 256
15. Rest & Relaxation 289
16. The Crew Chief 326
17. Heart of Darkness 330
18. Amongst Friends and Strangers 351
19. The Final Patrol (Operation Greeley) 360
20. For What it Was 371
21. Homecoming 374

Acknowledgements 394
About the Authors 399
Bibliography 401
Glossary 404
Army Ranks 408
1st Air Cavalry Division Structure 410

It is a different type of war than we've ever fought. Even the weapons are new. Only the names of the fighting units are old: The 7th Cavalry, the 8th Cavalry... the 5th, the 12th, and the 9th. Regiments born and forged in the Indian wars that now ride into battle, through the skies. It is a different type of country than we've ever fought in. Now flat and sunken with rice paddies, now rolling with hills and meadows, now mountainous and steep. It is hot, it is humid, it is thick with plants and vines. It is largely unpopulated, and in the military sense, it belongs to no one. Not to Viet Cong who roam it, not to the South Vietnamese. It is no man's land. In Vietnam today, you will hold only the ground you stand upon.

-*John H. Secondari, The Saga of Western Man, 1965*

To obtain the audio version of this book narrated by Will Stauff, please visit www.audible.com

To obtain a printed version of this book, as well as information about related events, reviews, and a collection of additional photographs, please visit the following websites:

www.thegroundyoustandupon.org

www.facebook.com/thegroundyoustandupon.org

To submit any additional information or corrections, email the author at:

joshbowe@hotmail.com

Thank you for taking the time to read our story. Customer reviews are most appreciated, please leave your own review on Amazon!

7th Cavalry Regimental Crest

We are the pride of the Army and a regiment of great renown, our name's on the pages of history, from sixty-six on down.

If you think we stop or falter while into the fray we're going, just watch the steps with our heads erect, while our band plays Garry Owen.

In the Fighting Seventh's the place for me, it's the cream of all the Cavalry; no other regiment ever can claim its pride, honor, glory and undying fame.

We know no fear when stern duty calls us far away from home. Our country's flag shall safely o'er us wave, no matter where we roam.

'Tis the gallant 7th Cavalry, it matters not where we are going. Such you'll surely say as we march away; and our band plays Garry Owen.

In the Fighting Seventh's the place for me, it's the cream of all the Cavalry; no other regiment ever can claim its pride, honor, glory and undying fame.

Then hurrah for our brave commanders! Who led us into the fight. We'll do or die in our country's cause, and battle for the right.

And when the war is o'er, and to our home we're going, just watch the step, with our heads erect, when our band plays Garry Owen.

5/7TH CAVALRY AREAS OF OPERATION 1966-1967

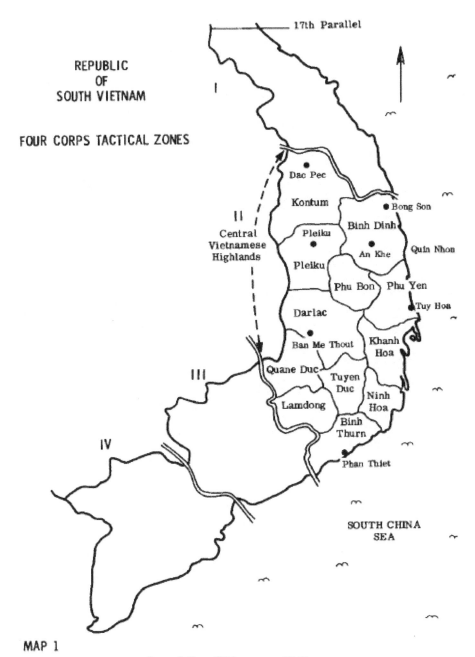

Republic of Vietnam, II Corps

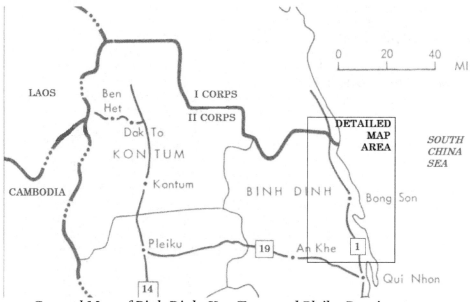

General Map of Binh Dinh, Kon Tum, and Pleiku Province areas

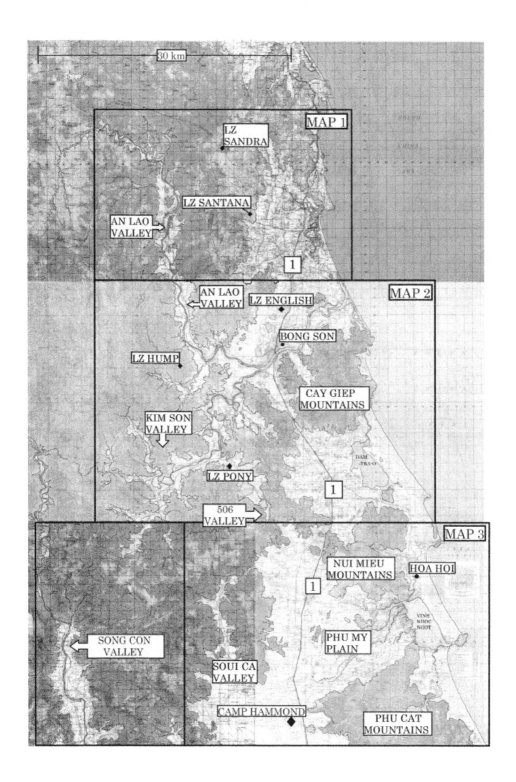

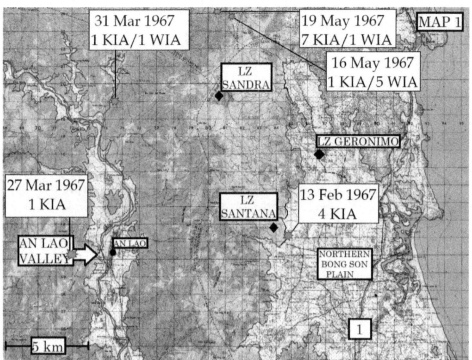

Map 1, Northern An Lao Valley and Bong Son plain regions

Map 2, Southern An Lao, Bong Son plain regions, Kim Son Valley (crow's foot)

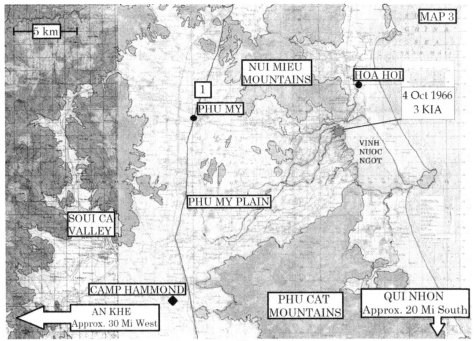

Map 3, Soui Ca Valley, Phu My plains

PROLOGUE

It is August 4th 2017 as I begin to write this introduction, fifty years to the day since my father returned home from war. From August of 1966 to August of 1967, he lived and fought in the Central Highlands and coastal plains of Vietnam. How do you write a story about something that happened over fifty years ago? I graduated a mere twenty-five years ago. All I can remember about that day is listening to some people talk, and a nice lady in a maid outfit serving meatballs at my party afterward. Imagine trying to remember what happened on a particular day a half-century ago, especially if it's a day you'd just as soon forget. As one would expect, my dad remembers images, bits and pieces, high points, low points, friends made, and friends lost.

Some of those images are rather grim, like that of a dead soldier being carried down the hill on a stretcher, his arm sticking straight up in the air from the effects of rigor mortis, or of their dead radio operator being loaded onto the chopper in the pouring rain. Others, however, are of a happier sort, like that of the Vietnamese children holding their hands out and exclaiming, "Give baby son, chop, chop!" Others are simply foreboding, like that of the San Francisco skyline disappearing into the mist as they sailed to Vietnam, a column of infantrymen swallowed by darkness while taking their first intrepid steps into the jungle, or that of a disheveled, abandoned firebase that had been overrun by the enemy. Others still, are just oddities that stick in one's mind, like that of a man running for his life through a flooded valley, or of an unusually tall soldier just standing atop a rice paddy dike amidst a firefight, looking around while everyone took cover in the muck.

When I began writing this book, I wanted to fill in the blank spaces, depicting exactly where my dad and his friends were, and what they did during their tour of Vietnam. Useful information was scarce, but I did stumble upon a map that documented the location of virtually every battalion in the 1st Air Cavalry Division on October 4th 1966, the date of his company's first fatalities. As I studied the map, I soon found the military symbol indicating the location of 5th Battalion, 7th Cavalry (5/7th Cav), my dad's battalion. Searching further, I found another symbol that indicated the location of his specific company, Alpha Company, 5/7th Cav, near what looked to be some kind of lake called "Dam Nuoc Ngot". All I knew from the books I had read, was that Alpha Company had been sent to sweep the area, eastward toward the sea, and at one point was sent to rescue a downed helicopter pilot.

Emotions are funny things. I had read a few accounts about what happened that day, the personal story of the first Alpha Company trooper to fall and the young family he left behind. Compelling as it was, it didn't quite bring me to tears. But as I studied this obscure map with military symbols showing precisely where Alpha Company had made contact with the enemy that day, knowing what happened there, realizing this was the very spot in the world where my dad first watched his dead fellow soldiers being flown away on helicopters – this is when I cried.

Through conversations with some of my dad's fellow skytroopers, I've come to realize that specific locations and dates aren't really all that important, not to them at least. For months, I've labored over how to describe places like the Bong Son and An Lao regions, Kon Tum and Binh Dinh Provinces, Highway 19 and the various mountain ranges, all places I've only read about. Those who survived in these places however, will tell you that a rice paddy is a rice paddy, the valleys, the mountains, the rivers and highways, they're all pretty much the same. The only thing that makes any of them special is what happened there. What they remember is their experience, the fear, the fleeting moments of joy and comfort, the bonds of brotherhood made, and the hardships of life in the infantry. In their mental scrapbooks they carry a disparate collection of anecdotes, reminiscences and legends, like stealing the colonel's jeep and heading toward town, crying beside a stream while trying to wash the blood from a fallen friend's radio, or the haunting vision of a dead soldier being carried to the chopper, his eyes suddenly opening as if he were still alive.

When I was a kid, our family would turn out the lights, make a bowl of popcorn, set up the movie screen, and click through photographs on our Kodak Carousel slide projector. Sometimes we would look at dad's pictures from Vietnam. My favorite was the one of him wading through a sea of six-foot tall elephant grass, carrying his rifle, unshaven, cigarette dangling from his lips. This photo was curiously absent from the collection of now digitized photos he sent me when I started this project. I think he was embarrassed to have a picture of himself smoking.

Clicking through each of the slides, he would mention the names of those in the pictures, which ones got killed, which ones made it. I never thought much about these unrecognizable faces, who they were before being sent to war, who they were to my dad. All I knew about the pictures was that they were from somewhere in Vietnam between 1966 and 1967. What I knew about dad's experience was that he was drafted and sent there on a boat, it was really hot, he got shot at, had some friends who were killed, and got a rock lodged in his arm that never came out. And by the way, it sucked. Like so many others, my father did his duty when called upon. For most of my life, that was all I needed to know.

The rest of the story, that of Alpha Company, 5/7th Cav, has since resided only in the fading memories of my dad and the men he served with. But what a tragedy it would be if that story were never told. My hope is for their loved ones to see this war through my dad's eyes, and learn something more about what they did there, and what they went through.

Although there were many pitched battles, it is not a tale of glory, nothing akin to the raising of the flag on Iwo Jima, as it were. Although there are Bronze Star, Silver Star and Distinguished Service Cross citations attesting to the valor of several of the men of Alpha Company, it is largely a story of drudgery, deprivation, and of walking through jungles and rice paddies waiting to get shot at. There is pain, death, and regret. It is also, however, a story of courage. Aside from the harrowing acts of valor, it is principally the daily acts of courage that I hope to convey, the courage to rise from the dirt each morning and continue the patrol, the courage to obey, the courage to simply show up.

To my knowledge, there are no books specifically about Alpha Company, 5/7th Cav that have been published. This will be the first. Forming a coherent timeline of events, bringing to life the young men of Alpha Company, describing the life of an infantryman in the Central Highlands; these things present a monumental challenge for someone who has never been to Vietnam, or been to war for that matter. Unqualified as I am, I hope to do their story justice.

The National Archives website maintains a record of all servicemembers killed in the Vietnam War. Pulling together the names and dates of deaths of those in Alpha Company, 5/7th Cav provided a starting point for research. It quickly illustrated those months and those days that were the toughest for Alpha Company. November 19th and 24th 1966, along with May 19th 1967 stood out as particularly dark days for the company.

I searched several military memorial websites, where fellow soldiers, family members, and hometown friends have posted their personal memories of those lost in Vietnam. I even stumbled across a posting my dad had left back in 2001, in remembrance of one of his buddies. Some of these people posted their email addresses, and I attempted to contact each of them. Many were kind enough to share their personal memories and backgrounds of the fallen. I'd like to thank each of them for their willingness to help. I have listed these generous people in the Acknowledgements section at the end of this book, noting each of their contributions.

There were three books written by former infantrymen of the 5/7th Cav that were of great assistance. In 1994, Captain Bernard E. Grady (Ret) published *On The Tiger's Back*, his own recollections of his time spent as Bravo Company's executive officer, then later as commander of Charlie Company. Another book was published in 2009, *1966 The Year of the Horse* by Robert K. Powers. Drafted around the same time, both of them grunts, both mortarmen, the experiences of Robert Powers and my dad were very similar. Like my father, Powers also became an electrician after the war.

Both books recount the tragic events of Thanksgiving Day 1966. Bernard Grady provided a possible explanation for why Alpha Company's soldiers would go for months on end without a change of clothing. In one chapter, he relates a story about how he came to know Father Tom Widdel, and what would become the Battalion Chaplain's second job. Serving in sister companies to Alpha, both Powers and Grady fought in many of the same battles, and their accounts helped me determine where Alpha Company was at certain times throughout their tour. Sadly, both Bernard

Grady and Robert Powers have since passed. If I could, I would thank them for what they wrote.

A third book was written in 2007 by Joe Sanchez of Alpha Company, 5/7th Cav, *True Blue, A Tale of the Enemy Within*. It is primarily about his experience as a cop in New York City, but also includes several recollections of his time in Vietnam, and the friends he made there. Aside from what he wrote in the book, he also shared with me many additional memories from both Fort Carson and Vietnam that added greatly to the story I have to tell about Alpha Company. He also helped my dad and me connect with a few additional skytroopers from the company. Thank you, Joe, for all of that.

One such trooper that Joe put me in touch with is Robert Matulac, who was their company's communications sergeant during their tour. We spoke for several hours on the phone. Now well into his eighties, he has an amazingly detailed memory of their many battles fought together. Those memories helped me to paint far more compelling and accurate portraits of their company's most harrowing moments.

Also of great assistance was Don Shipley. He was assigned to Charlie Company, in the same battalion. He is now the Vice President of Membership for the 5/7th Cavalry Association, a group of veterans from their old battalion who reunite every couple years. "So why hasn't Will been to any of our reunions?" was his first question for me. Like a shepherd searching for his lost sheep, he has dedicated much of his time to bringing wayward skytroopers back into the fold, and reconnecting them with their buddies. He and his colleagues in the association have been largely successful in their efforts over the years.

Much thanks is due to my loving wife, Misty, who encouraged me to finish this project since it began over a year ago, and who has shown great patience and understanding, as I have virtually been in another world throughout this process.

In reading the final draft of this book, I realized that I had forgotten to thank my mom, Carol. Sorry to say, but that would be typical of me. I suppose we sometimes take for granted all the love and support of those who are always there for us.

My mom accompanied my dad and me on our journey to the National Archives, spending long days scanning documents during our research there, while spending each night at College Park, Maryland's finest Super 8 Motel. She also helped to proofread several drafts of the entire book. When I was in grade school, I had aspirations of being an author, and she had always wanted me to write a book. So thank you, not just for all of that, but for helping and supporting both me and my brother, Nick, through all of the changes and challenges in both of our lives.

Most of all, I want to thank my dad for being willing to relive what could easily be considered the worst year of his life. In doing so, he's had to try to remember a lot of things that he would probably rather forget. I also want to thank him for all the letters and photographs he sent home from the war zone. Both have enabled me to bring this story to life in a way that would have otherwise been impossible. In fact, at least half of this book was written by him, in his own words, over fifty years ago.

When I started talking to him about this project, I asked if he still had those letters, most of which were written to his mother. Although he still had them, he said that the letters didn't really say much about what they were doing, and that they were really quite boring. Apparently, he had started reading them once and quickly fell asleep. After most of this book was written, or so I thought, I finally got around to asking if I could see them. He gave me a cardboard box, filled with letters still in their original envelopes, bound in rubber bands, all in chronological order. There were over a hundred letters.

I should have known better, as my dad always tends to understate things. His communiques were sent from some of the most remote valleys and outposts in Vietnam, written under the most austere of conditions, often scribbled in haste before another mission, or by flashlight, under a poncho in the rain. They would travel over eight thousand miles across the ocean, to be placed in a mailbox that stood across from a farmhouse, along a rural county road in Wisconsin. Reading each of his letters from beginning to end was the closest I will ever come to time travel.

His dispatches answered many questions as to where he and his company were and what they did throughout their year in Vietnam. They provided one answer in particular that I had been desperately searching for. It had to do with their mission on October 4th 1966, the date of Alpha Company's first fatalities, and their additional task of rescuing that downed pilot. I had corresponded with the daughter of one of the men killed that day. We exchanged whatever information we had, but neither of us knew if they had been successful in rescuing the pilot or not. My dad couldn't remember anything in particular about that day, nor could anyone else that I had spoken to until then. His letters revealed that their company had actually rescued both the pilot and his gunner that day. I was happy to share this news with someone for whom it meant so much.

During their time spent training at Fort Carson, the letters illustrated how utterly in the dark he and his buddies were about their fate. Rumors were their main source of information, and would continue to be so throughout their tour in Vietnam. Most importantly, the letters provided a window into who my dad was at this point in his life. Throughout this process, I had tried to keep in mind how young he was, and how different he may have been from the man I've always known. You see, my dad is universally considered a rather responsible and straight-laced fellow, a man who never drinks too much and hasn't touched a cigarette since before I was born. A pillar of reliability, he worked for over thirty years as a maintenance electrician at a local factory, and I can recall how each morning his lunch pail sat waiting for him on our kitchen counter, sandwich and apple inside.

As I read the first of his letters from Fort Carson, where he trained for war, it all hit me like a ton of bricks. He was just a kid. His concerns were that of a typical twenty-year-old, cars, girls, drinking and having fun, in pursuit of which he wasn't afraid to break the rules. And he was jazzed to become what was known as a *skytrooper*, flying into battle with a historic cavalry unit once led by General Custer. He even drew a picture of their Australian bush hat in a letter so his little brother could see what it looked like.

He may have been a bit embarrassed by the adolescent nature of some of the comments he made in his letters, not to mention some of the stunts he pulled. Then again, what grown adult wouldn't be embarrassed by a weekly recounting of all their thoughts and aspirations from when they were twenty years old? Had I kept a diary at that age, I would no doubt be mortified by it now, and loath to share it with anyone. But these are the things that give the story life, that make it real.

The letters paint a portrait of a young man, anxious to make his family proud, and utterly unprepared for the inglorious reality of this new war. He wrote at length about that first pitched battle they had fought on October 4th, asking his family if they had heard about Operations Thayer and Irving on the news. Entering into their third straight month of search and destroy missions, however, his recounting of their battles became vague, and eventually all but nonexistent. It's telling that he remembers nothing about the battle he wrote the most about, but wrote nothing about the one battle he still remembers most vividly, that of Thanksgiving Day 1966, his worst day in Vietnam.

The letters also portray a mother who was desperately concerned for the welfare of her boy, "Willie". Along with her many letters, she would send my dad packages of food, packets of Kool-Aid to make his water more drinkable, copies of the local newspaper, and at one point, a raincoat. She worried if he was eating enough, was he losing weight, was he cold, was he receiving communion, etc. Years later, she would confide in my own mother, her daughter-in-law, Carol, that she had been haunted during this time by the specter of a soldier in dress uniform, standing at her doorstep, telegram in hand. Of course, she wasn't the only one to be tormented by such a vision. She would correspond with other mothers in the area whose sons were in Vietnam, and would often inquire if Will knew where this guy was or where that guy was. And where exactly was he, because all of the firebases and remote outposts mentioned in his letters were not shown on the maps of Vietnam that were published in their local newspaper. It may well have been the worst year of her life as well.

One thing my dad always mentioned in his letters, was all the other people who were sending letters to him. I was surprised by this, and it was comforting to realize that there were so many people thinking about him at home. He may not have been as alone over there as I'd previously believed.

Something to keep in mind about the letters, of course, is that they tend to focus on the day-to-day life of a soldier, his personal thoughts, and questions over what was going on at home. With a few notable exceptions, they don't tell us in any great detail about the battles fought or the most terrifying of experiences. Some soldiers would, in fact, write at length about such things in their letters, but usually not in the ones addressed to their mothers, for obvious reasons. He did write at length at times, about the constant rain and their inability to ever get dry. Which brings up something else that's important to remember. To look at each of the photographs taken by my dad and his friends, one would get the impression that it never rained in Vietnam. Well, their cameras were typically kept in a small waterproof plastic bag in their rucksacks, and only taken out when weather permitted. It's also worthy to note the great effort that was required to get these pictures developed back then, and how many were forever lost, their film damaged from excessive moisture and heat.

When I was a kid, I considered my dad to be rather worldly. He had traveled to exotic places and fought in a war. He was a scuba-diver, and had been an astronaut at one time. As a construction worker walking on narrow beams high above the city, he helped build what is still the tallest building in Minneapolis, the IDS Tower. An electrician by trade, but also an amateur inventor and photographer, he is well-versed in astronomy, and an expert chess player. He can play both the guitar and the accordion. A jack-of-all-trades, he works on his own cars and builds things, and creates all manner of electronic gadgets. I later realized that he actually hadn't been an astronaut, the photos on our basement wall were actually of Neil Armstrong. Nonetheless, I still thought of him as a renaissance man.

By those who know him, he is regarded as a man of great integrity who can always be counted on to lend a helping hand. I remember more than one occasion when he has corrected a store clerk for giving him too much change or had forgotten to charge him for something. Whenever someone is in need, he is typically the first one to volunteer to help. I can recall him stopping to assist stranded motorists on the side of the road, once giving a ride to a woman with two kids walking along the highway in the winter. The one thing he's never been in any situation is a bystander. Today, he still spends many hours fixing and installing wiring in homes of his friends and family, and in our local churches.

Although he may not have been as straight-laced and responsible as he is now, his own words in his letters home demonstrate how his basic decency and regard for human life have always been cornerstones of who he is. Through all the death and brutality he was exposed to, it should be regarded as no small achievement that he always managed to keep this part of his character intact.

It is now May of 2018 as I finish writing this prologue. As mentioned before, in March of this year I took both my mom and dad to the National Archives in College Park, Maryland, just outside of Washington, DC. We had no idea what we would find there. We were hoping to find documents relating to my dad's company during their time in Vietnam. What we found were his battalion's daily staff journals and situation reports for every day of the battalion's first year in Vietnam. It was the final piece in the puzzle of sorts, detailing exactly where each company of the battalion was located and what happened on each of these days. The reports and journals illustrated exactly when and where many of the stories and events I had already written about actually took place, while bringing to light many other events I had not been aware of, some of them humorous, and others rather morbid.

We spent four days methodically scanning and taking pictures of thousands of documents, and one day visiting the monuments in Washington, DC. After our return home, I began sifting through the documents we had captured. Reading through each of the reports and journals was mostly mind-numbing and tedious, but every so often another piece of the puzzle would appear to help bring this story together. I had put off making the trip to the Archives until after I had practically finished writing this book, reluctant to travel so far with no guarantee of what we would find. It turned out to be a trip very much worth taking.

Notes on Revision, 2nd and 3rd Editions published June and November 2019:

The original edition of this book was published in May of 2018. The hardest part was actually finishing the project, as I continued to come across new information and new people with stories to tell, such as family members and friends of the fallen, as well as other former Alpha Company soldiers. At a certain point, I had to simply finish with the information I had at the time. I actually had a deadline of sorts. Many Alpha Company soldiers had already contributed much to this book and I had promised them that I would have print copies available at the 5/7th Cav's upcoming bi-annual reunion that was scheduled for August of 2018. Since that time, I've met a handful of additional Alpha Company soldiers, some at the reunion my dad and I attended, and others through email.

The catalyst for publishing this revised edition was a phone call I received in December of 2018. The phone call was from a gentleman named John Benson. Apparently, he had written an article in 2017 for his local newspaper commemorating the fiftieth anniversary of the death of an Alpha Company soldier who was killed in action, and who was a close friend of my dad's. A friend of his happened to be reading this book and recognized the name of the soldier from their hometown who John had written his article about. He called John to tell him about it, and then John called me. He provided me with details about this soldier's life before being drafted into the Army, as well as the text of his citation for the Silver Star that he was awarded for his actions during his final battle. Before this, I wasn't even aware that he had been awarded the Silver Star. John also put me in contact with one of the soldier's hometown friends. He spoke of their years growing up together, as well as the day he saw soldiers in dress uniform approaching the family home of his friend along with their priest. I'd always felt that this soldier, being good buddies with my dad before he was killed, deserved to have a more prominent role in this story - and now he does.

In addition to the revisions based on new information, I also tried to offer more colorful descriptions of certain events and scenes, such as the sights, sounds and smells of the city of Qui Nhon upon their arrival in Vietnam, a brief discussion of the soldiers' most popular and most loathed varieties of C-Rations, as well as the eerie atmosphere of their first foray into the jungle.

I also wanted to describe the new draftees' first encounter with their drill sergeants in more detail. For this, I actually drew mostly upon my own experience of basic training in 2007. Another thing drawn from my own experience is the description of what goes through one's mind while enduring severe homesickness and sleep deprivation. I've never been to war, but I have experienced both of these unpleasant things during my time in the Army.

Also since publishing the book, I've had the chance to read many other books written about soldiers' personal experiences in the Vietnam War. I found that it's often difficult to keep straight who everybody is in many of these stories, and it struck me that my readers would encounter the same difficulty. One book in particular, *The Boys of '67: Charlie Company's War in Vietnam*, took great pains to remind the reader of who each soldier was while referring to them throughout the book. It inspired my attempt to improve my own book in this respect.

Chapter 19 (The Final Patrol), takes place toward the end of my dad's tour. There were several battles during this time, but unlike those from earlier in their tour, for which I had gathered some very detailed personal accounts, I had very little to go on for this time from June to July 1967. Most of the soldiers I had talked to were no longer with Alpha Company during these months. Most had either been wounded, never to return, or had been transferred to other battalions. For the most part, I was left only with my dad's letters and the information in the battalion's daily staff journals. There were certain things I knew as facts, however. I knew where these firefights took place and the topography, as I could place each of them on the map. I also knew the weather for each day, as this was also noted in the reports. I knew how many were wounded and how they were wounded. I knew when and where artillery and air strikes were called in. I also knew that a large part of the company was now composed of brand-new replacement soldiers who'd just arrived in Vietnam, as discussed at length in my dad's letters home. For the sake of good storytelling, I wanted the account of those final months in the Central Highlands of Kon Tum Province to be more than just a recitation of these facts. And so, drawing upon the available information, I used my imagination to a certain extent in describing one of their last battles in the highlands, where two of the new guys get their first taste of combat.

In August of 2019, dad and I attended an Alpha Company, 5/7th Cav reunion hosted by Jack Fleming of 1st Platoon in Albuquerque, New Mexico. For the first time, I had a chance to meet and speak with my dad's friend from his mortar platoon, Martin Quinn. Like the aforementioned soldier who was killed, I always knew that he was good friends with my dad in Vietnam, and believed that he also deserved a more prominent role in this story. The memories he shared with us about his time at Fort Carson and Vietnam, along with his many recollections of my dad during this time, helped bring to light the friendship they shared. Also during and after this reunion, I met a few more soldiers from Alpha Company, including John Kruetzkamp, Royce Barrow, Barry Gallagher, and George Kalergis. Their memories are now part of this book as well.

1
THE LETTER

It was hard to stay awake, real hard. He could feel himself once again slipping into that half-awake, half-asleep dreamlike state that always seemed to take over while guarding their patrol base at night. The rain had stopped hours ago but the jungle was still dripping, as was the poncho over his foxhole. They had been attacked at night before, and he knew it would happen again, sooner or later. It was his worst fear, perhaps everyone's. With only weeks, perhaps days, left for him in "Indian Country", he only hoped the inevitable would occur after his departure. A cigarette helped him to stay awake. As it dwindled, a slide projector of sorts in his mind scrolled through the most haunting images of the last year, including the faces of his dead friends. The one image that kept reappearing, however, was from an earlier time when he would have been hard-pressed to find this place on a map - that of an unopened envelope sitting on the kitchen table. It had been delivered to a farmhouse in a little town named Tilden.

About as far as you can get from Vietnam, Tilden is a tiny farm town in northwestern Wisconsin. This is where my dad was born, literally, born in the farmhouse, and where he had lived his entire life. In October of 1965, he was still living on the farm and helping with chores when he could. He had recently started a job at Johnson Manufacturing, a machine shop in Chippewa Falls, working on a lathe and making parts.

Arriving home after work one evening, he found his mother cooking supper as usual, but he could sense something was amiss. His father was normally watching the evening news about this time. Now he sat silently, staring at an envelope that sat unopened on the kitchen table. "This is for you," he said. Will looked back at his mom as she prepared their meal. There were tears in her eyes. He sat down to open the envelope. The letter was from the President of the United States. "GREETINGS: You are hereby ordered for induction into the Armed Forces of the United States..." it began. A local board composed of his neighbors had selected him to serve his country. He was to report to the post office in the neighboring town of Chippewa Falls at 8:00 AM on October 26th. He was twenty years old.

Over the past year or so, Vietnam had been in the news as America's involvement was deepening. However, very few battles involving significant numbers of American ground troops had taken place yet. In fact, at this time it was rarely referred to as an actual war. It was a conflict that the Special Forces, Air Force, and Navy had been involved in since the beginning of the Kennedy Administration, mainly as "advisors" who provided weapons, training, and air support to the South Vietnamese. The Gulf of Tonkin incident had made headlines in August of the previous year, and President Lyndon Johnson could be seen on the television regularly, making the case for our continued involvement. Marines had landed in Da

Nang in May of 1965, while the Army's 1st Air Cavalry Division had established its own base in Vietnam's Central Highlands in July. A build-up of troops had begun and regular Army and Marine divisions were continuing to arrive in-country. The draft had recently been expanded, but until now, his life had been unaffected by the whole affair. Across the ocean and over eight thousand miles away from Tilden, this obscure place they talked about in newspapers called Viet-Nam would quickly turn his life upside down.

My dad is Wilbur E. Bowe, son of Edward and Mildred Bowe (Eddie and Millie). Born the third of four boys, Melvin, Darrell, Wilbur and Mike, he also has a sister, Diane. At the time Will was drafted, Melvin and Darrell were grown men and had been on their own for some time. Melvin was married to Delores and Darrell to Joanne. Both had several children of their own. Melvin had started his own farm up the road.

Darrell had joined the Army in 1954 and eventually became an airborne instructor. When Darrell completed his basic training, Eddie, Millie, Will, and three other relatives traveled to Fort Knox to see him graduate. While driving through Chicago on their way back, Eddie took a wrong turn at a stop-and-go light. After being pulled over by a policeman, he was informed that he had actually been driving on a sidewalk. The officer figured he was dealing with another drunk driver. Realizing that it was just a lost farmer in the big city, he would forgo writing him a ticket and instead helped him find his way out of town.

Twice during the 1950s, Taiwan came under attack from communist China. During the first of these attacks in January 1955, known as the First Taiwan Strait Crisis, Darrell's unit was called upon to go and defend Taiwan. With their bags packed and engines of their C-130s running, the mission was put on hold at the last minute. The engines were shut off and Darrell and the rest of his unit would sleep beneath the planes on the tarmac while diplomats negotiated a peaceful resolution to the crisis.

After leaving the Army, Darrell became a trucker. He and Will also had a joint venture of sorts, in which they had invested in a stock car they named PT-109, after John F. Kennedy's PT boat. Darrell did most of the driving, although Will gave it a go during one race in which he recalls finishing dead last.

Diane had suffered brain damage as a result of a severe fever at the age of five, and would remain at home with Eddie and Millie for as long as they could care for her. His little brother, Mike, was fourteen years old. Mike would eventually marry a girl named Donna Bohl, stay on the farm, and raise four of his own children there.

Despite growing up on the farm, farming would not be my dad's chosen profession. This was hard for me to understand as a kid, as I thought the farm was the greatest place in the world, with all kinds of equipment to climb on, cats and dogs everywhere, and very little adult supervision. We would ride the Honda three-wheeler all over the countryside, often flipping it. We would shock each other with the cattle prod and make forts out of bales in the hay barn. I would always find somewhere to hide out when it was time to go home. For Will, however, the farm was just a place where you did a lot of work. Instead, he would choose to be a tradesman.

Will graduated from a Catholic high school in Chippewa Falls in 1964, where he'd played fullback for the McDonnell Macks. From January to April of 1965, he attended Allied Machinist School in Chicago. It was the farthest he'd been from home. When he left for this school, his dad gave him a bus ticket and a twenty-dollar bill. Upon arrival, he needed a place to stay but didn't have enough money for his first month's rent. He made a deal with an apartment owner to pay it with his first check from the job that his school set him up with at a local chocolate factory. During his time in Chicago, my dad's younger brother, Mike, and his friend, Larry Geissler, (ages fourteen and eighteen, respectively) made the bus trip down from the farm to visit him. Millie had packed sack lunches for the boys. Upon seeing all the candy at the factory, the boys immediately dumped out their lunches and filled their bags with chocolate.

There are a few things you should know about the town my dad grew up in. Tilden is a small unincorporated town, located between Chippewa Falls, home of the famous Leinenkugel's brewery, and Bloomer, which happens to be the rope-jumping capital of the world. It is comprised mostly of dairy farms. It is exactly half-way between the Equator and the North Pole, a fact made known to all who pass by along Highway 53, thanks to a billboard constructed by my uncle Mike and some of his friends. Along with Chippewa Falls and Bloomer, it is one of a small handful of towns in the world where the name Bowe is routinely pronounced correctly, *Bo-vee*. There is a Catholic church, a motel, and two bars. One of these bars also serves as a banquet hall, and giant letters that spell "FOOD" are plastered on the highway-facing side of it. This is a place where our family has gathered many times over the years to celebrate anniversaries, birthdays, and a welcome home party for Mike's son, Neil, when he returned from Iraq in 2005. For a time, my uncle Mike served as Tilden's mayor/constable. When Eddie learned that his son was running, he decided to run against him. It wasn't that he actually wanted the job, he just thought Mike should have to run against someone.

The 1960s were known for protests. Wisconsin farm country had its own brand of civil unrest during this time. Will and about ten others actually spent a couple hours in jail for civil disobedience during a protest organized by the NFO (National Farmers Organization) over meat contracts. Later on, protests would erupt over milk prices. Fortunately, no blood was spilled during the demonstrations, only milk.

Along with Will, many young men in the Tilden area were either drafted or enlisted into the armed forces in 1965. His friend, Don Mc Ilquham, would become an Army artilleryman. His next-door neighbor, Allen Simon, was also drafted into the Army, along with his friend from Bloomer, Charlie Rubenzer, and Bill Leidel, his co-worker at Johnson

Manufacturing. His childhood friend, Ricky Mitchell, would join the Marines.

Imagining the world and the life Will had known when he received his letter of induction, you begin to appreciate the utter strangeness of the new world he would be thrust into. Like thousands of other farm boys across the country, including many from his own county, he would soon be transformed into a soldier trained to fight and kill in the jungles of a foreign land. The young Will's journey would include many firsts - his first train ride, his first voyage at sea, his first ride in an airplane, his first visit to a foreign country, and the first time he saw a girl in a miniskirt.

Edward Bowe's Farm

Aug 1964, jailbird Will Bowe in back of squad car during protest

1966, (back) Will, Darrell, Mel, Diane (front) Mike, Millie, Eddie

2
ARMY LIFE

We have a new platoon sergeant named Burtis. A good man and was a cotton picker in Alabama. I could tell right away he was a farmer.

At 8:00 AM on October 26th 1965, Wilbur Bowe reported for induction at the Chippewa Falls Post Office, along with dozens of young men from neighboring towns. Anticipating that he would be inducted, Will had already sold his '56 Ford Custom to his friend, Larry Schindler. As it was the first wave of the newly expanded draft, almost all of them were under twenty-five years old, not attending college, unmarried and without children. While standing in what would be the very first of countless lines in his Army career, Will met a fellow named Rodney Henning. He was from Eagle Point, a small farm town similar to Tilden, also near Chippewa Falls.

They were soon loaded onto a bus, bound for the Federal Building in Minneapolis, where the draftees would undergo a physical examination. Those found fit for duty would promptly raise their right hands and swear to defend the United States of America against all enemies. They would spend the night at the Andrews Hotel just a few blocks away. The next morning, they would board a train headed for Fort Leonard Wood, Missouri. Here they would be in-processed, issued clothing, receive a battery of shots, get haircuts, and take a written test to determine the occupational specialty they were best qualified for. As it has always been for soldiers going through in-processing, their main duty was to stand in line and do paperwork.

31 Oct '65

Hi Folks,

Well, here I am. Still haven't started basic yet 'cause we're still going through processing. We've been issued clothes and given tests and physical examination. It's been a lot of fun 'cause we ain't done nothing yet. There are six guys from Chippewa County I know quite well. Without them I'd feel alone. Some of our guys got drafted into the Navy. I think I would have went crazy if I was in the Navy. This is OK, so far, I hope.

Well, how's everything at home, do any combining yet? We've had good sunny weather down here so far. About Schindler, did he find the title for the car? Wish I was through with this part. We get 16 shots, some are given to you without the needle. They're blown into you. I'll get 4 of them tomorrow. Ain't much more I know, just having a lot of fun. I hate getting up at 4 in the morning. Well, who wouldn't. Oh yeah, we got a haircut too. $.80 those S.O.B.s charged us, then we get one every week, too. Well, see you in 8 weeks.

Willie

After less than a week at Fort Leonard Wood, Will and several others were flown to Colorado for basic training. They were headed to Fort Carson, where he and his fellow inductees would live and train together for the next eight months. They were herded from the airport onto buses and made their way to the post.

Shortly after rolling through Fort Carson's main gate, they could see rows of drab-colored barracks come into view. Eventually, they came to a stop and a drill sergeant appeared at the front of the bus and told them they had exactly one minute to get all their shit off of his bus. By design, their first basic training task was an impossible one. Anxious and bewildered, they struggled to escape the bus as fast as they could, olive-drab duffel bags in tow. "Put your bags over there," the drill sergeant yelled, "then form up over here - move your ass, privates!" Soon more drill sergeants emerged from behind the barracks, quickly descending upon the hapless gaggle of troops, each of them barking random questions, declaring what was wrong with them, or just telling them to move their ass. In their new green fatigues, the new privates stood at attention in a crooked half-baked formation as each of the drill sergeants walked up and down the lines. After their brief "get to know you" session, they were split up into platoons and informed that their sorry asses now belonged to Bravo Company, 1st Battalion, 11th Mechanized Infantry (1/11th Inf). Mechanized meant that they would learn to drive track vehicles, in this case, Armored Personnel Carriers (APCs). The 1/11th Infantry was part of the 5th Mechanized Infantry Division, commanded by General Autrey J. Maroun.

Here at Fort Carson, they would live in Army barracks, eat Army food, and live the Army life. My dad remembers getting his first Army paycheck. It was just over sixty dollars. In 1965, the Basic Pay for an Army Private (E-1) with less than four months time in service was $87.90 per month. Staff Sergeants (E-6) with over six years in service received $307.50, and Captains (O-3) with the same were paid $592.20. $1,939.50 was the monthly Basic Pay for a four-star General with over twenty-six years in service.

During their training at Fort Carson, the soldiers typically trained six days per week, with most evenings off. There was a movie theater and bowling alley on post, and the soldiers could occasionally hit the bars in the nearby town of Colorado Springs if issued a pass for the weekend. Overlooking Fort Carson is Mount Cheyenne, where NORAD, the North American Aerospace Defense Command is located.

The 1/11th Mechanized Infantry actually had a mascot of sorts, a female brown bear that had wandered into Canon City, Colorado as a small cub. She looked to be orphaned, and so someone brought her to the Pueblo Zoo. Having no need for an extra bear, zookeepers brought her out to Fort Carson where the 1/11th just adopted her, so to speak. The battalion's sergeant major couldn't tell if the cub was male or female, and named her

"Brutus" - officially, Brutus T. Bear (the T. stood for "the"). A Stars & Stripes article noted how Brutus, being good-natured for a bear, had once attained the rank of Specialist-5, but was later busted down for biting a general's finger. As one soldier explained, "There was a sign saying *Don't put your hand in the cage*, and he did. There was some discussion over whether she should be promoted or demoted because of the incident, but the general's view prevailed. We thought she should have gotten a medal." Brutus liked beer. At approximately one-year-old and 125 pounds, she had already earned a reputation as a heavy drinker. The article continued, "Although her Form 20 lists her Military Occupational Specialty as *Terrain Analyst*, her primary function is to assist in making this unit the colorful, high-spirited and well-known battalion that it is. Her Evaluation Report (DA Form 2166) reflects such rating factors as *Frequently fails to get along with others, both on and off the job*, and *Requires a lot of supervision in relation to what gets done*, but the members of this battalion have complete confidence in her ability to excel as a mascot."

Most of the battalion's young draftees expected to be sent to Vietnam, but no one would be officially told of where and when they were going until the very last week of their advanced training. Also left unknown to Will and his fellow draftees during basic training, was the job or MOS (Military Occupational Specialty) they would be trained for, as well as what unit they would be assigned to. Of course, there was no shortage of rumors.

Friday, 5 Nov '65

Dear Folks,

Bet you never thought I would end up out here, neither did I. Pike's Peak is right next to us, about 4-5 miles north. It's about 14 ½ thousand feet up and covered with snow. 90 of us came from Fort Leonard Wood by plane. Man what a ride that was. To look at the land below us was really beautiful. Especially when you didn't have to pay for it. Well, how's the weather? It's just perfect over here, cool and bright and sunny. I believe our platoon sergeant is very nice. We were standing in formation today and we told him the sun was getting hot, so he let us stand in the shade. We could have just as easily gotten the other one who is tough, mean, and a Karate-Judo expert. We got a pretty mixed up gang of 54 here. One from Guam, Canada, and 4 or 5 different states, ½ dozen Negros, and 2 Indians. The little guy from Guam is a real comic.

You know, ever since I have come in the Army I have been asked why I pronounce my name with the sound of a "V". Today I was asked again, and I said how to say it, and the guy says "you must be German," said he took German language in school. You pronounce "W" like a "V". So now I know.

How's everyone at home? Is Darrell getting his corn in? I hope you got my address right, 'cause I am expecting a letter from EACH of you sometime. Another thing, I took out a $5,000 life insurance for $1.00 a month. I don't *know what the catch is. I guess I better close now. My arm is still stiff from a shot I received yesterday. I got one in the ass last Monday, the needle was at least 1 ½ inches long and that ached for 2 days. We got 6 shots so far. Went to the dentist yesterday. I didn't have to, but some guys got 5 teeth pulled.*

So long for now,

Willie

Send your zip code also.

When they weren't training, they were either getting yelled at by their drill sergeants, cleaning things, or standing in line. The new privates learned early on that whenever you got a break in the Army, you smoked. Even if you didn't smoke, you smoked, as it lessened your odds of being tasked for some undesirable detail.

The soldiers would also learn how to march in formation, also known as Drill & Ceremony. As they marched about in columns, learning how to right-face, left-face, about-face and so on, one exasperated drill sergeant exclaimed, "Whew, there it is boys, I've found him already! Here's the one who's going to get his buddies killed in Vietnam 'cause he don't know his left from his right - there's one in every bunch!"

From November 1965 to early January 1966, they completed their Basic Combat Training, training that each soldier goes through regardless of the MOS they would later be assigned. They would be trained in basic combat, lifesaving, use of their gas mask, rifle marksmanship, and run several miles each morning. Will would qualify as an Expert Rifle Marksman. Before graduating from basic training, they would be fitted for their dress uniforms. While standing in line to be measured, Will met a tall barrel-chested guy from Seattle named Robert Wagner. "If I were just a half-inch bigger, I'd have a forty-inch chest," Will said.

"If I were a half-inch bigger, I'd have a forty-two-inch chest," Wagner replied.

Sunday, 21 Nov '65

Dear Folks,

Well, I am bushed right now. I had K.P. (kitchen patrol) all day. 12 hours of cleaning and mopping up the mess hall. Wasn't hard but it was tiring. Yesterday, I went to a football game. It was Air Force Academy against Colo. University. Colo. Won 19 to 6. I'll have to razz Gordy about that.

Tomorrow I'll be using my M-14 and march out 2 or 3 miles to the rifle range. We'll be doing this for the next two weeks. This physical exercise isn't nothing yet compared to my football exercise. I don't have anything to worry about compared to what I had in Chicago last winter. Man that was rough as hell there. I suppose it's going to get rougher, especially the weather. They say it gets mighty cold here.

The kid I sleep next to, said his hometown Superior, Wis. had six inches of snow. I imagine you got some too. I suppose it will be handy for deer hunting. When does it start? Say dad, you should go back to Colfax hunting. This place in the neck of the woods where the deer cross over a dirt road and into a path through the woods. Where Schwabs from Bloomer got their deer. I lay my money down on this neck of the woods before the deer cross the road. That's the very first place I would go.

Reason I called Larry Geissler was of some "wool" he tried to pull over my eyes. Why, there was no worry about me, the old Army will see to it that I am taken care of every minute.

You asked about Charlie Rubenzer. Well, he lives south of Bloomer on Hwy F. He got stuck at Fort Leonard Wood. This Henning kid from Eagle Point, we figure on going Airborne. I imagine you don't like the idea, but it ought to be a real treat to jump out of a plane, ha ha! I don't know for sure, but I think I will.

Say, about putting my name in the paper. I wish I would have told you before, but I am completely against it. It makes people think I am lonesome. If they want to write to me, they can find out my address.

What do you mean Mike dropped two subjects? He better sit on his ass and study. I don't give a damn how good he is at ball if he flunks out of school. He ought to know what he can get by with.

I'm sure glad Dad is getting his eyes tested. I was thinking about a pair of glasses for a Christmas present. I don't know if I'll be home for Christmas. You can't get military standby for ½ price during the holidays. $125 round trip by plane. Heck, I'll be home two weeks later anyway for ½ price, maybe even hitchhike on this 14-day leave. I guess I'll end now. We are having turkey for Thanksgiving. What are you having?

So Long,

Willie

30 Nov '65

Dear Folks,

It's almost 2 o'clock AM. We all have fire watch about once a week for an hour. So Ricky Mitchell is going over to Viet Nam. Two sergeants that take care of us 52 guys are going over also.

Oh, last week I had a good argument with our 3 sergeants and everybody in our barracks. They almost made a laughing stock out of me. I asked a question, if you held a rifle horizontal to the ground and a bullet at the height of the rifle in the other hand. You fire the rifle and drop the bullet at the same time, the two bullets will drop at the same time. Only one fellow knew for sure I was right, 'cause he took up physics in high school, and I got a few bucks I'll make on this bet. Father Rascey, when I was in the 4th grade asked that same question, and he better be right.

Did anyone get a deer yet? I am getting a little shooting myself, only it's targets. I guess I am fairly good at shooting. There is a right way and a wrong way and an Army way of shooting a rifle. If you ever call this M-14 a gun, it's 10 push-ups for you. Seven more days and I'll be done with the rifle range.

Say Mike, that's mighty good to sell 40 bars of candy, the most I sold was 2 and I ate them myself. Man those 2 you sent me, I was really starving for. I'll buy 2 more if you have any left.

All I can say for the Army, is it's still a bunch of horse shit. It's been pretty easy so far. The sergeants around here have never taught basic training before, and are about as dumb as we are.

Willie

5 Dec '65

Dear Folks,

I should wait until tomorrow night to write, I have such a hang-over. Been drinking all last night and this afternoon. We got paid a whole big $61 this last week. You know I got paid $13 too much, for a ½ minute anyway. You see, the lieutenant was counting the money and the First Sergeant asked me how do I get to say Bowe with the sound of a "V" instead of a "W". Anyway, I wasn't watching him count the money while I was explaining my name, until I got outside the door and I counted $74. About ready to take off running when the First Sergeant hollered, "Bowe, come here."

The Army has plans for us as artillerymen, such as tanks and heavy guns, that is if I don't go paratrooper, but I am. I'll be qualifying for the rifle range this Tuesday and Wednesday. Monday we'll go to the gas chamber to get a taste of tear gas. Next weekend I'll have a pass to go off post and hit the town of Colo. Springs. Some guys around here really get wild. They start to scrap every time they have a few beers. The beer is weak but the air is thin and it makes a big difference here.

How does Dad like his new glasses? How is Mike going to camp in the cold? I guess we might camp out next week also. So no one got shooting at deer except Dad. I am not coming home for Christmas, I am sure. It'll cost twice as much and so little time. I'll graduate from basic Jan. 15, so I'll be home for sure around the 17th and be home for at least 14 days.

That argument about this bullet is still going on. You know, which one drops first. Well, I guess I'll close for now.

Your Son,

Willie

Sunday, 11 Dec '65

Hi Mike,

I'll tell you what we all did the past week. Monday we went through the tear gas chamber. While we were in it we all took our gas mask off to give our name, rank, service number, date of birth, and where we live. Man, that was something else. You might say I was crying for an hour afterward, damn that was awful. Then Tuesday, went to the rifle range and I shot expert, boy am I ever good. You'll need me to shoot your deer next year. Did you get to shoot or see any deer? Thursday night we went through the infiltration course. That's crawling 86 yards over logs and barb wire while the machine guns are firing bullets 44 inches over our heads. 20th of Dec we'll go on our little old camping trip, carrying close to 50 lbs of equipment and during our march there will be planes shooting at us, if we don't get off of the road in time we'll be full of holes. Maybe if they'll give me a few bullets I'll shoot them down.

So how's the basketball games coming along? Yeah, I'd like to see how you got it set up. Is the ball in good shape yet? Looks like the Packers are either tied or ½ game ahead of Baltimore. I watched part of that game today. The Bears are a pretty hot club now, too. Hey, Ma says you still have a couple of candy bars left and I'll buy them if you haven't eaten them already! Where in the hell did you sell 40 bars of candy? Take 'er easy now. Write sometime this week.

Your big Brother Willie

Tue, 20 Dec '65

Dear Folks,

Well I thought I'd write a little letter this week so I could answer your letter sooner. I received your box today. The very first thing I did was open it and I was eating a popcorn ball in one hand and fudge in the other and the letter I received at the same time as the box. Here I was eating away and I read, "Do not open until Christmas." Oh well, I didn't open 2 of the boxes anyway.

I haven't had a chance to go to town yet. Had guard duty and K.P. the past two weekends. You might say tomorrow is our last day of basic training. Then our Christmas vacation starts. I'll be kept pretty busy during Christmas holidays. Going to the zoo and a hockey game, and maybe learn how to drive a tank. After that, it's just tests and monkeying around until the 12th of Jan, the date we graduate. Then I'll come home by the 13th for 14 days and then on my way to Airborne… Maybe Georgia or Carolina. I hope I can get into it. Henning is pretty happy today 'cause he thought he wouldn't make the 12-14 mile march. Now he's sure of going Airborne with me.

So Larry got picked up for speeding. Surprised he got away with it for so long. I received some cookies the other day from my foreman, Ronnie

Club. I was really surprised. Then I got Christmas cards from quite a few people. I wish I could send them one back, instead I'll have to write a letter. It makes it worthwhile to get up in the morning when someone is thinking of you. Yeah, I got Dad's and Mike's letters. They should write more often. Mike signed it "little Skeeter". Some guys called me that in high school also. Have you got the Christmas tree up? Yeah, we got one here too, to decorate. Sure wish I could ride home in Santa's sled. That would be a Christmas present and a half. Don't worry about me drinking too much. It's the last thing, it's the very last thing I can afford to do, except for New Year's Eve maybe.

Merry Christmas and a Happy New Year,

Willie

4 Jan '66 – 22 months left

Dear Folks,

Well I guess it's about time I write, too. Sure was glad to receive your letter. So far I still got heavy weapons. Many other guys got changed to it too. They say it's a pretty good deal. After this 8 weeks of advanced training in heavy weapons, I am still going Airborne. I'll be getting $55 a month more and I could use it.

I am sure of this now, I'll be home on the 13th of Jan. I am catching a plane to Minneapolis for $32. From there, Don Mc Ilquham's buddy will take me home. I am coming back here for 8 more weeks. I guess that will be alright. Just tell Diane to listen for a car about breakfast time on the 13th.

So a lot of guys are wondering where GI Bowe is. I bet they think I am either in the Navy or the Air Force. I heard that Allen Simon got into the Army, but wasn't too sure.

Sounds like everyone had a busy holiday. I almost forgot it was Christmas. New Year's Eve I didn't even get close to any bar, so us guys went to a Jerry Lewis show instead. Can't wait 'til I get home. It will be a treat but I tell you, I am by far happier in the Army even though it means, maybe, I'll end up in Viet Nam. I ate my best meal in the Army, and I ate my worst meal here, too (yeah, we got our "sea ration").

Larry Geissler wrote and told me he had blood poisoning from bare wire he used to pull a fox out of a hole. He said he almost went nuts 'cause he had to stay in the house for 3 days. Oh yeah, this Packer game I watched last Sunday was alright, and a week before when they took a close one from the Colts. I'll have to tell Larry Schindler about that one for sure. I guess I'll shave and hit the hay. Lights go out now at 9 o'clock and I've been writing for an hour in the can. I think this will be my last letter 'til I come home. So long for now and I'll be seeing you soon,

Willie

Robert Wagner, Christmas 1965 at Fort Carson

Fort Carson, Wilbur Bowe (left) and Rodney Henning (right)

At the end of basic training, each soldier would be assigned an MOS based upon his qualifications. Will was found exceptionally well qualified to be an infantryman, as was his buddy, Rodney Henning, the fellow from Eagle Point he met while reporting for induction at the Chippewa Falls Post Office. Most of them had stayed at Fort Carson through the holidays, and were allowed to return home in lieu of their traditional Christmas holiday leave. Will traveled home with Rodney. Although assigned to different companies, their paths would often cross, and they would become good friends.

For every infantryman in Vietnam, there were six or seven soldiers serving in other branches, such as artillery, aviation, engineers, transportation, signal (the military term for communications), and supply. It is therefore understandable that many had hopes of doing something besides pounding ground for the next year or so. One difference between enlisting into the Army and being drafted, was that those who enlisted could choose their occupation, so long as they qualified for it, while draftees could not. This left a large gap in the infantry ranks to be filled by draftees.

In January 1966, they would begin their Advanced Individual Training, or AIT. For this training, Will was transferred from Bravo to Alpha Company, 1/11th Mechanized Infantry, along with many of the same soldiers he would eventually go to war with, including Robert Wagner, Dennis Sherry, Richard King, Dale Erickson, and Bruce Madison.

Will would actually become an Indirect Fire Infantryman (11C), a special kind of infantryman known as a mortarman. Along with a team of three others, he would operate the 81mm Mortar. Mortars are sort of like portable artillery, inasmuch as they lob exploding projectiles at the enemy. They are more versatile than full-scale artillery in that they can be carried along with the infantry company, controlled by its commander, and fired with or without the use of a forward observer to spot and adjust the rounds. The 81mm mortar system stood just over four feet high when fully assembled. Weighing approximately ten pounds each, the mortar rounds were oblong-shaped with tail fins. They were "muzzle loaded", meaning they were simply dropped into the barrel, or tube, as it was called. Gravity and a firing pin at the bottom of the tube would do the rest, generating a very loud metallic "shunk" sound as each round was immediately propelled back out of the tube and into the sky. A typical infantry company would have one of its four platoons, typically 4th Platoon, designated as the mortar platoon, sometimes referred to as weapons platoon. In Vietnam, one good thing about being in the mortar platoon was that it was normally not in front of the company as it moved through the jungle, and thus, not the first to get shot at. The downside was all the extra equipment the mortarman carried. Along with his team members, Will would learn how to perform the duties of each position on the mortar team. They would break the gun down, set it back up, dig the mortar pit, and set the base plate and aiming stakes. They would rotate between each of the positions. They would split up the system and carry it on their many long marches out to the training ranges. Eventually, they would be tested and qualify as gunners.

Will would stay on the first floor of their barracks, becoming friends with a guy named Thomas Ragimerski and a few black soldiers, Carl Evans, John Bronson, Jr., and Willie Harris, as well as a couple Puerto Ricans, Robert Figueroa and Angel Reynosa. They all liked to sing, and would often harmonize to their favorite songs, like *Under the Boardwalk* and *My Girl*. Most of them were from the Bronx. Will also became close friends with Martin Quinn from New York City and Kurt Elmer from Harlem. Another buddy of theirs was Arnott Graham, a stocky black fellow who was a swell guy, but who had a big problem with authority.

Martin Quinn recalls vividly the day Will was transferred into Alpha Company to begin their AIT. With his unmistakable New York accent, he reminisced, "He and I hit it off from day one. I remember him coming into the platoon and that was it. We became bunkmates at Fort Carson. He was a farm boy, so I figured he knew everything about the outdoors. I thought he'd be a good pal to have where we were going. A real comedian, he was always cracking us up and never took anything too seriously." He also recalled how the sergeants would often make Will re-shave his face because he could never seem to shave his coarse beard close enough for inspection. "It would drive me crazy," he said, noting Will's tendency for messiness and disorganization. Will had a stocky frame with muscles developed from a lifetime of farm work and a few years of football workouts, while Quinn was tall and skinny. I imagine them as being a bit like *The Odd Couple*, with Will as the carefree "Oscar" and Quinn as the serious-minded "Felix". Although they had come from very different worlds, they forged an enduring friendship. The one thing they shared in common was their parochial school background, both of them being educated by Catholic nuns and priests throughout their childhoods. Quinn recalled the day he received his own draft notice in the mail, "Friday, October 15th 1965. I'll never forget it... with a token for the train. I told my boss, *As of 5 o'clock today, I am no longer employed here. I'm leaving for the service.*" Before he left, his boss gave him what he called a "miraculous medal". It was a medallion of sorts of the Virgin Mary, commemorating the Immaculate Conception. He would wear it on a chain around his neck for good luck.

There were also a few soldiers from the midwest in Will's platoon. One was Marvin Bierschbach, a Scandinavian fellow from a little town called El Rosa in central Minnesota. Like my dad, he was raised on a farm, unmarried, and had recently graduated high school, a perfect candidate for being drafted in 1965. Another was Gerald Anderson, a towering Nordic-looking fellow with glasses from Illinois. Al Patrillo was a quintessential country boy from Susquehanna, Pennsylvania. Unlike my dad, both Bierschbach and Patrillo had girlfriends back home to send letters to.

Growing up in rural Pennsylvania, Tom Ivey was a childhood friend of Al Patrillo who lived just across the street. Two years his senior, he recalls Al as being like an older brother to him, and how they would find all kinds of mischief to make around their small town and the surrounding countryside. They started out riding their tricycles together in the early fifties, and in later years they would play marbles, make clubhouses out of cardboard boxes, and fly balsam airplanes with long wind-up rubber bands. They both considered Tom's younger sister to be a pest, and would often find inventive ways to get rid of her, one time sticking a ball of prickly burdocks in her curly brown hair. Tom's mother cried over this as it was only one week before her First Communion, and she would have to have her hair cut short. On another occasion, they pushed her so hard on their swing set that she was sent flying and broke her arm. It was sort of an accident, they weren't *trying* to break her arm. As she was *his* sister and not Al's, Tom faced the brunt of the punishments for their many misdeeds.

When they were a bit older, Tom and Al would constantly roam the woods and stone quarries, at times finding baby crows and rabbits, bringing them back to show their parents who always admonished them to put the critters back where they had found them. They played hardball with several other kids on a makeshift neighborhood ball field, and Al was always chosen first when picking teams. They would ride their bikes five miles to the area lake to swim, where they would always get an "electrocuted hot dog" along with a bottle of Ma's Soda. There was a stream where they would often fish for trout, and Al would bring along his .22 rifle to shoot any woodchucks they happened to find. At the age of fifteen or so, Al Patrillo took up taxidermy. As Tom recalls, his first "mount" was a Flicker, a bird that looked like some sort of woodpecker. Al was very meticulous in his craft, explaining to Tom each step in the process.

Al Patrillo graduated from high school in 1963, went to work and soon bought his first car, a '57 Ford Fairlane hardtop convertible. He worked hard to fix it up with the help of one of his buddies. After that, Al and Tom spent less and less time together, as Tom still had two years left of high school. Upon receiving his draft notice, Al sold his car, which had become his pride and joy, to a friend.

Will's friend from Minnesota, Marvin Bierschbach had actually completed his basic training in Fort Leonard Wood and had been slotted as an artilleryman. His orders were changed at the last minute, however, and he was sent to Fort Carson to train with Alpha Company in the "God damn infantry" as he put it. Long before he was drafted, he had the wisdom to understand how utterly miserable an infantryman's life would be, and the forethought to avoid it. He had actually tried to enlist in both the Navy and Air Force, but they were all filled up. Shortly thereafter, he received his proverbial invitation from his friends and neighbors to serve in the United States Army. He cried when he received his draft notice. Nonetheless, he showed up. Another fellow midwesterner was Jim Hirschuber, originally from a small town named Stoddard, near the city of La Crosse, Wisconsin. He was nineteen years old when he was drafted, and recalls receiving his notice the day before his wedding, in October of 1965.

Up on the second floor of their barracks was another Puerto Rican fellow from New York City named Joe Sanchez. Eighteen years old and in search of adventure, he'd actually tried to join every service in the military but had been turned down. He wrote about this experience in his book, *True Blue, A Tale of the Enemy Within*. Even the Regular Army had rejected his application for enlistment, based on his physical. The standards for the Selective Service (the draft), however, were different. He was advised to go to his local board and request his draft be pushed forward. Being deemed unworthy for enlistment, but good enough for the draft, was actually a very common occurrence. Soon afterward, Sanchez would receive his own letter from the President of the United States. Upon completion of the very same physical he had failed several times before, this time he was accepted. At the time, his swearing-in would be the proudest moment of his life.

Sanchez was buddies with a Jewish guy, Alan Weisman, also from New York. Weisman was engaged, and Sanchez met his fiancé while they were stationed at Fort Dix for in-processing. He recalls that she looked a lot like Barbara Streisand. His first Army buddy, Sanchez looked up to Weisman who was a few years older than he, and had been impressed with his confidence in flirting with the stewardesses on their flight to Fort Carson from Fort Dix.

Alpha Company would claim young men from all across the country, including an unusually large contingent of twenty-six draftees from Kentucky. Nicknamed "Juggy", Guy McNay was from the town of Erlanger. It can be assumed that he may have had a rough upbringing. His sister, Annette Sebastian, who was married and fifteen years his senior, had been awarded temporary custody of Guy and his two brothers for mistreatment by their father and stepmother. Quinn remembered McNay as being a nice, quiet guy. The Kentucky group would also include a couple fellows who knew each other since grade school, Gene Cross and Donald Duncan. Another was Bill Purdy. At the age of eighteen, he was finishing high school and had just gotten into the ironworkers union when he and approximately twenty others from the surrounding communities received their draft notices.

Purdy remembers thinking of his friend, twenty-six-year-old Donald Rankin, as one of the "old guys" in their outfit. A devout Christian, he was the nicest guy you could ever meet. Along with his five brothers and one sister, Rankin had grown up poor, in a family of tenant farmers amidst the tobacco fields of central Kentucky. He had been the first in his family to attend college and was among a small handful of draftees in the company who had done so. He struggled to pay his tuition loans, however, and eventually dropped out with only one semester to go. Shortly thereafter, he was drafted. Among Donald Rankin's many friends in Alpha Company were Richard Cantale, Robert Matulac, and Royce Barrow from North Carolina, who would soon become his closest Army buddy.

Sent to Alpha Company from another basic training unit at Fort Carson was a small guy, Bobby Hansen from New Jersey. He was friends with Guy McNay (Juggy) from Kentucky, Alan Weisman from New York, and Jim Hirschuber from Wisconsin. The comparatively tall Hirschuber would describe Hansen as a guy who was "always the life of the party" and the two would become pals.

....

NCOs are non-commissioned officers, or sergeants. While commissioned officers make plans, write operations orders, and set policy, NCOs put those plans into action. Responsible for their direct supervision, they are expected to know their soldiers well, and to always place their needs above their own. In 2010, I held the rank of Specialist (SPC) in the Minnesota Army National Guard. Although I was not yet a sergeant, I was assigned to the position of team leader, normally held by a sergeant. I was a fairly inexperienced soldier when I joined Officer Candidate School (the Army's commissioning program), and I had recently washed out of the program. My new squad leader, Staff Sergeant (SSG) Brian Toohey said to me, "Well, Bowe, the officer corps didn't want you, but we're gonna make you an NCO." He had previously served in the 173rd Airborne Brigade during the initial invasion of Iraq in 2003. Anyone assigned to his squad would find him a competent leader who always put the needs of his soldiers before his own, but also one that you never wanted to cross. Failure to follow his instructions would bring repercussions both harsh and swift, the kind you never forget. His leadership inspired the perfect combination of fear, respect, and admiration that produced highly motivated soldiers, the kind that jump into action when given any kind of task.

SSG Toohey had assigned several tasks for me as a new team leader during our annual training in 2010, in preparation for our unit's deployment that was scheduled for the following year. Among them was to write down the serial numbers of all three of my assigned soldiers' weapons, and to take accountability of them twice per day. I was also tasked with recording each soldier's blood type and allergies, in case of emergency. Last of all, I was to memorize the *Creed of the Non-commissioned Officer*. I had accomplished all of this in short order, and stayed up late in our barracks that night memorizing the creed, which includes the following passages:

My two basic responsibilities will always be uppermost in my mind: Accomplishment of my mission and the welfare of my Soldiers; I will not use my position to attain profit, pleasure, or personal safety; I will communicate consistently with my soldiers, and never leave them uninformed; I know my soldiers and will always place their needs before my own.

I awoke the next morning with these words etched firmly in my short-term memory. SSG Toohey never asked me to recite them, however. Instead, he asked me what I knew about my soldiers. Basically, I knew their names and their blood types. While I had memorized the words of the creed, I had missed the point.

Although he was nearly ten years younger than me, I looked up to SSG Toohey, if not like an older brother, a more experienced one. And I'll never forget the last time I got smoked in my Army career. Getting "smoked" is when one of your NCOs dishes out punishment by making you perform push-ups, or to simply stay in the "front-leaning-rest", the starting push-up position, for an extended period of time, usually mixed in with any number of physical ordeals, until he's satisfied that you've gotten the point.

During that same annual training period, our entire detachment was staying in what we called the "pig barn" barracks on Camp Ripley. I don't think they were ever actually pig barns, but they were old, World War II vintage wooden buildings that were only used when all the other barracks were filled up. Our unit was typically on the bottom of the totem pole, and we considered ourselves the red-headed stepchildren of the brigade. Since the entire brigade was training at Camp Ripley at the same time in August of 2010, this is where we found ourselves.

SSG Toohey had instructed me to bring a big, dry-erase whiteboard to the field during our training one day. I had my guys load it into a big cargo truck called an LMTV on our way out. We were participating in an exercise engineered by a bunch of civilian contractors and Active Army personnel called XCTC, or "extasy" as our platoon sergeant, SSG Corbin, called it. We were in a convoy of Humvees and our mission was to clear a bunch of buildings in a recently-constructed Iraqi village with the help of some actual Iraqis who were role-playing as Iraqi Police. I was to have the small team of three or so of these Iraqi Policemen lead the way into our first building. Approaching the building, the Iraqis refused to go in, so I just barreled ahead and kicked the door as hard as I possibly could. There was no give to it whatsoever - I fell flat on my back and the door blew up. Now a casualty, I waited for the medevac chopper to come and get me. Well, I thought, at least I get to ride in a helicopter. When the mission was over, sweating in the August heat, we all gathered around to listen to one of the Active Army instructors tell us what we did wrong. Apparently, I was supposed to have grabbed that Iraqi Policeman and shoved him through the door ahead of us. On our way back to evening chow, I had my guys throw the whiteboard back on the LMTV.

Afterward, everyone was milling around the barracks and getting ready for the next day's training. SSG Toohey was looking for the whiteboard and asked me where it was. I told him that we had put it on the LMTV and forgotten to get it back after returning from chow. This is when the long-remembered smoking commenced, probably the worst smoking of my life. Although SSG Toohey was obviously not happy with my performance that day, he was actually quite calm while administering his punishment, and we had a very cordial conversation about life as I performed push-ups and other various exercises until the point of exhaustion. With me sweating profusely, our conversation continued after my twenty-minute or so smoking, and the topic turned to how I could be a better NCO. He wanted to impart to me the same kind of leadership style that he had mastered, that would make my guys jump into action without hesitation. This would require a more heavy-handed approach on my part, something that didn't come naturally to me.

Our platoon sergeant, SSG Scott Corbin had joined in the conversation at this point, remarking how being a team leader is the hardest job in the Army, how you needed to ride the "Joes" hard during training but also attend to their needs, how their problems were now your problems. Like SSG Toohey, Corbin was former active-duty and had also made the initial invasion into Iraq. He'd also spent several years as an air assault instructor at Fort Benning. We all looked up to him as a father figure. Then I remember SSG Toohey asking me, "Bowe, do you know how to dominate a room?"

At that moment, SSG Corbin interjected, "Yeah, like this..." and he proceeded to grab a folding chair and whip it across the room. "What the fuck!" he yelled, as the chair slammed against the wall. The entire barracks immediately fell silent and everyone fixed their gaze on SSG Corbin, like a bunch of deer caught in the headlights. "That's how you dominate a room, Bowe." Then everyone returned to what they were doing like nothing happened.

SSGs Corbin and Toohey were hard on their men at times, but they also took care of them. Like all the NCOs in our detachment, they never ate chow until they had ensured that each of their men had gotten theirs. It may seem a small thing, mostly symbolic, but it was really more of a mindset. At times, certain soldiers in our unit would be tasked out to train with other units, and those units rarely thought to make accommodations for them in terms of food or anything else for that matter. This mindset was meant to ensure that the needs of the "Joes" would not be forgotten by their leaders. We all respected SSGs Corbin and Toohey with the knowledge that they would do anything for us. At the end of that annual training, SSG Corbin actually rented out a couple of houses on post for all of us to have a party in, paid for out of his own pocket. To say the least, they were much nicer than the "pig barns" we had been living in for the past two weeks. For most of us, they were examples of what we wanted to be as future NCOs.

....

Among Alpha Company's NCOs were Staff Sergeants Donald Burtis from Alabama and Bobby Hayslip from Georgia. SSG Burtis had grown up on a farm, and my dad recalls him as the nicest and most laid-back of all their NCOs at Fort Carson. He was big and tall, spoke slowly and calmly, and wasn't always yelling at them like the others. Although he wasn't overly gung-ho, he was a career NCO who cared about and took good care of his soldiers. SSG Kenneth Gregory was a veteran NCO who had served in the Korean War. Bobby Hansen, the little guy from New Jersey who was always the life of the party, remembers SSG Gregory at the rifle range saying, "Are you guys having fun? Yeah, you'll see how fun it is when those targets are shooting back at you."

Just like Will and most of the other lower-enlisted soldiers (those in the ranks of Specialist and below), Joe Sanchez, the Puerto Rican from New York, had grown tired of being ordered around and made to do all the menial tasks that new soldiers typically do in addition to their training, like cleaning, scrubbing, polishing floors, and pulling KP (kitchen patrol), all while getting yelled at by their NCOs. On one occasion, the troopers returned to their barracks after a long day of training to find all of their stuff thrown out on the lawn because someone had forgotten to lock his footlocker. The soldier who had left his footlocker unlocked was made to carry it with him for the rest of the day.

In charge of Sanchez during their basic training was Sergeant (SGT) Bill Chapman. Noting Sanchez's unenthusiastic attitude toward cleaning, SGT Chapman invited him to "vent his feelings," as it were, "off the record." Thinking he was really free to speak his mind, Sanchez doubled down on the offer, swearing his sergeant a blue streak a mile long. Before marching out to the range the next morning, SGT Chapman gave Sanchez a very large forty-pound rock to put in his rucksack, so he could "work off some steam." He would carry the rock along with the rest of his gear for several miles to the range, and then back to the barracks that night. His Jewish buddy from New York, Alan Weisman, joked that P.T. Barnum must have been talking about Sanchez when he said there was a sucker born every minute.

A few of the soldiers possessed radios that helped kill the boredom of their downtime in the barracks. Will had one of his own and prized it dearly. Most of the music it played was of a familiar rock and roll sound he had grown up with. The Beatles were his favorite, while his buddy Al Patrillo preferred country music. Folk-rock artists such as Bob Dylan and Simon & Garfunkel had also become popular in recent years. Some of the sounds emanating from Will's radio however, were becoming very strange. Emerging onto the scene were a variety of new bands with odd names, such as Jefferson Airplane, The Grateful Dead, and Strawberry Alarm Clock. With cryptic lyrics that sounded at times like nonsense, they were ushering in a new sub-genre of rock, known as "psychedelic". Even the well-established Beatles had begun to adapt to the popularity of psychedelic rock. It was a sign that society was beginning to change. The America they would eventually return home to after their year in Vietnam would be remarkably different than the one they left in 1966.

A favorite pastime of SSG Hayslip and others, the soldiers would often gamble with dice or cards while stuck in the barracks. Marvin Bierschbach, Will's Scandinavian buddy from Minnesota, recalls how they would typically gamble until one of them was completely broke, and the other had all the money. In a basic form of loan sharking, the one with all the money would then lend the other money at a rate of two to one (borrowing $10 to owe $20), so he could continue gambling, or to buy cigarettes.

When issued weekend passes, they would hit the bars in the neighboring city of Colorado Springs. A shuttle bus would take them to town and back. A city-slicker of sorts from The Big Apple, Quinn thought of Colorado Springs as a hick town in those days. "The bars downtown were all up and down the sidewalk. Evans and Bronson would always go to this one bar in particular and have their girls lined up for Friday and Saturday night." In another part of town was the favorite spot of some of Alpha Company's officers, The Golden Bee, an Irish pub that was owned by a fancy hotel. Aside from the bars, the tattoo parlor was a popular destination for many. During one of their nights on the town, Will was kicked out of a bar after someone started a fight with him. While returning to post on a bus with other soldiers, an MP (Military Policeman) at the main gate demanded all the soldiers show their passes. Unfortunately, Will had not been issued a pass that day. The MP ordered all the soldiers without passes to wait outside the bus. The MP stayed on the bus to check the passes of those who had them. As the other three pass-less soldiers awaited their fate outside the bus as ordered, Will took initiative, slipping away into the darkness and sneaking back across post to his barracks. On another day off without a pass, Will and one of his buddies decided to climb the nearby Mount Cheyenne. This time, however, they would return to post by way of a culvert, in order to avoid the MPs at the main gate.

Ragimerski and Joe Sanchez also found themselves entangled in a scuffle with some local boys while leaving the bar one night. Outnumbered, they were chased all the way back to the bus terminal. Arriving at their barracks late, they knew they were in trouble. Sanchez slept on the second floor and Ragimerski slept on the first, where most of their buddies from New York were. Ragimerski's pals covered for him by making the bed look as if he were sleeping, but Sanchez was left to deal with his drill sergeant, who already had it out for him.

There was a USO hall at Fort Carson, and young women were bussed in from surrounding communities to attend dances there with the servicemen on Saturday nights. Joe Sanchez was there on one of these nights. One of his buddies picked out the most attractive woman in the hall, betting him that he was too chicken to ask her to dance. A bit younger than most of his Army buddies, Sanchez was inexperienced with women. He marshaled his courage, so as not to lose the bet, and more importantly, to avoid losing face. Her name was Teresa, she was twenty years old, and she lived in Denver. Not only did Sanchez persuade her to dance with him, he also got her number.

The next weekend, Sanchez called Teresa. She wanted him to visit her in Denver, which was an hour away from Fort Carson, but he didn't have a car. One of his buddies on base did have a car, however, and agreed to drive him there. Figueroa, Evans, and Willie Harris decided to come along. They went out dancing in some clubs in Denver with Teresa, her sister, and two other girlfriends. As it was getting late, Sanchez's buddy who had driven them there wanted to call it a night. The rest of them wanted to stay out, however, so Teresa said she would drive the boys back in the morning. Later that night, Evans, Figueroa, and Sanchez were in the lobby of a hotel, checking in. Willie Harris ran in and said, "Hey man, your girl's taking off." Sanchez ran out to find Teresa sitting in her car with the engine running. She asked him if he wanted to go for a ride. It was his first time with a woman.

10 Feb '66 – 89 weeks left

Dear Folks,

Don't have much to say. What I do have to say isn't good. I was in C Company, 1-11th by some mistake for 3 days and almost made a nervous wreck out of me. They're nothing but crazy and ridiculous. Now I am in A Company. Got the letter you sent me. Envelope all marked up. Looks as if it was all over post. This was how I got moved. From B Co to C, to A, to C, to A, to A Co 1-61st, back to A Co 1-11th. So you can see how the mail got mixed up. Thought I'd be getting into a good company. We can't even take a shit without letting the sergeant know where we are going. This is worse than Basic I went through. They're so damn scared we might take off. A guy I know went AWOL this morning. They're on your ass all day long and you can't even go anyplace. And doing work that's so meaningless is really bugging me. Just don't be surprised if I go over the hill.

Didn't do much this week. Still is a bastard of a company. Figure on starting AIT next week. I think we are getting this sergeant that was in the Marines for 9 years and just came back from Viet Nam. He puts on as if he is rough but I doubt it. You know, Rod Henning is just across the street from me and Don Mc Ilquham is just up about 4-5 blocks and we see each other every once in a while.

Will

17 Feb '66 – 88 weeks left

Dear Folks,

They seem to have eased off their "gung-ho, here we go" deal. Actually, I haven't learned anything yet since I came back from leave. All I did was drive this Armored Personnel Carrier for about a ½ hour yesterday. Then we had to qualify for our APC license and I passed my driver's test. Big deal! Everybody did. We had this one sergeant who was teaching us guys how to drive and he has never been inside one before. "Yeah," he says, "I'll have to get my license tomorrow, too." Huh? Well, that's the way they are around here. We got National Guardsmen right with us, and they've done less than we have. Next week I guess we learn some weapons or small artillery. We have a new platoon sergeant named Burtis. A good man and was a cotton picker in Alabama. I could tell right away he was a farmer.

This coming Sunday I figure on getting the gang together to go skiing up on Pike's Peak. We can rent a car and it should cost no more than 5 or 6 bucks for the car and skiing for the day. This guy I bunk next to has 4 years of college and a major in art, and can he ever draw. Usually he whips out pictures of fancy cars. We have quite a few Mexicans in our barracks and they all talk in Spanish to each other.

Say, I got me a sleeping bag. They're worth $18.00 and I am going to send it home whenever I get a chance. I didn't steal it or anything. You see, if you were missing any of your equipment you could get it replaced. I wasn't missing any, and I asked if they have an extra sleeping bag, and he said sure. Let me know about all that happens in the N.F.O., it sounds pretty interesting.

Will

21 Feb '66 – 87 weeks left

Dear Folks,

Well, my weekend is a flop. I had planned on going skiing but can't go on pass until one o'clock in the afternoon. So we've been hitting the town instead. I'll have a pretty good idea where I am going by next month or so. Rumors I heard say we might go to Germany. I hope so. I should be making E-2 pretty soon.

It's kind of lonely in the barracks now. Just about everybody is gone. Man, am I ever glad that I brought me that radio. It's really worth it. A lot of guys even want to buy it from me 'cause it is really the nicest radio around. I had it on guard duty one night. You know it's pretty big. An officer of the guard came to check on me. I was guarding these warheads with floodlights and live ammunition, so if I had gotten caught with the radio it would have meant a stiff fine. Wow, ask me if I was sweating when he was talking to me.

The National Guard are leaving March 11. This is one mistake I made. I should have joined the Guard or some reserve. But then again, I never wanted to take a back seat.

So Mike is a Tender Foot, ha ha, that sounds pretty cute. I'd like to step on them feet. Make him write a letter sometime. I almost forgot. Send me the rest of my clothes if you can. I'd like my sweater, the red shirt and short sleeve yellow shirt and blue pants. Well, so long for now. I am going to the show right now, it's only 35 cents or so.

Will

13 March '66 – 84 weeks left

Dear Folks,

Sorry that I haven't written. Just don't feel in the mood for it. Hope you're feeling better. I wasn't feeling too well today. I played hero and gave a pint of blood and I felt pretty weak in the stomach. I wanted the day off to see the pretty nurses at the hospital.

Rod Henning isn't going to Viet Nam. He is trying like hell to, though. Don Mc Ilquham might. So far I am not. Sometimes I wish I were going very much. You never know, I might yet. I hope not. About ¾ are on orders to be sent over on 22 of May. What is Kenny Mueller's address? I have to tell Ken what to expect. Nobody ever told me any advice. That pisses me off. You know that Larry Geissler might be drafted, don't you?

My clothes came in good shape. I want you to send my white shirt and two or three good ties, my good overalls and some of my underwear. So Mike really likes the sleeping bag. I slept in them twice and warm as hell. Mike wants that little scooter. Get it for him, it'll be a good hobby. How I wish I had one at that age. Keep him out of trouble, ha ha! Well, I'll sign off like he does.

From a Handsome, Muscular, Mighty, Great, Fabulous,

Willie

24 Mar '66 – 83 weeks left

Dear Folks,

Well, here I am for 2 weeks in the fields and it feels a little bit like home. The place used to be a big ranch and beautiful mountains around here. The first 2 nights we spent in tents. Was it ever miserable, cold and windy. We had 70 mile an hour wind one day. Thought I'd never live through it all. Now we are in insulated tents with heaters and it's a lot nicer. We had guard today and I was picked to be Colonel Orderly, and now I sit in this hut 'cause I was the only who knew how to type. Guess that was one time it paid off. Guys are suspicious about that sleeping bag.

Henning finally got his way and is going to Viet Nam. Don Mc Ilquham might go, doesn't know for sure yet. Sergeant was telling us guys tonight about when he was over there. It must have been something to go through alright. He was talking to us two guys for a couple hours straight. Interesting. He also belonged with the Green Berets or Special Forces.

Yes, Larry Schindler owes me exactly $100 yet. Do you ever hear anything about Larry Geissler getting drafted? No doubt he's scared. If it wouldn't be for the farm work, it would be the best place in the world for him.

I received those pictures and I really got a bang out of them. I tried calling you guys last Sunday about 5:30 C.S.T. but everybody was out visiting. Tried later, but was too busy getting ready for the field. Figure on coming back April 4th. I'll call the first chance I get back on base. Ask Mike what he wants, like helmets, bayonets, cowboy boots, only if he writes a letter. And Dad, too.

Your son,

Will

17 April '66 – 79 weeks left

Dear Folks,

About time I write again. Next Saturday I finish A.I.T. From here I am going to train in helicopters. We're going Air Mobile. Just travel in them, not flying them. I can't go Air Borne, short of men, so they say, but I am not going to give up. We will get paid $55 more if we train Air Borne.

I don't like to tell you this any sooner than I have to, but I think it best to say I am going over to Viet Nam by the end of the next 3 months. So I'll be home for 2-4 weeks this summer. Many guys here have orders to go in May. They showed picture slides of the country. Heck, I am looking forward to going over (for a day). I am really surprised to see that all of the guys are anxious to go. Our Captain has 4 Purple Hearts and was wounded 3 different times. He has pictures of the prisoners he has captured and killed. Our First Sergeant was over there and got wounded also. He says he made over $1,000 a month on extra pay and bounties, so I'll make a few coins while over there. It isn't as bad as it sounds. Viet Cong are only 5'2" to 5'4" tall, ha ha! No, I do look forward to going. I won't have 2 years of meetings when I get out of the Army, like otherwise.

Camp Red Devil made me feel how nice I had it back here. It's miserable out there. Back here I can relax with a can of beer, a bag of salty peanuts, with swing music and once in a while, a mild cigar. Tonight the colored guys are wild. Drunk as hell and 6 or 7 of them shaking dice, each with a fist full of bills. They're crazy. About the only thing a person can live for here is the nightlife, otherwise you'd go bugs. I am still glad I am in the Army. 18 months and I am FREE GONE. Man, I am just holding my breath for that day. Like waiting for Christmas when I was a little kid. Seems like forever. High school was the same way. I'll make it one day at a time, and life will be so wonderful again. Sigh.

My buddy's having his girl come out here and they're getting married. I got a hunch he'll want me to be his witness. He's a real swell guy. I think it's a good idea for him to be married. Maybe not, two ways of looking at it in the Army. We had our first rain out here the other day. Seemed nice to stand in rain and wade in the mud. Well I guess I'll hit the hay. They shut the lights off and now I am sitting in the can.

Will

21 April '66 – 79 weeks left

Dear Folks,

Be home in July. I believe in early part. Now all this is based on fairly reliable rumors. If I go Air Borne, it will be all changed again, but I doubt if I can go. Don't know if we will get $55 extra for Air Mobile. In B.U.T. (Basic Unit Training) we'll be in the fields 2 weeks, off 2, and back on 2, and it will be intensified. Two hours of physical training each day. "We will be TRAINED Soldiers" says the Captain. We'll graduate this

Saturday. Even heard rumors to go to Georgia for Air Mobile training. All the National Guard that took A.I.T. with us have their noses up in the air 'cause they're on their way home shortly. They'll be cooled down when they're alerted this summer or later. They were all in the Korean War, they'll be in this one too. I am glad I am not in with them, though.

One of my buddies went home on a 5-day pass to get revenge on his cousin's murder, should have been back last Sunday. Probably has himself killed. Yesterday, I seen my first mouse here. Well, I chased it a bit and I knelt on a cactus. Oh it's painful. They'll go through your boot and some guys get serious injuries from them. By the way, I missed the mouse. Wanted to stick it down someone's neck. If you have an empty box lying around, throw some cookies in it and stick it in the mailbox. Just make an extra-large batch the next time you make some.

Your son,

Will

While Will had generally mixed feelings about being in the Army and possibly going to Vietnam, he pretty much went with the flow. He figured that if he was going to be stuck in the Army for two years, he may as well be where the action was, and if possible, get paid extra to jump out of airplanes. He and Rodney Henning tried all they could to join the airborne corps, but to no avail. The one common theme in all these stories is that it really never mattered what any of them wanted to do. Whether they wanted to be where the action was, or specifically where the action wasn't, or just in any branch that wasn't the Army, or just in any job that wasn't infantry, or whether they wanted to jump out of airplanes, it mattered not to the Army. Their fate as ground-pounders had been predetermined.

Since most of the Army's main fighting units were already in Vietnam, many of them had planned on being sent over as individual replacements to various companies already in the field. As such, they all anticipated being split up and sent on their separate ways after their initial training. In fact, Royce Barrow had already received orders assigning him to the 4th Infantry Division in Vietnam. Unknown to them at the time was the fact that they would be desperately needed to fill out a brand-new battalion that was about to be formed mainly from those already assigned to the 1/11th Mechanized Infantry.

Mount Cheyenne, overlooking Fort Carson

Angel Reynosa, photo courtesy of Joe Sanchez

Fort Carson, (left to right) Molski, Elmer, unknown soldier, Figueroa, Sanchez, Willie Harris (in front), photo courtesy of Joe Sanchez

Martin Quinn at Fort Carson's Barracks

Fort Carson, Marvin Bierschbach with APC

3
AIRMOBILE

They say it is a pretty comfortable war, so they say. You go out and fight a little, come back, take a shower, go to the P.X. and have a few beers.

At the end of their advanced training, Alpha Company stood in formation outside in the company area in anticipation of an important announcement that would change everything. Their company, and in fact, their entire battalion would stay together and be sent to Vietnam as an intact unit. Those who had already received transfer orders to other units, such as Royce Barrow, would have those orders cancelled. The battalion would now be trained as an airmobile unit. They would also become the first soldiers on post to be issued the new M-16 rifle. Upon their deployment to Vietnam, they would be released from the command of the state-side 5th Mechanized Infantry Division in order to join the 1st Air Cavalry Division already in-country.

Since their arrival in July of 1965, the 1st Cavalry Division had built airfields, landing zones, and firebases throughout the Central Highlands of South Vietnam. The division's primary area of responsibility, that is to say, the land that it owned, was known as II Corps. Sandwiched between I Corps to the north, and III Corps to the south, it was basically the middle one-third section of South Vietnam. The initial group of 1st Cavalry soldiers had now been in Vietnam for approximately a year. Will and his fellow troopers were part of the first wave of draftees who would soon be trained and ready to continue the 1st Cavalry's mission.

At the time, the 1st Cavalry Division had been operating with three brigades. Each brigade commanded three infantry battalions, except for the 3rd Brigade, which had only two. Another battalion was needed to fill out the 3rd Brigade. To this end, the 1st Battalion, 11th Mechanized Infantry was officially re-designated as 5th Battalion, 7th Cavalry (5/7th Cav) in April of 1966, and would now belong to the 1st Cavalry Division's 3rd Brigade, also known as the *Garry Owen* Brigade. Within the 3rd Brigade, the 5/7th Cavalry would join the fight alongside the 1st and 2nd Battalions of the 7th Cavalry (1/7th Cav and 2/7th Cav), who had already been in Vietnam for the last year.

It should be noted that the regimental associations each of these battalions carried (7th Cavalry Regiment, 8th Cavalry, 5th Cavalry, etc.) were in name only. They had been kept part of each battalion's name only for purposes of heraldry and *esprit de corps*, military jargon for flair. Battalions in the modern Army no longer belonged to actual regiments, rather they belonged to brigades. Many cavalry and infantry regiments had been around since the time of the Civil War or even earlier. Brigades, on the other hand, had not been around that long in historical terms. Thus, they could not offer their subordinate commands the rich historical lineage that all of these old regiments could. And so it was that the names were kept, one of them being that of the famous 7th Cavalry Regiment.

The 7th Cavalry was indeed, a historic regiment. Formed exactly one hundred years prior in 1866, it had earned its fearless reputation during the Indian wars of the Dakota territories, under the command of then Lieutenant Colonel (LTC) George A. Custer. The 7th Cavalry would later see service in the Philippine-American war at the turn of the century, as well as in the Pacific Theater during World War II, and the Korean War. As portrayed by Errol Flynn in the 1941 film, *They Died With Their Boots On*, Custer had chosen the popular Irish drinking song *Garry Owen* as the regiment's official marching tune. "Garry Owen" would eventually become the phrase with which fellow 7th Cavalry soldiers would greet each other. The embodiment of cavalry esprit de corps, this Irish tune would be played at nearly every event where their band was present, and its rousing and infectious melody would become lodged in the memories of many generations of 7th Cavalry soldiers.

24 April '66 – 78 weeks left

Hi Hot Dog,

What do you say there kid, when are you going to drop a few lines to me? How's school holding out? When do those races begin? I think I'll see the races next Sunday in Colorado Springs. I should be home to see my car run this summer. Man, I miss the smell of burnt oil and the gunning of the engine.

You know this A Co, 1-11th will be changed to A Co, 5-7th. This is General Custer's cavalry unit. Going to wear an Australian Bush Hat (something like a cowboy hat), and wear jump boots. Oh, it's going to be sharp. It's going to be tough training. They're building a Vietnamese village outside of the Fort. That ought to be a laugh. We had a weapons firepower demonstration Saturday. From a .45 pistol to Armor. Shooting at junk trucks and tanks. Man the metal flew. It was quite some show. Heard some rumors today. Like, after B.U.T. we might take some jungle training, either in Georgia, Panama, or Hawaii. Sounds alright.

Henning and I and a couple other guys got stoned last night. We had to carry Henning back. I had K.P. with a big hangover today. This Ongsiner girl that chums with Carol Bresina, maybe you wouldn't know, but is her first name Sue? Henning and I have a $5 bet on it. He says it isn't. If you know, let me know. I might get myself a tattoo on my arm next week. A beautiful eagle with mountains in the background. Think I should? I always wanted one. I asked Darrell if he wished he could take his tattoo off, and he said, "yes," so I hesitate. Oh well, write sometime.

Will

28 April '66 – 77 weeks left

Dear Folks,

Well, I am in my Cowboy unit now. Getting our camouflage clothes next week. We're the only battalion on the fort to wear these. A new weapon's been issued to us, M-16. It's like a 22, the lead portion of the shell, but if you ever got shot in the foot with it, it could kill you. It's very wicked. Looks like a toy, very light, 6 ½ lbs. Weird looking. 2 shots could cut a man in two. An amazing rifle. I got a few pictures of it I'll send you next week. If you're worried about me going Air Borne, no need to. They're not letting anyone go. We start training Monday with a 15-mile march. We've been doing a lot of exercise this week and I am stiff. Be in shape by the time the march starts. Ought to make P.F.C. within a month or so. These sergeants that have their bellies hanging over their belts, oh are they hurting. They have to work out with us also, 40-50 years old and they're out running. They're pretty funny and we tease the hell out of them. Even the cooks work out with us, also the big "Bird" Colonel.

Ricky Mitchell got into a few close battles. That sounds exciting. He can handle himself OK. This may seem funny to you, but I am glad I am in, as much as I hate this. God made Hell. If I wouldn't have been drafted, I am quite sure I would have enlisted. I am in a platoon with a bunch of hoods from New York City. They're some "cool cats". We're right next to the P.X., which makes it handy. My buddy isn't getting married until he gets home on leave. We figure on being in the fields quite often now. There's a firebase in Viet Nam named Little Big Horn and our General's middle name is Custer. Ahem.

Adios,

Will

3 May '66 – 76 weeks left

Dear Folks,

I just took a shower, had a beer, and am sitting on my bunk with a big blister on my foot. I don't know why we march so much if we're Air Mobile. Guess we have to learn to run from the enemy, ha! Friday we're going to the pool to see if we can swim. If I pretend not to know, I might get time off during the workday to learn. I hope. Seen two guys parachute from a plane today. Ah, that was cool. By the way, give Darrell $15 for the watch I got from him. Told him he'd have to give it to me if I ever made it through Air Borne.

Adios,

Cowboy Will

The following article appeared in the May 6th 1966 issue of Fort Carson's newspaper, *The Mountaineer*:

Custer's Famous 7th Cavalry Returns To Life In New 5th Battalion at Carson

Fort Carson's new 5th Bn 7th Cavalry, first commanded by George Armstrong Custer 100 years ago, boasts a heritage of four Distinguished Unit Citations, two Korean Presidential Unit Citations, a Philippine Presidential Unit Citation, and the Chryssoun Aristion Andries, Greece's Gold Medal for Bravery. The 7th Cavalry was at the famous Battle of Little Bighorn in Montana June 25, 1876, when Custer's five troops of 264 cavalrymen faced more than 6,000 Sioux, Cheyenne, and Apache Indians. The result was history and 14 troopers were awarded the Medal of Honor. The 5th Bn 7th Cavalry comes to life again at Fort Carson, not too far from where it was first given the mission of guarding the western frontier in the days of Indian warfare.

The 7th Cavalry Regiment was constituted July 28, 1866 at Fort Riley, Kansas. Its motto, The Seventh First, signifies that the regiment and its successors came first in the actions of its members. The 7th Cavalry's regimental crest, a horse-shoe shape with four nailheads on the right and three on the left, boasts an arm and saber of the type used in the Indian campaigns. The blue and gold colors reflect the old cavalry. Across the top is "Garry Owen". The regimental name Garry Owen, Gaelic for Owen's Garden, comes from the 5th Royal Irish Lancers who frequented Garry Owen, a suburb of Limerick, Ireland. A tavern took the now-famous name and there the traditional song was born. Later, across the seas, General Custer approved the name and song so popular among the tough Irish immigrants and Civil War veterans in the 7th Cavalry.

They faced such famous Indian chiefs as Crazy Horse, Sitting Bull and Joseph of the Sioux. Indian campaigns were against Comanches from 1868 to 1875, in Montana in 1873, in Dakota in 1874, at Little Big Horn 1876-77, against Nez Perce in 1877, and at Pine Ridge 1890-91. Troops C, E, F, I and L were annihilated at Little Bighorn, where Custer made his famous last stand. Later they were in pursuit of Pancho Villa on the Mexican border. The regimental colors were flown in the Philippine Islands as far back as 1878. During World War II the 7th Cavalry won a Distinguished Unit Citation in Luzon as well as well as the Philippine Presidential Unit Citation. The 1st Cavalry Division made the initial entry into Japan and the 7th Cavalry had the honor of escorting General Douglas MacArthur into Tokyo. Twenty-eight days after Korean fighting started, the 7th Cavalry Regiment was at Pohang-Dong for the first of nine campaigns.

In basic training, the soldiers had all qualified on the old M-14 rifle, which had a wooden stock. The new M-16 was smaller and lighter, made of steel and plastic, and may have seemed a bit futuristic at the time. One feature of both rifles was a setting that allowed them to shoot rounds on full automatic, or "rock-n-roll" as it was sometimes called. Full automatic meant the rifle would shoot continuously as long as the trigger was held down, sort of like a machine gun. The rifle was less accurate in full automatic, however, and their ammunition clips only held twenty rounds. For the sake of accuracy and conserving ammunition, most would rarely use the full automatic setting. With their newly-issued weapons, the soldiers would once again have to qualify at the range.

One Alpha Company soldier from Kentucky, Chester Millay, recalled qualifying. On the rifle range, each soldier fires "iterations" or groups of targets in various positions. Millay was getting ready to start his next iteration of targets in the squat position. He forgot, however, that his rifle was still set on full automatic. He was surprised then, when he pulled the trigger and his rifle started firing on "rock-n-roll". He lost his balance and fell backward on his ass. "Luckily the drill sergeant was further down the line and didn't see my stupidity," he said, "the guys on my left and right had a good laugh."

Bill Purdy and others told of how their 2nd Platoon was tasked with assisting with a firepower demonstration in April. A lot of brass (Army slang for important people) would be there, including their battalion commander's state-side boss, General Autrey J. Maroun, commander of the 5th Mechanized Infantry Division. Everything was choreographed, Purdy recalled. One of the many things set to explode that day was a Claymore mine they had set up, a small landmine that was designed to spray bb-like metal pellets in only one direction. During the demonstration, one of 2nd Platoon's soldiers was taking a nap on the ground with his feet propped up on a log. When the Claymore detonated, a stray pellet was somehow sent back in the wrong direction, shooting straight through one of the snoozing fellow's size-13 boots. Their platoon leader, 1LT Harmon, was not happy. The errant pellet wasn't their fault, but now he would have to explain to CPT Wise exactly how his soldier managed to catch the pellet with the bottom of his boot. CPT Wise would have to explain it to LTC Swett, who would then have to explain the incident to General Maroun.

In preparation for their assignment to the 1st Air Cavalry Division, they would be trained in combat insertion and extraction by helicopter, known in the industry as Air Assault. On May 2nd 1966, the 5/7th Cav would begin what was called Basic Unit Training (BUT), in order to become an airmobile unit. Today Air Assault training is a special skill with a dedicated schoolhouse in Fort Benning, Georgia. Only soldiers of exceptional physical fitness are sent to the Air Assault school. Those who achieve course standards are awarded an Additional Skill Identifier and given wings to wear on their uniform. In 1966, air assault wasn't considered a special skill; rather, it was a basic part of the job for virtually every infantryman in the 1st Air Cavalry Division. It was, however, an entirely new concept in modern warfare. The new concept they were pioneering was called "Airmobile", and airmobile infantry soldiers were unofficially referred to as skytroopers. Rather than marching over long distances of contentious terrain, skytroopers would fly into battle on steel horses. The new skytroopers would come to learn, however, that despite being airmobile, they would still spend most of their time traveling by foot. This would be reflected in their training, as they would often march several miles to their training areas, rucksacks and weapons in tow.

With the advent of mechanized warfare in the First World War, the cavalry had traded in its horses for tanks. In preparation for the looming war in Indochina, they had swapped those tanks for helicopters. In 1965, the 1st Cavalry Division was officially renamed the 1st Cavalry Division *Airmobile*. A catchier name, it would become more commonly referred to simply as the 1st Air Cavalry Division. The 1st Air Cav would lead the way in developing airmobile tactics.

The airmobile concept had faced its first test in November of 1965 when the 5/7th's sister battalions of the 3rd Brigade, the aforementioned 1/7th Cav under the leadership of then LTC Hal Moore, and the 2/7th Cav, along with others, confronted a much larger communist force in the Ia Drang Valley of Vietnam's Central Highlands. The battle was depicted in the film *We Were Soldiers* and described in Moore's own book, *We Were Soldiers Once... and Young*. Surrounded by the enemy, it initially promised to be a repeat of another 7th Cavalry commander's last stand - when LTC Custer and his cavalrymen were butchered to the last man at Little Bighorn. And it would have been, if not for the massive amounts of air bombardment and artillery fire brought to bear on the enemy. The Ia Drang was the first major confrontation between regular American ground forces and their North Vietnamese Army (NVA) counterparts. The running five-day battle claimed the lives of over two hundred Americans and over a thousand NVA, and both sides claimed victory.

It wasn't just the infantry that would be transformed. The entire 1st Air Cavalry Division would become an organization comprised solely of airmobile units. Assigned to the 1st Air Cav were artillery, engineer, transportation, medevac, military police, intelligence, and signal units, all designated airmobile, with several helicopter battalions operating over four hundred aircraft to move them about the battlefield.

Despite all the airmobile hype, for soldiers like Will it was just another routine part of their training. They learned how to get on the helicopter, how to get off, how not to fall out, and how to rappel by rope out of a hovering chopper. With their bodies sweating and hearts pounding, and loaded down with nearly fifty pounds of gear, they leapt to the ground and immediately sprinted outward in all directions to secure the landing zone. Some would not become fully comfortable with the idea of flying during their training. As they would find out later on, however, getting shot at was a highly effective way of overcoming any lingering fear of heights.

Invented in 1956, the UH-1 Huey aircraft was also a recent innovation. Along with the CH-47 Chinook, it would become the modern soldier's lifeline for food, water, cigarettes, transportation, medical treatment, and mail. Eventually replaced by the UH-60 Blackhawk, some remaining Hueys continued their service in Army Aviation until 2016.

Over in the 5/7th's Bravo Company was First Sergeant (1SG) Dayton Hare, a veteran of both World War II and the Korean War. Significantly older and more experienced than most of the officers and NCOs in the company, he was small and wiry, grizzled by decades in the Army, a prototypical First Sergeant. Most of the time, he chewed upon an unlit cigar. By now, he could have retired and avoided a final combat tour. Captain (CPT) Bernard Grady was Bravo Company's Executive Officer at the beginning of their tour. In his book written twenty-five years later, *On The Tiger's Back*, he would recall that 1SG Hare's given reason for staying with the battalion was that he had yet to earn his Combat Infantryman's Badge (CIB). He had seen plenty of combat in both previous wars, but he had served as a military policeman in World War II, and as an artilleryman in Korea. The CIB is only awarded to infantrymen serving in infantry units in combat. Now the head NCO of an infantry company, this was his last and only opportunity to earn his own CIB. That was the reason he gave, but it is more likely that he simply could not bear to see his men, most of whom were half his age and had never seen combat, sail to Vietnam without him.

Alpha Company's First Sergeant and former Marine, John Potter, had also served in Korea, as had Alpha's company commander (also called C.O. for commanding officer), CPT A.J. Wise. A term of endearment, company First Sergeants are typically referred to by their men as "Top". 1SG Potter's face held scars from previous battles. Standing approximately five-nine, he was physically imposing, stocky and built like a soldier, while CPT Wise was long and tall.

The 5/7th Cav's Intelligence Officer, or "S-2" in Army lingo, was CPT Walt Swain. He was one of a select few in the battalion who had already served in Vietnam. As Grady recalled in his book, he had already survived two tours in the early sixties, in the swashbuckling days of remote Special Forces outposts, fighting alongside native highland tribesmen known as the Montagnards. Tall, square-jawed, blond and blue-eyed, Grady wrote of Swain's good looks, "If you needed to cast a green beret officer for Hollywood, Walt was your man." Swain thrived on adventure and danger, but also had a fatalistic streak. With a third combat tour looming, he doubted that his luck would hold out. He was said to have told his wife before departing that he didn't expect to come home alive.

Staff Sergeant Sam Daily was a squad leader in one of Alpha Company's rifle platoons. From Stringtown, Oklahoma, he was a career NCO. He was also the father of two girls, and had just learned that his wife was again with child. After the 5/7th Cav was formed in April 1966 in preparation for its maiden voyage to Vietnam, SSG Daily was informed that he would not have to go. As he had just spent over two years in Germany, he would be kept stateside for at least one year before being sent overseas again. Four young soldiers from his platoon came to his home to ask him if it was true, that he really wasn't going to Vietnam with them. They were terrified of being sent to war without their squad leader, and pleaded for him to go with them. As an NCO responsible for the welfare of his soldiers, he felt compelled to see them through the war he had prepared them for. He volunteered the next day.

SSG Robert Matulac was a veteran NCO who had enlisted in 1953, but had not yet served in Vietnam. He had served nine years in Germany, one in Korea, and the rest at various bases in the states. He was an Asian-American soldier whose mother, of Japanese descent, had been born in California. From the Philippines, his father had joined the U.S. Navy at the approximate age of fifteen, which he had to lie about to enlist, and served as a cook aboard its ships. A seemingly unlikely duty for a Navy cook, he told of a time when he was given a rifle and sent to fight the Germans in the Argonne Forest during the First World War.

As the communications NCO, Matulac was part of Alpha Company's command group, which included the commander, First Sergeant, radio operators, medics, supply staff, clerks, and drivers. In many ways, he was the right-hand man for both the commander and First Sergeant. He was friends with SSG Sam Daily, who was a few years younger than him. Daily invited him over to his house for lunch one day while they were training at Fort Carson. Sam Daily was very proud of his wife, and told him what a great cook she was. Matulac also recalls that Daily was a bit superstitious. As Daily drove them back to the battalion area on post, he took an unexpected right turn. "Where are we going?" Matulac inquired.

"Oh, nowhere," Daily replied. He then explained that a black cat had just crossed the street in front of them. What he remembers most about Daily, however, is how much his men respected him.

Sam Daily's family in Greeley, Colorado, prior to leaving for Vietnam

Another friend of Matulac's, Kazimierz Slomiany was from Wallington, New Jersey, and had only lived in the United States for five years. He had emigrated from Poland and served as his family's translator. During their time at Fort Carson, Matulac and Slomiany would often go skiing with a couple other guys, Earl Huber and Tom Gruenburg. Slomiany was drafted along with the others in 1965, and planned to apply for citizenship after fulfilling his obligation to the Army.

Now that Alpha Company was staying together and going to Vietnam as a unit, certain positions needed to be filled and additional duties assigned. Each of the four platoons within the company would need a radio operator, and their company commander would require two. This additional duty of radio operator would be assigned to certain infantrymen within the company. Royce Barrow recalled how he wound up as a radio operator for CPT Wise, and how it had nothing to do with anything radio-related. One of their sergeants came into their barracks, asking around for volunteers to help with some projects. Barrow had been soldiering long enough to know that, if you were smart, you never volunteered for anything in the Army. No one else volunteered however, and then the sergeant mentioned that he was looking for someone who could draw, or at least had some "artistic ability". Barrow was an avid drawer and had many artists in his family. And so, reluctantly, he volunteered to meet with CPT Wise in the company orderly room. He soon had him drawing up training aids, maps, targets, and other things that the company would use in their training over the coming months.

As CPT Wise got to know Barrow and liked him, he decided to make him one of his company radio operators, along with Donald Rankin, Bill Purdy's friend from Kentucky who'd been drafted shortly after dropping out of college. Barrow was from North Carolina and had also attended college. He had dropped out for a while to pay off expenses and save for one last year of tuition, and just like Rankin, received his draft notice shortly thereafter. The two of them would be trained by their communications sergeant, SSG Matulac, along with those picked by the platoon leaders to be their own radio operators. Amongst the platoon radio operators were Alan Weisman, Kenneth Rathyen, Phil Jones, and Dave Fedell. SSG Matulac was experienced, and taught the men everything he knew about radio communications. Barrow recalls how Kenneth Rathyen had worked at a camera shop before being drafted, and knew a lot about cameras. Barrow planned on taking a lot of pictures while he was in Vietnam, so Rathyen helped him pick out a small 35mm camera that fit easily in his shirt pocket.

Alpha Company was now also in need of medics. Trained at Fort Sam Houston for their own Combat Medic AIT, among the medics assigned to Alpha Company were Bill Garcia from California for 1st Platoon, Mike Walker for 2nd Platoon, Michael Handley, a tall farm boy from Central Illinois for 3rd Platoon, and Thomas Monnier for 4th Platoon.

Now that things were getting real, the young men of Alpha Company started thinking harder about their fate. Some would go AWOL (away without leave). For his part, Joe Sanchez's friend, Alan Weisman, struggled with the thought of going to Vietnam. He was known as one to speak his mind, and at one point got into a shoving match with one of the guys over his feelings about the war. He considered becoming a conscientious objector, and even spoke with a rabbi about it. The rabbi didn't exactly give Weisman the kind of counsel he was looking for, explaining that Jews have always answered the call to duty when their country is at war. Matulac recalls Weisman confiding in him that he was quite afraid. In an attempt to lighten the mood, Matulac said, "You have to go." Weisman asked him why, and he said, "Because you're the only Jew in our company."

"Yeah, I have to go," Weisman replied. The battalion commander took it upon himself to personally speak with Weisman about his concerns. What LTC Swett said to him is not known, but his words persuaded him to stick it out and do his duty.

Sanchez had developed major misgivings about what lay ahead as well. He began to regret his volunteering to be drafted and was seriously considering heading for the hills, going AWOL. He confided his fears and what he was thinking to Teresa, whom he had been continuing to date. She knew how much damage such a decision could do to his future. Whatever she said to him gave him the courage to carry on, and would alter the course of his life forever.

22 May '66 – 72 weeks left

Dear Folks,

Guess it's my turn to write again. We were only out into the fields just 5 days. Now we're going out this Monday for another 5 days. It was awful weather out there. The last day had about 2 inches of snow and cold. It's a laugh, those guys from the city are scared stiff of snakes. Killed a couple of them. Issued my bulletproof vest yesterday. Looks like something for the North Pole for clothing, but it can do a good job of stopping a bullet. We had an inspection of rifles today. I was the only guy that got inspected in our platoon and I didn't know our battalion commander had come for 'inspection arms'. Well, Lieutenant Colonel Swett stands in front of me, I give him a big smile, and he keeps staring. "Well, don't you know how to come to inspection arms?"

"No sir," I said. Asked me a bunch of questions. The platoon leader's face turned red. It wasn't my fault. Anyway, it was pretty funny.

Captain Wise, our C.O. (Company Commander) told us when we're leaving for V.C. land today. I wouldn't worry about it if I were you. My parents didn't raise no fool, even though you sometimes think so, ha! One of our sergeants has been over to Nam already. Rode shotgun (machine gun) on the helicopter. He wanted to sell me his pocket size camera today. Figure I'd wait 'til I get to Nam. By the way, we're going by boat. I can see

I'll be feeding the fish every time I get seasick. Takes about 4 weeks to get there. Brother.

Everyone knows this battalion is lean and mean. They step aside when they see our distinguished camouflage neck piece. Yeah man, tough, ha! Well, we do a lot of exercises and running. Bet there aren't too many soldiers that go through two years of basic training. My gosh, that write up of Allen Simon, ha, ha, ha! Is he a hero? Everyone has that type of training. Man!

Say, I might get a chance to jump. This friend I know made some 73 jumps before, and he goes to Denver and rents a plane. I helped pack his chute last Sunday. Know not for sure if I can jump, if I do I know I'll shit my pants, yeah.

Seen this show "Sound of Music". It was in this theater for 22 weeks straight now. Told Larry Geissler about wearing long underwear so we get used to hot weather. I guess he believed me, ha!

Dad, I want you to watch this racing car of mine. Just make sure they're taking care of it and don't let it sit idle, which I doubt they would. Did they race it tonight, how'd they do? Mike is darn lucky to be in the Boy Scouts. Man I wish I could have been in one. Might say I am in one right now, except a little bigger, that's all.

Your son,

Will

Martin Quinn recalled one night in particular, when their platoon sergeant rented out a room at one of the bars downtown. "It was just before going overseas. I was drinking rum and cokes and screwdrivers, and everyone got plowed. I don't even remember coming home that night."

5 June '66 – 71 weeks left

Dear Folks,

We had a platoon party the other night. Sergeant Burtis said before we left, "Don't fool with my German wife." The other said, "if anyone gets too wild and drunk, I'll smooch him in the mouth and kick him out," ha! We got to the bar and Elmer says to me, "Watch, I can speak a little German." He did alright. Now he'll be on detail for the next two weeks. The sergeant that warned us not to be too crazy, had his girlfriend instead of his wife spend the night, and spent the night in the cooler for drunken driving and speeding. The other sergeant got into an argument with some guy over a woman, and the woman pulled out a pistol and cooled them off. Can't wait until tomorrow morning to hear what they have to say, ha!

Our Lt. Colonel Swett is over in Viet Nam now, making reservations for us. He should not have too much trouble, ha! Hope the scenery is pretty and the fishing and hunting good. We are starting helicopter training now. This week especially, and then I guess two more weeks in the field.

Then we start flying in the choppers. We're in good shape. Can run 2 ½ miles and walk 8 miles with a 40 lb pack and still go bowling that night.

Henning's sister wants to pick us up when our leave comes. I told him you would, but I guess she still wants to. Better have the haying done. I doubt if I am physically fit for such heavy work. Be glad to see those green fields again. Only thing green in this state is the work clothes you wear. I increased my G.I. insurance another $5,000, making it $10,000 now. Costs only 2 bucks a month.

Will

13 June '66 – 71 weeks left

Hi Mike,

School is out now and you're spending your weekends camping, I suppose. They don't sell firecrackers in Colorado, so I can't get you any. Maybe I can sneak home a bomb. Maybe!

Working late all week, Wednesday up at 3 AM and to bed at midnight. Also, we'll be riding in helicopters. No more bivouac camping, whoopee! Just 14 working days left. We jumped off a 35-foot tower with a rope tied around us. Our platoon sergeant, Staff Sergeant Burtis, got on top and wouldn't come down. No lie, he was up there for an hour and a half, shaking like a leaf, ha ha! We were all nervous alright. We're receiving a lot of classes on Viet Nam. The guys go crazy over the movies we have about them. Guess we'll be stars someday, ha! Lt. Colonel Swett has taken some movie pictures of the exact place where we will be going. Be seeing them pretty soon. They say it is a pretty comfortable war, so they say. You go out and fight a little, come back, take a shower, go to the P.X. and have a few beers. By the way, I am pissed off 'cause they cut the free beer ration in half, from 6 cases to 3. Well, I guess you can't have everything.

Will

26 June '66 – 70 weeks left

Dear Folks,

Would you believe it if I said I was busy? Man, talk about losing sleep. But just one week left of training and we can hang it up. Wish I was in basic, it was 3 times easier then. I like them choppers though. Give quite a ride, fish-tailing around. Ride in them just about every day. Look on the map for the city of An-Khe, Viet Nam, it's where we will be stationed. Central Highlands, right in the middle of the action, ha! Hope you're not losing sleep over this. Isn't that bad. I am not worried, and no one else is either. Guess C Company got raffle tickets on which sergeants are going to be bumped off first. That seems a bit grim.

Got 8 months in this damn Army today and still no stripe. Most of us don't have one. Henning in D Co has had one for 2 months already. I am telling the C.O. to shove it. We're the best company in the battalion and still not treated right.

When are you sending the food? You know better than to ask a silly question like, do I want some cookies and doughnuts. Of course I do. When I get a chance, I'll send you some C-Rations, and I'll bet you'll never eat it cold. Have to make it out to a movie now.

So Long,

Will

1 July '66 – 70 weeks left

Dear Folks,

We finally finished training. Wow, does it ever feel good. We've got a week left, of what I don't know. A parade, packing, shots, and turning in our gear is about all there is left. Been a long hard time and I'll really be glad to get home. We're going to try like hell to rent a car this Sunday and Monday and watch the races at Pike's Peak.

Ricky Mitchell had a close call? Just cross your fingers. He'll be home in Jan. 67, way I figure.

Heard there might be an airline strike the 8th. I doubt if I can make it home with Henning. He is leaving Friday. So I'll make it home by bus from Minnesota. With any luck you can pick me up Sunday afternoon in Eau Claire. Yeah, I almost dropped my teeth when I received a letter from Darrell. Says the car is the fastest one down there. Can't wait to see it.

See you all soon,

Will

For reasons unknown, Joe Sanchez was transferred to the 2nd Battalion, 20th Aerial Rocket Artillery (2/20th ARA), a gunship aviation battalion of the 1st Air Cavalry, and sent to Vietnam in early July. Gunships were helicopters armed with various types of machine guns and rockets.

Also in July, Donald Rankin and twelve others were sent to attend special jungle training in Panama. While on his connecting flight back to Fort Carson, he wrote this letter to his family.

Chicago Airport - Tuesday Night

Dear Mom and Daddy,

We're finally almost back to Colorado. The flights have been smooth and pleasant. Panama was very interesting. We learned a lot, but the temperature, mud, rain, and insects were almost intolerable at times. I got hit in the top of the head with a rifle butt during the first day of training. We were jumping from a truck, and the guy behind me jumped too quickly. It was only a small cut, but they sent me to the hospital that day and later in the week. That cost me 100 points, and I didn't make Jungle Expert. I needed 800 points and I had 765. The people in Panama are so poor that it is almost unbelievable. The main part of town is about like Irishtown. They think of everything to get your money.

Our trip from Charleston to Panama was unbearable. We got off the ground once and had to turn around and come back because the landing gear wouldn't come up. They repaired that and then we took off again. I went to sleep while they were loading, so I didn't know when we took off. The second time we got full speed on the runway and bells started to ring. The engine right next to our window went out. They got us stopped and we went back to the terminal and stayed about two hours. Everyone was afraid to get on the third time, but we made it with no problems. We just left the ground in a United jet! It is smooth and the sunset is beautiful. It is red, orange, yellow, and then turns purple. We are flying toward it so we can see it a long time. We left four guys in Chicago. We thought we had an hour. But, we only had twenty minutes. Some of the guys' families were there and they didn't get to the ramp on time. They have tickets so they won't have any problem.

You should see my moustache. I really got quite a beard in the jungle, so I left the moustache. I'm sure the company commander will make me shave it off.

We wear a green and yellow scarf around our necks instead of a tie. There is an Airborne unit that has the same. We ran into them in Panama and they were going to whip us and make us take them off. However, we had plenty of guys, some knives and bottles, so they calmed down. One guy punched one of our men. Our guy punched him back and he ran. The Airborne really think they're something.

How are you all feeling? Is school out? I guess the weather is pretty now. I've been a little homesick the last few days. What do you all really think about Nancy and our age difference? Sometimes, I think that maybe I'd like to marry her but her family is such a bunch of goofballs. I'd hate to ask her to wait. But, it would be ridiculous to get married before going overseas.

They keep cutting our leave time. We're getting ten days before going to Vietnam. Have you heard from Jerry? Will he be home in July? This is about all. Write soon.

Love,

Donnie

The battalion's only female soldier, SP/4 Brutus T. Bear, was informed by her handlers that she would not be making the voyage with them. At just over a year old, she was deemed too young for combat by their commander. She may have been disappointed to see her friends go off to war without her. It was hard to tell though, as her face always wore the same blank expression, regardless of her mood. She would stay at Fort Carson for the time, and eventually travel to Vietnam after she had grown and matured.

Before departing for Vietnam, the soldiers were given a two-week pass to return home, make arrangements, write their wills, and say their goodbyes. A handful of soldiers would take the opportunity to marry their sweethearts back home. Among them was Will's squad leader, Bobby Hayslip who, as Quinn recalled, got married approximately ten days before shipping out. Another was twenty-one-year-old Charles Bradford from Newport, Kentucky. To his friends he was known as "Charlie Cool", and sometimes spoke with a stutter. The youngest of ten children, Bradford was known by his many adoring nieces and nephews as "Uncle Charlie". He was very protective, and quick to warn others not to mess with them. For whatever reason, he was not optimistic about his fate as he prepared for war, remarking that he may just come home in a box. "Aww unc', you're too mean to not come home," said one of his nephews. In any case, he wanted to ensure that his young bride, Peggy, was taken care of.

On the last day of his own two-week pass, Al Patrillo would catch up with his childhood friend and neighbor from Susquehanna, Pennsylvania, Tom Ivey. As Tom recalls, it had been a long time since they had last chatted. Much had changed and they had lost touch a bit, but Al was still like an older brother to him. Al told him he would be headed to Vietnam the next day, but didn't seem nervous or apprehensive. They talked about the classes Tom was now taking, all the crazy training Al had been through, and how he had shot "expert" at the rifle range. Mostly however, Al seemed enthused about a girl that he had been seeing. They had just gone out on a date the night before and he seemed pretty serious about her.

Sporting a cavalry-style moustache, Will traveled back to Tilden with Rodney Henning. By now, they had become good pals. On their caps, they now wore the arm and saber regimental crest of the 7th Cavalry, and on their shoulders, the bright yellow shield and black horse head patch of the 1st Air Cavalry Division. When it was time to return to Fort Carson, Eddie and Millie drove Will back to the airport in Minneapolis. His cousin, Alice, had ridden along to see him off. After exchanging hugs and kisses, he slung his duffel bag over his shoulder and made his way down the concourse. As she watched him disappear into the crowd of travelers, Millie asked Alice if she thought Willie would make it back alive.

April 1966, LTC Swett (left) and generals watching a weapons firepower demonstration at Fort Carson, U.S. Army Photograph

CPT A.J. Wise, first commander of Alpha Company, 5/7th Cavalry

UNEXPECTED ENTRY is the exercise in store for Pvt Teddy Olson, B Company 5th Bn 7th Cavalry, in combat survival swimming training. Blindfolds insure that each trainee derives maximum benefit from the simulated tactical situation. Olson's baseball bat simulates a rifle. Men unable to swim were given special training in basic strokes and water safety techniques. Assisting him is Lt Burnard E. Grady.

The Mountaineer, 13 May 1966

A.J. Wise and radio operator Donald Rankin, photo by Robert Matulac

Fort Carson, (left to right) radio operators Royce Barrow and Kenneth Rathyen, photo by Robert Matulac

The Mountaineer, 24 June 1966

June 1966, Fort Carson's rappel tower, U.S. Army Photograph

Air Assault training at Fort Carson, photo by Marvin Bierschbach

Albert Patrillo and Mom, Millie

Charles Bradford with bride, Peggy

4
SEASICK
...and that was the good part.

President Lyndon Johnson had dramatically increased troop levels since the beginning of the year when approximately 185,000 personnel were stationed in Vietnam. By August of 1966, that number had grown to almost 300,000, and would swell to over 385,000 by year-end. At the time, just over five thousand Americans had been killed throughout all the previous years of America's involvement. When the first soldiers of the 1st Air Cavalry Division were sent to Vietnam the year prior, in 1965, it represented a dramatic increase in the size and scope of the war. Before then, the conflict was the domain of the Special Forces and advisors who could call upon American aircraft to assist the South Vietnamese, who at the time were only faced with fighting the local Viet Cong guerrillas. Between that time and 1966, several regular Army and Marine divisions had been sent in from the United States, while thousands of regular North Vietnamese Army (NVA) soldiers had poured into the highlands via the Ho Chi Minh Trail. It was the beginning of the big war. The men of the newly-formed 5th Battalion, 7th Cavalry represented a massive doubling down in American commitment to that war, in keeping with the late President John F. Kennedy's inaugural declaration:

Let every nation know, whether it wishes us well or ill, that we shall pay any price, bear any burden, meet any hardship, support any friend, oppose any foe to assure the survival and the success of liberty.

Most of the young men drafted into service at this stage of the war or after would be sent to Vietnam as replacements. Going to war essentially alone, they would cross the ocean on a commercial-style military jetliner. Upon arrival, they would typically be sent straight to a "replacement battalion" in Vietnam, where it would then be decided which particular division and unit they would be assigned to. As such, they would typically arrive at their company already in the field. If they were fortunate, they might know some of their fellow replacements, but would generally start out as strangers in their new companies. This is how the experience of the original members of the 5/7th Cav differed from most others, and what made it special. Most had been drafted in 1965, trained together at Fort Carson, and now they would all go to war together with only their most senior leaders bringing combat experience along with them. Whether they knew it or not, however, each of these companies that comprised this battalion known as the 5/7th Cav would largely disintegrate over the course of the next year - and most of those who survived would return home alone, many of them broken in one way or another.

In Alpha Company, those who had been to war before included most of their platoon sergeants and some of their squad leaders. Among them were James Bonner, Marvin Hall, Harry Coit, Kenneth Gregory, James Evans, and Cleofas Madrid. Of these veterans, most had not been to Vietnam, but rather Korea. Their company commander, CPT A.J. Wise, had actually been a communications sergeant in the Korean War, and would occasionally remind Matulac, his own communications sergeant, of this fact.

On August 2nd 1966, the entire newly-formed battalion left Fort Carson in a mile-long caravan of buses. In the fog-laden San Francisco Bay, the aging USNS Gaffey awaited their arrival. Twenty-three years prior, she had first ferried troops to Guadalcanal during World War II, then to the Philippines and Okinawa. Like many of the 5/7th Cav's senior NCOs and officers, she had also been to Korea.

From a distance, the ship was a cacophony of noise and activity. By forklift and other means, massive loads of equipment, supplies, and food were being fed from the pier and over the gangway into a large opening in her massive grey hull. The soldiers would spend several hours napping on their duffel bags and smoking cigarettes before they were finally herded onto the vessel, one company at a time. Lugging their duffel bags on their backs, they were marched in a sort of half-assed formation into the opening in the ship's hull as the band played *Garry Owen* on the pier.

The approximately 180 soldiers of Alpha Company were led in a general state of confusion down dimly-lit stairwells, through long corridors, and into a large room filled with rows of bunks stacked four-high. The ship smelled dank, of sea salt and mildew. As soldiers claimed each of their individual bunks by throwing their bags on them, it soon became apparent that there were not enough for each of them. They were advised by their NCOs to start buddying-up. Known in the Navy as "hot-racking", they would share bunks and sleep in shifts for the next few weeks.

As the sun descended on the horizon, the ship's giant engines roared to life, belching black clouds into the sky, sending tremors through its frame, and arousing a renewed bustling and anticipation amongst those on deck. Along with hundreds of others, Will and his buddies gathered along the railing to watch the city of San Francisco disappear into the mist. For many, this would be their last view of American soil. Shortly thereafter, Will hurried back down into the ship to vomit in the toilet, as he was among the first to be hit by seasickness. They sailed out under the Golden Gate Bridge where many kind-hearted people had gathered to throw flowers and wreaths down to them - then into the Pacific, commencing eighteen days of constant up and down motion amidst its waves. Their first night and day of the voyage would be spent trying to find their sea legs, and most of the approximately two thousand soldiers aboard would quickly become seasick. To stave off the nausea, one of the cooks advised some of Charlie Company's soldiers on KP duty to eat an entire stick of butter. It seemed to actually work for some. Conditions on the ship were cramped and hot. To avoid overcrowding in their quarters below, no less than a third of the soldiers were required to be on deck at all times. Many would get over their seasickness after a few days at sea, but Will would remain ill. He tried some pills from the dispensary, and that seemed to help a bit.

Faced with the challenge of keeping a couple thousand soldiers out of trouble for eighteen days at sea, their leaders quickly set about tasking the men with duties. Kitchen duty, latrine duty, guard duty, and just about every kind of menial task, or "detail", as it is often called in the Army. To avoid these undesirable details, Bobby Hansen and his buddy, Jim Hirschuber, decided to spend most of their voyage hiding in one of the ship's lifeboats. To their good fortune, they would find that the lifeboats contained survival rations, and at times their buddies would bring them food from the galley. No one seemed to care that they were unaccounted for.

Hirschuber would explain how they actually ended up hiding out in the lifeboats. Their particular bunks were located just beneath an enormous heat pipe. It was already terribly hot in the bunk room, but he estimated the temperature under the pipe to be about 130 degrees. So, they went out to sleep on the deck. At about 3:00 AM, the crew began hosing down the deck and they were almost washed overboard. They climbed up and took cover in a lifeboat, and after that they just decided to stay there. He recalls a volleyball game being played on deck the next afternoon. At one point, the wayward ball bounced up and into their lifeboat. He could hear the voice of one of their company's platoon leaders, First Lieutenant (1LT) James Harmon, saying he was going to go get it. Anticipating an awkward situation, he threw the ball back out of the lifeboat. They expected to get caught at this point, but there was no further investigation.

The rest of the young men aboard would attend classes and briefings designed to prepare them for what they would face in-country. In the mornings, they would perform weapons training and exercise on the deck. There were even some impromptu boxing matches held. Will watched some of these, but was smart enough to not take part in them.

The following letter was sent by Donald Rankin from aboard the Gaffey.

August 12, 1966

Dear Mom, Daddy and all,

We're nearing Okinawa, and I can't wait. The voyage wouldn't be too bad if we weren't so crowded. I got seasick the sixth day and then had intestinal flu two days later. The sea is certainly boring after a few days. We've seen sharks, whales, and flying fish. The flying fish are unbelievable. There are 2,000 guys on the ship. Everyone gets along pretty well, and we're all in good spirits. They gave us GI haircuts again. It feels pretty good, but my head sunburns a lot.

You wouldn't believe how crowded we sleep. We are in double bunks, and we sleep head to toe. It is really hard to sleep with some of these smelly feet. Most of the guys are from my section that I sleep close to, so I make them take a shower at least every other night. Taking a shower is difficult because the shower room is at the end of the ship and it is very easy to get seasick up there. You have to hold on to the railing to stay seated on the commode. This is about all. I will write as soon as we arrive.

Love,

Donnie

Will also sent a letter home from aboard the ship.

13 Aug '66 – 63 weeks left

Dear Folks,

Haven't quite made it yet. Left San Francisco the 2nd and haven't seen land since, and won't until we hit Okinawa on the 15th. Just can't wait 'till we get there. Been seasick twice. I don't believe I could take Navy life. You know this boat, not worthy enough to be called a ship, is only going about 20 M.P.H. Imagine going to Minneapolis from home in a car at that speed. There are about 2,000 troops on this ship, about 600 of us guys (in our battalion). The weather is about 80-90 degrees. Got a very close haircut. Well everybody did, and my little moustache shaved off. We all look like we just got into the Army. Remember this colored guy I introduced you to, Graham? He's in jail for hitting a sergeant. Only guy in the cooler on the ship. It's pretty serious. So far, we've seen flying fish by the hundreds, and a few small whales and a few sharks. Seen the prison of Alcatraz and the Golden Gate Bridge. We have class about two hours a day and P.T. Rest of the time we lay around and play cards. Some games are for pretty high stakes. Got plenty of sleep, 10-12 hours. I guess by next Thursday we should be in Viet Nam. I'll be so happy to get there, just to get off this boat.

You know, it'll be almost a month before I'll be able to hear from you, since I left home that is. I hope you got my clothes and sleeping bag, and save them hats, they fit me well. My pants got dirty 'cause I was following a creek as the M.P.s were chasing me 'cause I went to town without a pass. Anyway, they didn't catch me, ha! I better sign off. The mail room is closing sooner than I expected. It is Sunday now, 6 o'clock PM. It's probably 8 o'clock and you're getting ready for church. Anyway, so long.

Up & down & up & down,

Will

Also sailing to Vietnam aboard the Gaffey was twenty-three-year-old Second Lieutenant (2LT) Winston Groom, fresh from his advanced training at Fort Bragg, North Carolina. He did not belong to the 5/7th Cav, but rather a psy-ops detachment on their way to join the 245th Psychological Operations Company in the Central Highlands of Vietnam. He had been appointed as "Rumor Control Officer" for the voyage over, so he started a rumor of his own amongst the soldiers aboard the ship, that they were being followed by an enemy submarine, just to see how long it took for the rumor to get back to him. In 1978, he would write one of the very first Vietnam War novels, *Better Times Than These*. The first part of his novel takes place aboard the Gaffey and was inspired by the events of his own voyage. In 1986 he would write another novel, entitled *Forrest Gump*.

Despite deep suspicions pointing to the two chaps who hid in the lifeboat, the identity of who caused the life vest fiasco remains a mystery to this day. A couple of weeks into the voyage, in what were relatively calm waters of the South China Sea, a signal came over the ship's distress frequency. A crewmember was sent to check the life vests, each of which was equipped with an electronic device that sends out a distress signal when deployed into the water. As expected, one was missing. Now every ship within the missing life vest's two-hundred-mile beacon would be required by maritime law to spend no less than four hours searching for it. As the ship circled back and searched for the life vest over the next five hours, the men were put on lockdown and forced to stay in their sweltering, overcrowded bunk rooms while officers and NCOs at every level took account of their men and reported their status up the chain of command. With every man accounted for, the question of who had thrown the life vest overboard remained unanswered. Out of sheer boredom, it had likely been thrown overboard as a joke. No one was laughing about it now, as they were to be kept on lockdown until someone confessed.

Interrogations persisted in vain until the ship encountered a massive typhoon that night. Anyone who wasn't sick at this time soon would be. Over and over, the ship rose with the swells, then crashed into the troughs, sending shivers, creeks, and moans throughout the length of its aging frame. At this point, it was too dangerous to go on deck for fresh air, and so they would stay in their steaming bunk rooms, passing the trash cans between them as needed. Marvin Bierschbach recalls holding on for dear life while trying to use the toilet, as seawater sloshed around and over the ankles of anyone trying to use the latrine. Hirschuber recalled how he and a couple other guys made their way through the ship's engine room that night; they weren't supposed to be there, of course. They found a trap door that opened up top and watched the many enormous waves rising above the deck. They thought for sure, they were going to sink. The ship's captain was known to later remark that it was the worst storm he'd ever encountered.

The storm eventually subsided, and they docked on the island of Okinawa the next morning. The soldiers were given a box lunch and kicked off to make way for the ship's resupply. As it was a military base, many tried to find the PX (Post Exchange, a military convenience store) to buy stuff or call home. Most, however, just got good and hammered with the free beer made available on the beach. One can just imagine the challenge of getting over two thousand drunk soldiers back onto the Gaffey that evening. The shore patrol would spend much of the night policing up stray troopers along the beach and elsewhere. The heat was stifling, and it persisted after darkness fell. Many soldiers slept on the deck that night in Okinawa.

They would sail for another two days before reaching Vietnam. It was Will's first voyage at sea. By all accounts, it was a miserable journey for everyone aboard, and especially him. He would not voluntarily set foot on an ocean liner again for another forty-five years. "How we survived all that, I don't know," Marvin Bierschbach joked over fifty years later, "...and that was the good part."

USNS Gaffey, photo by Marvin Bierschbach

Passing under Golden Gate Bridge, photo by Marvin Bierschbach

5/7th Cav officers and NCOs aboard the USNS Gaffey, 1SG Dayton Hare sitting second from left, front row (with cigar), LTC Ted Swett standing in back row (middle), photo by Royce Vick

Boxing matches aboard the Gaffey, photo by Marvin Bierschbach

5
SORRY ABOUT THAT

Seems funny, all these years I read about these people in geography class and here I am seeing it for real.

At approximately 4:00 AM on August 20th 1966, the USNS Gaffey arrived at the Port of Qui Nhon. Those who were awake on deck could make out the dark silhouette of mountains in the distance. By 8:00 AM, the heat was punishing, and the ship was again a giant beehive of noise, movement, clanking and yelling. Just before disembarking, the troopers were issued their rifles and forty rounds of ammunition, and they complained about not getting more. Because the ship was too large to dock, LCUs (Landing Craft Utility boats) were used to ferry the soldiers ashore. They looked just like the landing craft they had all seen in movies and newsreels about the D-Day invasion of World War II. After throwing down their duffel bags, they climbed down cargo nets into the landing craft. In the confusion of it all, someone had taken Will's helmet. The walls of the landing craft were high and the soldiers couldn't see where they were going. Rifles at the ready, many of the young men prepared to assault the beach under fire as the landing craft approached the shoreline. After a few minutes of anticipation, the ramp of the landing craft slammed down onto the sand. Surprise! There was the band again, playing their familiar theme song. This time they were flanked by a cadre of generals and other big-wigs, division and battalion flags on display, and a contingent of reporters taking pictures. People were lying about the beach, looking up at them in confusion.

Decades later, Bob Matulac would speak of the "vivid imaginations" of the young soldiers that day, and how so many of them thought they would be storming the beach. Don Shipley was a young trooper in Charlie Company, the first company to land ashore. He explained how it wasn't just their imaginations that were to blame. While aboard the LCUs, as a joke, many of their veteran NCOs had actually told them that they would be attacking the beach.

As hundreds of soldiers spilled out onto the shore, an NCO from Bravo Company, SSG George Porod, was now lighting up Will for not wearing his steel pot. What a way to start out his combat tour, he thought, with no helmet. Before long however, Alpha Company's 1SG Potter stepped in and advised SSG Porod to mind his own troops. The soldiers were immediately herded onto a convoy of 2 ½ ton trucks known as "deuce-and-a-halfs". They were transported to a nearby airstrip, and then crammed onto a giant C-130 cargo plane and flown to their base camp near the town of An Khe, Camp Radcliff. Will and a handful of other soldiers stayed behind to guard equipment until more trucks came to haul it all off. They helped load the equipment and send it on its way, then were taken to the airfield to spend the night. The next morning, another small convoy of deuce-and-a-halfs would bring them to base camp, where they would join their battalion.

As their convoy made its way through Qui Nhon, the new arrivals were immediately accosted by the smell of sewage, occasionally mixed with that of diesel fuel, burning garbage, and whatever the townspeople happened to be cooking. The streets were lined with vendors and pushcarts, and filled with hundreds of people on bicycles and scooters, which looked to be their main form of transportation aside from a handful of French-manufactured cars. With arms stretched to the sky, a gaggle of children ran alongside the truck, begging for candy. Some of the troopers threw C-Ration items and candy bars down to the kids and watched the ensuing melee. Soon the children were left behind in a cloud of dust as the convoy barreled out of the city and into the countryside.

Known as the gateway to the Central Highlands, Highway 19 was the main east-west route from Qui Nhon to An Khe, and beyond to Pleiku. Along its winding path, Will would take in the scenery, the rolling mountains and floodplains, and the patchwork of rice paddies that stretched through valleys toward dark tropical tree lines. Thatch-colored villas and huts could be seen along their banks. The dust cloud from the trucks in front coated the soldiers in a fine film of red Vietnamese dirt that clung to their sweat. It was approaching one hundred degrees and the sun was intense. Every so often, a lone farmer and his water buffalo could be seen working the fields. Women could be seen, sometimes in groups, working in the paddies or walking along the road carrying things and wearing conical straw hats. It seemed a rather peaceful scene. The forests however, were dark, foreboding and mysterious. Their thick canopies blocked out any hint of sunlight, even in the height of the afternoon, creating a dark abyss beneath them. Will imagined himself walking into that abyss, knowing not what lay inside.

The forests stretched further on, toward the mountains in the west, the highlands. They were headed into those mountains. After nine months of training, he was finally here in the backyard of the enemy, known to them as "Charlie". Now riding exposed in the back of the truck, he thought about how the enemy could be out there right now, watching him. In his mind, he pictured what he might look like, now in Charlie's crosshairs. He felt like an easy target. Before long, however, his thoughts returned to home, to the farm and his family. If they could only see me now, he thought.

Soon they found themselves winding their way through the mountains, and every so often they would pass a checkpoint manned by soldiers who looked bored. After what seemed an eternity but was actually only forty miles or so, they rounded a corner and someone spotted something bright and yellow atop a mountain towering in the distance. Eventually, they could make out the profile of a horse head within a yellow shield, and it was clear what they were looking at, the giant shoulder patch insignia of the 1st Air Cavalry plastered to the side of a mountain.

After a few more twists and turns through plunging mountain passes, they arrived at Camp Radcliff. Located in the heart of the Central Highlands near the town of An Khe, it was more commonly referred to simply as "An Khe". To the west loomed Hon Cong Mountain, displaying its giant 1st Air Cavalry patch on its side, leaving no doubt as to who owned the surrounding real estate. On its peak sat a security outpost and communications center for the camp. Scratched out of the wilderness by the initial wave of the division's soldiers to arrive in Vietnam the year before, An Khe was still primitive in terms of living conditions. Many of the permanent structures had yet to be built. This was the 1st Air Cavalry Division's headquarters and operating base, and here the new arrivals would behold the spectacle of the division's monumental operation. Chinook helicopters sling-loaded howitzers and crates of ammunition, while giant Sky Cranes hauled disabled Chinooks through the air. Communication and guard towers were scattered around the vast perimeter. All manner of war implements were on display, earth movers, tanks, artillery, supply trucks, fuel tankers, C-130 cargo planes, and endless rows of helicopters of all kind. It was a steadily moving colossus of lead, rubber, petroleum and steel.

In August of the previous year, the site that would become known as Camp Radcliff (An Khe) was selected by Brigadier General John M. Wright, Jr., after scouring the Central Highlands for a location suitable for accommodating aircraft of all sizes, including the over four hundred aircraft owned by the 1st Air Cavalry Division. General Wright knew, however, that an airstrip made of dirt would result in terrible dust storms with each and every take-off and landing. The underlying grass and brush would remain but would have to be cut very close to the ground. The general had not anticipated that his advance party in August of 1965 would be comprised of less than two hundred men, most of whom were high-ranking officers and NCOs. After they arrived, he gathered them in and began:

Gentlemen, you will all be issued a machete or a grub hook; they both do exactly the same job. We are going to cut brush until we have a golf course here. You may as well hang your rank insignia on a tree because until this area is transformed, we will all avail ourselves to this manual task. When the golf course is completed, you may then put back your rank insignia.

The airfield at Camp Radcliff would thereafter be known as the Golf Course.

Because the 5/7th Cav was new to the base, the battalion was simply given a large plot of dirt upon which they were to build their battalion area. On their first day there, the soldiers worked into the night erecting large tents that would serve as their barracks. Another would serve as their mess hall. Trenches were dug around each of them to prevent water from future rains running through their tents. Large holes were also dug by the men to act as bunkers in case of a mortar attack. Everyone was soon covered in the red dirt of An Khe. Just as an afternoon rain was approaching, all of the "old-timers", those who had been there awhile, stripped off their clothes, grabbed their soap and took a refreshing shower in the rain. The new guys ran into their tents to find their own soap and towels. When they came back outside however, the rain had stopped. They had just gotten wet enough to work up a nice soap and dirt lather and had no way to rinse off.

After evening chow, the men were relaxing when mortar rounds began to fall on An Khe. Most of them landed near the perimeter wire, but soon the rounds came closer to the road that ran through the battalion area. One round landed next to the colonel's tent, then another even closer to the road where many of the men had gathered. Most of them hit the dirt or took cover in the makeshift bunkers they had recently dug out of the ground.

Except for two in particular, most of the new battalion's men spent their first night at An Khe trying to sleep while the base's howitzers fired artillery rounds toward distant hills. Bierschbach had spent most of their first day working shirtless in the Vietnamese sun – not a wise decision for a Scandinavian guy with fair skin. With his back severely burnt, he would sleep on his stomach for the next few nights. Eventually, they would acclimate to the constant pounding of artillery, as well as the relentless heat.

Matulac related a story of two guys in search of a good time during that first night at An Khe:

Two men from Alpha Company got drunk. Bobby Hansen and Tom Gruenburg. Gruenburg decided they should go into An Khe (the town) and get some women. Hansen attempted to talk Gruenburg out of it, but he insisted. He climbed into Lieutenant Colonel Swett's jeep and they both took off down the road toward the main gate. At the gate, the MPs attempted to stop the jeep. Gruenburg gave it the gun and the MPs jumped out of the way. On to An Khe they went with MPs following them, sirens blaring. The two wayward troopers finally stopped, surrounded by MPs with guns drawn. Into the stockade they went. Captain Wise got a call from the MP in charge, and went to pick up the two drunks. The next morning, the two reported to 1SG Potter. I thought he was going to blow his top. He chewed both of them out and they seemed to melt under his wrath. Barrow, Rankin and I were in the same tent as 1SG Potter, behind a sheet that served as a door. We could barely keep ourselves from roaring with laughter.

Hansen would recall CPT Wise admonishing him that if the colonel ever found out about this, he would never get out of this place.

The following are excerpts from a letter Rankin sent the day after landing in Qui Nhon.

August 21, 1966

Dear Mom and Daddy,

We arrived at Qui Nhon yesterday. There was an Army band and villagers to greet us. The mountains are very pretty, but the villages are dirty and smelly. Our living quarters are a scream. We have tents with cots and a mosquito net. Last night, I didn't get out my blanket and almost froze. It really cools off here at night. Today, it is very hot but the wind is blowing.

The mortar shells burst about 1,000 feet away all night. The first few make you jump, and then you forget about them.

Our company area is safe. We have barb-wire barricades with land mines and machine guns out there too. Plus, a huge light about one mile up on a mountain that lights up the whole valley.

Everyone is in good spirits. We all have GI haircuts again. That and C-Rations for food are the biggest objections.

I will write as often as possible. Next week, we will probably start operations so there will be some long periods without writing. The helicopters will drop us our letters, even in combat but we won't always be able to send them out.

Tell everyone hello and write soon.

Love,

Donnie

Once the battalion area was set up, they would begin their 1st Air Cavalry "Division Training". Here they would train on a rappel tower, and again qualify with their M-16s. With all their gear, they would climb on and off a Chinook helicopter that hovered at over thirty feet using a rope ladder. They would also receive classes on booby-traps and Vietnamese culture and traditions. In a letter home dated August 26th, Rankin would remark that they spent most of their time digging ditches and going to class, but that the relationship between the NCOs and the rest of them had improved since their arrival, and they weren't giving them such a hard time as they had before.

In Bravo Company's tent, Dayton Hare, the wiry, cigar smoking First Sergeant who'd served in World War II and Korea, looked through a Pacific Exchange catalogue. The military's version of a Sears catalogue, it offered many of the same products at a lower price and was tax-free. 1SG Hare's wife had always wanted a set of fine chinaware, but it had always seemed a bit expensive. In his book, Bernard Grady, at the time Bravo Company's Executive Officer, recalls the First Sergeant showing him the picture of the Noritake chinaware set he had circled. It was the one he knew she would like, and after a couple more paydays he would have it sent home to his wife as a surprise.

24 Aug '66 – 51 weeks left

Dear Folks,

Finally getting a chance to write. It's like we expected, a lot of work. Got off the 20th. We expected to land on enemy territory, but as soon as we hit shore the band was playing. I lucked out and stayed back on detail the first day to guard equipment while everyone else flew to An Khe. I was at this airfield and hung a little jag on my first night here. We received our first operation order and we're heading out of camp here, maybe for a few weeks and come back in again. This place, Camp Radcliff or An Khe, is pretty secure and big, about a 40-mile perimeter. They're shooting artillery rounds off all night long, which is annoying. I think she'll be alright once we get settled, which will be in about 10 months. Get a tavern built after we get most of the work done. Had to eat C-Rations for two days. Now the hot meals we've been eating aren't too bad. Some ants around here are a little poisonous or something. Got up one morning and was bitten twice on the foot. Darn things sting. We get one Armed Forces Radio station out here. Have reruns of baseball games and fairly good music.

You'll notice I addressed the top of my letter with only 51 weeks left 'cause when I get out of Viet Nam, and if I still have to finish out my time in the Army, it will be like civilian life back in the states again. What did you ever do with my bombs, throw them away? Doesn't matter to me if you do. Before I forget, try and get Don Mc Ilquham's address. He was in the fields, so I didn't see him before I left Carson.

Well so long,

Will

30 Aug '66

Dear Folks,

Try to write a few lines before work starts. We haven't moved out on our mission yet, not until Friday. Guess it'll be for 2-3 months guarding a highway, which is the best job anyone can get. Hope we can keep this job for the rest of the 11 months. I just found out that this guy you met at the airport, Figueroa, Spanish guy, was one of the few who got to go to town (An Khe) last Sunday. Well, he shacked up with a woman and now he has the Clap (V.D.), ha ha! We're giving him a rough time about this now. This colored guy you met at the airport, Graham, is in the stockade in Saigon. Doubt if we'll ever see him again.

Received those snapshots yesterday. The guys got a kick out of them. Oh yes, happy anniversary to you guys and happy birthday to Mike. That's quite some birthday present he has. He'll need a license to drive it won't he? Better save it for me. Yeah, send me the newspaper for a few months. Rod gave me his Bloomer Advance. Some of the other guys are going to have the paper also. I'll be looking for them doughnuts today. I am going to sneak off with them so that I won't have to share them. I can taste them already.

Well, I better get ready for a little night patrol tonight. Last night 1st, 2nd, and 3rd platoons went out and it rained for about 2 hours straight. They were a sorry looking bunch this morning.

Will

20 August 1966, 5/7th Cav arrives at Qui Nhon, photo by Royce Vick

July 1965, initial wave of 1st Air Cavalry Division soldiers to arrive in Vietnam, source unknown

Aerial view of Camp Radcliff (An Khe), source unknown

Hon Cong Mountain, overlooking An Khe, source unknown

Joe Sanchez servicing gunship of the 2/20th ARA

·········

Since being transferred out of the 5/7th Cav, Joe Sanchez had found that being an infantryman in an aviation unit was not his cup of tea. His official job was to make sure the rockets on the gunships were mission-ready. He got to ride along in the gunships on a few missions, even though he wasn't supposed to. More often, however, he was made to be a cook for them. He had been trained to kill the enemy, and here he was cooking breakfast. After being ordered to get up early and pull KP duty for the third morning in a row, he refused. He was threatened with all kinds of punishment, including time in the stockade, but nothing came of it.

Picking up a copy of the Stars & Stripes, Sanchez noticed a front-page story of the 5/7th Cav arriving in Qui Nhon aboard the Gaffey, with photos of his former battalion coming ashore aboard the many LCUs. He walked across base camp to the 5/7th Cav's headquarters tent and requested they take him back. He managed to get the ear of their battalion commander, LTC Swett, who directed he be assigned to Bravo Company. Afterward, he ran into CPT A.J. Wise, who he remembered from Fort Carson. He explained how he really would prefer to be with Alpha Company again if possible, and so it was that he would return to his old company. Arnott Graham, the guy who had a problem with authority and punched an NCO while aboard the Gaffey, also happened to be there in the battalion headquarters at the time. He made it clear he thought Sanchez was nuts to come back to the infantry. Sanchez walked back to the 2/20th ARA to pack his stuff and get his paperwork started. The battalion clerk was typing up his transfer orders. "Going to the 5/7th, huh?" he remarked grimly, "better send your mother some flowers."

Still at An Khe during their first week, certain platoons would be sent outside the perimeter of the base camp. In these "get to know you" patrols, they marched overland for miles, learned how to cross fast-moving rivers using ropes, and set up ambushes for any approaching enemy. In a way, they served as preparation for future patrols in more remote and dangerous areas. Make no mistake, however, these were not simply training missions. In 1965, the communications center atop Hon Cong Mountain had been overrun by Viet Cong sappers, soldiers trained to infiltrate and sabotage base camps and firebases. The enemy was known to harass and probe the perimeter of An Khe, and as they had already found out, mortar attacks were frequent. In fact, if the enemy mortar teams were close enough, they could sometimes hear the metallic "shunk" sounds of their rounds being dropped into the tubes several seconds before raining down and exploding, and the soldiers learned to take cover.

Sanchez would soon find himself on one of these first patrols with his platoon and a fellow named Rocco, who carried an M-79 grenade launcher. As usual, it was raining. They crossed some rice paddies and went into a village. Rocco didn't have his poncho with him. "Extra weight," he said, so they had to share Sanchez's. After setting up their listening post for the night, Sanchez kept watch for three hours and then woke Rocco up for his turn at guard. Before he could fall asleep himself, he could hear Rocco snoring.

....

Will and the others in 4th Platoon were sent out on their own patrol outside the wire at the end of August. After moving through a village and crossing a river, they set up a night ambush and waited for the enemy to show up, but only encountered rain.

31 Aug '66 – 48 weeks left

Dear Mike,

Well, I guess you might say I have arrived in the Paradise Island as you call it. Paradise for snakes, bugs, and mosquitoes. Bugs come in three sizes: 4, 5, and 6 inches. The other day we climbed up and down a ladder on a two-engine helicopter that hovered at 20-30 feet with 90-100 MPH wind. You should have been with me last night. I never had such a miserable time since the time I had K.P. on the ship. We had this little patrol, just like on T.V., crossing rice paddies and sewage drains, and it rained about 3-4 inches anyway, in 3-4 hours. We then set up an ambush and waited most of the time. Took turns sleeping in the rain and it was cold. Went through a small village with houses made of mud and grass roofs. Seems funny, all these years I read about these people in geography class and here I am seeing it for real. I am getting some pictures of this place before I leave.

Hey Mack, tell me how did you swing this cycle? You're not even old enough to drive it. You're 15, right? You're going to drive to school? Let me know the first time you're picked up, ha! Say there old buddy, how about doing me a big favor? Send me some Kool-Aid packages, 20 or 25 packs would be alright. This will kill the taste of the water over here. We get water in rubber barrels and it tastes like rubber. I took my chance to write now 'cause it's drizzling this afternoon. Well, I just came back from supper, got two beers and two pairs of jungle boots, and I am ready to hit the sack as soon as I seal this letter.

Take it easy,

Will

At 5:00 PM on September 1st, the battalion received a request from 3rd Brigade to provide one company for a counter-ambush mission for 1st Battalion, 8th Cavalry (1/8th Cav). At the time, the 1/8th Cav was running a security mission along Highway 19. Departing An Khe on a convoy of trucks the next morning, the 5/7th's Charlie Company was sent to assist. Later that day in the battalion headquarters tent, staff officer CPT Martin Frey briefed an inspection team on the deployability of the new battalion. They also began detailed planning for the 5/7th Cav's first battalion-size mission set to begin in just a few days, when they would assume control of the entire Highway 19 security operation from the 1/8th Cav.

It was a balmy seventy-eight degrees, and a full moon shone over An Khe on the night of September 3rd. For once it wasn't raining. As the soldiers of the 5/7th Cav slept in their recently constructed tents, eight platoons from the 1/12th Cav were on patrol and in ambush positions outside the perimeter of the camp. At approximately 9:50 PM, the first of over a hundred 82mm mortar rounds began to rain down on the Golf Course, destroying dozens of the 1st Air Cav's helicopters. As sirens sounded throughout the camp, base defenses went on high alert and the response was launched. Two aerial rocket artillery (ARA) gunships took off in search of the enemy mortar team, as searchlights from the guard towers scoured the vast area outside the perimeter. Artillery batteries shot illumination rounds over the same areas while firing several high explosive rounds on preplanned targets outside the perimeter. By 9:55 PM, the mortar attack had ended and the enemy, still undetected, was attempting to escape.

At 10:13 PM, a platoon from Bravo Company, 1/12th Cav spotted a retreating Viet Cong mortar platoon. A firefight ensued, but the enemy soon slipped away. At 10:30 PM, Bravo Company, 2/5th Cav, the base camp's reaction force, was air assaulted into the area in pursuit of the enemy. At 11:00 PM, two guard towers detected enemy small arms fire and responded with machine gun and mortar rounds.

Known at the time, was that the mortar attack had come from somewhere north of the Golf Course. The area was kept lit throughout the night with spotlights from guard towers and AC-47 Spooky gunships, as well as illumination rounds from the artillery. Among the dead were four soldiers of the 15th Transportation Corps (an aviation supply and maintenance battalion). Seventy-six had been wounded, and seventy-seven aircraft had been damaged or destroyed.

As the sun rose, many more infantry companies would saturate the area in search of the enemy. All they would find, however, were four impressions left by 82mm mortar base plates in the ground just outside the wire along the northwest corner of the camp, along with three unfired mortar rounds. Ammunition expended in response to the mortar attack included 2,810 high explosive artillery rounds, 428 aerial artillery rockets, 144 high explosive mortar rounds, as well as 9,600 7.62mm rounds fired, and two 500-pound bombs dropped by the Spooky gunships.

In another letter dated September 4th, Rankin would note how the mortar attack kept them up until 2:00 AM the night before. "This place is so pretty. It is a shame that these people can't get settled and enjoy the beauty and natural resources."

The following appeared in the September 9th issue of the *Columbus Enquirer*:

Moment of Truth is Near for 1st Cavalry's Newest Battalion

AN KHE, Viet Nam (UPI) – The moment of truth is fast approaching for the 1st Air Cavalry Division's newest battalion – the moment when its men will face death in the jungle battlefield hell of Viet Nam.

Some of the men are worried. Maybe pint-sized PFC [Private First Class] Timothy Payne is too, but he doesn't show it. "Man, those V.C. can't kill me," he said. "I owe too much money. I'm paying alimony." Payne is from Galien, Mich. He is a little guy. And he has his troubles because of it. Like this afternoon when he and his buddies were standing in line to get an issue of jungle boots. "Man, they've just got to have a size four and one-half," he said. The quartermaster did, and he and his companions laced up shiny new boots. They took a couple of tentative steps. By then, the new leather and canvas boots, designed to dry quickly after a sudden rain or after wading in streams and rice paddies, were caked in oozy mud. The thick, black mud is everywhere this time of year in the central highland home the new unit – the 5th Battalion, 7th Cavalry – is hacking out of the jungle for itself.

So far, the men of the battalion have not faced the enemy. They arrived in Viet Nam on Aug. 20 to bring the brigade up to strength. But they know that any day now, they will trudge out into the jungle hunting for Communists to kill. They know, too, that some of them may not come back. Like some of the guys that they have replaced. "But they're more than willing," said Sgt. Maj. Robert Meyer, a giant of a man from Newport, Kentucky. "Morale is exceptionally high. We're ready."

PFC James B. Harmon of New Boen, Tex., is one of the battalion's riflemen. He wants to start using it. Maybe this has something to do with the fact that lately he has mostly been using a shovel. It takes a lot of digging to set up a new base camp, and it is men like Harmon who do the work. "When we get through with all this digging, though, we will be able to get out and get those Viet Cong," Harmon said. "I'm ready to go."

The battalion was formed in April at Fort Carson, Colo. Harmon said that he wouldn't mind the Communist booby-traps too much. He said he figured the cactus back at Fort Carson "is worse than these punji stakes over here." A couple of his buddies laughed. They said they figured he might change his mind later. The punji stake used by the Viet Cong is a needle-sharp sliver of bamboo that can cut through a man's boot and inflict a dangerous wound. At times, the stakes are tipped with buffalo dung which causes a rapid infection that can and has been fatal.

Since the battalion was formed, the men have had extensive physical training. They believe they are in good fighting condition. Lt. Col. Ted Swett of Columbus, Ga., battalion commander, could not be prouder of his men and their intensive training program. "Even 18 days on a ship coming over has not taken the edge off," he said. "Could you believe that 85 laps around the sundeck on that ship is three miles?" Besides the running and physical training aboard the ship, the men fired their M-16 rifles off the fantail and attended lectures to learn more about the war they will soon be fighting – and the enemy they are out to kill, and who is out to kill them.

"There are advantages of coming to war as a unit," Swett said. "One of them is that you know all of the men personally. There's one problem, though. Some of them are going to get hurt." As he said this, the battalion commander's grin disappeared for a split-second. Then it reappeared, and he added: "But we feel we are big enough to take it in stride." The colonel said he could not ask for better troops. Three-fourths of his officers, he said, hold the Expert Infantryman's Badge, and more than half of them have had Ranger training. "Fort Carson outdid itself to give me the cream of the crop," he said. "The ultimate result is that more troops will stay alive."

The battalion base camp is located only a couple of miles from the once sleepy village of An Khe which now is a G.I. honky-tonk haven where soldiers can buy anything from cold beer to female companionship. But only a few of the men have seen An Khe. Passes are few. There is too much work to do putting the finishing touches on a modern military fighting machine and its home camp. For example, there's a 1st Sgt. Haskell Westmoreland of Beckley, West Virginia. He's busy night and day whipping Charlie Company into shape. "We're over here for just one thing," he said. "And that's to kill Viet Cong."

 At noon on September 4th, Charlie Company returned to An Khe from assisting the 1/8th Cav in their counter-ambush mission along Highway 19, just in time to get ready to go right back to the same place with the rest of the 5/7th Cav the next day. In fact, an advance party had already been sent out to the area to coordinate the 5/7th's takeover of the Highway 19 mission.

 As the young men of Alpha Company readied their packs for the field, the stocky former Marine, 1SG Potter hauled a sack of mail into their tent. Everyone was hoping to get something from someone. Soldiers milled about the tent, reading their letters, curious about any goodies or packages their buddies may have received. Amidst the bustling, Will's good mortar platoon friend from Pennsylvania, Al Patrillo, just sat on his cot, looking at the ground. He'd just had the unfortunate honor of receiving Alpha Company's very first "Dear John" letter since their arrival in-country. He took it hard, real hard they say. I know this to be true because everyone I've talked to seems to remember this. What a rotten thing to do to a guy, Will thought, with a whole year to go in a place like this, "Sorry about that."

The following article and photos appeared in the September 15th issue of the 1st Air Cavalry Division's newspaper, the *Cavalair*:

'Mules' Replace Tracks, 5/7 Grasps Airmobility
Story and Photos by PFC Harold Morris

Twelve months after the first Skytroopers arrived in Vietnam, a new unit became a working part of the 1st Cav's airmobile striking force. On August 20, the 5th Bn 7th Cav joined the 3rd Brigade at An Khe, just four and a half months after beginning the transition from a mechanized infantry battalion to an airmobile fighting unit. The battalion came from Fort Carson, Colorado, where as the 1st Bn, 11th Inf (Mech), it had trained with track vehicles on the wide-open spaces until April 1. On that day it received its new designation and began training for the future trip to Vietnam. Armored Personnel Carriers and other tracked vehicles were turned in, and jeeps, "mules" and scooters were drawn in return. The M-14 rifles were exchanged for M-16s. All winter clothing was turned in, and mosquito netting and flak jackets were drawn. The training began. Tower rappelling, firing the M-16, the M-60 machine gun, 81mm mortar, 90mm recoilless rifles, field training, grenade throwing – all these had to be completed. In addition, twelve men per company were sent to Panama for jungle training.

On August 1st the 5/7th was ready. The next day they boarded a troop ship, the USNS Gaffey, for the trip across the Pacific. On board the ship the men were given classes on terrain and tactical situations found in Vietnam. They also fired their M-16s and rappelled down the cargo hold of the ship. On the 20th of August, the Gaffey docked at Qui Nhon, and a plane trip from Qui Nhon to An Khe placed the 5/7 in the Division that same day. Tents had to be put up, trenches had to be dug, mess facilities had to be established.

Then the in-country training started. The men of the 5/7 visited the firing range, a hot 5-mile march from camp, several times. On the first trip they zeroed their individual weapons – M-16s and 45 automatics – and threw hand grenades. The "Garry Owen Troopers" fired a quick-reaction course. As they moved through the woods they were "attacked". The purpose was to see how quickly these soldiers could react to enemy encounter and bring immediate fire on him. Also on the agenda was a static display of helicopters used by the "First Team" and demonstrations by the Pathfinders. Classroom instruction included prevention of malaria, types of snakes in the Republic and treatment of snakebites. A very impressive demonstration by the Explosive Ordnance Demolition (EOD) team showed the newly-arrived Skytroopers the types of booby-traps and mines used by the Viet Cong. The point stressed in the demonstration – leave no duds on the battlefield or "Charlie" might shoot it back at you. MACV Commander, General William C. Westmoreland paid a visit to the 5/7 during their first week in-country to welcome them to Vietnam.

Gen. Westmoreland spoke to the men on the background of the communist insurgency here.

Night patrols were a major concern during the training. Those going on the first patrol were "nervous but not scared." The final day of training was presented by members of the 228th Aviation Battalion with Chinook helicopters. The men of the 228th demonstrated the capabilities of a Chinook, and also stressed the importance of continual radio contact from ground to helicopter when the chopper is coming into a landing zone. After the presentation, two Chinooks hovered above the ground and each dropped two troop ladders. The men of the 5/7 then climbed up one ladder into the aircraft and down the other ladder to the ground, putting their new knowledge to use. When asked about the men of the 5/7, Sgt. Maj. Robert O. Meyer said, "The morale is very high – they're eager and ready for action."

WELCOME — Gen. William C. Westmoreland, MACV Commander, welcomes the "Garry Owen" troopers to their new assignment.

ACADEMICS — Men listen attentively to instructor discuss map reading. They also learned about snakebite and booby trops,

LET'S GO— Ready for the real thing, "Garry Owen" troopers start out on their first patrol.

6
INTO THE JUNGLE
(Operation Roadrunner)

Yeah, I got, let me see, 27-28 notches in my gun now.

The opening scene of the film *We Were Soldiers* depicts the final defeat of the French during the French-Indochina War by the communist Viet Minh. It had taken place in 1954 along a stretch of Highway 19 (then Route Colonial 19) approximately eight kilometers west of what was known as the Mang Yang Pass. Winding through the Central Highlands, the Mang Yang Pass is located between An Khe to the east and Pleiku to the west. Flanked by spectacular mountain rises on both sides, it was the site of many enemy ambushes during both the French-Indochina War, and the Vietnam War that we know. The battle was a slaughter, and relatively few of the French troops managed to escape. Over eight hundred soldiers of Mobile Group 100 were hastily buried near Highway 19 in the aftermath of that final battle.

During the previous summer, in 1965, the newly-arrived battalion commander of the 1/7th Cav, LTC Hal Moore, had walked this same battlefield along Highway 19, contemplating exactly what he was getting himself into. In his hand, he held a copy of the book *Street Without Joy: The French Debacle in Indochina* by Bernard Fall, which described that final battle in detail. Still visible from the highway were the white crosses marking the graves of those who died defending the French empire, a mere twelve miles from their new base camp at An Khe. In his own memoir written decades later, *We Were Soldiers Once... and Young*, he recalled the Vietnamese adage, "He who controls the Central Highlands controls South Vietnam." He also knew that whoever controlled Highway 19 controlled the Central Highlands. In fact, the North Vietnamese communists had once planned a major offensive in which they would utilize Highway 19 to split South Vietnam in two. The arrival of the 1st Air Cavalry in July of 1965 delayed these plans for approximately ten years.

The following appeared in the September 15th 1966 issue of the *Cavalair* regarding a typical incident along this fabled highway:

Iceman Made Fatal Error When He Cheated Charlie

Ice was a premium commodity when the Cav first arrived in An Khe. The ice arrived in an ancient truck from Pleiku, and the loss from melting amounted to nearly ¾ the original load – the truck was not insulated, save for a worn tarpaulin that covered the load. The iceman grew prosperous on the inflated prices the Americans would pay for his cooling product, but one day he made a fatal mistake. Some military policemen, accompanied by their Vietnamese counterparts, went out to check on a stalled vehicle a few thousand meters outside of town. They found the vintage iceman's truck. Inside was the iceman, bullet hole in head and very much dead. He had cheated, said a note in Vietnamese on the hood of the truck, and "grown rich on the dirty money of the Americans." This was bad enough, but the real crime, according to the note, was that he had tried to cheat the Viet Cong tax collectors who then controlled the road. So there was no ice in An Khe that day, nor the next, nor in fact for quite some time.

Aerial View of Mang Yang Pass, photo by Harald Hendrichsen, 604th Transportation Company

5 Sep '66 – 47 weeks left

Dear Folks,

Don't have time to write 'cause we're leaving this morning. If I don't write for a while, don't worry. I'll write when I get a chance to. No big thing.

So long,

Will

At 7:10 AM on September 5th 1966, the skytroopers of Alpha Company departed An Khe, once again in a convoy of deuce-and-a-halfs. The rest of the battalion would follow at intervals throughout the day. Dubbed Operation Roadrunner, the 5/7th Cav's first mission was to secure this long and winding road known as Highway 19, from An Khe to Pleiku, including the infamous pass, where another deadly communist ambush had occurred just two years prior on ARVN (Army of the Republic of Vietnam) forces.

Pleiku and An Khe were major bases, and many military convoys were made each day between the two. There was also plenty of local civilian and merchant traffic along the route. The 5/7th Cav was now responsible for controlling the movement of these convoys, and for keeping both the military and civilian traffic safe. They would patrol and clear the surrounding jungles and mountains all along the highway, in an effort to keep the Viet Cong (VC) at bay.

After traveling a few miles, the trucks came to a halt and the skytroopers jumped out. Now into the jungle to search for Charlie. The sun was beating on them hard as sweat stung their eyes. The shade almost seemed inviting, if not so ominous. Once again Will found himself staring into the darkness of the jungle, as one squad after another became swallowed by it. With their hearts now pounding, he and his mortar team would soon follow. Entering the forest they would find a dark, damp, pungent-smelling world, teeming with insect and animal life that made strange and exotic sounds - monkeys screaming, the mating calls of geckos and other lizards, and all manner of bird noises. The air was like that of a sauna, and with each breath the troopers would feel their lungs fill with moisture. The foliage was covered with droplets of water, and within minutes their fatigues were soaked. Beams of sunlight filtered through the canopy here and there, and within those beams of light they could see the moist particles of jungle debris, seeming to float in the air. It was creepy, dark, and unwholesome, but after a day's worth of plodding through the jungle with no sign of the enemy, it became just exhausting and boring. And so began what would become an endless daily routine of hacking through dense forests, slogging through rivers and rice paddies, and climbing over mountains in search of Charlie.

The infantryman carried his standard-issue M-16 rifle, a machete, and on his load-bearing vest, at least three twenty-round clips of ammunition, at least two frag grenades, at least one smoke grenade, and perhaps, one or two white phosphorous grenades. In his helmet, he carried letters from home, and at times, photographs of his girlfriend, or perhaps, those of a girl he wished was his girlfriend. Strapped to his helmet, he often carried a small bottle of bug juice or a pack of cigarettes. Quinn carried Marlboros when he could get them, while Patrillo carried Pall Malls. Will favored Camel non-filters. On his back, he carried his rucksack, to which was attached a shovel called an "entrenching tool" and a flashlight. The rucksack held a poncho that was used both as a raincoat and for shelter. As they would come to learn, it could also be used for covering dead bodies, or at times, as a makeshift stretcher for carrying them. Also in his rucksack, he carried a light blanket called a "poncho liner", cans of food called "C-Rations", and a few personal hygiene items such as a toothbrush, razor, and a bar of soap. Although issued a small inflatable sleeping mat, he would likely forgo this because of the added weight. On the same necklace that held his dog tags, he would carry his P-38 can opener for opening C-Rations, an absolute necessity. In addition to his dog tags and P-38 around his neck, Quinn carried the miraculous medal of the Virgin Mary that his boss back home had given him before he left. In one of his fatigue pockets, Barrow carried the small 35mm camera that fellow radio operator Kenneth Rathyen had helped him pick out before leaving Fort Carson. No extra fatigues were carried, as he would rely on helicopters to bring these. Aside from these necessities, the typical infantryman would also carry a pen and notebook for writing letters, a small Bible or a Rosary, candy, comic books, Playboy magazines, good luck charms, and perhaps, condoms.

Radio operators Donald Rankin, Royce Barrow, Kenneth Rathyen, Alan Weisman, Dave Fedell, and Phil Jones would carry the PRC-25, a twenty-three-pound radio telephone more commonly referred to as the "Prick-25". With its three-foot antennae constantly bouncing back and forth above the radio operator's head, it was like wearing a sign that said to the enemy, "shoot me first!" As assistants to the commander and platoon leaders, radio operators had to be calm under fire, and it helped if they could read a map. They soon became a hub for both official information and the rumor mill. A bond of sorts was formed amongst them, especially between Rankin and Barrow. They were always together since being chosen by CPT Wise as his own radio operators while training at Fort Carson. They were like peas in a pod, and they had become best friends. Specifically, Rankin handled communications between Alpha Company and the platoons on what was called the "company net", while Barrow communicated with the 5/7th Cav battalion command post on the "battalion net". Weisman was the radio operator for Alpha Company's 2nd Platoon and worked for their platoon leader, 1LT James Harmon. In 3rd Platoon, Phil Jones served as 1LT William Nelson's radio operator.

Machine gunners Bobby Hansen, Bill Purdy, Guy McNay, and Robert Wagner would carry the twenty-three-pound M-60 machine gun and chains of ammunition, while grenadiers such as Al Patrillo would carry the M-79 grenade launcher. Resembling a sawed-off shotgun, the M-79 wasn't that heavy, but its ammunition was. In addition to the standard infantryman's load, those in the mortar platoon would each carry part of their team's mortar system. One soldier would carry the tube while another would carry the bipod, another the ammunition with each round weighing about ten pounds, and another would carry the base plate, which was the most awkward to carry. Each component weighed over thirty pounds. Still others in the company would carry Claymore mines to place around their patrol base at night, as well as extra blocks of C-4 plastic explosive to clear landing zones. On their backs, the infantry company carried a slow-moving arsenal of weaponry, lead, steel, and explosives. Perhaps the most eloquent description of this was written by Tim O'Brien in his book, *The Things They Carried*, "...they carried it on their backs and shoulders — and for all the ambiguities of Vietnam, all the mysteries and unknowns, there was at least the single abiding certainty that they would never be at a loss for things to carry."

On Will's mortar crew was their team leader, SGT John Fulford from Fernandina Beach, Florida, Marvin Bierschbach, his buddy from Minnesota, and John Bronson, the tall, lanky black guy from the Bronx. Their squad leader was SSG Bobby Hayslip.

Like most every infantry company, Alpha Company was comprised of three rifle platoons (1st, 2nd and 3rd Platoons) and one mortar platoon (4th Platoon). Each platoon was led by a platoon leader, a 1st or 2nd Lieutenant, and supervised by a platoon sergeant, a Sergeant First Class or Staff Sergeant. SSG Donald Burtis was the platoon sergeant in charge of Alpha Company's mortar platoon. 1LT Sam Cathcart was their platoon leader. Each platoon had four squads, led by a Sergeant or Staff Sergeant. Each squad had two teams, typically led by a Sergeant. The head NCO of Alpha Company was 1SG Potter, responsible for running the company as directed by its commander, CPT A.J. Wise, who would bear ultimate responsibility for the actions of his soldiers, and their welfare.

Although they would occasionally occupy a rudimentary hilltop base with bunkers overlooking the highway during Operation Roadrunner, most days and nights would be spent in the wilderness, or "Indian Country" as it was often called. Each platoon was responsible for guarding a checkpoint along the highway, as well as patrolling the surrounding jungle. As one squad in each platoon manned their assigned checkpoint along with a nearby hilltop overlooking that checkpoint, the other squads would patrol the surrounding forests and villages. As both Will and Marvin Bierschbach recall, one of their first nights in the jungle was spent taking shelter in a tiny abandoned cement building. It was raining hard and water was running through the mud floor of the building. To avoid lying in the water, they sat on their helmets and attempted to sleep while leaning against the wall. Their attempt was largely unsuccessful.

On a typical patrol, the company was on its own and moved as a unit, with each platoon following the other. In open areas, the soldiers in each platoon would form a wedge or "V" shape, and spread out in such a way as to prevent a single grenade or mine from killing more than one of them. When patrolling through dense forest, they would move in a single file so as not to get lost. The company moved with two of the three rifle platoons in front, followed by the command group and the mortars in 4th Platoon, and one rifle platoon taking up the rear. This allowed for the company commander to direct mortar fire in support of the rifle platoons when they encountered the enemy.

Before nightfall, CPT Wise would choose a defensible position, usually on some high ground, upon which they would set up their patrol base or "bivouac". The troops would form an oval or cigar-shaped perimeter and dig in for the night. Each team of two to three soldiers would dig a foxhole along the outside of this perimeter. Emplacements for the machine guns would be dug. A trench would also be dug in the very middle of the patrol base to serve as the company's latrine. Each position along the perimeter served as a guard post of sorts, but trees and other vegetation often blocked the view. Therefore, "fields of fire" as they were called, would need to be hacked out in front of each of these positions. Also each night, several Claymore mines would be set out in all directions beyond the perimeter. The Claymore was an anti-personnel mine, shaped like a large, thick, curved plate, the convex side imprinted with the words: FRONT TOWARD ENEMY. It was to be placed wherever one thought the enemy was likely to approach and driven into the ground using its built-in stakes. Detonation wire would be strung back to the operator's guard position. When activated by its remote detonator, the mine would explode in an outward direction, spraying metal balls in a shotgun-like pattern. Trip flares would also be set out beyond the company's perimeter. When the enemy, or in some cases, an animal, stepped on or into its wire, a bright burning flare would be shot straight up into the air, illuminating the surrounding area. On most nights, small teams of soldiers would be sent farther out, in ambush positions, "listening posts" or "stakeouts" as they were often called. The purpose was to detect any approaching enemy before they could attack the company's main body.

The poncho each soldier carried was basically a large plastic sheet with a hole and hood in the middle, so as to be used as a raincoat. When buttoned together with two other ponchos, and with the use of some sticks, they would form a crude and tiny tent-like shelter, known as a hooch. While two of his buddies slept in their hooch, one soldier would keep watch. They would take turns through the night, each soldier earning two hours of sleep for each hour spent on guard duty. At times, circumstances dictated only two men per foxhole, in which case they'd get one hour of sleep for each hour on guard. Quinn especially hated the chore of digging in at night. "Will was good at digging foxholes though," he remarked, "and getting through the rocks and roots was hard, especially after a day of humping the hills. I'd set up the tent while Will dug a little trench around it to keep the rain from flowing in." He laughed as he recalled how Will was more likely to use his helmet for cooking than for protection when they were setting up for the night. When it was on, it was always crooked, "John Wayne style" with the chin straps dangling. "I'd say to him, *Will, you might want to strap that thing down. Charlie's out there and your head is a mighty big target for him.* And he'd just say... *aw, why bother.* He was a character and took everything very lightly, and I was a nervous wreck most of the time. But all of his joking around did so much to lift the spirits of everyone in the platoon."

As to be expected, the company was on edge during their first few weeks in the jungle. In fact, the entire battalion seemed to be as one of Bravo Company's platoons spent a great deal of ammunition one night, in response to what was believed to be a tiger "or something" approaching their perimeter, as noted in the battalion's daily situation report, or SITREP. Bobby Hansen recalls seeing a black panther stalking by Alpha Company's perimeter one night during their mission along Highway 19. He also spoke of a Vietnamese armadillo, or Pangolin, that gave them an unusual amount of trouble. As he recalled, many flares were spent lighting up the area around the armadillo, as its movement made a noise very similar to that of enemy soldiers shuffling along the ground.

Will's worst fear was to be attacked at night, but the darkness offered a welcome reprieve from the heat. Except for the occasional sounds of animals, it was mostly quiet and peaceful. I've tried to imagine what goes through your mind while guarding the perimeter at night, staring into the darkness, watching for movement, and waiting for your chance to rest. In the quiet and solitude, this is likely where your mind starts to wander, recounting exactly how it was that you ended up here. I imagine this is where you feel about as far away from home as you can possibly get.

Because no one was killed by the enemy during Operation Roadrunner, I had previously thought of this period of time as relatively uneventful. Reading the first two daily situation reports from this operation changed that belief. The fact was that Charlie had wasted no time in welcoming the newly arrived skytroopers to the war zone.

HEADQUARTERS
5TH BATTALION, 7TH CAVALRY
1ST CAVALRY DIVISION (Airmobile)
APO US Forces 96490

6 September 1966

SUBJECT: Battalion Commander's Daily SITREP

TO: Commanding Officer, 3rd Brigade, 1st Cavalry Division (Airmobile)

1. OPERATIONS SUMMARY:

5th Battalion, 7th Cavalry located coordinates BR 240-530 continues mission of securing Hwy 19 and convoy movement control.

At 10:25 PM, Sep 5th – Company A reported an enemy probe of its perimeter, coordinates BR 095-549, object believed to be a man, set off 2 illuminating devices, was engaged with small arms fire and set off one more device. Negative further contact.

At 1:52 AM, Sep 6th – Company D reported incoming light weapons fire with negative enemy contact at coordinates BR 240-530.

At 7:45 AM, Sep 6th – morning sweep of Hwy 19 completed. Reported Green [clear].

At 12:25 PM, Sep 6th – 2 unidentified personnel were seen heading west from CP [check point] 3 and 200 meters from Hwy 19. When elements from Company A attempted to apprehend individuals, they avoided apprehension.

At 1:50 PM, Sep 6th – ¼ Ton M-151 vehicle turned over on Hwy 19 vicinity of CP 7 fatally injuring SP/4 Gary D. Jefferis, and seriously injuring PFC James C. McDonugh, both members of this unit. MEDEVAC was called and individuals were lifted out of area at 2:10 PM. SP/4 Gary D. Jefferis was reported DOA. Injuries of PFC James C. McDonugh not confirmed at this time.

At 4:50 PM, Sep 6th – Convoy EU 306 departed CP 12. One round sniper fire was received by convoy EU 306 coordinates BR 273-473. Company B sent squad size element into area to search and seize; negative contact.

2. STATISTICAL SUMMARY:

    a. Friendly Casualties: KIA 0, WIA 0, MIA 0, killed non-hostile 1, injured non-hostile 1. Cumulative figures for Operation ROADRUNNER: KIA 0, WIA 0, MIA 0, killed non-hostile 1, injured non-hostile 1.

    b. Enemy Casualties: None

    c. Friendly Equipment Losses: None

3. CURRENT FRIENDLY DISPOSITION: See enclosed overlay.

4. This report covers period 7:01 PM, Sep 5th to 7:00 PM, Sep 6th.

FOR THE COMMANDER:

WILLIAM R BROWN JR
Capt, Infantry
Adjutant

HEADQUARTERS
5TH BATTALION, 7TH CAVALRY
1ST CAVALRY DIVISION (Airmobile)
APO US Forces 96490

7 September 1966

SUBJECT: Battalion Commander's Daily SITREP

TO: Commanding Officer, 3rd Brigade, 1st Cavalry Division (Airmobile)

1. OPERATIONS SUMMARY:

5th Bn, 7th Cav continues mission of securing Hwy 19 and convoy movement control. Patrols and ambushes were sent out to areas along Hwy 19. Company A reported one M-79 [grenade launcher] round fired in 4th Platoon area from west at 9:55 PM, Sep 6th, round landed at BR 095-549.

Company B reported sniper fire vicinity BR 294-463 at 8:05 AM, Sep 7th, do not know if VC or bandit. Patrol from Company B discovered punji stakes at BR 262-475. At 11:00 AM, Sep 7th B Company patrol found fresh tracks heading from northeast, also one 80mm dud, one 105 HE or illuminating dud. EOD notified and neutralized at coordinates BR 2770-4740. Company B patrol reported 35 old emplacements with overhead cover, negative contact, negative equipment found at 1:50 PM, Sep 7th coordinates BR 239-475.

2. STATISTICAL SUMMARY:

    a. Friendly Casualties: KIA 0, WIA 0, MIA 0. Cumulative figures for the operation: KIA 0, WIA 0, MIA 0.

    b. Enemy Casualties: None

    c. Friendly Equipment Losses: None

3. CURRENT FRIENDLY DISPOSITION: See enclosed overlay.

4. This report covers period 7:01 PM, Sep 6th to 7:00 PM, Sep 7th.

FOR THE COMMANDER:

WILLIAM R BROWN JR
Capt, Infantry
Adjutant

On September 7th, Bravo Company was sent into the Mang Yang Pass area to improve security there. Here, one of its soldiers would be wounded while placing a Claymore mine. Later that night, Alpha Company's 4th Platoon would take sniper fire twice, at 10:20 and again at 10:26 PM. They responded by firing their mortars and calling in artillery strikes on the suspected enemy positions. At 2:30 PM the next day, a half-ton truck carrying MPs was engaged by machine gun fire from both sides. Nine rounds hit the truck and one MP was wounded in the attack. The highway was closed for an hour while artillery and ARA gunships pummeled both sides of the road from where the attack came. Afterward, Bravo Company searched the area but did not find the enemy. Each of the companies of the battalion would continue to be attacked, probed, and harassed throughout the weeks spent in the jungle near the highway. At 1:45 AM on September 9th, a soldier from Bravo Company would become the first of the battalion to take an enemy bullet, shot in the leg during another sniper attack.

8 Sep '66 – 47 weeks left

Dear Folks,

Here I am in a pup tent and it's pouring out. It drizzled just about all day now, and every day. Having a hard time getting my clothes to dry. Have to wash them by hand in a creek below the hill here. The last bunch of guys that were in this position were here 35 days, so they had everything pretty well set up when we got here. Half of us stay up at night to guard, that's the night shift. The first night here, everyone was trigger happy. They would stare into the dark, and then would swear that this tree or that bush moved. We'd shoot a flare up and shoot a few more rounds. Boy, everyone was a nervous wreck that first night, me too. Man, what a life.

I finally received your doughnuts today. Well, to say the least, they were a bit moldy. We didn't get any chow yet today, and we were all starving, so we ate about ½ the box, mold and all. One of them said, "If we die of food poisoning, we'll die together." We're supposed to get two hot meals a day, but it hasn't been the case so far. Glad I brought some candy along. Say, I would like you to do me a big favor, please. Send me a pair of overboots, and a good raincoat. Then I would really be in business. We got one raincoat, but it's so awkward and clumsy. It would be worth $1,000 in this weather. Send it as soon as possible and I'll be walking like a king. Guess I best get some sleep now. For the size of them boots, have them fit a size 7-W shoe and I'll be waiting. The coat, 32 sleeve length, and 37-40 chest. Hurry!

Will

12 Sep '66 – 46 weeks left

Dear Folks,

Still raining out. Haven't seen the sun, except for a few minutes, since we got here. The only problem is that we have a hard time to dry our clothes. Getting hot meals 3 times a day. Sometimes it is real good, sometimes it ain't. The other day we went on a patrol through these hills. Seen how some of the people live. The houses are about 3 or 4 feet above the rice paddy and made of grass. You know, no matter how hard I may have it in life, I'll always be thankful to God that I was born in the U.S. We live like kings back home.

Last Tuesday, a guy got killed and two injured below our hill when their jeep turned over on a curb. Our doc had to administer 1st aid to them. I guess the first big case he ever had. It's a damn good road top. Blacktop and a lot of traffic. Mostly all Army vehicles.

Found a fishing pole in front of my bunker with a line and hook. Tried a little fishing down by the creek. Fishing poles here are as big as 3 inches in diameter and as high as 30-40 feet. We use them a lot for stakes and poles. The area on this hill is about an acre. Figueroa and I tent together and help guard the west side.

How long did Leonard and Ken stay? I tell you, those two guys can join the Navy if they like. I had my belly full when I was on the ship for 18 days. I'd rather have my feet on this firm muddy ground. How did Ken's car look, pretty sharp? You know, if I bought a car over here, there'd be no tax whatsoever on it. Do you know how much tax or money I could save, well let's say on a new GTO?

Will

Here is some money that we get. It is not Viet Nam money, but military money we can only spend 'cause of some reason or other. It feels like I have $500 in my pocket.

The following are excerpts from Rankin's letters home between September 12th and 17th.

Dear Mom and Daddy,

Received eight letters today. Boy, do I feel better. Everything is relatively quiet here. Today, one of our Jeeps was fired upon. They have stopped the Jeep, but we don't know any particulars. That was our camp that was attacked. They're still firing on it, but they usually don't do too much damage.

We're doing pretty good. I'm so accustomed to being dirty and wet now. Today, I had a narrow escape of my own and three other guys' making. We built a large bunker of sandbags and logs. My tent has been down for about three days, so I decided to sleep in the bunker. It was pretty comfortable. The driest night's sleep that I've had for a while. But, I got up this morning, walked out and the thing collapsed. It covered up my helmet, weapon, duffel bag and everything. It shook me up to think I might have been under there but it broke my heart because it was such an awful job building it.

The natives have been unfriendly the past few days. That is a good indication that there are VC in the area. This camp has been very quiet. I hope it continues.

I really feel a little homesick tonight. The day has been good, but sometimes the loneliness gets to me. Whalen and Earlywine are at my immediate position now. It is good to have someone from home, but we aren't real close. I guess because of our ages. But, I'd probably be lost without them.

Our unit hasn't encountered any bad action yet. Today, one position received "sniper fire" but he was soon run off. They think the Viet Cong are holding off until the monsoon gets worse.

I'm feeling better about everything mentally and physically each day. My arthritis is bad on cold rainy days, and I have a very bad cough at night. Today, they gave me some antibiotic pills to try to get rid of the cough. I think that a lot of it is due to talking all day and half the night on the radio. I'm learning my job pretty well. I've slowed down on being so "gung-ho". There is little chance of me making E-5, so I'm just sort of enjoying myself.

The commander got up yesterday morning in rare form. He grumbled and growled, stormed and had a regular temper tantrum. I just stuck my head out of the tent and laughed. He doesn't have it any harder than we do.

Yesterday, I took a bath in the creek. Did it feel great. It was cold but wonderful after being dirty for 14 days.

Also, send me that Cumberland College catalogue sometime. I want to start working on this now. The Army pays $100 a month, and I might get out three months early to go to school. This is about all. Tell everyone hello.

Love,

Donnie

3rd Platoon medic Michael Handley recalled one of their first patrols near Highway 19. Their platoon leader, 1LT Nelson, was leading them through the jungle following what he believed was a blood trail along a narrow walking path. After some time, in great anticipation they rounded a corner of the path to find a couple old women chopping weeds and chewing on beetlenuts, a popular practice among old Vietnamese women. The beetlenuts would turn their teeth black, and the juice they spit out apparently looked a lot like blood.

Bill Purdy of Alpha Company's 2nd Platoon told of a night patrol his squad went on during this time. They were being led by a tall sergeant they called "Stretch". While leading the patrol in the darkness, Stretch fell ass-over-teakettle into a deep ravine with water running through it. He was shaken but okay. He had dropped his M-16 in the fall, however, and for the life of him, couldn't find it. They all climbed down into the ravine and began feeling around in search of the rifle. Purdy recalls hearing the voice of CPT Wise over the radio, "don't even think about coming back without that weapon."

Crawling around in the muddy water of the ravine, Purdy thought to himself, "It's only going downhill from here."

On September 15th at 1:58 PM, Charlie Company's 2nd Platoon was air assaulted to an area known as LZ (Landing Zone) Quick. Aside from one punji stake wound, their patrol was without incident. During their subsequent extraction, however, their helicopter crashed, killing one and wounding four others. They would stay at the crash site through the night, and until the wrecked chopper could be recovered the following afternoon. Bravo Company would suffer two more wounded in action when enemy grenades hit two of its soldiers who were guarding a bridge along the highway at 8:50 PM on September 17th.

Also on September 17th, Alpha Company received word that they would soon be sent out on their own company-size operation. It would be dubbed Operation Golden Bee, in honor of their favorite bar in Colorado Springs. In a briefing attended by SSG Matulac and the company's platoon leaders and platoon sergeants, CPT Wise advised them that they would soon be preparing for their first air assault mission.

Matulac awoke in his hooch the next morning to a fierce burning sensation in his right foot. He went to the company medic, Bill Garcia, to have it checked out. Removing his jungle boots revealed two red bite marks. It looked to be a snake bite, but he was advised that it had been from some kind of millipede. After packing up his stuff, he headed down a trail toward the highway. His ankle was now beginning to feel numb and before he knew it, he was tumbling down a hill. Having rolled his ankle, he was soon flown to Pleiku. With his foot in a cast, he reported back to CPT Wise the next morning, but would not be able to go on the company's first air assault.

18 Sep '66 – 45 weeks left

Dear Folks,

Thank you, thank you for those cookies. Man, you couldn't have timed it any better. I just got back from patrol that morning and with little food the day before, I was starving. It was in good shape and the Kool-Aid really covers up the pill we put in our canteen for the water we get from the creek. It sure cost a lot to send it. The newspaper is sure good to read. Everybody else wants to read it also. At least I can read what's going on in Viet Nam. Did you get my little newspaper? The chow is getting better and the sun's shining a little more, and it's beginning to look real good.

I got a letter from Allen Simon yesterday. He is in a 4.2 mortar platoon, which is bigger than the one I operate. He says he's guarding Highway 19, the same one we are guarding. I couldn't make out rightly what he wrote, but it seems like he's in Pleiku, and I am only 10 miles from him now. Sure would like to see the old boy. Those boots and raincoat on the way yet? Take the cost out of that $25 check. What did you guys do with those shells I brought home? That 79 round, I figure to make a gear knob out of it.

Will

At 3:00 PM on September 20th, Alpha Company's platoons displaced from their positions, replaced by elements of Bravo and Charlie Companies. They now moved to the battalion's forward command post known as the Eagle's Nest overlooking the Mang Yang Pass, in preparation for Operation Golden Bee. In military parlance, "forward" means in the field where the action is, as opposed to "in the rear with the gear." A couple hours later, they were informed that the operation had been indefinitely postponed.

21 Sep '66 – 45 weeks left

Dear Folks,

I bummed these papers and envelope off of Henning. The last few days on our hill, we had a little excitement. Some V.C. or innocent hunter pulled a trip flare and we shot into that area with everything we had. It was supper at the time. The guy who delivered the chow was in the creek taking a bath, and he jumped back in the jeep with no clothes to man the machine gun, ha! I was shooting my gun and eating a tough steak sandwich at the same time.

We moved from our last position and moved on top of the hill Rodney Henning is on. We were supposed to go on a big mission, but now it is canceled. Hard telling where we are going. Rod is going on a little patrol today. My old squad leader joined the long-range patrol, and now he is in charge of Rod. He is the most sure-footed Sergeant I know, and Rod is damn lucky to have him. Wish I still had him. I found out the other day that this guy that got killed in the jeep accident below our hill was a good friend of Rod, and a good man. I knew him a little, also. It sure is a bad way to go.

We've been getting our lifeline packs pretty regular now. Razor blades, candy, soap, toothpaste, cigarettes, but no beer. They're supposed to be free, but I heard they've been selling them to locals on us, back at camp. So we buy it off the Boom-Boom wagon that goes by on our road.

To get back to my last letter, we guys were discussing what to do with my shells back home. The 79 for a gear shift, 50 Cal for a radio knob, mortar round as a hood ornament, and I could put James Bond out of style. Well anyway, our platoon sergeant and platoon leader came over and the guys mentioned about my shells in a kidding way. Platoon leader says, "God damn Bowe, did you really sneak all them home?" I say, "Well you see, no comment, sir." Anyway, they all got a little chuckle out of it.

I received those boots and raincoat the other day. I couldn't hardly wait for them to get here. Now if it would only rain. Well, if it doesn't rain in the next 45 weeks, that would be alright too. Our Lieutenant was bitching 'cause of the heavy box, and the newspaper and letter he had to carry up the hill for me. I got them all willed out, in case I get bumped off. Now I have to worry about being knocked off by my own friends. I know the packages you have been sending are expensive to send, so you keep track of it from the money I send home. You may say it's alright, but not with me 'cause you have expenses and I don't. Also, next month or the one after, chip in $20 to the church for me. Not that I think the church needs it so much, but the Good Lord might give me some luck. I hope.

Old Pro,

Will

21 Sep '66 - 45 weeks left

Hi Fuzzy Face,

Mike, I'll be square with you. I haven't told anyone what's really going on here or I'd have them all worried. I know I can trust you. Like the last hill we were on. It wasn't too bad, most of us survived. I always told you I dug ditches, but I didn't say what for, did I? Burying V.C.s. I remember the time John got killed. His arm torn off. We thought we sent it home with him. But it was the wrong one, it was Andy's arm. Guess we all make mistakes. Like this last mission we were going on, they named it Suicide Mission. Thank God we didn't have to go. They were ready to give the last sacrament. Yeah, I got, let me see, 27-28 notches in my gun now. I suppose my days are numbered. When you gotta go, you gotta go. Now wait a minute. You're not believing all this shit, are you? Seriously, the biggest enemy here is the rain and the ants. Like that one day that trip flare went off and we put a lot of bombs and lead into that area. I doubt if we got anybody, but I know we killed a hell of a lot of ants.

You shave yet before you went to school today? Or, old Grip will make you dry shave in front of the class. Bet you couldn't wait to get back to school. I know I couldn't, so I could get out of filling the silo. What do you have for subjects? I know, Phy-Ed, Girls, and skipping classes, and General Science. Remember how good I was at it. All of them A's. I always believed in doing a good job at my studies, or not doing them at all. Does Grip still tell stories of me, how good I was in football? The touchdowns, the tackles, the interceptions. Of course, this was only during practice. In the real games, I always let the other guys play hero. My weak point was being too modest. Like Darrell says, "I could have been a star, but they already had lights."

I got them pictures you all sent. What color is that cycle of yours, how does she run? Wish they all would have been in color. Would like to read the newspaper, but don't have my baggage with me. I see Jerry Bresina is doing good in football, co-captain and all. Heard Green Bay won two games. Wish we could have brought our radios with us. What's the hit song back home? How are the races coming? Say thanks to Ma and Dad for sending the clothes, I almost forgot. It was just as I wanted. Really, I couldn't have done better if I picked it out myself.

Your hero,

Will

Donald Rankin also penned a letter home on September 21st.

Dear Mom and Daddy,

Everything is still going fine. We moved again yesterday. We are now on top of a mountain in the Mang Yang Pass. It is so beautiful. I wish that I had a camera to take some pictures. There were three thousand Frenchmen killed on this mountain about 1955. How the Vietnamese ever did it, I can't see. Everything is going well. We've only had three casualties from the enemy. They were minor. We had two guys killed in accidents. One in a Jeep and one in a helicopter. This is about all. Tell everyone hello and write.

Love,

Donnie

On September 22nd, after two days of securing the battalion command post at the Eagle's Nest, Alpha Company was notified that Operation Golden Bee was on again, now set for September 24th, and they resumed their preparations.

·········

There was an interesting film made by John H. Secondari as part of an anthology series for ABC Television, *The Saga of Western Man*. You can easily find the full-length episode on the internet today. Filmed in 1965 when the big military build-up had just begun, unlike other Vietnam films, its perspective is not jaundiced by hindsight or knowledge of the eventual outcome. Against the backdrop of an armada of helicopters flying over the mountains, the narrator observes prophetically regarding Vietnam's highlands, "...it belongs to no one. Not to Viet Cong who roam it, not to the South Vietnamese. It is no man's land. In Vietnam today, you will hold only the ground you stand upon."

The film follows an airmobile infantry company of the 1st Air Cavalry Division - Alpha Company, 1st Battalion, 8th Cavalry - from their air assault landing on a hilltop, to their burning of enemy encampments, and their wounded being flown away. It also features their own turn at guarding and patrolling along the unpredictable Highway 19. This particular Alpha Company is remarkably similar to that of the 5/7th Cav and is led by CPT Theodore Danielson, who is tall and looks to be about thirty. Congenial yet blunt, he speaks with a deliberate southern drawl. "In rappelling, a man can reach the ground from sixty feet in about four seconds... and if somebody's shooting at him, I guarantee he'll try to make it faster." The film portrays what CPT Danielson's company shares in common with all the airmobile infantry companies fighting in the Central Highlands.

The narrator concludes, "Alpha Company, 1st Battalion, 8th Cavalry marches off again. One company and one company commander, in an army composed of companies... and they all are pretty much alike. They man the outposts, and with their lives they buy the peace we shall enjoy tonight."

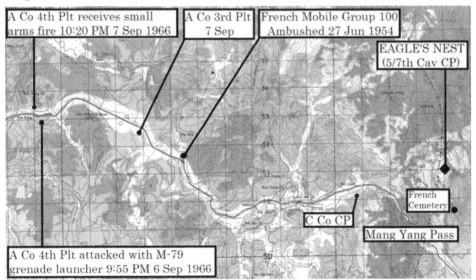

Highway 19 area of operations, each grid square equals 1 kilometer

Rice fields along Highway 19, photo by Robert Matulac

Indigenous tribesmen of Central Highlands known as Montagnards, photo by Robert Matulac

Outpost on hilltop along Highway 19, photo by Robert Matulac

Bronson carrying base plate, photo by Marvin Bierschbach

Gerald Anderson (left) and Kurt Elmer (right), photo by Wilbur Bowe

.50 Caliber machine gun emplacement, photo by Bill Purdy

Marvin Bierchbach's hooch

Alpha Company Commander, CPT A.J. Wise, photo by Bill Purdy

Marvin Bierschbach carrying bipod

Alpha Company moving out into highlands, photo by Robert Matulac

7
AIR ASSAULT
(Operation Golden Bee)

Wish you could have seen us all. Boy, I tell you we sure were bad looking, beard, mud, and torn clothes, but I am in good shape.

While the 5/7th Cav secured Highway 19, other battalions of the 1st Air Cavalry Division's 1st and 3rd Brigades launched Operation Thayer on September 13th 1966. In what was the Army's largest air assault operation to date, 120 Huey and Chinook helicopters airlifted five fighting battalions into positions surrounding the Kim Son Valley. Known as the Crow's Foot, the Kim Son is actually comprised of several valleys with rivers that converge in the shape of a crow's foot. From fourteen mountaintop landing zones, the skytroopers descended into the valleys, searching and clearing their respective hillsides, forming a steadily tightening noose around the enemy. Allied ARVN battalions were placed in blocking positions at the north end of the valley to prevent the enemy's escape.

Thayer was the first operation of the Binh Dinh Province Pacification Campaign, designed to destroy the Viet Cong and North Vietnamese infrastructure that had been established throughout Binh Dinh Province. An important part of the strategy was to deny the Viet Cong access to the rice harvests that they would confiscate from the rural population. As this was nearly their only source of food, this tactic would prove effective in encouraging abandonment and surrender amongst the enemy. The campaign would march on throughout the year and continue through 1967. Within ten days of its launch, Operation Thayer had successfully dislodged the enemy from the Kim Son Valley. Now separated from their supply bases, the enemy fled eastward with several battalions of the 1st Air Cavalry's 1st Brigade in relentless pursuit. On September 23rd, the NVA launched a failed nighttime attack on an ARVN command post, then moved even farther eastward into the coastal plains. Retreating on foot, the enemy could not outpace the skytroopers who pursued them through the air. Within days, the two enemy battalions were trapped in an area of the Phu My plains between the Phu Cat Mountains to their south, and the Nui Mieu Mountains to their north. To their east was the South China Sea, and to their west, the Americans.

The 5/7th Cav however, would not join this large, multi-brigade, multi-national operation until the beginning of October. As Operation Thayer grinded on in the eastern coastal plains, Alpha Company kicked off its own company-size Operation Golden Bee, air assaulting into a jungle area approximately thirteen kilometers north of An Khe. It was initially planned as a three-day operation.

23 Sep '66 – 44 weeks left

Dear Folks,

Best get this letter written before dark. All I want to say is I am going on a 3-day mission. So I won't be writing. Well, I don't write that often, so it doesn't make that much difference.

This is one of his buddies finishing his letter, as he is going to get our chow for tomorrow. When I get out of the service, I plan to visit you people.

PFC Quinn

Donald Rankin would also send a letter home before their mission.

Dear Mom and Daddy,

A very slow, cool, pretty day. It is the easiest day that we've had since our arrival. They were fattening us for a kill. Tomorrow, we are going on a full company operation. They haven't given us any details. So if you don't hear from me for awhile don't worry.

Is there enough money for you to make it on? If not, I think that I could arrange for the bank to give you part of my monthly payments. If I survive, I will get those others paid. If I don't – it won't matter because the insurance will cover it. This is about it. Write when you can.

Love,

Donnie

At 8:51 AM on September 24th, the first choppers began lifting the men of Alpha Company from the PZ (pick-up zone) at Eagle's Nest. Amidst the whine of their engines and the thumping of their blades, the men moved through a storm of reddish-brown dust toward their flying steel war horses. The troop-laden choppers vibrated as they strained upward, and for the first time, the soldiers would view their new home from the sky as they sped at over one hundred miles per hour, skirting the treetops. Picturesque rolling hills, plains and meadows, winding brown rivers, triple-canopy massifs, mountains and valleys. In addition to the view, the open-doored choppers also provided temporary relief from the heat.

I've often tried to imagine the spectacle of an American air assault from the enemy's perspective. As a Viet Cong soldier, you may have fought with the communist Viet Minh against the French in previous decades. The French however, did not use helicopters, and traveled the battlefield mainly in trucks and armored vehicles, which had limited their ability to get at you. In contrast, the Americans could descend from the sky to strike virtually anywhere at any time - so long as they could find you.

It would seem a rather dreadful affair to witness this terror from the sky for the first time. Artillery bombardment would have shaken the ground and shattered trees only yards away from where you hide in your valley sanctuary. Then dramatic plumes of white phosphorus would explode all around you, setting everything ablaze, and signal the end of the shelling.

Soon after, fighter jets would descend from the sky to drop cartwheeling canisters of napalm. Exploding upon impact, they send up walls of orange flames several stories high that engulf the surrounding trees. You soon feel the hot thermal wave of the blasts, then the air around you being sucked into the vacuum created by the rising heat.

An armada of helicopters would appear over the ridgeline. On its flanks ride the gunships, who now drop headlong into the valley like angry hornets, spraying a hail of lead and rockets into the area surrounding the landing zone. Those who had given away their position by taking shots at them are now hunted relentlessly by the attack helicopters - each laden with over a thousand pounds of hate, 7.62mm machine gun rounds for killing men and aerial rockets for destroying dug-in positions and bunkers. Spewing bullets at over six thousand rounds per minute, some gunships carry Gatling gun-style armaments known as miniguns. With its red tracers, the minigun's torrent of lead takes on the appearance of a red snake.

As the gunships circle, the main body now moves into a stepped formation and descends into the valley. Door gunners on each chopper strafe the surrounding tree lines and hillsides with their M-60s as they approach the valley floor, and you are forced to take cover. As the din of the machine gun fire tapers off, you raise your head and count ten aircraft hovering over the rice paddy, blowing the reeds flat while spraying and rippling water outward in all directions. You know that each one is filled with skytroopers trained to hunt and kill you. Close enough to make out their unshaven faces, they look filthy but well fed. The most eager are leaning out and standing on the skids, one arm clinging to the chopper, the other clutching a rifle. One has a pack of cigarettes strapped to the side of his helmet and is the first to jump into the muddy water. Through the grime on his shoulder, you detect something yellow. These are the horse soldiers.

You could still choose self-preservation and disappear, and that's what the majority of enemy soldiers did at this point. Those who chose to stay and fight the skytroopers had extraordinary courage, and most of them would die. But the enemy had advantages of his own. The enormous firepower carried by the Americans was heavy, and so it was not difficult for the enemy to outpace them while they were on foot. Such air assaults precluded any attempt at stealth, and Charlie was rarely taken by surprise. All of this allowed the enemy to choose when and where to fight the Americans, an advantage that would prove decisive.

As it were, Charlie would not challenge the men of Alpha Company on their initial descent. Their first air assault was not without incident, however. The hillside that was to be their landing zone was an area covered with both trees and elephant grass. It had been blown up with artillery preceding their assault, and jagged remnants of splintered trees and branches were everywhere. It was a wicked mess of a landing zone. Prepped not only with the standard high explosive artillery and white phosphorus, exploding barrels of tear gas had been dropped on the LZ from Chinook helicopters to give the first wave of troops extra stand-off from the enemy. The initial wave would therefore jump into battle with their gas masks.

The whole gas mask thing is more challenging than one might expect. In my training, I've only had to use a gas mask but once per year, whenever qualifying on the M-4 at the rifle range. The Army needs to know that you can shoot your rifle while wearing a gas mask, and that's about it. At fifty meters, we would typically just shoot the closest target on the range several times over to prove this. The masks are difficult to see out of to begin with, and it only gets worse as they inevitably fog up. In addition, you can never get the rifle close enough to your face to use the sights because the bulky mask gets in the way. I figured I would be pretty useless if I ever had to use that thing in combat.

The first wave of choppers descended on LZ Brenda at 9:16 AM. The men were told that they would be assaulted onto a hill where a force of Viet Cong was believed to be holed up. Yelling over the noise and thumping, each chopper's crew chief would advise the men aboard to get out the right side of the aircraft, closest to the hill. For whatever reason – perhaps because he had been trying to don his gas mask over his glasses at the time – a young and eager lieutenant in 1st Platoon didn't get the message. As the rest of the men jumped out the right side, he took a flying leap out the left shouting "Garry Owen!" and taking his radio operator with him. They fell about twenty feet and the lieutenant broke both his ankles. The troopers soon learned how deceiving the tall elephant grass could be, making you think you were closer to the ground than you really were. As each wave of soldiers jumped out of the choppers, they sprinted outward to secure a perimeter, just as they were trained. Their training had not prepared them for landing on and running across such a ragged and blown up landing zone, however. The last wave of the air assault was dropped onto LZ Brenda at 10:46 AM. A testament to the harshness of that particular LZ, four others were injured while jumping out of the choppers. Bill Purdy would recall being one of the first of Alpha Company's troopers to suffer the pain of a punji stake wound, as one went straight through his hand and broke off during their subsequent patrol that day. He also recalls one of their scout dogs being wounded by one of these countless punji stakes.

While the platoon sergeants were largely combat experienced and well-respected by their men, the lieutenants were a mixed bag. As platoons often moved independently in this "small-unit war", at times called a "platoon leader's war", land navigation skills were more critical than they had ever been before. Some of their young lieutenants, however, had a hard time reading a map. The Army Infantry Officer's motto is "follow me," but as Matulac recalled, one of their platoon leaders was more apt to shout, "move up, move up!" from the rear of the formation he led, unaware of the situation his men in front faced.

In stark contrast to this was the leader of Alpha Company's 2nd Platoon, 1LT James Harmon. A West Point graduate, both smart and tough, he was universally respected by his men. "He was head-and-shoulders above the others," remarked Bill Purdy, one of 1LT Harmon's soldiers in 2nd Platoon. As Purdy recalled, he wasn't what you would call a "spit-shine" soldier, and CPT Wise would have to remind him to shave on occasion. He remembers him as an officer who rarely barked out orders at his men. Rather, he would tell them what needed to be done, and they always felt compelled to oblige.

True to their name, skytroopers would kick off their missions by air. They were still infantry however, and would spend the vast majority of their time trudging over the Vietnamese landscape on foot. At 11:06 AM Alpha Company set out from LZ Brenda along what was called "Route Red" to begin their search and destroy mission. Assisted by a scout dog platoon attached to the company, they would spend the next five days pursuing Charlie through dense jungle, encountering several small hamlets, enemy camps, and river crossings. They continued their movement during their first day of the operation well into the evening hours. At 6:55 PM, they would stop to bivouac for the night. As the sun rose the next morning, they continued their patrol. At 7:55 AM the scout dogs picked up the enemy's trail, leading the company to an area where at least ten Viet Cong had slept the night before. At this time a request was sent from the company, through battalion, to the 3rd Brigade command. The request was granted, extending the operation for an additional two days. The next morning, on the 26th of September, they moved out again at 7:04 AM toward a suspected Viet Cong controlled village complex. The next two days brought more of the same, taking only light contact from their elusive enemy, reluctant to fight in force.

It was during this time that my dad recalls his first firefight. Searching for Viet Cong on a hillside of burnt-out trees defoliated by Agent Orange, he heard the sound of AK-47s coming from somewhere in the distance, and the whistle of bullets flying by his head. There was some yelling, and along with everyone else, he hit the ground. He tried to take cover behind a skinny dead tree. The smell of rotting wet undergrowth filled his nostrils as he lay on the ground and readied his rifle. He returned fire, having little idea where the enemy was. As the soldiers got on line with each other and the machine gunners emplaced their weapons, the sniper fire was answered with a punishing explosion of lead in the enemy's general direction while a blue-ish gun smoke haze enveloped the platoon. The forest's pungent odor was quickly overwhelmed by that of burnt gun powder. Cease-fire was ordered... then it was over. It has been said, "All war is hell, but contact's a bitch." This is what was considered "light" contact. Will and his friends now knew what the war looked like, what it felt like, and what it smelled like. It wasn't exactly what they'd imagined it to be, though I suppose it never is for anyone. Mostly, it just felt like mass confusion and noise, and they couldn't even see the enemy. As they moved out to continue their patrol, Will looked at the pathetic tree and briefly contemplated its uselessness. He promised himself that next time, he would find a better place to take cover. Fortunately, Alpha Company's superior firepower had provided all the cover necessary to survive that half-hearted attack. Though anticlimactic, it was a small victory. No one would die today.

The following are excerpts of two articles that appeared in the October 8th issue of the *Cavalair*:

5/7 Unit Succeeds in 1st Combat Test/Search Led By Angry Lieutenant
By SP/4 Jerry Condon

Co. A of the 1st Air Cav Division's 5th Bn, 7th Cav destroyed major elements of an expansive Viet Cong supply network north of An Khe in a five-day sweep mission tagged Operation Golden Bee. The operation, which ended Sept. 28, was the first combat test of any of the battalion's companies since its arrival in Vietnam August 20. Until now the unit's forces have held prime responsibility for the security of Hwy. 19 between the Cavalry base camp near An Khe and the city of Pleiku. The sweating skytroopers kicked off Golden Bee Sept. 24 with a five-wave air assault into landing zone Brenda, 13 kilometers north of Camp Radcliff. Artillery splattered the knotted jungle minutes before ships began carting the heavily equipped 'Garry Owens' into the landing zone.

Throughout the operation communications and quick troop movement were hampered by densely foliated hills strewn with punji stakes and narrow paths that the company had to cut out of the jungle itself. "It's really difficult to maintain control of a tactical formation in vegetation as thick as this," remarked Capt. A.J. Wise, the company commander, during the operation's second day. While direct enemy contact was light, the company destroyed 53 enemy work and sleeping huts, dozens of bunkers, concealed crop fields, large amounts of harvested crops, and thousands of newly made punji stakes. Automatic weapon ammunition, rice caches, meat animals, and crude punji stake factories were also uncovered. An estimated 20 guerrillas were pushed out of the supply channel as Alpha Company humped through 15 kilometers of jungle and broken trails near the banks of the Song Ba River.

German Shepherds of the 25th Inf. Scout Dog Platoon attached to Alpha Company were used to track fleeing enemy soldiers and seek out trails and paths. "We'll shoot anything that moves," radioed the angered leader of the scout dog platoon, Lt. Teddy D. Hampton. "Tell everyone to lay down and be quiet." Moments earlier, four Viet Cong had escaped him and his sergeant following a close-range firefight. The pair was seeking the source of previous enemy sniper fire in the jungle as elements of Alpha Company checked out scattered huts and bunkers near crop fields further to the rear.

Lt. Hampton and Sgt. Manuel Ybanez began their tedious search on a hidden path while their four dog teams awaited further instructions at the jungle entrance. Four pajama-clad soldiers had popped out of an adjoining trail just 10 meters ahead of the tiny 'recon' patrol. "It was the first time 'Charlie' has walked right into us," Hampton said afterward. "Two of them had automatic weapons, probably AK-47s, and the other two had carbines." Hampton and Ybanez hit the ground and opened up with their M-16s and grenades as enemy bullets bounced in the trees around them. One Viet Cong clutched his chest and sank to the ground, but was carried away by the others as they escaped into the thick jungle. Capt. A.J. Wise brought two squads into the area and blanketed the jungle with M-79 and automatic weapons fire. Then Capt. Wise sent a 10-man search party after the guerrillas, but the two dog handlers soon spotted drag marks and blood on a path the foursome used as an escape route.

Bundles of bamboo still moist from cutting were found on secret enemy trails, indicating that 'Charlie' had fled moments before the company advance. Artillery fired from the Cavalry base camp potted portions of jungle in the path of the oncoming infantrymen. "It's not a heavy troop concentration area," pointed out Lt. James Ulrich, a forward observer attached to the unit from the 1st Bn, 21st Artillery, "but they must have thought the best place to store supplies was right under our noses."

Capt. Walter L. Swain, battalion S-2 (Intelligence Officer), stated that "original intelligence reports indicated that the area had a drug collection point. But nothing we have found as of yet can substantiate this."

Lt. Hampton and his sergeant hurriedly grouped three dog handlers and a radio operator around them. After confirming by radio that all friendly troops in the area had ceased search efforts and remained stationary, the patrol set out with a rusty-brown and black German Shepherd named Prince in the lead. Prince, handled by PFC Darrel G. Melton, was wounded earlier by one of the tens of thousands of punji stakes scattered throughout the area. As the scout patrol followed a blood trail left by the retreating guerrillas, Prince alerted his followers to enemy booby-traps and led the patrol through a maze of complicated paths. The rear man of the Viet Cong foursome haphazardly planted punjis behind his group as they raced through the torrid jungle. More than an hour later the patrol surrounded three sleeping huts and a bunker complex where the four had stopped "to pick up food, packs, and a new supply of punji stakes," according to Lt. Hampton. The little village contained cotton supplies, corn rations, musical instruments, batteries, and miscellaneous trinkets. "They're headed toward an aid station across the river," the lieutenant remarked. But night closed in and the weary platoon leader decided to wait until morning to continue the chase.

Member of Company A directs landing of helicopters before assault.

Troopers Assault onto gas prepped LZ Brenda.

Capt. A.J. Wise directs movement of his company before fire touched off during operation.

Heavily laden motorman trudges through jungle.

Bunkers and tunnel complexes have to be searched.

An instructor at one of my non-commissioned officer courses had a particularly apt description of what "search and destroy" meant, "Basically, it's walking around looking for a fight." There was a method to the whole thing, but to the infantrymen on patrol it often felt like they were just wandering around, waiting to get shot at. By all accounts, the lower-enlisted men had little idea where they were, where they were going, or when they would get there. All they knew is that they were on their way.

The company commander would receive their orders from the battalion, when to commence movement, what areas to search, what to look for, what routes to take, and the location of their final objective. He would be advised by CPT Walt Swain, the 5/7th's Intelligence Officer (S-2), of suspected enemy locations. 1LT James Ulrich, his forward observer mentioned in the first *Cavalair* article on Operation Golden Bee, would advise him of what assets were available to assist them should they encounter heavy resistance. The gunships, which were Hueys modified to carry armaments rather than troops, were popular choices in these situations as they offered enormous and accurate firepower. Huey gunships were eventually deemed too slow, however, and too easy for the enemy to shoot down. In 1967, the AH-1 Cobra would be introduced as the attack helicopter of choice. With only two seats and no cargo or passenger space, it was designed specifically as an attack chopper. Made apparent by its alien appearance, the Cobra had but one purpose in life, killing. Artillery batteries held outposts throughout the region and could also be called upon, either by the commander or by the aforementioned 1LT Ulrich and his team of FOs (forward observers). This FO team included his Recon Sergeant, as well as his radio operator, Danny Garrity. They were attached to Alpha Company from the 1st Battalion, 21st Field Artillery (1/21st FA). Binoculars, compasses, maps and radios in tow, the FO team moved with and fought with the company as they made their way through the jungle.

After their company patrol base had been bivouacked each night, CPT Wise would typically brief the command group, the platoon leaders and platoon sergeants of the next day's mission. The platoon sergeants were to then brief their squad leaders, and they in turn, were to brief their own men. At times, Matulac would inquire of the lower-enlisted soldiers in each platoon as to what they knew about the next day's operation. He was usually disappointed but not surprised to find that they knew very little.

While on patrol, snipers would often take a few shots at them and then slip away. In this deadly game of cat and mouse, Charlie was outgunned but not stupid, and rarely challenged the skytroopers in full force. They typically only killed one to three soldiers at a time. Their objective was not necessarily to overrun the Americans, but rather to simply demoralize them. The troopers would often remark, "It ain't much of a war, but it's the only one we've got." There was a unique frustration about fighting such an invisible enemy; bullets whizzing and crackling through the foliage, your only recourse to fire blindly into the jungle, often while your buddies lay wounded or dying. They would come to learn however, that you didn't have to see Charlie to kill Charlie. Though they seldom saw the enemy alive, they saw plenty of their dead, and counted them all.

There were many ways one could die in Vietnam, and enemy fire was just one of them. There were frequent encounters with booby-traps and explosive devices. Many were made from grenades, artillery and mortar rounds, or anything else that could explode, hidden in the ground and activated by unseen trip wires. They were psychologically devastating because just like the enemy, they were invisible, yet unlike the enemy, there was no way to fight back against them. Not the deadliest, but perhaps the most feared of these was known as the "Bouncing Betty". Activated by three tiny prongs that were easily concealed in vegetation, the relatively small mine had two charges. The first popped the mine up about three to four feet, waist high - or more to the point, ball-sack high - before the second charge exploded, sending shrapnel into the victim's midsection and groin. Many areas were riddled with punji stakes, which were also usually invisible until it was too late. They were often smeared with feces so as to infect the victim with gangrene.

In addition to poisonous scorpions and millipedes, over thirty species of venomous snakes inhabited the region, including bamboo vipers and the fabled "Two-Step" Snake, named for the number of steps its victim would take before dying. Bobby Hansen recalls a time he was sitting around bullshitting with the guys when he felt something moving underneath him. He stood up to find he was sitting on a snake, and everyone just ran off without their rifles. Bob Matulac recalls a buck sergeant, SGT J.C. Jackson, who had the misfortune of having a cobra spit in his eyes. Rendered totally blind, he was flown to a field hospital. When the wounded were flown out of the field, their gear would be gathered by the medics, and their weapons and ammunition placed in a locked cage near the field hospital. Eventually, SGT Jackson recovered his sight. Before returning to the field, he was brought to this cage to retrieve his weapon. Amidst the stacks of countless M-16s he could not find his own, so he simply grabbed one that looked functional. When it was discovered that he no longer had his issued weapon, he was made to pay for it out of his Army paycheck. Although he was the only soldier Matulac recalls to get spit in the eye from a cobra, he was not the only one to suffer the injustice of having to pay for a lost weapon after being wounded.

The soldiers carried an enormous amount of explosives and firepower, leading to many wounds and deaths at their own hands. The battalion's records would account for many such incidents, pistols and grenade launchers discharging into soldiers' feet, Claymore mines exploding prematurely, and ammunition dumps catching fire. A particularly fickle mistress was the M-72 LAW, or light anti-tank weapon, a rocket launcher that functioned as a mini-bazooka. They were designed to blow up tanks, but in Vietnam they were mainly used for destroying dug-in bunkers. Bill Purdy told of one soldier who was firing the LAW but hadn't properly aligned something in the mechanism. The LAW had misfired and the soldier lay wounded, and they all thought he'd been killed. This soldier had a buddy, and they had some kind of agreement wherein one would get the other's stuff if he got killed. His buddy was going through his pockets when the wounded soldier said, "Hey man, I'm not dead yet!" Another one of Purdy's friends from Kentucky in 2nd Platoon, John Kruetzkamp, recalled one of the company's lieutenants shooting off a flare. He was underneath a tree (his first mistake), and the flare went up sending branches down on the lieutenant. He had also gripped the flare mechanism too high, resulting in a severely burnt hand. He laughed as he recalled how the lieutenant was awarded a Purple Heart the next day.

On occasion, the company would take surrendering enemy soldiers prisoner. Bound and blindfolded, they would be interrogated with the help of ARVN interpreters. At times, they would encounter enemy soldiers seeking to surrender before a fight even started. Their malnourished bodies would emerge from the bushes, often waving a white cloth and making motions toward their mouths that signaled their hunger. They would call out, "Chieu Hoi!" in reference to the Army's "Open Arms" program that gave amnesty to those who voluntarily surrendered. Those granted amnesty under the program would be cared for and fed, and then used for intelligence. The Chieu Hoi program was promoted by psychological operations units, such as that of psy-ops officer and future author, 2LT Winston Groom. They would drop thousands of leaflets over enemy areas, encouraging their soldiers to surrender, with the promise of good food and humane treatment. In a memoir written for the *Smithsonian Air & Space Magazine* in 2013, Groom recalled, "I dimly remember one of the infantry platoon leaders telling me over drinks in the tent that passed for an officers' club that the North Vietnamese soldiers were using our leaflets as toilet paper — his men had stumbled on an area in the jungle littered with the evidence. This led to us discussing a plot to embed the leaflets with itching powder or some other unpleasantness, but nothing came of it." A 1st Air Cavalry Division Operational Report from 1967 even contemplated the use of cigarettes to promote surrender amongst the enemy:

Psywar Cigarettes. The effort to make VC/NVA read Chieu Hoi Messages could reach a new dimension in effectiveness if persuaded to read leaflets. While the VC/NVA may destroy leaflets, he would certainly be reluctant to destroy cigarettes with psywar messages on them.

WHERE IS THE ZONE OF LIBERATION?

Actually, you are living in a zone of liberation. The area of forests and impure water, where you must hide out, move secretly at night, is the zone you call 'liberated'. The regions under VC control no longer exist because a million inhabitants fled the VC-controlled villages to go to live in areas under government control. Your zone – as you well know – has no security. The government and Allied forces can carry out a search and destroy operation at will. No spot escapes the bombardment of the Allied forces. You are short of food. Things will get worse because the Allied soldiers have seized all your reserves in the caches and the inhabitants of remote villages cannot supply you. Under such miserable circumstances, how can you win? What must you do to survive? There is only one way – and that is to rally under the CHIEU HOI Program of the government, to be warmly welcomed, to be well treated and get the chance to build a new life in free South Vietnam.

Chieu Hoi leaflet with translation, from the National Archives.

Known as the "Breadbasket of Vietnam", the coastal plain regions are among South Vietnam's most fertile. Within II Corps, this included areas known as the Bong Son plain to the north, and the Phu My plain to the south. Their terrain being practically identical, both of these coastal plain areas were often referred to simply as "Bong Son".

Rice paddies are virtually everywhere in these regions. These are open valley areas where rice is grown, flooded with water. Earthen "dikes" that rise less than a foot or so above the water crisscross each of these paddies. While they could provide quick and easy passage across the paddies, they were seldom used as it was safer to remain low and walk through the gray-colored muck. The muck was thick and sticky, and rife with enormous bloodthirsty leeches. The best way to remove them was to burn them with your cigarette lighter, if it wasn't waterlogged. Their teeth were razor sharp and their bite could not be felt, yet they would cause a great amount of bleeding. After crossing a rice paddy or river, Matulac would often look back at the men and notice blood soaking their legs or crotch area. He would ask if they'd been wounded, and they would invariably answer, no. They would then look down to realize they were being made a meal by any number of leeches that had found their way into their trousers. Despite their enormous size, these leeches could flatten themselves to the point where they could invade even the most tightly-laced jungle boots. Checking their bodies for leeches would soon become part of each soldier's morning routine, and incorporated into their ten-minute smoke breaks while on patrol.

I used to wonder why so many soldiers in Vietnam carried their cigarettes on their helmet. I know now that it was the only place on their body that wasn't constantly wet. Waking each morning soaked from the morning moisture, they would then walk for hours through dew-covered foliage. The wetness of their environment would start to evaporate in the late morning heat, only to be replaced by that of their own sweat. In these conditions, they found that wearing no underwear was preferable to wet underwear.

Rice paddies just happened to be great places to get shot at. My dad recalls crossing one in water just above his knees when his platoon started taking fire from the adjacent tree line. As rounds whizzed by their heads, everyone crouched in the water and returned fire, hunkering down behind the dikes wherever possible. Except for Tall Lee Roy, an exceptionally tall soldier who towered above the others. Lying in the muck behind the dikes, everyone yelled, "Lee Roy, get down!" but he just stood there on the dike, looking around. Will could see the green tracers streaking by Lee Roy on each side. Tall Lee Roy would mysteriously survive the incident without a scratch.

Despite its dangers and constant wetness, the rice paddies of the coastal plains were still preferable to their dense forests, which also had to be patrolled and cleared. The jungle's thickness reduced the infantry company to fighting on par with the enemy. Their mortars were often rendered useless amidst the tangled vines and bamboo, and attack helicopters could rarely be used as both enemy and friendly were hidden beneath the jungle's canopy. Calling for artillery support was particularly problematic in these conditions. Imagine trying to keep track of your own location and determine the enemy's grid coordinates when you can only see a few feet in front of you. In the nightmare scenario where your company encounters a battalion-size force of five hundred or more, reinforcements would be called upon, but this was severely complicated when there was no place for the choppers to land. In the depths of the jungle, the infantry company was on its own.

River crossings represented yet another opportunity for the enemy to attack, but also the soldiers' only opportunity to bathe. When they felt it was safe, or were simply desperate enough, they would take off their clothes and wade into the river, bars of soap in hand while others pulled security. At times, they would even attempt to wash their fatigues in the river.

As there were different forms of malaria, there were a couple different pills given to the soldiers. A white pill was taken daily to prevent a particularly virulent strain of the disease known as falciparum. For the more common form of malaria, they were given another pill every Monday. Large and orange, this is how they knew which day of the week it was. Well known to the soldiers, malaria's symptoms included fever, uncontrollable shivering, convulsions, and jaundice. In severe cases, the disease caused damaged vision, kidney failure, and brain dysfunction. After several months in the field, however, some soldiers would avoid ingesting the pills in hopes that they would contract the disease and be sent to a hospital where it was comfortable and dry. To ward off dysentery, they were also given water purification tablets to put in water derived from streams, resulting in a particularly loathsome swill known as "Iodine Kool-Aid".

As their division, brigade, and battalion commanders moved them around the chess board that was II Corps, the skytroopers would find themselves chasing rabbits known as Viet Cong in the strange and exotic wonderland known as the Central Highlands. Unlike those chased by Alice, these rabbits were particularly vicious, and had developed an elaborate system of tunnels throughout the country. These tunnels had already been used by the Viet Minh with great effectiveness only a decade prior, during the French-Indochina War. As both the NVA and Viet Cong mainly moved at night, this subterranean network served as their refuge during the day. Many were found to contain command centers, medical facilities, and even mess halls. Throughout their tour, the skytroopers would encounter many of these tunnels while on patrol, and each of them would have to be searched, and then destroyed. The openings to these tunnels were hidden beneath the brush, usually covered by a trap door, and often booby-trapped. Most of these tunnels turned out to be empty, but not always. Those who did not surrender or escape would meet a particularly gruesome death inside the tunnel itself, by way of flamethrowers or white phosphorus grenades. Matulac would recall that regular grenades were often ineffective at removing the enemy from tunnels, as their blast did not go around corners. He would advise his soldiers to use white phosphorus whenever possible, as it would continue to burn while sucking out all the oxygen from the tunnel. Finally, the bodies of enemy soldiers who met their fate in the tunnels would have to be removed, counted, and stacked. Considered worse than that of the actual killing, this most unpleasant task of entering the tunnels with a flashlight and pistol, then dragging out the charred enemy bodies, was usually given either to the lowest ranking or newest members of the platoon.

John Kruetzkamp carried an M-79 grenade launcher and a .45 pistol. He said he liked having the .45 with him at night, the only disadvantage being that whenever they found a tunnel, he was made to go in and search it. He recalled crawling into one tunnel with his pack still on. He was deep into the tunnel when someone dropped a grenade in the other end, sending a wave of agitated fruit bats flying at him. In a panic, he tried desperately to turn himself around and get out as the bats accosted him, but his entrenching tool attached to his pack was caught on some rocks. The bats were all over him in the pitch blackness of the tunnel and for a while, he felt like he couldn't breath. It took him some time to calm down after he finally managed to shimmy his way out. Not long after this incident, Kruetzkamp gave his .45 to one of the new guys in their platoon, he seemed pleased to have it. Later on, when they came upon another tunnel they called him up to go in and search it out. "Here's your pistol," the new guy said, trying to give back the .45.

Kruetzkamp just replied, "Why do you think I gave it to you?"

Also during their search and destroy missions, they would frequently come upon hamlets, which they would have to search. Entering was dicey, as they were sometimes occupied by enemy soldiers. These tiny villages in the countryside consisted mostly of crude wooden houses with grass roofs and dirt floors, though some stood on stilts above the paddies. Some were fortunate enough to have a functioning well nearby. They were inhabited mainly by women, children, and old men. They had virtually no possessions, and subsisted on whatever the land could provide. Most of them worked harvesting the rice.

Men of military age were conspicuously absent. They would be conscripted to fight, either with the ARVN or the Viet Cong. Any military-age men they encountered would be interrogated by an ARVN interpreter attached to the company. The interpreters had to be monitored carefully however, as they were often inclined to settle personal vendettas with those suspected of being Viet Cong. If weapons were found, the village would be burned and its inhabitants relocated. Unpleasant as this task was, villages used by the enemy to store weapons and food were legitimate military targets. One might question the wisdom of this policy, as it often alienated many otherwise neutral or even friendly villagers. Nonetheless, the men of Alpha Company didn't get to make policy. This is simply what they were ordered to do in service to their country.

The soldiers had little more than pity to offer the villagers, who were caught in an impossible position. The Viet Cong and North Vietnamese would confiscate their rice, force the men into service, and often rape the women. Resisting them meant death. If found to be cooperating with the communists however, their homes would be destroyed by the Americans, who would then attempt to relocate them as humanely as possible.

Their true loyalties could not be known, nor could they be distinguished in any meaningful way from the enemy, yet they were to be treated with a certain level of respect and dignity. Sent to Vietnam by some guy they didn't know to kill some other guy they didn't know, and admonished not to kill anyone that didn't deserve killing, our soldiers were led by commanders under constant pressure to produce increasingly impressive enemy body counts. Caught in this morally treacherous circumstance, the character and the humanity of these impossibly young skytroopers would be tested. To fail such a test, to become calloused to the suffering of the innocents, to treat them like cattle or worse, would have been understandable. It is known that in some situations, perhaps led by commanders of lesser caliber, some American units would at times, fail to abide by the laws of war, and even the norms of human decency. By all accounts however, the young men of Alpha Company, and for that matter, those of the entire battalion, seem to have acquitted themselves admirably in this regard, treating the villagers with as much compassion as they could.

Particularly troubled by the plight of the rural inhabitants they encountered, was CPT Wise's radio operator, Donald Rankin. He would often write to his old college roommate, in whose wedding he'd been the best man and who had been the last person to see him off on his way to Vietnam. In his letters to his friend, he often spoke of the heartache he felt for the poor people of rural Vietnam.

The helicopters that brought supplies were called log ships. They were the infantryman's sole source of food, clothing, and ammunition. The log ship also represented their only connection to "The World" (the world outside Vietnam), as it would often bring bags of mail and current issues of the Stars & Stripes newspaper. The log ships also brought Lifeline packs, packages that contained various personal hygiene items, as well as candy, chewing gum, and cigarettes. For some reason however, they rarely had fresh uniforms for Alpha Company's soldiers.

On most days, the choppers provided one hot meal for the soldiers in the field. Otherwise they ate C-Rations, which had been invented at the beginning of World War II. Most of the C-Rations they were fed were of Korean War vintage. The Pound Cake was good, but even better with Peaches in Heavy Syrup poured over it. Quinn was always the first to the chopper to unload the C-Rations, hoping to find his favorite meal, Spaghetti and Meatballs, a bonus if it contained his favorite dessert, the Pecan Roll. If Lifeline packs were aboard, he hoped to get one that contained Chuckles candies. One wildly unpopular C-Ration item was the Ham and Lima Beans, often called Ham and something rather profane by the soldiers - you can look it up. Also universally scorned was the peanut butter, which was usually rock hard with all of the oil separated. Many found that adding C-Ration Cheese Spread or Tabasco sauce was the secret to making certain meat items edible. Each meal box contained a Meat Unit can, a Bread Unit can, and a Dessert Unit can, as well as an accessory pack that included salt, pepper, instant coffee, gum, toilet paper, and four commercial-grade cigarettes of varying brands. They never knew what brand of cigarettes they would get in their C-Rations, but would often make trades to get their favorite. C-Rations could be heated by lighting a small amount of C-4, a putty-like plastic explosive material. The C-4 would burn fiercely when lighted, but would not explode without the use of a detonator. As an explosive, larger amounts of C-4 were often used to clear landing zones for dust-off (medevac) choppers when no open area was available.

Usually the soldiers would eat their meals straight from the can. At times, however, some of them would use their creativeness and ingenuity to make gourmet meals, and in fact, several C-Ration cookbooks have been published in this effort. Quinn recalls on several occasions crawling from his tent at first light to find Will using their helmets to cook some sort of concoction. On the first of these he asked, "What the hell are you doing with our helmets?"

"What does it look like," Will replied, "I'm making us breakfast."

On a precious few occasions, the log ships would also bring a chaplain, accompanied by an assistant. Aside from setting up the service, the chaplain's assistant was also tasked with protecting the chaplain, who traveled unarmed. Military chaplains are unique from their civilian counterparts in that they are responsible for ministering to soldiers of all different faiths, regardless of their own affiliation. Many soldiers tend to find Jesus during their months in basic training, as it is a good way to get out of the battalion area and avoid work detail on Sundays. In the fields of Vietnam however, service wasn't necessarily held on Sunday, but rather whenever the chaplain could make it there. The services would be held at the patrol base or outpost, typically using boxes of ammunition or C-Rations as an altar. Each chaplain was typically responsible for tending to the spiritual needs of an entire battalion scattered throughout an area of over three thousand square miles. The services were few and far between, short on ceremony, with abbreviated sermons. They were, nonetheless, especially meaningful to the soldiers who attended. One chaplain of the 1st Air Cavalry, CPT Henry C. Hilliard, conducted over five hundred services in the field. He would earn his Air Medal several times over, as well as two Bronze Stars for Valor. He would also be awarded the Soldier's Medal, for rescuing a wounded pilot from the flames of his burning helicopter. Firebase Mary actually had a small, roofless chapel put together by the artillerymen who manned the outpost. Named in honor of the patron saint of the artillery, Saint Barbara's Chapel was surrounded by a small picket fence. A row of little wooden benches served as pews, and on its altar of stained ammo boxes was placed a brass cross, carved from a 105mm canister.

The 5/7th Cav's chaplain was a Catholic priest, Major (MAJ) Thomas Widdel. In his mid-forties, both a soldier and a priest, he was built more like a soldier. His manner, as to be expected, was more that of a priest. When not holding services in the field, he would stay at his tent at LZ English, a major outpost near Bong Son with an airfield and field hospital. This is where most of the dead and wounded of the 5/7th Cav would initially be flown into from the field, and this was the reason he stayed there. Father Tom requested that he be notified of any incoming casualties. When called, he would make his way to the medical tents. In his book, Bernard Grady spoke of the many trips he made to the medical tents with Father Tom during the later months of their tour, when Grady served as the Battalion Adjutant. Often waiting as the dust-off landed, Father Tom would do his best to comfort the wounded, most of whom were only half his age.

Last in the row of medical tents at LZ English was the Graves Registration unit. Graves Registration is the military term for the morgue. Parked outside the Graves Registration tent was a refrigerated truck, used for storing the bodies of the dead until they began their journey home. This tent is where the dead were first brought, and where Father Tom often found himself. Graves Registration personnel could usually identify the dead by their dog tags and name tape, but military regulation required two individuals to independently identify each body by physical recognition. Although identifying the dead of his flock was not an official duty of his, it would become a rather routine one.

On September 28th, the soldiers of Alpha Company would use ropes to cross the large Song Ba River as they reached their final objective of Operation Golden Bee, arriving at PZ Linda at 2:30 PM. Smoke grenades were set off to signal the incoming choppers. They smelled like sulfur, not necessarily a pleasant scent, but one that would become welcome, often associated with the end of a long mission. By 4:10 PM, the final lift was bringing the last of the company's soldiers back to An Khe, ending their first air assault operation.

Meanwhile that same day, the rest of the battalion was preparing for their own return to base camp. That morning, a coordinating party from the 2nd Battalion, 12th Cavalry (2/12th Cav) arrived at the Eagle's Nest to plan their own take-over of the Highway 19 mission, scheduled for the next day. At 5:17 PM, the 1st Air Cavalry Division Commander, Major General John Norton, arrived to be briefed on the battalion's experiences and recommendations. On September 29th, the rest of the battalion returned to An Khe, just in time to prepare for their next mission, where they would join the rest of the 3rd Brigade and others in a much larger and more dangerous mission that would be a continuation of Operation Thayer.

28 September 1966, Will Bowe carrying base plate followed by Angel Reynosa, crossing Song Ba River, photo by Fred Brodosi

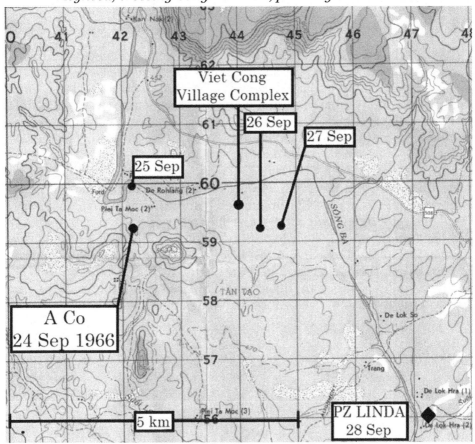

Operation Golden Bee, 24-28 Sep 1966

29 Sep '66 – 43 weeks left

Well, we finally made it back from our mission yesterday. We had a couple of injuries from punji stakes and broken bones. Then after we came back to An Khe, we heard what we did on the radio. What a blow up. First music I heard since the 5th of this month. We are going to Bong Son tomorrow, a long ways from here, so not much of a rest. This last mission we ran into about 4 V.C.s, killed one or wounded him bad. Burnt down a bunch of houses. Wish you could have seen us all. Boy, I tell you we sure were bad looking, beard, mud, and torn clothes, but I am in good shape. I doubt if I lost any weight. I don't know how often I'll be able to write, so don't worry. What I'd like to do is send some V.C. souvenirs home if I could.

The guys wrote to a girl in our newspaper, Berg from Spring Street. She announced her engagement and about 20 of us guys signed our letter to her. Everybody reads my paper. I always keep forgetting to mention, you only need a 5-cent stamp on the letters and it still goes Air Mail. Now you can write 5 letters for the price of 2. Say, how much money did you guys get from the Army, $203? Can't be that much. I got your candy and long johns and paper. This letter may be a little mixed up, but I am in a hurry and mixed up too. I'll write the next chance I get. Don't know when.

Will

It was the end of September 1966. Alpha Company's men had survived each of their many jungle patrols along Highway 19, as well as their first air assault operation. Several had been wounded, but so far there had been no fatalities for the company. All the while, they had managed to shoot up a few Viet Cong and take some prisoners. As a battalion, the 5/7th Cav had suffered many more wounded, but only two fatalities, resulting from Delta Company's overturned truck and Charlie Company's helicopter crash.

To their east, the 5/7th Cav's sister battalions of the 3rd Brigade, the 1/7th Cav and 2/7th Cav, were closing in on the dislocated and desperate enemy regiments that had been pursued from the Kim Son Valley (Crow's Foot) and into the soggy coastal plains of Phu My during Operation Thayer. The operation ended on October 1st 1966 with over two hundred communist soldiers killed, at a cost of thirty-five American lives. In terms of body count, it was a success, and the enemy had been expelled from the Kim Son Valley. Operation Thayer had prepared the battlefield. The next phase of the Binh Dinh Pacification Campaign would exploit it.

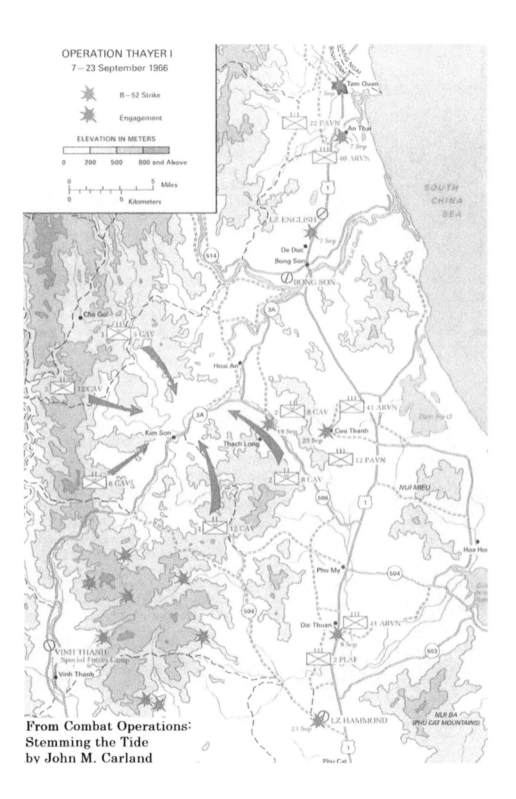

From Combat Operations: Stemming the Tide by John M. Carland

Choppers loading in preparation for air assault

Soldiers en route to LZ, photos by Wilbur Bowe

Aerial view eastward toward coastal plains and South China Sea beyond, an inlet lake can be seen in the background

Air assault into valley, photos by Wilbur Bowe

Alpha Company patrolling through rice paddies in wedged formations, photo by Wilbur Bowe

River crossing in Binh Dinh Province, John Bronson in foreground, photo by Wilbur Bowe

Soldiers crossing creek while on patrol, photo by Wilbur Bowe

John Curtis investigating tunnel, photo by Robert Matulac

Viet Cong fighter pulled from tunnel, photo by Marvin Bierschbach

Marvin Bierschbach enjoying C-Rations

SGT J.C. Jackson, photo by Bill Purdy

Marvin Bierschbach amidst burning enemy huts

Bronson (left) and Evans (right), photo by Wilbur Bowe

Punji stakes near ARVN command post, photo by Wilbur Bowe

Father Tom Widdel and assistant, preparing service at Alpha Company patrol base, photo by Marvin Bierschbach

8
THE FIRST TO FALL
(Operation Irving)

I know my soldiers, and will always place their needs above my own.
-Creed of the Non-commissioned Officer

In Alpha Company's 3rd Platoon, Bobby Hansen shared a foxhole with a fellow from Milwaukee named Donald Smith. Smithy, as he called him, would have been better suited for a typewriter than life in the infantry, he recalled.

At 9:00 AM on September 30th 1966, after spending only one day back at base camp, the 5/7th Cav moved out for its next operation. Again in a convoy of trucks, the battalion forward command post headed for Camp Hammond while each of the companies – Alpha, Bravo, Charlie and Delta – headed for PZ Bradley, just off Highway 1. Running anywhere between ten and twenty kilometers inland from the South China Sea's coastline, Highway 1 was the main north-south route through the Phu My and Bong Son plain regions. Camp Hammond was located just west of Highway 1, near the town of Phu My. Approximately fifty kilometers north of Camp Hammond along Highway 1 was LZ English, near the town of Bong Son. Though smaller than those at Pleiku or An Khe, both LZ English and Camp Hammond were major outposts with airstrips that could accommodate both helicopters and large fixed-wing aircraft.

From the pick-up zone, the companies were airlifted to separate LZs along a north-south axis approximately three kilometers west of Highway 1, north of Camp Hammond. Charlie Company was flown to the northern-most LZ Suzie, Bravo to LZ Hooker, and Delta to LZ Thomas. Alpha Company was flown to the southern-most LZ Ike at 2:25 PM with its final lift arriving at 3:25 PM. After the lifts were completed, each company conducted patrols in its own area, while key leaders attended briefings at Camp Hammond on what was to be a massive operation the next day. A reconnaissance platoon was attached to Alpha Company, while pathfinder and engineer teams were attached to others. It would be the 5/7th Cav's first battalion-size air assault. At night, teams were sent out to ambush positions. The patrols and ambushes made no enemy contact. The enemy was on the other side of Highway 1, where they would soon be sent.

Commencing the next day, Operation Irving was a continuation of Thayer, with the objective of finding, fixing, and finishing the communist forces that had fled into the coastal plains from their sanctuaries in the Kim Son Valley. The enemy was scattered and desperate, but relatively intact. It was deemed a new operation as in this phase, the 1st Air Cavalry's 1st and 3rd Brigades would now be joined by both ARVN and Republic of Korea (ROK) forces. Also joining the 3rd Brigade for the first time in this next operation was the 5/7th Cav. Just as in Operation Thayer, Irving kicked off with five battalions of skytroopers air assaulting into battle positions in the early morning hours of October 2nd 1966.

At 6:45 AM Bravo Company lifted off from its position, air assaulting at 7:11 AM onto LZ Opal, atop a hill just northwest of where the Song Ca and Siem Giang rivers would meet, then separate again, in the middle of the Phu My plain. The Phu My plain was a vast, soggy, lowland area bordered by the highlands on the west, the Nui Mieu Mountains to the north, the Phu Cat Mountains to the south, and on the east, a large inlet lake of the South China Sea named Vinh Nuoc Ngot (shown on map as Dam Nuc Ngot). Around this inlet was where the enemy was known to be. Alpha Company lifted off at 8:16 AM, air assaulting onto its own hill, LZ Topaz, at 8:31 AM. Located betwixt the two rivers, Alpha Company's LZ was approximately 1 ½ kilometers southwest of Bravo's. At 9:23 AM both Charlie and Delta Companies air assaulted into LZ Bloodstone, another two kilometers southwest of Alpha Company, securing what would serve as the 5/7th Cav's battalion command post. Early that afternoon, the battalion command group arrived by Chinook to set up shop at LZ Bloodstone. From here on the southeast bank of the Siem Giang River, LTC Swett and his staff would direct each of the companies during the impending battle.

On the far northeast side of what would soon become a vast battlefield, battalions of the 1st Brigade took up positions near the coast, surrounding enemy regiments who were holed up in the village of Hoa Hoi, just north of Vinh Nuoc Ngot. The 1st Brigade began its attack immediately. A few hours into the fighting, leaflets were dropped on the village, warning its civilian inhabitants to evacuate and its occupiers to surrender. The offensive was paused at one point to allow approximately two hundred villagers to escape what would soon become a bloodbath for the NVA soldiers holed up there.

As the battle around Hoa Hoi raged on, those units massed to the southwest, including the 5/7th Cav, waited for the call to move out. During this time, each of the companies conducted search and destroy missions in their own areas of operation. Only two enemy fighters were killed by the 5/7th Cav on this day, but over fifty were taken prisoner.

In the early morning hours of October 3rd, the battalions of the 1st Brigade reattacked Hoa Hoi ferociously, while soldiers of the 5/7th Cav and 1/7th Cav continued their own localized patrols. For its part, Alpha Company conducted patrols in a loop pattern, returning to LZ Topaz before dusk. As the sun set on the battlefield, ambushes were placed in strategic areas by all elements to catch any exfiltrating enemy soldiers. Of the approximately three hundred enemy soldiers that occupied the village of Hoa Hoi, over two hundred were killed and over thirty were taken prisoner by soldiers of the 1st Brigade.

3 Oct '66 – 42 weeks left

Dear Folks,

You wouldn't believe what we did this morning. We watched combat from the top of a big hill. Must have been at least 1,500 men and 12 armored vehicles blowing the hell out of these villages below us. Just like watching a movie. Some joker yelled out, "Popcorn, peanuts and sodas, get them while they're hot!" You might have heard of this operation, named Irving. Might take a week or more to finish. This other unit cut off a battalion of V.C. last night, something like 160 V.C. got killed with the help of the Navy. No one in this company has been hurt so far in this operation. Even we killed a couple V.C. and captured a bunch of them. Man, I tell you there are more choppers around here than there are birds. Sure am glad I am in the mortars. You see a little action, and yet you're fairly safe. We've got to make a drive 6-8 miles to the sea, and about a million villages to clear out. So that's the story so far. I received one of your packages, and you know a mouse chewed a hole in it. That didn't make a darn bit of difference.

Combat Will

Donald Rankin would also write home on October 3rd.

Dear Mom and Daddy,

We're now a part of Operation Thayer. We're on top of another mountain. The sea is on one side, with rice paddies and palms on the other three sides. Today I had to carry a baby up this horrid mountain. Yesterday, we captured 41 VC's, killed two and wounded two. In these two days we've found medicine, documents, and everything. Tonight, we are moving elsewhere. The 12th Cavalry killed 169 VC where we're going. We're still doing okay. No deaths and few casualties from the enemy.

Received a lot of mail tonight. That makes the day better; you, Suzie, Nancy, Bob Schweitzer, and a guy from college. I wish I had sent all my money home. I'll probably get it wet and ruin everything in my billfold. Tell everyone hello. Save one of those pictures to send to Nancy. This is about all. Will write when I can.

Love,

Donnie

Donald Rankin carrying child, photo courtesy of nephew, Tony Rankin

Alpha Company received its final mission briefing on the morning of October 4th. Their mission was to finish what the 1st Brigade had started. Both the 5/7th and 1/7th Cavs began their push northeastward in the direction of the previous day's fighting, searching villages and taking prisoners. The reconnaissance platoon and ARVN troops moved on Alpha Company's right flank, while Bravo moved along the left. Farther north, ROK soldiers moved in the same direction.

It started out like any other search and destroy mission for Alpha Company as they made their way down the hill from LZ Topaz and into the soggy, flooded battlefield of the Phu My plain. 3rd Platoon led the way followed closely by 1st Platoon. In 3rd Platoon, Wagner and McNay took turns carrying their machine gun. Will and his four-man team that included Bierschbach, Bronson and Fulford, lugged their mortar pieces along with the others in 4th Platoon. Tom Gruenburg and Earl Huber would always find SSG Matulac to let him know they were heading out with their platoon. As a lucky insult of sorts, Matulac would tell them, "go get shot," or, "catch a grenade." It seemed to work, as whenever they did this they would both return unscathed.

Intelligence had reported that a regiment-sized force was occupying a small fishing village just south of Hoa Hoi. On the map this village is called "An My". Located near the northwest corner of the Vinh Nuoc Ngot inlet, this village was to be their final objective. The terrain here was at sea-level and dominated by both rice paddies and mangroves. Mangroves are trees or shrubs with twisting exposed roots that grow in salty tidal backwaters.

As the forward company for the battalion, Alpha was to lead the attack on the village after covering several miles on foot. They moved through a wide valley laden with water and dotted with many other small villages. Here the water was nearly waist high, or higher for those short of stature like Bobby Hansen. Alpha Company trudged along for miles between the two rivers that ran in the same direction as their advance. To their left, Bravo Company moved in the same direction on the other side of the Song Ca River. On Alpha Company's right, their attached reconnaissance platoon and ARVN forces moved with them along the other side of the Siem Giang River.

As the village of An My came into view, so did the South China Sea. The river on Alpha Company's right flank, the Siem Giang, went through the middle of the village and eventually emptied into the inlet. This is when Bobby Hansen recalls overhearing traffic from one of their radio operators; Bravo Company had come under attack and taken two wounded in action. Above them flew an H-13 Light Observation Helicopter or scout ship, in search of enemy positions. The H-13 is a small, bubble-shaped chopper with just a machine gun for weaponry, seating only a pilot and gunner, and no passengers. The scout ship was there to direct the attack of the gunships and to draw fire from enemy positions so they could be targeted. As they continued through the water-filled valley, the H-13 flew toward the village and disappeared over the trees.

Hansen recalls a soldier was on his left, followed by a CBS reporter, as he moved through the branches of the mangroves. As they moved closer toward the village, the lead platoons came under vicious fire from fortified bunkers just outside the village. At the same time, enemy soldiers erupted from spider holes to shoot at the troopers, then quickly disappeared back into the ground. As Hansen recalls, it was like a u-shaped ambush and he watched the soldier to his left take three rounds that nearly flipped him over. He could see the reporter lying next to him in the water, but it was unclear whether he had been wounded as well. Troopers of the lead platoons were scattered about the dikes of the rice paddy, and many were getting shot. Now everyone was lying in the water, taking cover behind the rice paddy dikes and desperately trying to return fire. Many of their rifles were jamming. What had moments before been a fairly organized formation of Alpha Company's platoons had dissolved into chaos. Soon the platoons and squads were all mixed up with each other, and their sergeants struggled to keep control of their men as they fought for survival. The fighting had just begun, but already this new operation had made their previous one seem like a walk in the park. The enemy they faced in Operation Golden Bee had been more intent on fleeing than fighting. On this day, escape was not an option for the enemy; they would have to surrender or fight.

Hansen could see two enemy soldiers coming at him from about a hundred yards in front. He only got off two rounds before his own weapon blew up. The company's grenadiers attempted to take out the bunkers with their M-79 grenade launchers. They would also find many of their own weapons useless as they had recently been submerged while taking cover as the fighting began. The only weapons that seemed to be working were their M-60 machine guns. The muck was so thick, it seemed the harder they tried to pull their feet out, the harder it tried to suck them back down. At one point, Hansen would become immobilized in the mud, and two others would have to pull him out.

In the midst of the fighting, at approximately 2:30 PM the H-13 scout ship was shot down by enemy machine guns. In addition to taking the village, Alpha Company was now faced with a rescue mission. CPT Wise radioed 1st Platoon, directing them to extract the pilot and his gunner wherever they were, alive or dead. Although somewhere in the vicinity, the chopper was out of sight and they would be forced to search for it as intense fighting continued. All they knew was that it went down somewhere near the east edge of the village. After some searching, the helicopter's gunner came rushing to them through some brush. He was supposed to have stayed with his pilot, CPT J.D. Twenten, whose back had been injured in the crash and was immobilized. He was understandably terrified, however, with their position known and so close to the enemy. He led Alpha Company's 1st Platoon up toward the downed chopper that lay crashed in the water amidst the mangroves with its injured pilot, near the southeast corner of the village. To get to the chopper, however, they would have to cross the Siem Giang River, and then a wide-open area of deeply flooded salt water paddies or salt dikes, as they were sometimes called. They were somewhat like cranberry bogs. With the help of the reconnaissance platoon securing the river crossing, they began making their way across the salt dikes and toward the chopper.

Approximately half-way through the flooded salt dikes, they were attacked again. This is where 1st Platoon's SSG Sam Daily, who at the pleading of his men had volunteered to go to war with them, found himself in a dangerous situation. He attempted to lead his squad in a flanking movement toward the enemy, but became pinned down by machine gun fire from one of the many fortified bunkers. Sam Daily and his machine gunner, Charles Bradford, along with a third unknown soldier, directly assaulted the bunker, placing enough cover fire to allow the rest of the squad to move to safety. In doing so, they had exposed themselves to the enemy's automatic weapons. Hansen recalls that both Daily and Bradford were off to his left, and the guys were yelling at them to get down just before Daily was hit. The initial round that hit Daily was said to have knocked him back and off his feet. Bradford nearly made it to the enemy bunker while unloading his M-60 before being struck down himself.

3rd Platoon's medic and farm boy from central Illinois, Michael Handley recalls how he helped to save one of the many wounded that day, a soldier named Jessie Lane. He also recalls his vain attempt at saving Daily as he lay in the mangrove swamp, but he was too far gone, as was Bradford. Will had briefly known Bradford, who'd married his young bride while on their two-week pass before departing for Vietnam. From Newport, Kentucky, he was twenty-one years old.

The third soldier who had joined in the assault was also wounded. Sometime later, he felt compelled to write to Sam Daily's wife, explaining the circumstances of their final moments together. Over time, the letter was lost, but his wife still recalls some of what was written:

Your husband died a hero. I am telling you how it happened. We were in a rice paddy when we were attacked. Sergeant Daily ordered us to go for cover. He said, "get back, get back, that's an order!" Two of us disobeyed him and stayed with him. We were all shot, but we are trained to play dead. Some Vietnamese soldiers came to make sure we were dead. One of the soldiers said, "shoot them in the head." The other soldier said, "why waste the bullets? We already kicked them, and they are all dead." So, they all left.

PFC Bradford would be posthumously awarded the Silver Star, and SSG Daily the Bronze Star with "V" Device (for Valor).

Staff Sergeant Sam Daily distinguished himself by heroism in action on 4 October 1966, while serving as a squad leader during the extraction of a downed helicopter pilot from hostile territory in the Republic of Vietnam. As his company came under intense enemy fire from several fortified bunkers and dikes, Sergeant Daily led his squad in an aggressive flanking action, but heavy enemy fire pinned the squad down before it could reach the objective. Exposing himself directly to enemy fire, Sergeant Daily executed a one-man assault on the bunker which had effectively halted the forward progress of his squad. He was successful in suppressing the enemy fire sufficiently to enable his squad to resume its advance, but was mortally wounded while doing so. Sergeant Daily's determination, devotion to duty, and concern for the welfare of his men are in keeping with the highest traditions of the military service, and reflect great credit upon himself, his unit, and the United States Army.

"He saved my life that day at the cost of his own," said Barry Gallagher about his soldier, Charles Bradford. 1LT Gallagher was leading 1st Platoon as Alpha Company's first replacement soldier. He had just recently taken over for the lieutenant who had broken his ankles during their first air assault in September.

Gallagher had volunteered for the draft shortly after graduating college with the guarantee of Officer Candidate School, and had married his high school girlfriend during his basic training. Upon his commissioning as an infantry officer and completion of airborne training (jump school), he had volunteered for service in Vietnam so that he could choose which division he would be assigned to. At jump school, he had watched soldiers of the 1st

Air Cavalry going through their own airmobile training with their helicopters at Fort Benning, and had decided this was the division he wanted to join.

Gallagher recalls being pinned down behind the dikes near 2nd Platoon's leader, 1LT James Harmon. They both said, "John Wayne" before they rose up, yelling at their men to follow them forward into the fire. Their men having such little combat experience, the two leaders may have wondered whether the men would follow, or if they would be left to run through the flooded expanse alone. In any case, their men rose up from the water and fought like hell, and eventually overran the enemy.

As his own weapon was useless, Hansen used Daily's rifle as their mission continued. Although 1st Platoon is credited with the rescue, troopers from 2nd and 3rd Platoons were there as well. After nearly three hellish hours of fighting, searching, and more fighting, the pilot was finally rescued at approximately 5:20 PM. Hansen recalls a fellow 3rd Platoon soldier, Dennis Sherry, using a small reed boat he had found to ferry the injured pilot out of the knee-deep water of the mangroves. He was eventually put on a field stretcher and carried out to a waiting dust-off that had been called in by Matulac, who was with the command group at the rear of the company.

1st Platoon's 1LT Gallagher recalls how he and a few others also used one of these reed boats to bring one of his own wounded soldiers along with the body of Charles Bradford out of the flooded battlefield. As the sun was setting they became separated from the rest of the company, having only a .45 pistol, two M-16s, and one non-functional radio between them. Eventually they were missed, and a few soldiers were sent back to lead them out.

Hansen's buddy, Smithy, had been wounded before the fighting even started and would be flown out on the same chopper as the injured pilot. He had suffered a large gash in his hand from his own machete while stabbing into a stack of hay that was bunched up around a pole while marching through the valley. Perhaps not realizing that the pole was inside, his machete got caught on it, causing him to lose his grip. In the command group, radio operator Royce Barrow recalls how they were still taking sporadic fire from some NVA fighters scattered amongst distant spider holes when the first medevac chopper came in. They were ordered to lay down a suppressive fire on those positions to protect the incoming dust-off, and they let loose with everything they had.

SSG Cleofas Madrid, a veteran of the Korean War, continued to lead the attack on the village, taking out many of the occupied spider holes. He would be awarded the Silver Star for his actions on this day.

As fighting continued, Alpha Company's mortars were set and firing on the village. Soon thereafter, Bravo Company was flown to the opposite side of the village as a blocking force. Robert Powers was a soldier in Bravo Company, and recalled the battle in detail in his book, *1966 The Year of the Horse*. He described a chaotic scene as their Hueys descended into the landing zone. The door gunners opened up with their M-60s, strafing the perimeter and tree line, while he and other Bravo Company troopers jumped into the rice paddy six feet below. They were instantly stuck in the paddy's thick bottom-layer of muck, exposed and unable to move. Bullets whistled by as they struggled to move their legs. They were soon engulfed in a blue haze, as the smell of gun powder filled the valley.

Just like Joe Sanchez, Powers had failed his enlistment physical while attempting to join the Army Reserves, but was soon after deemed fit for the draft. He was one of the battalion's first replacements who had just arrived in Vietnam a few days earlier. It was his first taste of combat.

Eventually Bravo Company's troops made their way toward a tree line, regrouped, and walked through the jungle to a clearing where they would establish their fighting positions. On the opposite side of the village, Alpha Company was pushing the enemy up towards them. They quickly emplaced their mortars and began lobbing shells while the rifle platoons unleashed their machine guns.

Trapped and desperate, many enemy soldiers attempted to escape the village by crossing the Vinh Nouc Ngot inlet, some swimming, others in little fishing boats. Their attempts were unsuccessful. The enemy was engaged with massive force until cease-fire was ordered. A Navy battleship could now be seen positioned in the South China Sea, out of range of the NVA's weapons. Within minutes, it began shelling enemy positions within the village of An My. After approximately an hour of bombardment, the companies dug in and prepared for a long sleepless night.

It was almost dark when the next medevac arrived under fire to fly out Daily, Bradford, and several more of Alpha Company's wounded. Among them was the soldier who had been shot near Bobby Hansen as the fighting started. He had taken three rounds in the leg, which would eventually be amputated. From Seattle, Robert Wagner had taken a bullet through his ear that also ripped through his chinstrap. Also wounded, were Jessie Lane, Jerry Brown, Danny Rogers, Rolland Slocum, and Sergeant First Class (SFC) Marvin Hall.

Infrequent gunfire and artillery bombardment continued on the village where the enemy was held up as darkness fell. Illumination rounds were also lobbed by the battleship throughout the night to light up the village and prevent the enemy's escape. Illumination rounds are artillery shells that burst high in the sky, then burn brightly as they slowly descend by parachute - each round emitting a piercing hissing sound along with a smoke trail that spirals above. They can light up over a square mile of terrain. As they rock back and forth beneath their parachutes, so do the shadows of everything on the ground. The thumping of helicopters could be heard constantly. Guided by flashlight and radio, medevac choppers landed, then quickly disappeared into the darkness with more of the battalion's dead and wounded.

One of the many Alpha Company soldiers from Kentucky, Gene Cross would recall walking along the dikes of a rice paddy that night when he was shot in the head. The bullet went through his helmet, but somehow only grazed his scalp, leaving a scar that remains to this day. All he remembers is seeing a flash of light or "stars" as it were, then waking up in the muck as a medic revived him. Apparently, he had been storing all of his letters from home in his helmet. Although they were believed to have possibly helped save his life, his letters had been mostly ruined.

At first light, Alpha and Bravo Companies would move into the village. They expected resistance, but encountered none. What they found instead was a smoking apocalyptic scene. As the battleship sailed away, they searched the destroyed village. Several dead North Vietnamese were found in dug out emplacements and trenches, their bloody bodies crumpled and in awkward positions. Whatever survivors there were had escaped with the weapons of the dead. The men were surprised to discover that many of the enemy machine gunners had been chained to their gun emplacements, so as to prevent their retreat. Their commanders may have sensed that an overwhelming force was coming for them. Unlike the Viet Cong who typically wore black pajamas, many of these NVA regulars had khaki uniforms and pith helmets. At 8:20 AM on October 5th, after clearing the village and destroying the enemy's rice caches, Alpha Company was airlifted to Camp Hammond and replaced by Charlie Company, who would be left to count and stack the bodies.

Later that day, a log ship would eventually arrive at Camp Hammond, this time with fresh clothing. The soldiers stripped off their grime-laden fatigues that they had worn since leaving An Khe in August. As would become their common practice whenever new uniforms arrived, they piled their old fatigues on the ground and set them ablaze. Unbeknownst to the men of Alpha Company, they would have to make these new fatigues last even longer. The men were also given showers. After recovering at Camp Hammond for the afternoon, Alpha Company was flown back to LZ Opal to continue search and destroy operations.

There was one other fatality suffered by Alpha Company on October 4th. PFC Donald Smith, Jr., Hansen's buddy "Smithy" who had been wounded by his own machete. He was en route from Camp Hammond to An Khe for medical treatment, along with soldiers of several other units. While flying through a dense fog near An Khe, their C-7B Caribou, a military transport plane, crashed into the side of Hon Cong Mountain. There were no survivors. Smithy was twenty years old.

6 Oct '66 – 42 weeks left

Dear Folks,

We finally got started with our drive to search out these villages, Oct 4th I guess it was. It was going along fine, seeing how these people live. We took a bunch of prisoners. It was late in the afternoon when the N.V.A. shot down a chopper. We (A Co) went out to rescue the two pilots. It took about two hours to get there and when we did we got attacked. A Sergeant and a PFC I knew quite well got killed while the company got closer to the chopper. Six or seven got wounded. It's something I never want to live through again. We rescued the pilots. One thing I am glad we got is those choppers with rockets and machine guns, and also the medical ships. They really saved the day. We didn't fool around to see how many V.C. we killed. Yesterday we showered and shaved and got clean clothes. Now we are back as a reserve.

I received your long letter yesterday. I put it in my helmet and had the helmet upside down and now it's soaking wet. We get envelopes and paper in our Lifeline packs and now it is coming in pretty regular. To answer your letter, I am not starving. I doubt if I lost any weight, or very little. It rains an awful lot where we are now, and it gets darn cold at night. No, it isn't true what I wrote to Mike. I said in the letter that I was just kidding. We guys make up all kinds of silly stories like that. Sorry if I had you worried.

I got to talk to Rod about 2 weeks ago. Yes, he might get to train in the Green Beret camp for 6 weeks. This is because he is on long-range patrol and I am not. No, I didn't see Allen Simon. I guess I was about 10 miles from where he was and he might have seen me if he drove past the little place where we were along the road. Larry Geissler said Allen saw me too. He might have.

Looks like the hog prices are very good, is that the highest it's been all year? I am eating the package of popcorn and marshmallows. The marshmallows got a little sticky this morning 'cause I left them in the sun. You won't have to bother with these packages every week 'cause lifeline packs come pretty often now with the free candy bars.

Will

SGT Larry Abegglen (left) and Michael Handley (right)

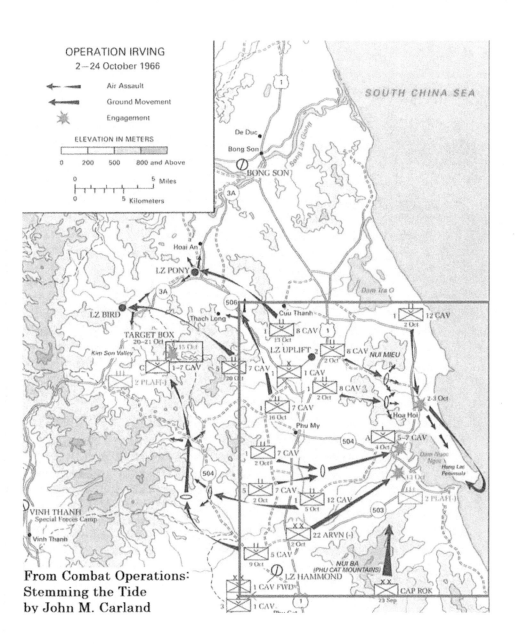

From Combat Operations: Stemming the Tide by John M. Carland

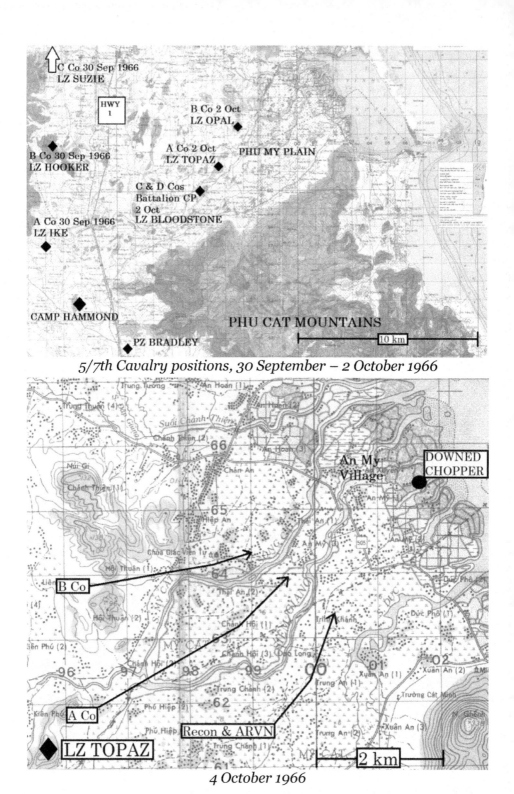

5/7th Cavalry positions, 30 September – 2 October 1966

4 October 1966

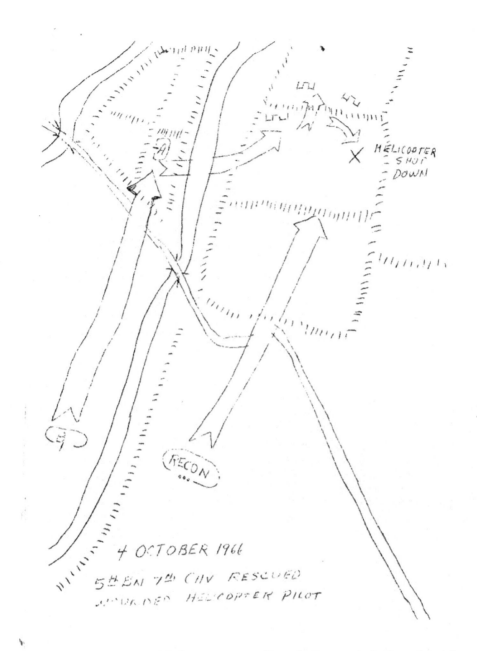

4 October 1966, hand-drawn map of battle from 5/7th Cavalry After Action Report

1LT Barry Gallagher

4 October 1966, Sam Daily leading his soldiers as fighting commenced

Sam Daily

Charles Bradford

Donald Smith

Soldiers on hilltop outpost watch aerial rocket artillery being fired into valley below from distant chopper, photo by Wilbur Bowe

Bell H-13 Light Observation Helicopter (scout ship), source unknown

Enemy occupied village, photo by Robert Matulac

Alpha Company moving in to attack as bombs fall on enemy occupied village, photo by Robert Matulac

1LT James Harmon and 2nd Platoon with enemy prisoners, photo by Robert Matulac

Regrouping after firefight, photo by Robert Matulac

CPT A.J. Wise with villagers after firefight, photo by Robert Matulac

Medic aiding wounded villagers following firefight, photo by Robert Matulac

9
DELIVER US FROM EVIL

Now we don't have to make up war stories like we did before.

Most soldiers that have been to war will tell you that the worst part was not the fighting, but rather the living conditions. Few of us can fathom what it feels like to endure two months in a humid and filthy environment with no change of clothing. The saturation of one's clothes with sweat, earth, and bug dope makes it feel like you're wearing greasy rags. Worse than this deprivation however, was that of virtually never having dry socks, and the condition of the skytroopers' feet could be counted as a torture in its own right. Many soldiers suffered from both ringworm and trench foot, or jungle rot as it was called. The endless daily marching through rough terrain exacted a heavy punishment on their feet, and their constant wetness exacerbated the pain and deterioration. Of course, it wasn't just their feet that would suffer. Although the leeches themselves were not painful, the bleeding wounds they left were. Unable to heal in the constant moisture, these wounds would simply fester. If they weren't walking through leech-infested rice paddies, they were walking through elephant grass, their sharp blades inflicting cuts along their arms and hands, or through thorny jungle vines and bamboo that did the same. Like those left by the leeches, these relatively minor wounds would cause constant pain as they became infected, often oozing puss and refusing to heal in the dampness of the jungle. Sooner or later, they would all encounter the wrath of Vietnam's fire ants. Unlike that of the leeches, the fire ant's bite was felt immediately. They would build their nests in trees, and if disturbed would attack en masse, their bites leaving welts that would also itch and ooze for weeks. Martin Quinn recalls how his own hands and arms were becoming infected with jungle rot. Their medic, who he remembers as being a rather small fellow, would pour some sort of antiseptic or something on them to kill the infection, and it would sting like hell.

I've tried to get my head around what your body feels like under these conditions. The most time I've ever spent in the same uniform is about one week, and I thought that was absolutely miserable. The farthest I've ever had to march with my rucksack is twenty miles, on a relatively flat road and with dry boots. After the first ten miles, my leg muscles began to stiffen and my stride shortened. It took a couple days for my body to fully recover. Now I imagine that same trek, carrying an M-16 and mortar tube, with wet boots, through swamps and over hills, knowing that I would do it all again the next day. During a few training missions, the longest I've ever had to endure without sleep is, perhaps, forty-eight hours or so. One of the first things you learn about sleep deprivation is that you can start dreaming while you're still standing and with your eyes open. To say the least, it messes with your mind. Considering these physical ordeals along with the leeches, mosquitoes and countless other parasites, the fire ants, the heat, the dysentery and various fevers, the many skin rots and molds, the lack of basic sanitation, the weight they carried and the fear that followed them, one can scarce comprehend the misery of an infantryman in the Vietnam jungle. The fact that some men were willing to inflict serious wounds upon themselves in hopes of getting out, should at least give us some indication of the utter hell that it was. For those of us who have not been to war, the best we can do is to simply understand that we can never understand.

Following the battle of October 4th, the companies of the 5/7th Cav would continue search and destroy missions throughout the Phu My plain. On the night of October 5th, Alpha Company would set up in blocking positions near LZ Opal to screen any soldiers fleeing from Bravo and Charlie Companies' search and clear missions. The next day, Alpha Company's troopers moved out on their own patrol. Meanwhile, Bravo Company would take fire from another village near An My. Several secondary explosions were seen and heard as the village of approximately thirty huts was burned to the ground the next morning. An entire squad from Charlie Company was reported lost at 2:30 PM. By 3:55 PM they had been found and were flown to their company's command post. On October 8th, Alpha Company moved out again, this time closing on LZ Ruby, atop another hill approximately four kilometers southwest of LZ Opal. That night, Charlie Company soldiers would kill two Viet Cong passing through their ambush positions.

The next morning, Alpha Company moved back down into the valley to cordon and search a village known as Vinh Nhon near the banks of the Song Ca River. They returned at dusk to LZ Ruby with one prisoner who was found hiding in one of the huts. Will was placed in charge of guarding the prisoner as they waited for intelligence folks to take him away. He was warned not to turn his back on him. Now sitting Indian-style on the ground, he didn't look like much, scrawny and maybe seventeen or eighteen years old at best. Whether he was Viet Cong or not, he was of military age and that made him suspect. In South Vietnam, young men were not simply allowed to sit out the war.

As Will stood guard over the hapless captive, he noticed a lone man in black pajamas, perhaps a Viet Cong, perhaps an innocent farmer, walking along the dikes of a rice paddy far across the valley. He motioned to Patrillo, who came over and offered Will one of his Pall Mall cigarettes. Whoever the man was, he wasn't supposed to be there according to the ROK soldiers who happened to be patrolling along the other side of the valley. As they opened fire, geysers of water and mud sprang up all around him as he dashed for cover. Several seconds later, they could hear the distant shots echoing across the valley. They watched the man sprint across the tops of the dikes, falling once into the muck, then stumbling and running again toward the tree line at the edge of the rice paddy. Will had never seen anyone run so fast in his life. It is not known if the running man survived. What was known, is that it was a good thing the Koreans were on our side. Days later, Bierschbach would notice some soldiers ahead of him stopping to look at something on the ground as they entered a hamlet recently searched by ROK forces. He couldn't tell exactly what it was at first, but he figured it was something dead by the many flies swarming about it. As he approached, it became clear that it was the head of a Viet Cong soldier. He had been buried up to his neck by the Koreans and left to die, a practice the Viet Cong themselves routinely inflicted on suspected government sympathizers. He had been dead for some time.

10 Oct '66 – 41 weeks left

Dear Folks,

You know that big fight we had? This guy got shot in the helmet and the bullet came out the side and it just scratched his head a little. He told me he was shaking like a leaf after that happened. We had a couple of heroes too. One dragging his buddy back to safety after being hit. Another bringing back a machine gun under heavy fire. Now we don't have to make up war stories like we did before.

Just sitting on the big hill and searching the villages below us. Then we move to another hill, and another one. Down in these flat lands is where most of the people live. Coconut trees all around, sugar cane, peanuts, onions, and a few other crops they raise besides those darn rice paddies. Caught a guy yesterday. Our interpreter claims he is a draft dodger from the South Vietnamese Army. Just like some of us back home. This little book is what the village chief gave me. He is up on the hill with us. He brought his bike along with him. This is their main transportation. They have cement houses in some villages, usually the church or chief's house. These were made, I guess, by the French people that were here. Well, I guess I'll go dry my clothes out while the sun is still out. Every morning we wake up soaking wet.

Rice Paddy Daddy,

Will

On the 10th of October, Delta Company prepared for a raid on another village near An My, set to commence at dawn the next morning. Meanwhile, Alpha Company continued searching and destroying in the Phu My plain, returning to LZ Ruby at dusk on the 11th. While pulling guard duty that night, Will's platoon sergeant came to him with an unusual question. SSG Burtis stood before him along with PFC Bruce Madison, asking if he would teach them how to pray. It is not known exactly why he chose to come to my dad with this request. I suspect that SSG Burtis knew his soldiers well, and was likely familiar with my dad's background attending Catholic school. As darkness fell upon them, quite literally in the valley of the shadow of death, the three skytroopers joined hands and bowed their heads as my dad led them in the same prayer that Jesus taught to his disciples.

Our Father, who art in Heaven, hallowed be thy name. Thy kingdom come, thy will be done, on Earth as it is in Heaven. Give us this day, our daily bread, and forgive us our trespasses, as we forgive those who trespass against us. Lead us not into temptation, but deliver us from evil.

12 Oct '66 – 41 weeks left

Dear Folks,

Did you ever hear of our Operation Thayer? There have been about 3,000 killed in this operation so far. Life here seems so cheap, just makes you sick. But the village people are happy to see us come. Some of the people here too, are Catholic. In this hut, they had a picture of Christ and Mary. Thing is, they both had slanted eyes. Went to Mass yesterday, the 4th time since I was back on leave. Been to protestant service twice. I go every time I get a chance to. Everybody goes now. My platoon sergeant is a Catholic and told me before the Mass started that he never was to church in 20 or more years. He mentioned about confession and so I encouraged him to go, and so he did, received communion also. Last night I pulled guard with him and Madison, and had to teach him a lot of prayers. He wears a rosary around his neck now. I think everyone says his night prayers out here. I am glad I did some good for him.

Just waiting as a reaction force today. I am a bit tired from sitting up ½ the night B.S.-ing. This one cat from college knows quite a bit about flying saucers and people that live underground called the Dare-rows, hypnotism, and reincarnation. Man, he sure made it sound so real, and he's a real smart guy too. He said there were 2 buildings in N.Y. with bottomless elevator shafts. Also, a cavern in Colorado that over 1,000 people never returned from. This guy has 3,500 pictures of flying saucers. I don't know man, but it seems to me that it mustn't be true. I'd sure like to check into this when I get back to the states.

It's been almost a year since I've been in the Army. Doesn't seem like it. Seems more like 100 years since I was back in Fort Leonard Wood. Boy what changes I went through since high school days. I read in the last newspaper you sent that Melvin got picked up for a traffic fine. Ha!

Will

After a few more days of searching and destroying in the Phu My plain, the 5/7th Cav moved its operation northward. On October 15th most of Alpha Company was air assaulted to LZ New Diamond on the southern edge of the Nui Mieu Mountains. 4th Platoon however, was flown elsewhere, to an artillery firebase known as LZ Garnet. Here they would catch a short break from the constant patrols. That night, a trooper from Bravo Company would go missing. Three small patrols and an H-13 observation chopper would search for him through the night.

By now everyone had grown quite accustomed to the leeches and knew how to remove them quickly and painlessly, either with a squirt of their bug dope, which did little to keep away bugs, or by burning them with their lighter. After a patrol one day, however, Quinn noticed something in his pants. He wasn't surprised to find a leech, but he was disturbed to find where it had dug itself into, the right side of his ball sack. He was horrified to discover that the creature was dug in deep, and neither bug dope nor fire would remove it. He walked over to the medic. "I've got a problem Doc," he said, dropping his drawers. The look on the medic's face didn't give Quinn any confidence. By now the leech was fully engorged, writhing every which way and weighing heavily on his scrotum. After much discussion with the other medics, it was decided that the bloodsucker would have to be cut out. Doc began sterilizing his tools, first with alcohol and then with his lighter for good measure. Before he could cut into him, however, the victim would need a shot of Novocain. Quinn stared in apprehension at the needle as Doc tapped the air bubbles out of the syringe, imagining just where it was that needle was headed. It was perhaps, not the most traumatic medical procedure he would ever endure, but it was one that he would never forget.

The outposts that served as artillery firebases were often referred to as LZs (landing zones), such as LZ Pony, LZ Hasty, LZ Hump, etc. The artillerymen who lived on these outposts would refer to them as firebases, while the infantryman who came to visit called them LZs. Of course, most LZs were actually just landing zones and nothing more, unoccupied places suitable enough for choppers to drop infantrymen into at the start of a mission. The artillery outposts, or firebases, represented a rare opportunity to rest. Typically located on a cleared-out hilltop, it was relatively safe compared to the areas they patrolled. They were still pulling guard duty and sleeping in shifts in the dirt, there were typically no buildings or showers, but at least they weren't slogging through the bush all day. It was the perfect opportunity to write letters home. Sanchez and Bierschbach would write to their girlfriends and Hirschuber would write to his wife, while Will would write to his mom, Millie. Matulac didn't have a girlfriend to write to, but was pen pals with a girl in San Francisco. Instead of placing a stamp, they would simply write "FREE" in the corner of each envelope and they would be delivered. Before long however, Sanchez would receive his own "Dear John" letter from Teresa, saying she met someone else, as would his Jewish buddy from New York, Alan Weisman, from his fiancée.

By the standards of most soldiers, these outposts would easily be considered "in the field", based on their primitive living conditions and remote locations. It's noteworthy however, that the infantrymen would typically refer to their time spent at these outposts as "in from the field", as their life here was relatively comfortable compared to the surrounding wilderness where they spent most of their days and nights. A few firebases were more developed, such as LZ English and Camp Hammond. These had larger perimeters, were accessible by road, and may have featured a medical aid tent or field hospital, a chow tent, and even at times, a beer tent or "clubhouse". In fact, LZ English had a tent in which soldiers could see movies. Most, however, were small affairs with no such luxuries, located on mountaintops and accessible only by helicopter. They would have dug-in artillery positions surrounded by sandbags, and bunkers constructed by the artillerymen who lived there. Around their perimeters would be more bunkers and foxholes built by the transient infantrymen.

During the battalion's operations, one company would often be designated as a "reserve force" and kept on call at a nearby firebase while the remainder of the battalion carried out search and destroy missions. When one of its sister companies encountered fierce resistance, the reserve company could be immediately air assaulted into a blocking position to prevent the enemy's escape, or to simply aid a company that was in over its head. The advantage to being on reserve was that you could rest while the other companies humped the hills. When your company was called into action, however, you could count on being dropped into an LZ under fire. At times, the flight crews would inspect the blades and body of the aircraft for damage while flying out the company in waves. The skytroopers would come to recognize this as a tell-tale sign that they would soon be jumping into a hot LZ.

During their times spent on the various firebases, the soldiers had an infinite amount of time to get to know each other. They would read the Stars & Stripes and talk about what was going on in the news, read the funnies, exchange dirty jokes, play cards and smoke cigarettes. It sure beat patrolling the jungle, but after you've read and re-read all your letters from home, written and sent your replies, played several hands of poker, and smoked all your cigarettes, the boredom was crushing.

Will spent a lot of time on the outposts talking with Al Patrillo. He joked around a lot and always smoked Pall Malls. He carried an old fedora in his rucksack that he would wear whenever not on patrol. Patrillo's mother was also named Mildred or "Millie", and also like Will's mom, would often send packages of goodies to be shared. Patrillo would also receive many letters and coffee tins filled with homemade cookies from the mom of his childhood friend and neighbor, Tom Ivey. Tom himself recalls that he was never very good at sending letters to Al. Patrillo and Will often talked about what they were going to do when this was all over. An amateur taxidermist, Patrillo said he planned to move to Wisconsin to start a taxidermy business with Will. My dad figured he was joking, but could never be sure. Instead of a rifle, Patrillo carried an M-79 grenade launcher. They were called "thumpers" for the sound they produced. Approximately the same size as a rifle, one disadvantage of the M-79 was that its grenades would only detonate after traveling thirty meters, a problem for close-in fighting. As such, thumpers also carried a .45mm pistol.

Being on his mortar team, Bronson was another good friend and was quite a comedian. He would often remark how Will never complained about anything. Even when it was raining, "at least it was a warm rain." He joked that Will would even sleep on the dike of a rice paddy without complaint. Oddly enough, they would find themselves together in that very situation at one miserable point in their tour.

Bobby Hansen recalls talking with his good friend Alan Weisman about the cars they were going to buy as soon as they got back to The World. Hansen planned to buy himself a '68 Plymouth with a Hemi engine while Weisman planned to buy a '67 Jet with a 428.

The Army has a way of bringing together people of extremely disparate backgrounds. As a soldier, you'll often find yourself in close quarters and forming bonds with those you would have never associated with in your civilian life. And unlike a normal job where you spend eight or so hours with your coworkers each day, in the field you'll spend every waking and sleeping minute together.

·········

Matulac's position as Communications NCO was at the company level, and as such, he got to know almost all of the soldiers from each of the platoons, at least a little bit. In 2013, I accepted a full-time position as Admin NCO with my own National Guard unit. Prior to this, I knew the guys in my own platoon fairly well, but not so much the rest of our company-sized detachment. Working at the company level, you quickly learn which soldiers have personal problems, which ones have drug and alcohol issues, and which ones have problems with the law. Whenever a soldier got himself in trouble, I was always among the first to know about it. At one point, our Readiness NCO, SFC Adam Petersen, took to calling our area's county jails each Monday, to see which of our soldiers had gotten into trouble over the weekend.

I remember looking out on the drill floor of our armory during one drill, amazed at how I not only knew the names of each of the hundred or so young men who milled about the floor, but could also tell you something about each one of them.

I mentioned before how we in the military often find ourselves becoming friends with the most unlikely of folks. The Army is also a place where those who don't fit into most social circles, often find the most acceptance and appreciation. It reminds me of a young soldier named Joseph Parker-Widga. He was barely out of high school when he showed up at our annual training in 2010. He was very quiet, kind of reclusive actually, and seemed a little scared of his sergeants. He spoke with a sort of Elmer Fud-like impediment. I don't know if socially awkward is the right term to describe him, it was more that he just wasn't interested in social activity. Our platoon sergeant, SSG Corbin, had an aversion to long names, and so he dubbed him "P-Dubs".

One year, after another annual training at Camp Ripley, P-Dubs and I were back at the armory in Anoka, our last stop on our way home. He was the only one there aside from myself. He couldn't see out of one eye as it had become infected with some kind of God-knows-what from the field. He wore glasses that are often referred to as BCGs or "birth control glasses", the very non-fashionable eyewear issued to soldiers by the Army. He was the only soldier I ever knew to actually wear these after basic training. They weren't pretty, but they were sturdy and practical, and they were free. I didn't think he should drive, so I offered him a ride home. "No thanks, sawgent," he said, "my brothos picking me up."

As different as he was from most of us, P-Dubs found friendship and appreciation among the young men in our detachment, probably more than he ever found in the world outside the Army. He was proficient with radio communications, and with the plethora of digital equipment we commonly use nowadays as forward observers. Most of all, he was a good friend to his buddies in his platoon, known as someone who would never refuse a helping hand.

I was the only one in the office the day before drill, when my friend and boss, SFC Petersen, called to inform me that P-Dubs had killed himself. It was October of 2016, and we had all known P-Dubs for over six years. He had recently been on temporary full-time orders through the summer, and helping out our supply sergeant, SSG Adam Walton, in the supply room. Only about a month or so before, those of us in the detachment full-time staff had gone on an outing to a Twins Game in Minneapolis. We brought P-Dubs along. While watching the game, we talked for hours at a bar within the stadium that overlooked the field. He seemed like his usual self, in good spirits. I tried to convince him into letting me take him to the topless bar afterwards. I thought it would be good to get him out of his shell. He wasn't interested, said he needed to get up for work the next morning. Even before asking, I knew this would be his response. He went home early while the rest of us got drunk that night.

He had planned his death meticulously, organizing his belongings and tying up loose ends, leaving letters for a few people he worked with regarding where to find certain things. To SSG Walton, he left his rifle. He didn't want to put anybody out. It was as if he were simply making arrangements for an extended trip.

In the week after October drill, I was once again alone in the office at the armory. Late in the day, I received a call from a military chaplain in the Minnesota National Guard, the one who would be presiding over SPC Parker-Widga's funeral. It was to be held the following morning at the Fort Snelling military cemetery. As it was, he didn't have much to go on for the soldier's eulogy. I told the chaplain that I would try to gather some information that would be useful and send it to him. I looked through his personnel records and found a recommendation for the Army Achievement Medal that P-Dubs had been awarded following his deployment with the unit in 2011. That was helpful, but I also thought his family should know at least something about what he did during his time with us, and what he meant to us. I didn't intend to write his eulogy, but that's just how it worked out.

It's sad to acknowledge it, but it would have been an extremely small gathering if not for all his fellow soldiers who showed up to see him buried. If it weren't for the Army, I would never have gotten to know a person as unique as P-Dubs. Having known him is one of the things that makes me glad I joined.

·········

Will would describe his own company as a mixed-up bunch. Bierschbach was from a farm like my dad, but many of the other soldiers were from the big city, places like New York, Philadelphia, Harlem and the Bronx, and most of them were scared to death of snakes. Before the war, my dad had never really known anyone of other races, or who had exotic northeastern accents. Now he was part of an infantry company cobbled together with blacks, whites, Italians, Puerto Ricans, as well as native Hawaiians and Eskimos. Sent to this hell from farms, cities, trailer parks, suburbs and ghettos all across the United States, few of them were there by choice, but they all depended upon each other now for survival.

After a long terrifying night lost in Indian Country, the wayward PFC Lee returned to Bravo Company at 6:55 AM on October 16th. Later that day, giant Sky Cranes descended on LZ Garnet to carry off all of the artillery where 4th Platoon was pulling security. Soon the artillerymen departed in their own choppers, ending 4th Platoon's brief reprieve. They were quickly flown back to LZ New Diamond to rejoin Alpha Company.

17 Oct '66 – 40 weeks left

Dear Folks,

No, I am not in the hospital if that's what you're thinking. It is just an envelope and paper the Red Cross gave us. Good news, this operation I believe is almost over with. Rumors are going around saying we might go in tomorrow. We in the mortars platoon had been guarding an artillery unit for 2 days. Man, what I wouldn't give to be in the artillery. Good food and lots of it, sit on the top of a hill and take it easy. Now we're back with the company. Our C.O. it seems, doesn't give a damn about us in the mortar platoon 'cause we have it a lot easier than the rifle platoons. That's why it seems we always get cheated out of our supplies. I think he's getting too big-headed since that big rescue mission we (the company) made. It hasn't rained now for almost a week. It quit just like that. Otherwise, we were wet 26 hours out of the day. Now everyone is getting a real fine tan.

I read in our newspaper you sent, about our company rescuing those helicopter pilots. This battalion calls our operation Irving, the Koreans call it Tiger. Also, we had the South Vietnamese Army out here and a couple of other battalions, and they called this whole operation Thayer. Some of the guys said in their letters from home, that we were on the Chet Huntley Program, making the news.

I got to see Rod a couple of days ago. Actually, we took over their position guarding artillery and they were teed off. Rod and the rest of his guys that belong to the Long Rang Recon Patrol are all going to quit 'cause they aren't getting all the privileges that they were told they would get. Rod says he got himself a shotgun off a dead V.C. I guess he can send it home if he likes. I hope I can get a V.C. rifle to send home.

I got your package of fudge and doughnuts. I just munched away for an hour and ½ last night while on guard. If you're going to send tomatoes, send them in a coffee can. The shoe boxes always get pretty squashed. The next package you send, send a stick of summer sausage and a big chunk of cheese. The cheese the N.F.O. sent us, you know who got it? The generals and colonels, we'll never see it.

Hey, I might be going on a 5-day vacation on the 28th of this month to Hong Kong. This is called R&R, rest and recuperation. If my name turns up, my buddy Quinn said he would lend me a large sum of money. He and Figueroa claim they're going to visit our farm after the service. Two big city slickers from New York that have never been on a farm before. My buddy Brodosi got his pictures back, and the picture he took of me crossing the river, and I am sending it to you. I think this picture was taken 28 Sept.

I am sending a little package for Mike. Well, I best not say. Hey Mike, if you don't have anything to do after school, ask the public librarian for the Government Blue Book, or Project Blue Book. Also, the book named The Shafer Mysteries. Also, books from an author named Charles Fort. These *books all tell of flying saucer sightings, and of the people named Dare-rows. Let me know what you find out, OK? I got your letter Mike, but you can't put a back address as just the city. It doesn't make any difference anyhow, as long as the Zip Code is on it.*

I guess the Orioles sure did a job on the Dodgers, huh? I read about them in the Army newspaper. Heard about Willie Davis making them errors, and Larry Schindler is all for the Baltimore team. Did the Yankees really finish in last place? If so, tell Larry Geissler about that.

You know when we got nothing else to talk about, we talk about our plans when we get out of service. This is my plan (subject to change). First, I am going to take a 48-hour bath. Then I am buying a set of fine clothes and then I'll jump into my '67 Thunderbird car that I had ordered from Viet Nam tax-free, and drive home from California. Then I'll raid the refrigerator for 3-4 weeks if Ma hasn't kicked me out of the house by then, ha! Then instead of working at Johnson's, I'll work in Minneapolis or Milwaukee for more money and overtime so I can pay for the car. Then I'll slow down a little, after I get a little money in the bank, and take advantage of this G.I. Bill that will pay $110 a month for 36 months of schooling. Don't know what I'll take up, but it'll be something. And then for a hobby, I am going to take up astronomy and build a 6 to 8-inch lens telescope. I'd like to, that is. But you never know what I might end up doing.

This I am sure of. June '67 the battalion will start rotating back to the states, starting with the lowest ranking, E-1 first. If I have less than 90 days before my E.T.S. date (25 Oct '67) when I land in California, I'll be discharged from California. When the 1st of June comes near, I am going to try like hell to get busted to E-1.

Chow time now. Sounds like a big bargaining center. Trade 2 cans of this for a can of that. I can get some good trades, you'd be surprised what I would trade for a fruit cake. Well, I must eat now. Man, is it ever hot out.

Will

One of the most dangerous parts of taking a team out from the company patrol base to conduct ambushes or listening posts was returning to the company in the dark. Known as a "passage of lines", the team leader was responsible for informing those guarding the patrol base that they were leaving, and when and where they would return. Guard duty ran in shifts however, and the message didn't always get passed on to the next guy. At 8:18 PM on October 18th, two soldiers from Bravo Company were shot by their own men while returning to the company area from ambush positions. It was dark and it was raining, and their dust-off was delayed. Under extremely poor flying conditions, they were both finally medevaced out at 9:44 PM. One would die before reaching the field hospital.

At 4:10 PM the next day, Alpha Company was air assaulted to an entirely different area, westward to LZ Buckner, high in the Central Highlands between the Kim Son, Soui Ca, and Song Con river valleys. This was where other battalions of the 1st Air Cavalry had commenced Operation Thayer on September 13th. The terrain here was much different, steep, rugged, and thickly vegetated. Just like Phu My however, it was still very wet, with many rice paddies and flooded streams running through the fog-laden valleys below. The rest of the battalion would fly into their own LZs in the same area the following day, the 20th of October, with the battalion forward command post setting up shop at LZ Duz.

This new area in the Central Highlands represented the most frightening type of terrain to patrol for Will and most others. It was known to be riddled with land mines, booby-traps, and punji stakes. It also featured many more challenging natural obstacles for an infantry company on patrol. Open areas were few and far between, and landing zones would be extremely hard to come by. The troopers could only see a few feet in front of them as they hacked their way through the dense tangled vines and vegetation. The terrain was particularly punishing as they were never walking on flat ground. One night in particular, they found themselves forced to set up their patrol base on an extremely steep mountainside, making their attempt to catch what little sleep they were afforded all but impossible. Each platoon moved in a line formation. Here the vines were thick, tearing at their arms, hands, and faces with their thorns. Sometimes called "wait-a-minute vines", they would seem to just latch on to their rucksacks, making their slow progress extremely frustrating. My dad felt like they were going to be ambushed here under the jungle canopy, where no attack helicopters or artillery could come to their rescue. Although they searched intently for the enemy, no one actually wanted to find him under these conditions.

Black clouds darkened the sky on October 21st. The rains that had briefly subsided now returned in torrential fashion. On this day, Alpha Company found itself on the west side of the southernmost claw of the Crow's Foot (Kim Son Valley). Through this particular claw of the Crow's Foot ran the Soui L`on River. The open area of this valley was only five hundred meters wide in some areas, and on the other side loomed a dark and enormous jungle-covered hill where enemy encampments were suspected. Over a thousand feet above the valley floor, its peak disappeared into the low-hanging clouds. Brigade headquarters had ordered the 5/7th Cav to search and clear that hill. The plan was to attack upward from all directions at dawn the following morning, with Bravo Company advancing on the hill from the opposite side, Charlie from the south, and an attached company from the 1/7th Cav advancing from the north. Each company would leave one platoon back as a blocking force.

21 Oct '66 – 40 weeks left

Dear Folks,

Now I am teed off, 'cause the chopper came by and blew the letter I was writing to you, and I can't find it. We didn't go in like I figured, and it started to rain again. Son of a gun. We went closer to Bong Son, still a lot of leeches around here. I don't know if Rod got his raincoat or not. Wish I had mine out here, but it's too much to carry when your moving. Food is picking up. Haven't been hungry for a long time.

Wet Will

It was still raining at 6:00 AM the next morning when the companies moved out from their patrol bases to surround and search the hill. Moving in from the west however, Alpha Company would have to cross the Soui L`on River, which had now developed into a raging torrent that suddenly widened and engulfed nearly the entire valley, including their patrol base. By now it had become very deep and would prove impossible to cross. The attached company from the 1/7th Cav would run into the same problem while moving in from the north. An airlift was contemplated to get Alpha Company across the river, but the relentless downpour prohibited such an attempt. Both Alpha Company and the attached company from the 1/7th Cav would spend the night in blocking positions along the flooded rivers as showers continued. The rain finally eased, and at 9:31 AM the next morning, October 23rd, they were airlifted across the river to commence their attack on the hill. The jungle was wet, dark and extremely dense. Its ground was exceedingly steep, muddy, covered in soggy deadfall and rife with jagged rocks. The company's movement was agonizingly slow, and most of the troopers had no idea what direction they were going, only that they were going up. As they reached the top, they would find that the enemy had fled, but had left behind many rice caches. Normally this rice would be airlifted out and distributed to the local villagers from whom it had been confiscated by the Viet Cong. Unfortunately, no landing zone was available here, and so the rice would have to be destroyed.

Also on the 23rd, Donald Rankin would write to his younger brother, Wayne.

Dear Wayne, Martha and children,

Received your letter with those cute pictures several days ago. However, it has rained for three solid days and nights. Yesterday, the river overflowed and we were in knee-deep water before we knew what happened. We are in very jungley territory between Phu My and Bong Son. We haven't seen too many Viet Cong, but the mosquitoes, rain, ants, and leeches are enough. The leeches are four and five inches long sometimes. They are really hard to keep off.

I guess Jr. is glad to be home. With luck, I'll be home by this time next year. That really seems far away now. I received the card and letter from

Wayne about a month ago. I thought that I had answered. But, we move around here so much that it's hard to remember anything. Tell everyone hello. I'll write more later.

Love,

Donnie

The next morning, Alpha Company continued moving eastward through the jungle and down the opposite side of the hill in search of the enemy. They set up their patrol base on the banks of the Nuoc Lang river, in a valley that formed yet another claw in the Crow's Foot of Kim Son. This particular river valley was even narrower than the previous, only about two hundred meters across in the area where they camped. Here they would have very little stand-off from any approaching enemy. Rankin wrote a letter home as they prepared for another airlift, set for the following day.

Dear Mom and Daddy,

Received your letter this afternoon. A nice easy day. Very hot, but tolerable. I got about nine letters. Everybody, Sarah Jane Bell, Gene's sister, Mrs. Gibson, you, Suzie in California, Suzie Crockett, some woman in Arizona I don't even know, and several others.

Tomorrow we're going into a "hot" landing zone, so it'll be a few days before I write probably. I don't even know the area. This is all. Will write more later. Tell everyone hello.

Love,

Donnie

The looming air assault would mark the beginning of another major operation for the 1st Air Cavalry Division. Despite hopeful rumors of returning to base camp at the conclusion of Irving, Alpha Company and the rest of the 5/7th Cav would be kept in the field as the division rolled into its next operation, through November and well into December.

Operation Irving officially concluded at midnight on October 24th 1966. It was a resounding success in that the displaced enemy was largely killed or captured, and organizationally dissolved. Over two thousand enemy soldiers were killed and over 1,400 were taken prisoner by allied forces. Over fifty Americans had given their lives to make it happen. In this new kind of war, with no semblance of defined battle lines, progress could not be measured in terms of territory. As it had been said, "In Vietnam today, you will hold only the ground you stand upon." Territory occupied by the enemy was not the actual objective as it had been in conventional wars, rather the enemy himself was the objective, and success would therefore be measured in terms of body count. It should be noted that armies have always used body count as one particular measure of success or failure. The Vietnam War, at least during the tenure of General Westmoreland, was unique in that body count would become virtually the only measure of progress. By this measure, Alpha Company and the entire 1st Air Cavalry were winning.

As night fell upon them on the 24th of October, the soldiers of Alpha Company had suffered only three fatalities in their first two months of combat operations, though many more had been wounded or fallen sick. This was just the beginning. The deadliest month was yet to come.

Rice paddy with dike running along foreground, photo by Wilbur Bowe

Alpha Company soldiers being extracted from rice paddy, photo by Wilbur Bowe

Crossing river in Bong Son, photo by Robert Matulac

Scout dog and handler, photos by Robert Matulac

(left to right) Robert Matulac, Kenneth Paquette, A.J. Wise

10
LIFE AND DEATH IN THE JUNGLE
(Operation Thayer II)

Just one of those mental pictures that stick in your mind, I suppose.

As Operation Irving was terminated, Operation Thayer II officially commenced on October 25th 1966, although the 5/7th Cav would not join in the area of operations until the next day. It would be more of the same search and destroy missions throughout the highlands and coastal plains for the soldiers of Alpha Company. November brought with it the monsoon season, characterized by daily downpours that fell in sheets, excessive wind-driven storms, increased humidity, and an opaque early morning fog that blanketed the lowlands.

Toward the end of October, Royce Barrow was being sent out for a week of Rest and Relaxation, or R&R as it was called. Each soldier was entitled to one week of R&R during their year-long tour. Barrow was going to Hong Kong. He didn't have any money, however, as he had the Army deposit almost all of his paychecks into a savings account. He asked his best friend and fellow radio operator, Donald Rankin, if he could borrow some cash. Rankin was more than happy to lend him sixty bucks for his trip.

On the morning of October 25th Alpha Company was airlifted from the banks of the Nuoc Lang River, where they had bivouacked the night before. Flying about four kilometers west, at 9:50 AM they air assaulted onto LZ Falcon, atop another large hill just to the west of the Soui L`on River. With Bravo and Charlie Companies set in blocking positions in the valley below, Alpha would spend the day moving northeast along a jungle-covered ridge, ending its patrol on the banks of a rice paddy in another portion of the Crow's Foot labyrinth of valleys.

On October 26th, the battalion would be flown into the Thayer II area of operations, approximately eight kilometers southwest of the Crow's Foot area they had been patrolling. At 8:10 AM, Chinook choppers lifted the battalion headquarters along with Delta Company, to LZ Pluto. They were soon followed by Bravo Company air assaulting into LZ Venus, then Alpha Company into LZ Mars, and Charlie Company into LZ Mercury. Except for LZ Mercury, which was located down in the valley of the large Song Con River below, the LZs were at high elevations. Alpha Company's LZ Mars was located on a cleared-out area along a saddle leading up to the area's highest mountain that peaked at an elevation of over three thousand feet. Approximately four kilometers southwest of the LZ, the Song Con River could be seen winding through an expansive valley that approached five kilometers at its widest point.

The rain had slowed to a drizzle that filtered through the trees. It was Will's turn at guard. Where clouds parted in the distance there was some moonlight, but little more than the skyline of mountains across the valley could be made out. The foreground before him was nothing but black shapes. He would watch those shapes, study them, waiting for one to move. The vast void was filled with constant insect and occasional animal noises. Filling the void in his mind were images of home. He saw his dad filling the silo, his mom in oven mitts, putting a roast into the oven, the football field where he'd played fullback, and his little brother Mike riding past him on his bicycle. The odd thing was that he wasn't even thinking about home. In fact, he was trying like hell not to. Yet the images were just there, randomly, a psychological effect of severe homesickness. Before long, the images were morphing into some kind of dream, and he began to hear conversations in his head. He wasn't exactly dozing off, his eyes were wide open and staring straight ahead. And yet, these dreams persisted until he came to, shaking them out of his head. Minutes later, they would start again. Perhaps a cigarette would help him stay alert. He lit one beneath his poncho, careful to keep its glowing end out of sight. Sleep deprivation was taking its toll.

On October 27th Alpha Company set out in a northwest direction across the mountain range, headed toward LZ Venus. Venus sat atop a mountain that towered 1,496 feet above the valley. The troopers spent the morning hacking their way through approximately three kilometers of densely forested ridges. They then crossed a small stream before beginning their nearly 1,400-foot ascent to LZ Venus. The mountain was extremely steep. Weighed down by their extra equipment, 4th Platoon was struggling to keep up with the rest of the company, and at times would drop their base plates or other mortar pieces while negotiating the rocky terrain.

The vegetation here was such that each man had to follow the other extremely close to avoid separation. In the depths of the jungle, the man in front of you represented your only connection to the civilized world and being separated and lost was one of their worst fears. Will was carrying the base plate and following close behind Quinn, and would occasionally grab on to Quinn's belt to keep from falling behind. He said finally, "Will I know that base plate's heavy but I can't carry both of us up this hill!"

A lieutenant of one of the rifle platoons was growing impatient and began accosting the men of 4th Platoon as they approached the top. Hansen recalls their journey up that same mountain as one of the worst; burdened by chains of extra M-60 ammo, he was walking on point, the first in line, and chopping through the vines and bamboo with his machete. He remembers being particularly aggravated and exhausted as they reached the top. Here, dozens of huge five-hundred-pound bomb craters could be seen about the mountain and in the valley below.

After reaching the top of the mountain, they moved down a short distance toward a cleared area on the other side. They had reached LZ Venus. The battalion command chopper was en route with LTC Swett and some of his staff officers to discuss the day's events and receive Alpha Company's after-action reports. They were also transporting three new replacement soldiers. New guys were sometimes referred to as "fresh meat" or "FNGs". As Matulac neared the LZ, he could see two soldiers of the rifle platoons standing around, smoking and joking with one of the engineers. As the command chopper approached, Matulac made his way toward the three to admonish them of the danger of their situation as the area was yet unsecured. He was within a few feet of them when two were cut down by machine gun fire from some jungle-covered high ground above. Matulac then saw the chopper's door gunner jumping around and trying to avoid the bullets while maneuvering his own weapon. Matulac leapt for cover into a nearby crater as the company frantically attempted to get its collective shit together and return fire. Bobby Hansen and Larry Raynaert had just finished digging their foxhole and Hansen had been making his way toward the landing zone in hopes of getting some mail. He had left his weapon behind and found himself laying defenseless on the ground as the bullets came in at the LZ. Matulac and Rankin returned fire at the enemy while leap-frogging each other up the hill. Upon landing under fire, one of LTC Swett's staff, MAJ Victor Bullock, rushed to help one of their medics, Specialist-4 (SP/4) Bill Garcia, care for one of the wounded soldiers.

Meanwhile, Will and Quinn had been preparing to dig in for the night while SSG Burtis stood reading a newspaper a few feet away. They were arguing over whose turn it was to dig their foxhole when the shots rang out. Dropping their entrenching tools, they ran for cover and hit the ground. CPT Wise was already on the radio, calling in gunships. As they blindly returned fire into the forest, Will noticed that Burtis wasn't with them. He could hear him crying for help, but couldn't see where he was. Bullets were still flying, mostly from their own company at this point. For a moment he hesitated, unsure of where Burtis was or how to get to him amidst the hail of flying lead. Jumping out from his position, 1SG Potter ran out to Burtis through the cloud of gun smoke and promptly dragged him back to safety as Will and Quinn and the others did their best to provide cover fire. The company continued sporadic firing into the jungle until the gunships arrived to pummel the enemy positions. SSG Burtis had taken two bullets in his stomach. The front of his fatigues soaked in blood, his arms and hands were shaking uncontrollably. As soon as the enemy had been chased away, they carried him back to the LZ where he and the other wounded soldiers could be evacuated, and their medic started hooking up an IV for him.

Once the fighting stopped, supplies were quickly unloaded, but the terrified three new soldiers refused to get out of the chopper. The other three who had been wounded minutes before, including SSG Burtis, were lying on the ground and waiting to be loaded on. Matulac had to physically remove the three replacements from the aircraft. Three soldiers in, three soldiers out. Within minutes, the chopper dipped its nose and began its ascent, blowing a storm of dirt in the faces of the squinting troopers. Will and Quinn continued to watch as it disappeared into the sky with their platoon sergeant.

Will wondered if Burtis would survive. He'd known him since their time at Fort Carson. A fellow farmer, he was nearly the only NCO to treat him and the other draftees with some degree of respect and compassion. Will remembered his fear of heights and how he refused to climb down the rappel tower, and how just recently, he'd taught him how to pray. Though it was utterly inconsequential, that brief moment of hesitation during the firefight now filled him with deep regret. Burtis was more than his platoon sergeant, he was his friend, and he should have been the one to drag him to safety, he thought. SSG Burtis would survive his wounds, as would the other two soldiers. He would stay on light duty at An Khe for the remainder of their tour, however, as SSG Hayslip took over as platoon sergeant for 4th Platoon.

Chester Millay recalled how after the wounded were lifted off that day, they were all ordered to march back out to find the snipers. Dejected and exhausted, they trudged back into the jungle in search of the enemy. Finding nothing, they returned to LZ Venus a few hours later as the sun was setting.

Alpha Company's troopers would set out from LZ Venus the next morning, again moving northwest. They were moving mostly downhill this time, and would cover approximately two kilometers before stopping on a hill near the Song Con River. Here they would cut out another landing zone with the help of the engineers, dubbing it LZ Sun.

28 Oct '66 – 38 weeks left

Dear Folks,

I hope you guys got my last letter, 21 Oct. You see, we were camped along this river and we had a flash flood. Some of the guys got their letters back and I didn't, so I don't know if it got through or not. I had sent those pictures back, so let me know if you received them. I lost the first page of that letter when a chopper flew over the tent. Oh well.

The sad part of this letter is my platoon sergeant got shot, but is in good shape. It came from some snipers. We've been really humping the hills lately and it's been really rough going. You want to know why we get wet every day, well, almost every day? It's because we are always moving and there's not always time to build a decent shelter. Yes, I do have my raincoat, but not with me. It will come in handy once we get into base camp. I believe around Dec 15th for about 3 months or so. I think I've only seen Rodney twice since 5 Sept. Did you ever read in the paper about the 1st Cav Division or Operation Irving? Well, that's us. It is us in the 5th of the 7th Cav, along with the 1st of the 7th, and 2nd of the 8th, combined with the Korean Army and Vietnamese Army, and it's also called Operation Thayer. It's hard to explain.

Did you get the picture of me crossing the river? I got those pictures of Mike, Darrell and Diane. I see you still have those letters hanging up and Mike is trying on my shirts, ha! Yes, he can wear all my clothes, except for those hats, OK? Also, I see Darrell needs a shave and the lawn needs a cutting. You guys better shape up. I really like them pictures, wish I could keep them. I missed R&R this month. I have a chance for Bangkok on 12 Nov, or Tokyo on the 24th. Maybe. If I get R&R, I sure will call home, you better believe I will. I'd best close, it's starting to pour rain.

Jungle Will

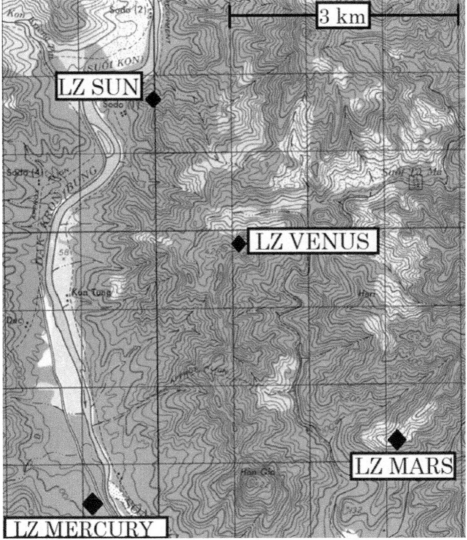

Song Con River Valley area, shown on map as Dak Kron Bung

27 October 1966, MAJ Bullock (left) and medic Bill Garcia (right) caring for wounded soldier, photo by Robert Matulac

The search for the enemy continued on the 29th of October as Alpha Company turned eastward, covering five kilometers into the mountains. As a battalion, the 5/7th Cav had been searching for the enemy in the Kim Son and Song Con Valleys for nine days, finding only rice caches and punji stakes, and taking infrequent contact from snipers. On this day however, they would encounter two mines, wounding nine of the battalion's men.

The search would drag on in the Song Con area for another day, and on October 31st Alpha Company would be airlifted to Camp Hammond. While the other platoons pulled security, 1LT Barry Gallagher's 1st Platoon was designated as the quick reaction force for the 3rd Brigade.

Barry Gallagher recalls how not much was happening the next day, November 1st. He was told that he could send a few of his men in to see a USO show starring Nancy Sinatra. He sent five of them up to a pick-up point from where they would be flown to An Khe to see the show.

Shortly thereafter, at approximately 1:30 PM, 1LT Gallagher's radio crackled with an urgent call from CPT Wise. Two helicopters of the 1/9th Cavalry had been shot down and one of their scout platoons had run into an entire battalion of Viet Cong. They were pinned down near a village southwest of Bong Son, between Highway 1 and Dam Tra-O Lake, just south of the Cay Giep Mountains. As the brigade's quick reaction force, Gallagher's 1st Platoon would be flown in to assist. The five men who thought they were going to see Nancy Sinatra that afternoon were quickly diverted. They met up with the rest of 1st Platoon as they air assaulted into a hot LZ in a large rice paddy.

On the other side of that rice paddy lay the village where the Viet Cong were holed up. After crossing the paddy, they immediately found themselves pinned down by machine gun fire from dug-in bunkers. As the gunfire erupted, Rocco, the fellow who Joe Sanchez recalled going on his first night patrol with, started running back through their lines toward the rice paddy. He barreled right between Gallagher and his radio operator, Ray Malinowski, busting the cord that ran between the handset and the radio. Fortunately, Malinowski was always prepared. He had an extra cord and was able to fix it.

Gallagher could see there was some cover they could use at the edge of the village if they could just make it there, so they pushed on, low-crawling through thick grass beneath the gunfire. One of his men, PFC Stoflet, was out in front of their assault and pushing on toward the bunkers when he was hit. Amidst the deafening gunfire, he heard a cry for "medic!" and watched SP/4 Garcia rise from the ground to make his way toward Stoflet. He didn't get very far before he was shot in the head himself. Gallagher recalls trying to save Garcia as he lay dying in the muddy grass. His reflexes were still working as he attempted to call in a dust-off, but the area was now too hot for them to come in. Moments later, he felt a surge of wind blowing from a chopper's downdraft at his back. He recalls, "I turned as a helicopter suddenly landed behind us. Two men jumped off and grabbed SP/4 Garcia under heavy fire and put him on the chopper and took off. The two men were Colonel Swett and Major Jennings. That is how much they loved their men."

At 4:17 PM, the 5/7th's Bravo Company was assaulted onto a nearby unoccupied hilltop, LZ Suzan, from where they would join the assault. A downpour commenced as Bravo Company began its own advance across the wide rice paddy toward the village. Night fell as the battle continued. After nine hours of intense fighting, the skytroopers managed to overrun the enemy, though most had escaped into the mountains. They had killed over forty Viet Cong, all of whom had been left at the scene by the retreating enemy battalion, a sign that they had been beaten badly.

Three soldiers of the 1/9th Cav had died, as had seven from Bravo Company, 5/7th. Among Bravo Company's dead was their beloved First Sergeant, Dayton Hare. Several Viet Cong had been concealed in spider holes dug beneath a hedgerow approaching the village. They had waited until the First Sergeant and a handful of others were right upon them when they opened fire. Forty-four years old and having survived two previous wars, he now lay dead in the pouring rain, near a village named Quang Ngheim. He and the others were evacuated in the dark. He was posthumously awarded the Silver Star and Purple Heart. He had also finally earned his Combat Infantryman's Badge. Shortly thereafter, some of his friends pitched in to send his wife the Noritake Chinaware set he had picked out for her.

The two soldiers from Alpha Company's 1st Platoon to be killed were SP/4 Bill Garcia, twenty years old from Pacoima, California and PFC Michael Stoflet, twenty-one from Elkhorn, Wisconsin. Stoflet was awarded the Distinguished Service Cross for his bravery.

The President of the United States of America, authorized by Act of Congress, July 9, 1918 (amended by act of July 25, 1963), takes pride in presenting the Distinguished Service Cross (Posthumously) to Private First Class Michael Howard Stoflet, United States Army, for extraordinary heroism in connection with military operations involving conflict with an armed hostile force in the Republic of Vietnam, while serving with Company A, 5th Battalion, 7th Cavalry, 1st Cavalry Division. Private First Class Stoflet distinguished himself by exceptionally valorous actions on 1 November 1966, while his unit was being airlifted to reinforce a besieged American unit. As his platoon proceeded north from the landing zone to assist the friendly unit, it came under intense automatic weapons fire from several fortified Viet Cong bunkers. Private First Class Stoflet's squad continued to advance until it was pinned down approximately 75 meters short of the hostile positions. Realizing the perilous position his comrades were in, he dauntlessly began a one-man assault on the insurgent emplacement. Despite the murderous volume of fire directed at him, Private First Class Stoflet succeeded in safely reaching the bunker, and immediately found an opening through which he could get inside. His first attempt to secure the position was nearly fatal, as a burst of automatic weapons fire sent him reeling backwards with a slight head wound. Momentarily stunned, Private First Class Stoflet again disregarded his safety to vault back into the small opening. In this courageous effort to overcome the enemy, he was mortally wounded. His unimpeachable valor in the face of overwhelming odds enabled the platoon to overrun the Viet Cong position and accomplish its mission. Private First Class Stoflet's extraordinary heroism and devotion to duty, at the cost of his life, were in keeping with the highest traditions of the military service and reflect great credit upon himself, his unit, and the United States Army.

As the torrential rain continued, soldiers from Alpha's 1st Platoon and Bravo Company searched the village. The next day, Bravo returned to LZ Susan to recover while Charlie Company was flown in to search for the enemy along with Alpha's 1st Platoon. They continued through the 3rd day of November with Bravo Company rejoining the search, and Alpha's 1st Platoon moving to LZ Carol. They ended their mission just after noon on November 4th, searching and clearing a village on the banks of Dam Tra-O, another inlet-type lake near the South China Sea. Afterward, with the exception of Delta Company pulling security at LZ Crystal, the 5/7th Cav regrouped at Camp Hammond.

2 Nov '66 – 38 weeks left

Dear Folks,

We finally got a little rest. We're pulling guard at a French security camp (Hammond). Very little worry, and can see for miles around. We don't know for how long. Might leave again soon 'cause of some fighting going on again. If we stay here much longer, I've got a stack of letters to catch up on. So tell Darrell and Mel, Mike, Schindler, Ronnie, Larry, Doris, Pat, Connie, and Steve I'll write them all a letter when I get a chance to. I tell you, those summer sausages and cheese you sent sure came at the wrong time. When we got to this camp, I ate so much that I couldn't move, and then the sergeant came with two packages for me. Well, I didn't open it until the next day. Then I took my old dirty, rusty, dull 15-inch machete out, cleaned it and sliced off a couple chunks of meat and cheese. It's been a long time since I had a taste of spiced meat and a lot of cheese. It was really good, even though we weren't too hungry. The guys here said to send more out. I still have a couple of packages of Kool-Aid left. The water is good and the food is getting a lot better the past couple of weeks.

I guess you misunderstood me. Astronomy is not an animal, it is the study of the universe. Remember the time I wanted to learn how to stuff animals (taxidermy)? Well, this guy Patrillo from Pennsylvania took it up, and he made it sound really interesting. I wish I would have tried it out. This is what dad and Mike could do for a little hobby. Just get the address out of Sport & Field. For only 10 bucks, they'll show you how to mount all kinds of animals. I know I am going to try it when I get home. If you want me to buy you Chinaware or a souvenir, let me know, OK?

May God take care of you all,

Will

Looking at a photograph of son William Garcia, Jr. is Mrs. William Garcia. She accepted the Purple Heart Medal posthumously presented to son during ceremonies Friday at Fort MacArthur. Garcia, 20-year-old medical corpsman, was killed on November 1st, 1966.

Michael Stoflet

1SG Dayton Hare (B Co)

With the exception of 1st Platoon, Alpha Company had been pulling security at Camp Hammond for the last five days. The following are excerpts from a letter that Rankin sent on the 5th of November:

Dear Mom and Daddy,

We're still at the Forward Support Area. It is really great! It gives us some time to relax and catch up on our letter writing. Yesterday, I got a package from Martha Barnes Lee and Dr. and Mrs. Simpas in Paris. Also, the day before, Carolyn sent me a fruit cake from North Carolina. Everyone has really enjoyed it all. I have too much so about all the company gets a share. Sometimes, I feel kind of guilty. The price of the stuff and the expense for mailing it is outrageous. Should anyone mention a box, tell them not to spend money on soap. The Army sends us an accessory pack and soap is the only item that there is enough of.

Things have been quiet for us except for 1st Platoon. They were committed the other day and had two killed and two wounded. It really ticked us off. They should commit us as a company. They sent them to help a battalion that isn't too swift anyway. I'm sure 1st Platoon was being typical aggressive "A" Company and had no back up support. That platoon has suffered all the killed in action and 12 of our wounded. I was part of that platoon until I was made the radio operator. "B" Company also had heavy losses in that battle. I'd hate to know who they were. Those two real close buddies from Michigan are in that company. We were together all the time until we became A Co, 5/7th.

An NBC news cameraman went with us on a short escapade yesterday. Look closely at the news, and you might see some of my company. I don't think that I'm in any of them. This is about it. I'd better close because I have about 15 letters to answer.

Love,

Donnie

Later that afternoon, Alpha Company would be replaced by Bravo and sent out on another mission. The men were told to load up into the back of some deuce-and-a-halfs, and at 2:15 PM they departed Camp Hammond moving northward along Highway 1. Turning right onto Highway 504 at the town of Phu My, they headed eastward, back into the vast coastal plains and steaming rice paddies where they had fought their first major battle. After traveling approximately six miles along the muddy Highway 504, the convoy stopped at a small bridge that spanned the Song Ca River. Here the troopers jumped out and prepared for another search and destroy mission. To the southeast, the Song Ca's twin river, the Siem Giang, was less than a quarter mile away. On its banks, they could see what was left of the village of An My, where they had fought on October 4th. They had returned, but this time alone, as Bravo Company pulled security at Camp Hammond, Delta secured LZ Crystal near Bong Son, and Charlie Company prepared for its own recon-in-force mission along the Song Lai Giang River, also near the town of Bong Son.

Over the next two days, Alpha Company's skytroopers would cover over thirteen miles on foot, making their way around the Vinh Nuoc Ngot inlet. On November 6th, they set off to the north, crossing another river that emptied into the inlet, then making their way into the jungles of the Nui Mieu Mountains. They would climb nearly one thousand feet up the mountain range's southernmost peak before descending back down toward the sandy Hung Lac peninsula that separated the Vinh Nuoc Ngot from the South China Sea. Along the way they would take a surrendering Viet Cong prisoner. Moving south along the peninsula, they bivouacked their patrol base amongst its dunes and set out ambushes for the night. There was a lot of beauty here along the sea, with its turquoise water, white sand beaches and palm trees. For once, it wasn't raining, and the scenery was a welcome change. Traversing around the southern banks of the inlet, they moved inland at daybreak. While crossing more rivers and searching another village, they made their way back up to where they had started out the day before. With one captured Viet Cong to their credit, they set out their ambushes and spent one last night in the Phu My plain.

The next morning, November 8th, smoke grenades were set off to mark their position and soon Chinooks arrived to lift them off. By 7:45 AM they were at LZ English. By 8:37 AM, Hueys were dropping Alpha Company's troopers onto LZ Catalina, atop a mountain on the north edge of the Cay Giep range, where the Song Lai Giang River empties into the sea. Here they would search for remnants of NVA regiments fought by Charlie company in their recon mission the night before. It had been a fierce battle, with gunships, artillery and naval gunfire being brought to bear on the enemy. No enemy were found on Alpha Company's patrols however, and the next day the battalion once again regrouped at Camp Hammond, with Delta Company continuing to secure LZ Crystal.

On November 10th Alpha Company would be sent out again. Again they would scour the Phu My plain in search of the enemy, this time along Highway 504 where they would find several bridges burned by the Viet Cong. They would return to Camp Hammond in a convoy of trucks on the 12th.

Soldiers would often arrive to take the place of the dead and wounded, as well as those who had fallen ill. They would typically arrive in the log ship choppers. In mid-November, Donald Duncan arrived while Alpha Company was being resupplied in the field. He was the Kentucky grade school friend of Gene Cross, who had taken a shot through the helmet on October 4th and survived. Unlike the others who had just arrived in Vietnam, Duncan had come over with them in August on the USNS Gaffey and had been working in the 5/7th Cav battalion supply shop at An Khe since their arrival. Apparently, he'd gotten into a serious disagreement with his boss and wanted out. He actually volunteered to come out to the field. Will was perplexed by his decision to give up a swell, relatively safe job back at base camp. "Why would anyone want to come out here and live with us?" he thought. He figured Duncan had lost his marbles. Back from the stockade, Arnott Graham would also rejoin the company in November. Leaving the company was Robert Henry. He had a brother who had just been sent to Vietnam as well. The Army didn't want to have both serving in a combat zone at the same time, so Henry was sent to Korea.

13 Nov '66 – 35 weeks left

Dear Folks,

Guess it's been a while since I wrote last. Wrote to Mel and Darrell. I'll have to write to Darrell again 'cause I wasn't in a good state of mind. We've been moving a lot and now we're here at Camp Hammond. This morning, this Vietnamese interpreter was teaching me Judo. Man, he weighs 30-40 less than me and he threw me all over the place. I can handle myself against anyone in my platoon, but this cat's too good. Been having a lot of fun with these Soul Brothers (colored people), they're out of sight. Singing and telling jokes, make you die laughing. I get more sleep and rest when we're humping through rice paddies or jungles. Here we're either playing poker, rolling dice, singing, or getting canned up. And then in the next day or so, we'll go chase V.C. Last week they pulled a dirty trick on us. Told us we had to attack this hill with 80 V.C.s on it. Man we were scared, and all there was on the hill was N.B.C. taking movies of us. Talk about pissed off. I'd like to... can't say. But the next guy with a camera will be a guy without a camera.

This letter just got wet from the little shower we just had, and this dang tent just ain't too good either. Man, it's getting hotter than hell out now. I don't care how hard it rains or how many hills and rice paddies we go through, as long as we don't have to fight. When the weather is bad or we're tired and miserable, I always say it could be worse. In fact, the guys here don't understand me. One cat said if I slept in a rice paddy it would be OK, as long as the water wasn't flowing, ha! As long as I don't go through another day like Oct 4th I'll be happy. I remember the first time we searched a village. We were sharp, on our toes and scared. Now we stumble into a village, flop down in their yard, and make ourselves at home. Only people left are just the young kids, women, and old men. Kids here are like the kids back home. Give one kid a piece of candy or gum and you got the whole village holding their hands out. The old men will give us coconut juice. When these people get old, they look like they're 150 when they might only be 50 years old.

We got a guy here, Henry, leaving for home. Lucked out. Man, I sure hate to see him go. Graham is coming back from the stockade. He'll be back in again, ha! Figueroa bought a $25 watch from a Vietnamese. Very nice watch, but does not work, ha! Just shook hands with Henry. Wish I could come home. That old fart got my razor too. Says he'll send it back. Yeah, I bet he will. Oh well, I got another one back at camp.

No, Rodney doesn't read the Chippewa paper. Not mine anyway, 'cause I very seldom see him. But I guess his mother sends him the Bloomer paper. I don't know why Rod is discussed. The only company that hasn't fought yet. I guess that's why he always wants to see some action. He should be in A Co. We've seen and been in the most action so far.

About 35 shopping days left until Christmas, huh? If you guys send me a watch for Christmas I'd be real happy. The watch I had in Colorado went haywire. If you do send a watch, have it with illumination dials. It comes in real handy at night, for guard duty. Heck, they're singing Christmas carols already. Wish they wouldn't, makes me feel bad. If I get on R&R, I'll send you all kinds of presents.

Will

Donald Rankin also happened to write home on the 13th.

Dear Mom and Daddy,

Just returned from four days of tramping around the China Sea area. We've been there so many times that it's getting like home. The people recognize us and try to give us food. We captured four VC men and two women. One patrol killed a VC and got his weapon. That area is east of Phu My. It is supposed to be pacified now. The 9th Division is going to move in and occupy the area. Then, we'll move on to some other VC stronghold. Today, we're going to go to church services and get our equipment ready to go to Bong Son for four days. We will be a blocking force there. That is usually a very easy job.

We're beginning to get a lot of new guys in the company. They are beginning to take seven or eight at a time from the 5/7th Battalion and put them in others. This is because we're all due to leave Viet Nam the same time. Should we all stay together, they would have to replace a complete battalion next August. Everyone is really angry that we're getting split up.

Several of the guys made E-5 yesterday. Sometimes, I think about being a fire team leader or squad leader and realize that I'd be responsible for the lives of about nine men. However, someone has to do it. So, if the opportunity comes, I might take it. The Captain told me last week that if I could get into Warrant Officers school, he would release me. I'd sure like to be a helicopter pilot but three more years is a long time. Probably, eight to ten months of that would be over here.

Did I send you Nancy's address? Send her a picture. It is a real pretty morning. There are a lot of low flying clouds, and the sun is half shining. It is good that the clouds are here. The temperature must be 100 degrees already. This is about all. Tell everyone hello and write soon.

Love,

Donnie

On November 13th, Alpha Company would air assault another LZ, this time in the Bong Son plain near Dam Tra-O Lake. Again they would search and destroy, while a civic action team provided medical services to a nearby hamlet just east of Highway 1. Again they would return to Camp Hammond on the 16th of November.

While waiting as a reserve force at Camp Hammond on the 17th, the company was alerted at 3:25 PM to respond to contact made by the 1/9th Cav. By 4:25 PM choppers filled with Alpha Company skytroopers were descending onto a mountaintop between the Kim Son and another valley just east of the Crow's Foot, called Valley 506. In pouring rain, they moved south through the mountains, eventually linking up with a platoon of the 1/9th Cav. Now following a creek bed, they kept moving until late in the night and bivouacked in the jungle. The next morning they moved to the northwest. Again they would come up empty-handed, and again they would sleep in the jungle.

In his New Jersey accent, Bobby Hansen would remark, "Everybody remembers that day," while recounting the events of November 19th 1966. He also recalled that a few days earlier, his squad leader, SSG Elvin Wideman, had received a Dear John letter from his girl. Hansen himself had a girl to write home to for a while, but after a couple letters he never heard from her again. Early in the day, LTC Swett had flown out to visit Alpha Company in the field. He also happened to bring with him a very important communique for Alan Weisman. The letter informed Weisman that his aunt had passed away, and that she had left him over a million dollars. He joked that he would be the only millionaire sleeping in the Vietnam bush that night.

After more fruitless searching on the morning of November 19th, Alpha Company was lifted approximately five kilometers southeast and assaulted into a sea of elephant grass along a ridgeline that jutted northward from the massive Nui Hon Giang hill mass at 10:07 AM. For whatever reason, the landing zone was not prepped with artillery and bombing in the normal fashion, perhaps to maintain some degree of surprise on the enemy. Despite the open area on top where they landed, the sides of the hill were dark and densely forested.

As Matulac recalls, his buddy Earl Huber had forgotten to get his lucky insult that day. The command group, 1st Platoon, and mortar platoon moved south from the landing zone, eventually making their way to the rice paddies in the 506 Valley at the base of the ridgeline. They continued moving around it. Meanwhile, 2nd and 3rd Platoons split up and made their way through the jungle across opposite sides of the same ridgeline. After nearly four hours of searching, 2nd Platoon radioed to the company that they had found human shit on the ground, a sign that the enemy had been there recently. They kept moving. Shortly thereafter, they found themselves face to face with a company of Viet Cong. They had been waiting in fortified bunkers and were dug in deep in the hillside. For a half-second or so, they just looked at each other, both sides taken aback at how close they now were to each other. Then the gunfire erupted. It was strange that the enemy had not been expecting them. The only explanation is that the jungle surrounding the camp was so thick that it insulated the enemy camp from the sound of the choppers landing only a half-kilometer from their position.

As they took cover, 1LT Harmon told his men to keep their heads down under the hail of lead. Next to him was his newly-wealthy radio operator, Alan Weisman. During a lull in the gunfire, Weisman looked up briefly, attempting to locate the enemy positions as he talked to CPT Wise on the radio. He was shot in the head, and died soon thereafter.

2nd Platoon held its ground for the next hour, and at 2:30 PM 3rd Platoon was picked up by choppers and flown down to a position from which they could reach them. They would have to make their way uphill, and still lying between 3rd Platoon and 2nd were broken trails and thick jungle, a large ravine, and eventually a large knoll. Going around this knoll would lead to 2nd Platoon's position, where they were trying to get to. Led by 1LT William Nelson, among those in 3rd Platoon were Bobby Hansen and his buddy, Jim Hirschuber, as well as their squad leader who'd just received his Dear John letter, SSG Elvin Wideman - machine gunners Robert Wagner from Seattle and Guy McNay (Juggy) from Kentucky who was raised by his older sister, Annette - riflemen Earl Huber, Bill Boyce and John Fitzpatrick - radio operator Phil Jones - and a new guy, Eddie Woodruff, a replacement who had just arrived the month prior.

The 5/7th Cav would later be recommended for a Presidential Unit Citation based upon the battalion's activities from September 1966 through March 1967. In that recommendation were narrative descriptions of many of their battles, including that of November 19th 1966. According to this narrative, "Link up with the platoon in contact by the air assaulted platoon was not possible because of the dense vegetation, darkness, and a large ravine separating the elements." The real reason for their failure to link up with 2nd Platoon, as Hansen recalls, is that they were sent up the wrong trail.

As they moved up and around the knoll, they could see footprints. Huber was on point, a few feet in front of Hansen when he said, "Hey, there's some bunk..." and before he could finish the word "bunkers" the whole forest in front of them exploded. They had been sent around the wrong side of the knoll, right in front of the enemy bunkers which were now only fifteen feet away. Huber was the first to go down, shot in the leg. The pistol grip of Boyce's rifle was splintered by an enemy's bullet that also ripped through his own leg. Just to the right of Hirschuber, Fitzpatrick was shot in the chest. Hirschuber credits his own survival to the fact that he happened to be standing behind a small "nub" in the ground that held a large tree when the machine guns opened fire on them. SSG Wideman called up his machine gunners, Wagner and McNay. As they moved up, Wagner fell into a hidden pit filled with punji stakes, one of which went through his leg. Soon after, McNay was shot in the shoulder. Meanwhile,

Hansen found himself pinned down in a fold in the ground next to a tree. As large fragments of bark and branches from the tree rained down on his backside, he would watch the tall grass before him being mowed short by the enemy's machine gun fire. Moments later, Hansen was bandaging Huber's leg as the others in the platoon got on line. Huber was hurt badly, but smiling with the knowledge that he would soon be getting out, one way or another. Hansen joked, "hey, why don't you shoot me in the leg and I'll go with you!"

Soon Jones came on line, just to Hansen's right. "Jones, come on with me," SSG Wideman said, and they made their way toward the bunkers. As they crawled through the brush, Jones was hit by four bullets, one through his helmet, one through his pack, another shot the wire of his radio, and yet another shot off the antennae. All of this left Jones, himself unscathed. Wideman continued in his effort to take out the enemy bunkers, but was not so lucky. Their platoon leader was still yelling at them to move up, not realizing that most of them had been badly wounded. As their squad leader, SSG Wideman lay impossibly close and exposed to the enemy bunkers, Hansen prepared to recover his body along with Jones by dragging him back by his ankles. He was surprised to see that Woodruff, the new guy, had already moved up in front of him, toward Wideman. "It should have been me to go up there with Jones to get Wideman," Hansen remarked about the new guy, Eddie Woodruff, "but he was already up there, he just stood up and got shot."

Hansen and Jones could see that Wideman was already dead, but Woodruff was still alive with a sucking chest wound. They managed to pull him back down into the brush by his ankles. Lying only about four feet in front of them, Wideman was too close to the enemy to be recovered. Promising to come back, Hansen and Jones wanted to carry Woodruff back down the hill to get him medevaced, but their platoon leader wouldn't let them go.

Bravo Company had been flown into a blocking position to the northwest, in the 506 Valley. Charlie Company had been alerted and was standing by at Camp Hammond, but rain and darkness prevented their take-off.

It was getting dark by the time Huber and the rest of the walking wounded made it down the hill. As the battle was ongoing, only those who could make it down on their own could be medevaced at this point. The worst of the wounded, as well as the dead, would have to wait until morning.

As fighting commenced, 4th Platoon had set their mortars. As the battle continued, they lobbed their shells at enemy positions and continued to do so throughout the night. Artillery could not be used as 3rd Platoon had gotten far too close to the enemy positions. Darkness fell, and 2nd and 3rd Platoons held their positions while the mortar teams shot illumination rounds to expose any escaping Viet Cong. Will and his buddy Marvin

Bierschbach would recall this as one of their longest sleepless nights in Vietnam.

"I got a million-dollar wound," Huber said to Matulac while waiting for the chopper, which would not arrive until approximately 1:00 AM. After that day, his buddy Gruenburg would never forget to get his lucky insult from Matulac, and would never be wounded himself.

Matulac would recall this as one of his most terrifying nights spent in Vietnam. He was responsible for calling in the dust-off for the wounded. The night was pitch-black, however, and he would need to guide the dust-off to the casualty collection point near the edge of the rice paddy using flashlights and ground flares. With the enemy still fighting just up the hill, he was no doubt making himself a target.

They advanced on the enemy bunkers at daybreak, only to find many dead bodies and weapons left behind. The new guy, Eddie Woodruff, had died during the night. "We could've saved him," Hansen reflected.

Mangled enemy bodies were scattered about the blood-soaked ground, and many blood trails could be seen leading away from the bunkers and into the jungle. Staggered about the hillside, the bunkers were found to be rather elaborate affairs, fortified by large logs and packed down with dark, reddish-colored mud. Most emptied into tunnels, and inside the troopers would find enemy weapons and many more dead bodies lying in pools of semi-coagulated blood. Now it was time to start stacking.

Matulac recalls many of the battle-weary men from 2nd and 3rd platoons filtering back down the hill through a trail, to the base of the ridgeline where the company was gathering near the banks of the rice paddy in the 506 Valley. Many were badly wounded. One of them was 3rd Platoon's radio operator, Phil Jones, who had a hole shot squarely through the front of his helmet. He seemed fine. As Jones walked past, he noticed another hole in the back of his helmet. "Are you hurt?" Matulac asked. No, was the reply. Hirschuber would recall a fellow named Curtis Zechman. His neck was bleeding, but he was unaware that he had been shot. The bullet had managed to lodge itself just beneath his skin and was still stuck in his neck. He didn't believe it until he felt the bullet for himself. My dad remembers watching the dead being carried down from the hill that morning. As rigor mortis had set in, an arm of one of the dead troopers was sticking straight up as he was loaded onto the chopper. Just one of those mental pictures that stick in your mind, I suppose.

Matulac and three other exhausted soldiers carried SP/4 Alan Weisman's body to the chopper. Muscles weak from a night of fighting, they bumped his head on the chopper door as they lifted him in. "Sorry Alan," Matulac said reflexively, forgetting for a moment that he wasn't really there.

With five of their men killed, this was the most fatalities Alpha Company had taken in a single day. Also among the dead were PFC John Fitzpatrick from Franklin, Wisconsin and 2nd Platoon's SP/4 Coley White from Wiley Ford, West Virginia. From Saint Louis, Missouri, SSG Elvin Wideman would be awarded the Distinguished Service Cross.

The President of the United States takes pride in presenting the Distinguished Service Cross (Posthumously) to Elvin Joseph Wideman, Staff Sergeant, U.S. Army, for extraordinary heroism in connection with military operations involving conflict with an armed hostile force in the Republic of Vietnam, while serving with Company A, 5th Battalion, 7th Cavalry, 1st Cavalry Division (Airmobile). Staff Sergeant Wideman distinguished himself by exceptionally valorous actions on 19 November 1966 while serving as a squad leader with elements of the 7th Cavalry on a search and destroy mission near Bong Son. When the lead element became heavily engaged with a Viet Cong force, his platoon moved forward to provide fire support. As the unit maneuvered into position it was suddenly pinned down by intense automatic weapons fire from several fortified bunkers to their immediate front. Pinpointing the insurgent positions, Sergeant Wideman directed three of his men to cover him as he dauntlessly crawled forward alone. When he arrived at a point near one bunker, he threw a grenade into it and destroyed the emplacement. With complete disregard for his safety, Sergeant Wideman then ran through the fierce hostile barrage to another emplacement where he killed all the Viet Cong with his rifle. Unmindful of the inherent dangers, Sergeant Wideman courageously advanced toward another bunker a few meters away. As he raised up to toss a grenade, he was mortally wounded by machine gun fire. With the last effort of his strength, he flung the grenade into the emplacement, killing all the insurgents inside. His conspicuous gallantry saved many of his comrades from death or injury and contributed immeasurably to the defeat of the Viet Cong force. Staff Sergeant Wideman's extraordinary heroism and devotion to duty, at the cost of his life, were in keeping with the highest traditions of the military service and reflect great credit upon himself, his unit, and the United States Army.

Over thirty Viet Cong had been killed and an enemy camp destroyed. Amongst the enemy items captured that morning were a ChiCom grenade (a grenade with a wood handle), nearly fifty rounds of ammunition, fifteen pounds of clothing, and an inch-thick stack of documents. At 10:00 AM Charlie Company was flown in to replace Alpha. As Alpha Company returned to Camp Hammond, Bravo and Charlie would continue to search the surrounding area for what was left of the enemy. Over the next two days, they would find many more bodies of dead Viet Cong in the surrounding jungle, along with vast amounts of weapons and equipment that had been abandoned by the enemy, including more frag grenades, AK-47 rifles, machetes, mines, anti-tank grenades, rocket launchers, Bangalore torpedoes, more documents, over a thousand rounds of 7.62mm ammunition, and over a ton of rice.

Donald Rankin would write this letter home the next day.

November 21, 1966

Dear Mom and Daddy,

Yesterday, we returned to the forward support area after a very gruesome week. Most of it was spent cutting through the jungle hunting the Viet Cong. Sunday, our 2nd Platoon went on a patrol and walked right into the middle of a Viet Cong camp. Our 3rd Platoon was flown in to help them, and they ran into an even larger group. They fought for about two and a half hours. It got dark and both platoons had to stay in the jungle all night. They flew the remainder of us into the bottom of the hill where we stayed all night. We fired mortars around our two platoons all night to keep anyone from getting to them. Yesterday morning, the rest of A Company, along with another platoon from another company, went up to bring out the dead and wounded. We had five killed and eight or ten wounded. It was sure a sad morning yesterday, but we are lucky that all of those two platoons weren't killed. There was at least a company of Viet Cong hidden in the thick trees and vines with bunkers that our mortars would hardly shake.

Yesterday afternoon, they brought us back in. We're all doing pretty good. My feet are kind of rotten. We get ringworm and impetigo all over us if we don't put zinc oxide on every little scratch. My left ankle is swollen, but the soreness has gone. I guess it is from the rough walking and jumping from the helicopters! The other day, we jumped from the helicopter and ran for cover. I tried to jump what I thought was a small puddle. I tripped and went in up to my neck. We all got a big laugh out of it. That afternoon and night, we walked for six and a half hours along a creek, through thick jungle, rain all the way, to get to a platoon that had encountered the Viet Cong earlier that day. We didn't encounter any action but were we beat.

I'm still receiving a lot of mail and packages. There are about ten or twelve letters in my helmet that I haven't had a chance to answer. Suzie sent me a box yesterday. I'm about sick from eating so much. We stuff ourselves after having C-Rations for six or seven days.

I'm still considering being a helicopter pilot. What do you all think? I would probably be back in the states by January. Go to Alabama for nine months and then be reassigned. Also, I'd probably have to come back here for twelve months. That wouldn't be too bad. The VC don't like to shoot at helicopters because they carry some really potent machine guns and rockets. Should I do that – I would get E-5 pay, clothing allowance, and if I didn't get my commission, I'd still be E-5 and get a good job. My commander talked about it last night. At first he wouldn't say much, but twice in the last three weeks he has suggested that I try it.

Yesterday, I got a new uniform. I had worn the other one for two and a half months. It was beginning to be a little frayed. The weather has been unbearably cool and rainy. Some nights, we almost shook our teeth out. Jones had a close call the other day. A bullet went through his helmet, shot his radio antennae off and cut the handset off. He didn't even have a bump on his head. This is all for now. Maybe I'll have time to write more after this week.

Love,

Donnie

    A few days later, a log ship would arrive with supplies and a couple more soldiers from the battalion's rear echelon. Like Duncan who had arrived a week or so before, they had also been working in the battalion supply shop at An Khe. Unlike Duncan, they had not come to the field by choice. One was a thin black fellow named Robert Cain. The other was Russell Ferrebee. Nicknamed "Porky", he was a chubby disheveled soldier whose helmet was usually crooked, and who seemed to always be getting yelled at by someone. Both of them were nice kids, as Matulac recalls. It is not remembered what they had done, only that they had managed to piss somebody off at base camp, and as a result, had been sent to the field.

    Just like SGT Jackson, Bill Boyce, the soldier who had his own rifle shot up with splintered fragments stuck in his leg, was not able to find his weapon after recovering from his wounds. He would eventually receive a bill from the Army. He opted to make payments on his debt, sending the Army exactly one dollar each month.

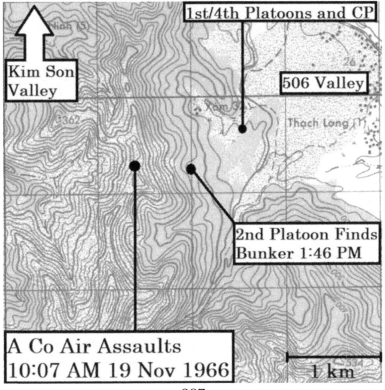

John Fitzpatrick

Coley White

Elvin Wideman

Alpha Company's 1st Platoon on Chinook, photo by Robert Matulac

Bill Boyce, photo by Robert Matulac

Tom Gruenburg, photo by Bill Purdy

Alpha Company soldiers taking a break after a firefight, photo by Robert Matulac

(left to right) Howard Garrison, Danny Whalen, and Kazimierz Slomiany, photo by Robert Matulac

Observing artillery strikes, photo by Wilbur Bowe

(left to right) King, Lussier, SGT Abegglen, photo by Wilbur Bowe

Airstrike over hill, two soldiers watching in foreground, photo by Marvin Bierschbach

Another airstrike over same hill, photo by Marvin Bierschbach

(left to right) Angel Reynosa, Fox, Spaur, photo by Wilbur Bowe

Martin Quin holding captured Viet Cong weapon, photo by Wilbur Bowe

11
THANKSGIVING

Today the heavens cried for him.

It was like any other morning as Alpha Company's men rose from beneath their ponchos to greet the dawn on Thanksgiving Day 1966. Surely, in the little sleep they were afforded, some of them had dreamt of home and were disappointed to find themselves waking once again in filthy wet fatigues in this no-man's land known as the Central Highlands. They would do all the normal things that soldiers in the field do in the morning. Relieve themselves, shave, perhaps, brush their teeth, perhaps, smoke a cigarette or two. Some were fortunate enough to have packets of instant coffee that could be heated with a balled-up wad of C-4 and shared with their buddies.

As the others milled about, CPT Wise's radio operator Donald Rankin penned another letter to his old college roommate back home. He wrote about how he planned to return to Vietnam after it was all over, to help the poor villagers recover from this terrible war. Already addressed and in its envelope, he stuck the letter in his pocket, intending to send it on its way with the next log ship.

Well into their third straight month in the field and in nearly constant rain, their feet were in bad shape, and many were falling ill from a variety of tropical diseases and infections. Weary from the constant trudging through rice paddies and jungles, they had been promised a reprieve, showers and new fatigues, soon. They knew not when these promises would be fulfilled, only that today they would be a blocking force for Charlie Company's sweep through a village, then fly to Camp Hammond for their Thanksgiving dinner. That was the plan, at least.

The day before, Alpha Company had been air assaulted into the mountains between the Kim Son Valley to their south, and the An Lao to their north. Perhaps the most beautiful region in the Central Highlands, the valley of An Lao also had a reputation as the deadliest. It was dominated by steep mountains covered with dense triple-canopy jungle. A wide river valley cut straight through the towering mountains on both sides. At its southern-most reaches, the valley curled sharply to the west, then back to the north, creating a fish-hook shape. Following their air assault the previous day, Alpha Company had patrolled moving north, approaching the southern edge of the An Lao Valley's fish-hook. They had dug in on a small hill overlooking an enormous rice paddy that lay in the valley, perhaps a half-mile wide. Bobby Hansen would recall it as the largest rice paddy he ever saw. From here they would begin their advance north down the hill, then through the expansive rice paddy on the 24th of November. On the other side, a battalion of NVA was believed to be occupying a large village of about twenty or so small huts. The village, known as Van Hoi, was flanked on the south and west by the vast L-shaped rice paddy they were slogging through. A small river ran through the village, and to its north rose lightly wooded foothills which intermittently cradled terraced rice paddies of their own, and eventually led up to the enormous and densely forested Nui Dat Set Mountain. As this was the monsoon season, the rice paddies were all deeply flooded.

That same morning, Joe Sanchez was waiting to board a Chinook log ship that was headed out to deliver ammunition and other supplies to Alpha Company. He had been sent in to LZ English for some kind of medical treatment or something, and was to return to the field that morning. The crew chief told him there was no room for him on the chopper, and he would have to wait until tomorrow.

Alpha Company was on its own as the soldiers made their way north across the rice paddy, toward the village of Van Hoi, still in the early morning. As they approached, slow-moving fixed-wing fighters were busy strafing suspected enemy positions surrounding the village with machine gun fire. One of the pilots gave Matulac a thumbs-up as he flew by. Expecting to get shot at, he felt his own radio operator, Kenneth Rathyen, was following too closely. "Spread it out," he told him, just as large casings from one of the aircraft's machine guns landed on Rathyen's helmet, causing him to go cross-eyed for a moment.

The plan was for Alpha Company to make its way around and position itself on the opposite (north) side of the village and act as a blocking force for the 5/7th's Charlie Company, who would sweep through the village from the south side. Charlie Company's landing zone, dubbed LZ Springfield, was to be just south of the village, in the middle of the same rice paddy that Alpha Company was now crossing, and so Alpha Company's 3rd Platoon was left here to secure that landing zone in the middle of the wide-open paddy.

After crossing a ravine on its southern edge, Alpha Company's 1st, 2nd, and 4th Platoons, along with their command group, skirted their way around the palm tree laden hamlet cautiously, wheeling clock-wise around its western edge, surprised that they had not yet taken fire. As they made their way around the village toward their blocking position on the north side, they did not enter it as this would be Charlie Company's task. However, they did encounter a small group of approximately six huts in their path, about five hundred meters west of the main part of the village. They searched these few huts, finding nothing but the usual women, children, and old men. It was unusually neat and tidy, however, with the earthen floors of the huts packed smooth. Matulac would find a cave, into which he threw a white phosphorus grenade. It turned out to be empty. Suspecting the wells had false bottoms, with enemy munitions stored beneath, he blew them up as well. Nothing but water.

After moving through the small group of huts, Alpha Company waded through more rice paddies, eventually arriving at their blocking position at the base of a long-rising foothill about three hundred yards northwest of the main part of the village. They would wait here for several minutes while Charlie Company was en route by helicopter. At approximately 9:00 AM, the first wave of Charlie Company's platoons arrived at LZ Springfield, on the opposite (south) side of the village. As they descended onto the LZ secured by Alpha Company's 3rd Platoon, all hell broke loose. Machine gun fire erupted from the village at the choppers carrying Charlie Company's soldiers. In 3rd Platoon, Bobby Hansen recalls that as Charlie Company's soldiers leapt into the rice paddy, he couldn't even hear the machine gun fire beneath the thumping of the choppers, but could see by the expressions on their faces that they were getting shot at. 3rd Platoon's job had been to secure that landing zone and they thought they had. The enemy, however, had waited for the choppers to arrive before revealing himself.

CPT Bernard Grady, Bravo Company's Executive Officer when they arrived in-country, had been recently put in command of the 5/7th's Charlie Company. He described his own experience during this battle in his book, *On The Tiger's Back*. As he and the other Charlie Company troopers came in under heavy fire from machine guns on the south edge of the village, the choppers banked evasively to the right and ascended, and he and his soldiers were forced to jump out at a height approaching twenty feet. With only the earthen dikes providing cover and a wide expanse to cross, Charlie Company began their advance northward toward the village. For the time being, Alpha Company's 3rd Platoon would be fighting the enemy alongside Charlie Company.

From the opposite side, Alpha Company now moved back toward the village. Machine gun fire was now coming at them from its northwest corner. Along with the others, Matulac lay in the water, taking cover behind an earthen dike. Water erupted approximately fifty yards in front of him, toward the village. He watched as another round splashed about ten yards closer, then another only five yards in front of him. As he searched for the sniper's position, he recalled reading something about the battle that occurred in the Ia Drang Valley the year prior, and how many snipers had taken up positions in trees. Marvin Bierschbach would also recall sniper fire coming from the trees. There just happened to be a row of trees just outside the north-facing side of the village. From left to right, Matulac began firing rounds into each one. After putting a few rounds into the fourth tree, he saw a rifle drop. He shot a few more rounds into the same tree and watched a body fall to the ground.

As the battle heated up, throngs of civilians could be seen evacuating the village. Charlie Company's platoons struggled to make their way across the rice paddy as the village was pummeled by artillery and mortars. Many of Charlie Company's men already lay wounded in the muddy water. Fighting continued with little movement for about twenty minutes until two bombers descended from distant clouds to their south. While manning the radio, Barrow could hear the drone of their engines growing louder as they approached. Troopers in both Charlie and Alpha Companies had marked their positions with smoke and were taking cover in the muddy water behind the dikes. The jets ripped the enemy positions with their guns while dropping several canisters of napalm in and about the village. Radio operator Royce Barrow could see green tracer rounds shooting up at the bombers from the village. He watched in awe as the bombs dropped, shaking the earth and sending ripples through the muddy water he was immersed in. A third jet would arrive just as Charlie Company was preparing to assault the village. Both of its bombs would land tragically short, directly on top of one of Charlie Company's platoons. Those who were just outside the blast zone would feel the intense thermal wave flash across their skin while watching mud, helmets and men sent flying in all directions before them. Amidst confusion, screaming, and the smell of napalm, like that of burnt rubber and gasoline, they would wade through the paddies to find that one of their troopers had been killed instantly and several others were severely burned. Barrow was manning the battalion net (the radio used to communicate with the battalion command post) at the time, and recalls hearing Charlie Company's angry commander yelling over the radio, "Drop the bombs on the damn village, not us!"

CPT Grady stayed on the radio, desperately trying to call off the final jet, but to no avail. The jet banked for its final run at the village, then dropped its last canister of napalm. It landed at the base of a palm tree on the south side of the hamlet. It impacted the arc of the tree in such a way that it was, in effect, lobbed back out into the paddy. The giant oblong canister wobbled through the air above the troopers for several seconds before belly-flopping in the water in front of them, splashing many of them with mud, each of whom would have been incinerated had it detonated. Fortunately, it did not.

Once the heaviest of the fighting had subsided, 3rd Platoon began making its way by foot to rejoin the rest of Alpha Company. As they approached, CPT Wise rose up along with Rankin, his radio operator, and prepared the company to move out. He had radioed the platoon leaders, advising that they were preparing to move through the village, and was still holding the handset that was attached to the radio on Rankin's back. As his radio operator followed, CPT Wise took only two steps before a sniper's bullet meant for him struck Rankin in the head. He was killed instantly.

Now that it had been sufficiently pummeled, both Alpha and Charlie Companies advanced through the destroyed village. The huts were thoroughly cleared, the enemy's weapons gathered, their dead counted. Little was left of the hamlet aside from burning huts, bodies, and parts thereof. Marvin Bierschbach still recalls the bodies of NVA snipers hanging from trees surrounding the village. In a suicide mission of sorts, they had apparently tied themselves in place, so they could keep firing their weapons as long as possible, even after being shot by the Americans.

Shortly thereafter, Alpha Company's 3rd Platoon was airlifted to a position far to the northeast of the village to prevent the escape of any remaining enemy fighters. At 1:17 PM from Camp Hammond, Bravo Company was flown in to take over 3rd Platoon's blocking position and 3rd

Platoon was lifted back to join the rest of the company. Meanwhile, Alpha Company's 1st, 2nd, and 4th Platoons and the command group were making their way back to their original blocking position, at the base of the long-rising hill where they had initially taken fire. Martin Quinn and a few others carried Rankin's body, now wrapped in a poncho, through water in the paddies that was chest-high at times. He remarked how at this point in the day, exhausted from the fighting, the feeling that gripped him was one of numbness rather than fear.

As 3rd Platoon descended near Alpha Company's position, Matulac watched green tracers from a distant tree line rip through the choppers as 3rd Platoon's soldiers jumped into the muck below. The choppers seemed to be magnets for enemy bullets, and again they were under fire. They were supposed to have jumped out from the side away from the enemy, but Bobby Hansen recalls jumping out the wrong side of the chopper with his ammo bearer. Matulac would recall the sight of a 3rd Platoon ammo bearer who wore thick glasses, Brian Ravese, trying to link up with his machine gunner after being separated during their landing. Sergeants were yelling at him to go one way then the other, as he desperately struggled through the muck. Geysers of mud and water exploded all around him as he splashed through the waist-high water, changing direction several times before making it to a safer position.

During a lull in the fighting, they resumed their advance up the hill. Will, Bobby Hansen, and two others now carried Rankin's body with them. As they reached the top, a dust-off chopper descended. Again, bullets erupted from somewhere in a distant tree line. Ammunition was hastily unloaded as Rankin and several wounded were loaded onto the chopper under fire. As my dad remembers, part of Rankin's skull was missing.

Meanwhile, at LZ English, a chopper that had been preparing to bring Alpha Company's Thanksgiving dinner was quickly re-purposed as men threw out the food containers in exchange for crates of ammunition.

On the other side of the hill lay another rice paddy, and beyond that, a dense jungle ascending into the mountains. Alpha Company's 1st Platoon passed through the command group to lead the way down the opposite side of the hill and through the rice paddy. Matulac would recall one of their sergeants saying to his platoon leader, "I see something moving in the brush up there." The lieutenant told him to keep moving, however. They had waded nearly all the way through the paddy when a barrage of automatic fire exploded from the dense forest before them. In an L-shaped ambush of sorts, machine guns to both their left and front were unleashed at the same time. Several troopers in the lead squad of 1st Platoon fell immediately. A scene of chaos ensued as fighting resumed. 1SG Potter walked out into the rice paddy to retrieve one of the wounded and drag him back to the command group where Matulac and the company medic were located. The seemingly bullet-proof First Sergeant then went back out for another of their wounded.

The enemy was pursued by Charlie Company through the jungle for approximately two miles to another small village near Bravo Company's blocking position. Eight of the enemy were taken prisoner here. According to CPT Grady's account, they had shed their uniforms and weapons, but were determined to be North Vietnamese regulars. Under intense interrogation by the ARVN interpreters, none would give up where they had hidden their weapons.

When it was over, several of Alpha Company's troopers had been cut down in the rice paddies. Six had been killed, and many more were wounded. Will, Bierschbach, and a handful of others had used their own ponchos to cover their bodies. One was that of Gene Cross's grade school friend, SP/4 Donald Duncan, the supply clerk who had volunteered to join Alpha Company in the field just a week before. Also among the dead were SP/4s Robert Cain from Sumter, South Carolina and Russell Ferrebee from West Union, West Virginia, the two guys who had been sent to the field for pissing someone off at base camp. It had been their first combat operation. Also killed, were PFCs Thomas Erickson from Saint Paul, Minnesota and Malcolm Brouhard from Wheatfield, Indiana. Brouhard had just gotten married prior to departing for Vietnam. As a recent replacement, he had been with Alpha Company for exactly one month. Private-2 (PV2) Eddie Lopez was the Charlie Company trooper killed by the friendly napalm airstrike.

The dead were still lying in the field, and Matulac had called in another dust-off. As the chopper circled above, the pilot radioed Matulac, asking when their last contact was. "About an hour ago," Matulac advised. The pilot wouldn't come in, he was spooked and for good reason. The dead would have to wait. He was still carrying Rankin's radio, which was covered in blood. He tried to find someone else to take it, but to no avail. Until this point, even during the tragic events of the 19th, he had managed to keep his emotions under control. He found a stream in which he attempted to wash off the blood and brain matter from his friend's radio. This is when he broke down and cried.

Night was approaching, as were rain clouds. Alpha and Charlie Companies remained at the scene for the night to stack bodies and mop up, while Bravo was airlifted to Camp Hammond along with the prisoners. A torrential rain soon commenced. Alpha Company set up their patrol base at the edge of the valley. As Bobby Hansen recalls, no sooner had they dug their foxholes, than they became completely filled with water.

It was dark now, but it was still Thanksgiving, and a chopper was en route to Alpha Company with the day's special meal. Although there was a shortage of both body bags for the dead and ponchos for the living, there would be no shortage of food for the day's survivors. Box-shaped "mermite" containers filled with turkey, gravy, mashed potatoes, cranberry sauce, and all the fixings were on board. As the chopper approached, it was taken under fire by snipers. The crew began hastily throwing down the insulated containers of food as they hovered approximately twelve feet from the ground. As the containers dropped, Robert Wagner, who had been wounded on both October 4th and November 19th, desperately tried to keep them from falling over and spilling. Except for some spilled gravy, he succeeded in his effort. After the sniper fire was suppressed, the chopper eventually landed and the rest of the food was unloaded. Matulac informed the pilot that he needed to take out their dead. The pilot explained that he couldn't because they would have to decontaminate the chopper before hauling more food, and that takes hours. Matulac was desperate and near tears, and threatening to have his men open fire on his chopper if he refused. Finally, the pilot obliged, and the dead were loaded on. There was more than enough food to go around. As the rain poured down on the skytroopers and their meal, it's hard to say what they may have given thanks for.

Royce Barrow remembers this meal vividly. They hadn't eaten anything all day and he was starving - and yet, he couldn't eat. His best friend was dead. He still owed him the sixty dollars he'd borrowed from him for R&R. Years later, he would remark of Donald Rankin, "He was liked by everybody, not an enemy in the world, and he was my best friend and good buddy." CPT Wise had lost a man who he considered a damn good radio operator, but more importantly, a good friend. They had become close in the months since he had chosen him as one of his radio operators. One soldier remarked how it seemed like something inside CPT Wise broke on that day when Rankin was killed.

Sanchez was still at LZ English. That afternoon, he had watched a medevac chopper land with the first of Alpha Company's dead and wounded. Frantic activity commenced about the field hospital, a large tent surrounded by sandbags. Another Alpha Company soldier was there with him. Through the rain and mud, they rode a mechanical mule, a small utility vehicle, toward the medical tent. As they approached, they saw a row of jungle boots in the mud outside the tent. Next to the boots were helmets filled with rainwater and blood, some with bullet holes in them. Sanchez's fellow Alpha Company soldier was in tears. Amidst the blood and agony of the scene inside the hospital, they saw many familiar faces.

SP/5 Richard Cantale was an Alpha Company soldier who also happened to be at LZ English that day. He may have been the same soldier that Sanchez now recalls riding in the mule with, but I can't be sure. In any case, he was there at the field hospital and wrote this letter home about the events of that day. It was featured in the book, *Dear America: Letters Home From Vietnam*, edited by Bernard Edelman and published by W.W. Norton & Co. The book was later made into an HBO documentary.

25 Nov 66

Hello dear folks:

It's going to be hard for me to write this, but maybe it will make me feel better.

Yesterday after our big dinner my company was hit out in the field while looking for VC. We got the word that one boy was killed and six wounded. So the doctor, medics and the captain I work for went over to the hospital to see the boys when they came in and see how they were.

The first sergeant came in the tent and told me to go over to the hospital and tell the captain that six more KIAs were coming in. When I got there, they asked if anyone from A Co was there. I just happened to be there, so they told me that they needed someone to identify a boy they just brought in from my company. He was very bad, they said. So I went into the tent. There on the table was the boy. His face was all cut up and blood all over it. His mouth was open, his eyes were both open. He was a mess. I couldn't really identify him.

So I went outside while they went through his stuff. They found his ID card and dog tags. I went in, and they told me his name – Rankin. I cried, "No, God it can't be." But sure enough, after looking at his bloody face again I could see it was him. It really hit me hard because he was one of the nicest guys around. He was one of my good friends. No other KIA or WIA hit me like that. I knew most of them, but his was the first body I ever saw and, being my friend, it was too much. After I left the place, I sat down and cried. I couldn't stop it. I don't think I ever cried so much in my life. I can still see his face now. I will never forget it.

Today the heavens cried for him. It started raining at noon today and has now finally just stopped after 10 hours of the hardest rain I have ever seen.

Love,

Richard

In his own book, *1966 The Year of the Horse*, Robert Powers of Bravo Company would recall guarding one of the wounded NVA soldiers they had taken to Camp Hammond that night. Lying on the ground, the wounded enemy prisoner was visibly in pain. Powers covered him with his poncho, and waited for some military intelligence officer to arrive and pick up the prisoner. His small act of compassion was acknowledged with a pained nod of the prisoner's head. Their own Thanksgiving meal had just arrived, and Powers would struggle to eat as much of it as he could before the rain washed it all off his paper plate. By the time he had finished, the prisoner was dead.

Back in the field, it was still raining as Alpha Company prepared to sleep in shifts on the night of Thanksgiving 1966. As Will and others had given up their only form of shelter to cover the dead, they consolidated whatever ponchos they had left. Under a makeshift tent of sorts, they huddled together as the downpour continued through the night. At about 3:00 AM, a shot rang out from within the company's perimeter. Bobby Hansen recalls hearing the shot followed by a scream of pain, and how he thought they were once again under fire. In fact, one of their new replacements had shot himself in the ankle, in hopes of being evacuated from the hell he now found himself in. His foot shattered, he was treated by the company medics, but the kid would have to wait until morning to be medevaced. Amidst the pouring rain, his cries of pain could be heard throughout the night as the men of Alpha Company tried to sleep, and so ended my dad's worst day in Vietnam.

27 Nov '66 - 32 weeks left

Dear Folks,

I am finally getting to write. I am just going to say I am in bad shape. Ain't been dry for almost a week and have very sore feet. Man, am I ever getting sick of this damn rain. I guess we're going back to base camp for a couple of months. You must know by now that I spent a night with Rod on one operation. Well, I am sending this letter now. Write more soon, and I will have plenty of time. I hope.

Will

Royce Barrow

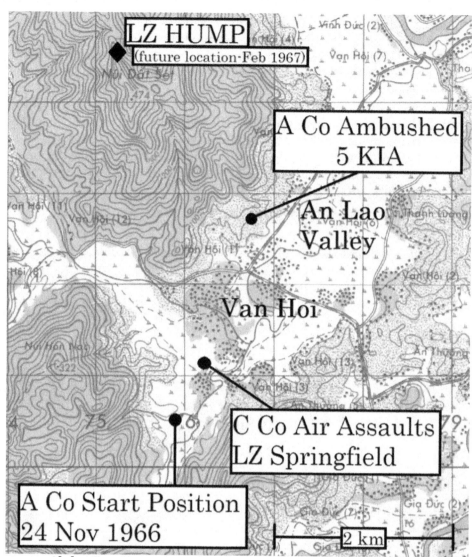

Alpha Company area of operation, Thanksgiving Day 1966

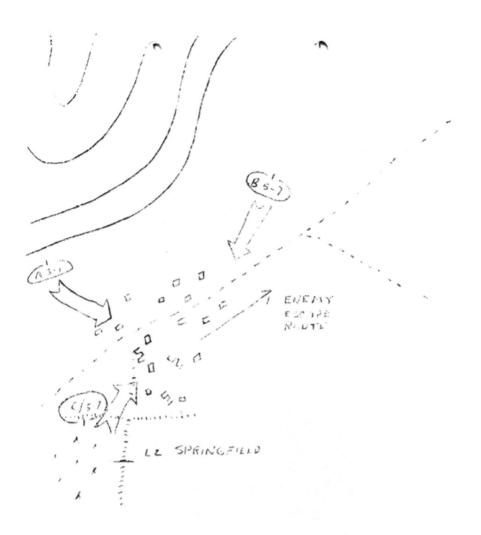

24 November 1966, Hand-drawn map of battle from 5/7th Cavalry Operations Summary

Thomas Erickson

Eddie Lopez

Donald Rankin

Robert Cain, Russell Ferrebee behind, photo by Robert Matulac

12

THE BEST DAY

How some people make a career out of the Army I'll never know.

Rain continued throughout the day after Thanksgiving. The battalion had planned to bring both Alpha and Charlie Companies back that day, but poor flying conditions prevented their extraction. Alpha Company would move a short distance up into the jungle-covered eastern side of Nui Dat Set Mountain, spending another night in the area. The next morning, on November 26th, they moved back down into the An Lao Valley and were airlifted back to Camp Hammond at 11:37 AM. Alpha Company would spend the rest of the month pulling security at Camp Hammond.

On December 1st, LTC Trevor Swett relinquished command of the 5/7th Cav to LTC Charles Canham. Like many, he had fallen ill and could no longer continue as commander. LTC Swett had commanded the battalion since their days at Fort Carson when they were still the 1/11th Mechanized Infantry. Battalion commanders in Vietnam were not typically held in high regard by the lower ranks, but LTC Swett was an exception to this. Barry Gallagher said he was like a father figure to many of them, recalling how there was "not a dry eye in the formation" during the change of command ceremony.

Also on December 1st, Bravo Company would lose six of its troopers in the Kim Son Valley, in a confrontation known as the Battle of Phu Huu II. One of the six, PFC Lewis Albanese, would be awarded the Medal of Honor.

3 Dec '66 – 32 weeks left

Dear Folks,

Sorry for not writing as often as I should. We were pretty busy last Nov. Well, we're about two or three days from going back to An Khe. Right now I feel pretty sick. First time since I've been to Viet Nam. I should be alright tomorrow. We've been here at Camp Hammond for almost a week. Rodney is the head of his company? Maybe his platoon, but not his company. He is pretty sharp. I know, he can carry a radio. Yeah, I got a letter from Don Mc Ilquham the other day, and you know he is going to be in the very same place I am right now, Camp Hammond.

Hey guess what, the Bloomer High School Freshmen Homemakers of America girls sent me a shoe box full of goodie bars. Man, I thought that was really nice of them. Now I'll have to write a thank you letter back. What makes you think I can play that recording you sent? I think I can play it on this guy's tape recorder. Someone just told me I got a box from a church. Guess I'll just go way up to the C.P. tent and get it. It's about supper time now and I only ate a can of fruit so far today. Wondering how

I (or we) get beer? The Army sells it, beer from the states, and the Vietnamese have beer of their own.

Hey, how about finding out how much tax money a person pays on a new car. Thinking about buying one while over here, it's all tax-free.

So Mike got lost while hunting, ha ha ha! Well, you still have a chance to get one yet. I should be getting a letter from Larry Geissler soon, telling me about his buck.

R&R is 5 days, but it takes about 10 for travel and getting ready and all. I hope I go in Jan. or Feb. All I am looking forward to is rest, the Bob Hope show, and some good times. Also, a lot of letters to catch up on.

Will

7 Dec '66 – 31 weeks left

Dear Folks,

And now we are very sure of going back to An Khe. A 5% chance of going. This makes the 999th rumor so far. Well, that's about all for now. Forgot to say that ½ of the company is sick or something.

So long,

Will

Now into the first week in December 1966, Alpha Company and the rest of the battalion had spent three straight months in the field. At this point, their clothing was coming apart at the seams and literally falling off their bodies. At 10:45 AM on December 8th, the exhausted battle-weary battalion began its journey back to An Khe in a convoy of trucks for their rotation of Camp Radcliff defense. The base defense mission was officially named Operation Dazzlem, but was more commonly referred to simply as Green Line Duty.

In the time since they had left An Khe for the field in September, engineers had built wooden barracks for the battalion. They had also constructed a mess facility. Named Hare Hall, a small three-foot-tall cement pedestal and plaque had been placed just outside its entrance in memory of Bravo Company's fallen First Sergeant, Dayton Hare, who was killed along with twelve others, including Alpha Company's Michael Stoflet and medic Bill Garcia, near the village of Quang Ngheim on November 1st.

Although a drastic improvement from their life in the field, An Khe was not exactly Club Med. The troopers worked long hours in the oppressive heat, guarding posts and manning towers along the perimeter, as well as performing other base duties, such as burning cans of waste from their wooden outhouses. Also during their time at An Khe, teams of soldiers would again be sent out on night patrols, just as they had during their stay in August. At least they could come back into base camp in the morning. Compared to what they had endured in the field, their standard of living here seemed out of this world. Observing the routines of those who worked primarily on base, it became clear to many of the infantrymen that they had chosen the wrong profession.

In the Army, those in the artillery, armor, and other *combat arms* branches will often refer to those in *non-combat arms* branches, such as supply or signal, as POGs, short for "People Other than Grunts". It should be noted however, that infantrymen consider anyone not in the infantry to be POGs, combat arms or not. In Vietnam, they had a more colorful acronym: REMFs, for Rear Echelon something or other. You can probably guess what the last two letters stood for. They envied the easy life they lived compared to their own, all while earning the same paycheck. Despite the contempt some may have had for the REMFs, most would have traded places with them in a heartbeat if given the chance.

For the first time in months, the soldiers of the 5/7th Cav would get hot showers, cold beer, and three hot meals per day. Battalion supply would provide them all with new fatigues, for most, their first in over two months. There was even a chapel where movies were shown at night, and a clubhouse where soldiers could get beer. Freshly showered, and in his new fatigues, Will lay on his bunk. He left his boots off, however, allowing his throbbing and deteriorated feet to luxuriate in the air. Despite all their ruck marches at Fort Carson, nothing could have prepared their feet for the conditions they had endured. Most were in dismal shape now, and infected with God knows what. Some soldiers, such as Leonard Pelullo, were suffering from trench foot or jungle rot, as it was called. Pelullo lay on his bunk, letting his feet heal while enjoying the Christmas cookies sent by his family in Philadelphia. He listened to a tape recording of his mom, dad, and sister that they had mailed to him. "I'm not going to die here," he said to his buddy Joe Sanchez afterward. "Of course," Sanchez replied, "we're going to both make it home together." Al Patrillo had a tape recorder as well, and recorded a message to send to his own family.

Quinn related a memory of Will during that same time at An Khe, remarkably similar to Joe Sanchez's memory of Leonard Pelullo. "I can still see it in my mind as if it were yesterday... Will was sitting barefoot on his footlocker at An Khe in December, in those new wooden barracks we only saw maybe once or twice." He continued, "He was writing a letter home and I could tell he was depressed and upset about something, can't remember what it was about, maybe it was just the holidays. Unusual for him because he was usually the one cheering us up. I just said, *Don't worry man, it'll all work out.*" Quinn also recalled how there were certain tents at base camp occupied by soldiers who "liked to party" and how he could smell the pot smoke a mile away.

They would soon get the opportunity to visit the town of An Khe, and would be briefed of the off-base rules by their NCOs. As venereal disease was a big problem, each soldier was required to purchase a condom in order to receive a day pass. Taking a military bus into town, they would find lots of little shops and restaurants, most of them catering to the American soldiers. Though small for a city, only a few blocks long in each direction, it bustled with activity. Some stores would sell military "surplus" supplies and uniforms. While soldiers of the 5/7th Cav had a hell of a time getting clean fatigues in the field, the shopkeepers in An Khe seemed to have plenty. There were also numerous laundry shops, where rear echelon soldiers could send their uniforms to be cleaned, pressed and starched. The shop owners would provide free beer for the soldiers as they waited for their laundry. Universally remembered about the town of An Khe, were the ever-present throngs of children in the street, many offering to shine boots, some simply begging, while others tried to pimp their "sisters" to the visiting Americans. In the seventeen months that U.S. forces had been stationed near the city, its economy had become quite dependent on American money. There was a red-light district nicknamed Sin City, comprised of a series of small buildings with bars in front. It was cordoned off from the rest of the town, and an MP would check passes at the gate. This is where local girls would meet and entertain the soldiers.

After three months of constant tropical dampness, many of the company's soldiers were sick. Despite the big orange pills they took every Monday, many had contracted malaria, including Guy McNay. He was also still recovering from being shot in the shoulder on November 19th.

A few days into their stay, Will fell ill with some kind of food poisoning, or perhaps, dysentery. Whatever it was, it is remembered as the worst case of food poisoning in his life. A cold sweat set in and his face turned pale and clammy. His bowels churned, then loosened violently. To further complicate matters, his new platoon sergeant who had replaced SSG Burtis, SSG Hayslip was sending him on a night patrol. Fortunately, SGT Fulford, the leader of his four-man mortar team intervened, insisting that he stay back and recover. Will was forever thankful for this. So much so, that it's one of the few things from his experience that he still remembers half a century later. Fulford had actually been drafted into the Army along with the handful of rank-and-file soldiers assigned to him. The draftees appreciated having an NCO who was one of their own. He was an all-around good guy and friend to Will.

As Operation Thayer II continued in the field, the 5/7th Cav assumed responsibility for the defense of base camp from December 10th 1966 through February 3rd 1967. In doing so, a revised defense plan was implemented and several new LZs and security outposts would need to be developed around the outskirts of the camp, with access roads leading to each.

13 Dec '66 – 30 weeks left

Dear Mike,

Now that we're back at An Khe, I am getting my teeth checked. Sure is nice here. First night I slept without waking up once in 3 good months. Last night was the first time I seen a T.V. since I left the states. Qui Nhon is where they broadcast the programs. First time I heard music in over 2 months, too. Man, was it nice to listen to the radio again. Turned the knob, "click" and music. Wow, outa' sight, heaven. They've got a movie screen set up here too, which I seen a couple of nights ago. They had a beer tent and sold hamburgers and hot dogs. Even though it rained and we got pretty wet, we enjoyed it. Been doing a little card playing. Won $30.50, which should break me just about even. Gen. Norton is coming to visit us. Lately, we've been on perimeter guard, me and all the platoon. We have the Division dump grounds nearby and it stinks. Now that we've got it easy and there's not much to do, they've turned us into an engineer company. They've got us building roads, believe it or not. We're supposed to be having a little rest. Yeah, on the first day we worked ½ the day and the road wasn't even supposed to be there. How some people make a career out of the Army I'll never know.

Yes, we've been going on all kinds of operations before we came back to camp. Some real bad ones, too. B Co. went on one, got about 60 V.C.'s killed and 6 of their own people killed. Captured about 100 pieces of equipment. They made a big haul. Altogether they killed 154, and A Co. killed 83, C Co. about 60 or so, and D Co. 15 V.C.'s. It was Rod's platoon that killed the 15, too. A guy in B Co. I knew, got the highest medal award, Congressional Medal of Honor. Wounded 3 times, saved two of his buddies and killed 8 V.C.'s, runs out of ammo and charges the V.C. bunker with a .45 pistol and he gets killed. Well, now he's a hero. Wish he was more careful. Some of our guys didn't make it either. I doubt if you saw us in battle 24 Nov. They might have mentioned it. Well, we should be taking it pretty cool here for a while.

A bunch of our guys got transferred to 1st of the 7th Cav. I wish now that I would have been sent there. The guys say it's great. Over in our mortar platoon, we have 5 leaders and 6 workers. The rest of us are either sick or transferred. I'd sure hate to leave my friends, but I can't stand these big heads. Say, I am going to try and be a door gunner on a helicopter in Feb. Chances are very slim that I'll get it.

So, no deer this year and you got yourself lost, ha! I really had a good laugh when Ma said that. It won't be the first time, either. Basketball is well in season now. How I wish I could handle the basketball. I can just get that feeling of the ball at my fingertips and "swish" through the net it goes. So you have a team going this year. I know it ought to be great.

...Today's the 14th. The dentist hardly did any work on my teeth. They were in good shape and I only brushed my teeth 3-4 times. Did you get my Christmas card? Don't believe that card, the only chapel we ever had was an open field with cases of C-Rations for an altar. Actually, we never came close to a church. Now I am listening to this radio station. I can't see how any station can be so darn messed up. They play rock and roll 1-5 in the morning, and this horrible classic jazz when we're just starting to take it easy in the evening. What can you expect when it's an Army station. Our sergeant swears my radio was on 24 hours a day back at Fort Carson,

Colorado. You know, I heard the Packers and Colts game. What a game. Be sure and mention the game to Larry Schindler, he sticks up for the Colts. Are the champion of the NFL and the champion of the AFL playing each other in the Super Bowl? Be some game alright.

I hope we get to town one of these darn days. Our C.O. is so chicken to let us go. We might make it to the town of An Khe before Christmas. If I do get there, I'll buy some Christmas packages to send home. I hope. I bet we don't get to see the Bob Hope show. Something will come up, I know. I heard Phyllis Diller is coming with him, man that ought to be a real pair.

Hey tell me, are you going to learn taxidermy? I know you're busy, but how about dad? He's taking it easy this time of year. I got a Christmas card and letter from Mrs. Henning, she says I should write more often to my folks. I know, that was just in Nov., it won't happen again. Hey, ask Dad if Larry Schindler paid everything on my car. No doubt he has.

Wish I had a little drink here. The last time, Rod and I really hung one on. And I got sicker than a dog that night, whew. I guess I don't have any worries for a while. A little roof over my head, keeping dry and warm, and plenty of candy, everyone is healthy and the cows are giving plenty of milk. So now I'm going to sack out, or listen to some crummy music, or write another letter. So next time let me know how school's going and send a picture of your modern art, OK? Oh well, Fuzzy Face, ha! How do you like my electric razor?

Easy Sailing (so far),

Will

An Khe, (left to right) Quinn, Elmer, King, Anderson, Fulford

An Khe, (left to right) King, Anderson, Fulford, Bierschbach

An Khe, Amundson (left) and Bright (right), photos by Wilbur Bowe

Troops trading goods from their Lifeline packs, photo by Wilbur Bowe

Leonard Pelullo recovering from jungle rot, photo by Joe Sanchez

Shops in An Khe

Nunez outside the bars of An Khe, photo by Wilbur Bowe

Sin City, An Khe, photo by Wilbur Bowe

At one point during their stay at An Khe, Joe Sanchez was ordered to guard a buck sergeant from Alpha Company who had gone AWOL. "I'm not going back out there, I need to go home to my wife," he said to Sanchez. He had gone off base and made his way to the airport in Saigon. He was planning to buy a ticket and board an airplane back to the states, until he saw that he would have to get through MPs who were posted en route to the airfield. He tried to run but was caught by the MPs. Sanchez just felt sorry for him.

Later in December, several soldiers from Alpha Company were transferred to the 1/7th and 2/7th Cavs. Among them was Sanchez, who protested to SGT Chapman, wanting not to leave his buddies. Many however, felt that the 5/7th, being the new battalion in the brigade, had been singled out for the worst of the action in order to "get their share" as it were. Going to one of the other battalions might be a good thing. Thinking the same, SGT Chapman threatened to kick his ass if Sanchez didn't leave as ordered. The 2/7th Cav however, would prove to be no safer than serving in the 5/7th. In his own book written in 2007, *True Blue, A Tale of the Enemy Within*, Sanchez describes the events of his twentieth birthday in January 1967 while serving as radio operator for a forward observer in the 2/7th Cav:

After dinner, I settled back and started a letter to my mother. I told her all the stuff that sons in a tight place make up to tell mothers they don't want to upset: how nice the weather there was, how quiet things were at camp, how safe I felt – anything that would make her think I wasn't really in harm's way. Just as I was writing this, I looked up and saw helicopters in the direction we had just been brought in from. They were firing ARA (aerial rocket artillery) rounds at the target below.

"Saddle up," we were told. There was enemy activity and we'd have to go back out in the field. The lift choppers arrived. We were put aboard, four to six per chopper. They took us back to where we had been that afternoon and put us off near a village. We were to search out a suspected VC camp. The enemy was nowhere to be seen – and that's the worst kind. We heard him, though, and pretty soon we were likely to feel him.

Sporadic automatic fire broke out whenever a patrol got too near the enemy's position, but so far, nothing had really popped. Fred Booker, our forward observer and a British Army veteran, was on an embankment. Then some of us started down the embankment. Our platoon leader went ahead. I stepped aside to let him pass. Some of the group followed him, and I wound up picking up the rear.

That was when the grenade came at us and exploded. I remember calling out in Spanish, "Oh, my God, Mom, I've been shot in the head," and thinking I was going to die. I felt burning sensations in my arms, legs, groin. Then everything went from fast to slow-motion. I saw Booker tumble down the embankment to my right, and to me, he looked like a store mannequin floating in some Twilight Zone. Even the leaves blown off the trees seemed like they were hovering instead of falling. I was coughing from the battle smoke, and then it seemed like I couldn't move at all. I suppose my brain had shut down from the concussion – that's what they said later. All I know is I was aware of everything, but my body wasn't moving or responding at all, and it was only when I heard the ringing in my ears I realized I was actually coming back to life.

In fact, I could move now. I managed to limp out of the crater I was in and I saw a trooper on the ground taking cover. Then someone came up to me, forced me to the ground, and called for a medic. As I was lying on my back being treated, I could see jets flying overhead and bombing the area near us. It turned out four of us had been seriously wounded by shrapnel, and that we had killed four Viet Cong in return, but I didn't know that yet. I don't remember much about being airlifted out except that the medevac pilot gave me a thumbs-up.

·········

In the middle of December, Martin Quinn took his chance to go to Hong Kong for his week-long R&R. He found that jewelry was cheap there, and so he bought himself a gold star-set ring with a couple of diamonds for thirty-five dollars.

Meanwhile, on December 19th Will's mortar platoon was transported to a short and wide, densely forested hilltop about a half-mile from An Khe's perimeter. The 5/7th Cav's new base defense plan called for many new fortified outposts to be established along an expansive ring around An

Khe's perimeter. As part of this plan, their job was to clear the area and establish a new security outpost on the hill, to be dubbed LZ John. This involved cutting brush and blowing up trees as the entire hilltop needed to be cleared for visibility. For protection, they would also begin constructing rudimentary bunkers made of earth and sandbags. His buddy Rodney Henning and about a dozen others from Delta Company would join Will's mortar platoon in establishing the outpost. Their work on LZ John would continue for nearly two months. The only enemy encountered during this time would be a seven-foot boa constrictor, killed by CPT Wise's M-16 during one of his visits to the outpost.

21 Dec '66 – 29 weeks left

Dear Folks,

Been working quite hard lately. On a small hill and building bunkers and clearing the land surrounding it. We worked almost two days before they realized that they needed a dozer. It's just outside the base camp. It's still quite safe and we'll be here 'til late Jan. or so. It sure seems nice not to be humping and to be safe. I got a package from Larry Geissler and he had a coconut in it. We got a charge out of it. As if we don't get enough of these in this country, ha!

I wonder if we'll have Christmas Day off. Seriously, the way things have been going, it'll be the first day we've ever gotten off work in Viet Nam. We won't see the Bob Hope show for sure, and I counted on it so much. It's so close to Christmas and it seems like it's the middle of July. Wish the Hennings a Merry Christmas for me. We were only given a few cards to send. Hope you all have a fine Christmas and New Year.

Will

Christmas Eve would be spent in the rain on LZ John. On Christmas Day however, Will, Elmer, and two others were allowed to go back to An Khe for Christmas dinner. The bane of many an infantryman in the Central Highlands, ringworm was now infesting the feet of both Will and Elmer. Contrary to its name, ringworm is not actually a worm or parasite of any kind. Thriving in the constant dampness of the infantryman's feet during the monsoon season, it's actually a fungus that forms a ring shape. On the day after Christmas, they both took the opportunity to get treated at the aid station at An Khe. Afterward, they were sent to the dispensary to pick up their supply of ointment. They were to report back to the company immediately after picking up their medicine. Instead, they decided to go see Bob Hope's show. On a large stage, he was walking about with his golf club in hand. They managed to get close enough to hear his jokes. Other celebrities were there to entertain the troops, including Phyllis Diller, Anita Bryant, and Vic Damone. Later, the Korean Kittens, Joey Heatherton, and some other Playboy models showed up to remind the boys what they were fighting for. They couldn't have picked a better time to have a ringworm infection. When the show ended that evening, they finally made it back to the company. For not reporting back when they were supposed to, they were put on KP duty for the rest of the night. Given what their normal day at the office was like, they didn't really consider this much of a punishment. It was well worth it for an afternoon of laughter and pretty girls. To this day it is remembered as my dad's best day in Vietnam.

27 Dec '66 – 29 weeks left

Dear Folks,

Rod and I spent Christmas Eve together, listening to Christmas carols on my radio. It was rainy out and mud ankle deep, and we felt so damn lousy that night. I sometimes get so damn sick of this damn Army, words can't describe. But guess what? I had a wonderful time on Christmas. Five of us were allowed to go into base camp on Christmas, so I had my one foot checked and I had ringworm on it. Doc gave me a 48-hour profile.

Christmas dinner was out of this world, very good. Oh yes, and I seen the Bob Hope show while I was back there. Ended up on K.P. 'cause Elmer and I sneaked off. Oh well, it was worth it by far. Man, did we have a blast there. That Hope is really crazy. And Phyllis Diller, wow, she was out-of-sight, and the other sexy women, wow. Say, don't forget we'll be on T.V. Jan. 18th, so don't miss it. I had a wonderful time, far more than I expected. With a lot of luck and a bit of pull. And poor Rod is out with our platoon, helping us build this outpost. About 11-12 with him, helping us. He came in on Christmas Day, also with us. Man, was he ever pissed 'cause Elmer and I had a profile, ha ha!

No I am not in the fields, those are other units of the 1st Cavalry. We, 5-7th, are next to An Khe. Our platoon is outside of camp, about a ½ mile. We are building a well-fortified outpost. On this outpost, we have about 35 guys. We built a bunker, took 3 days to build and it fell down 3 times. We killed a big, over 7-foot long Boa Constrictor. And by the way, our chapel is the ground we stand on, any place, 'cause we don't have one yet.

I was very happy I received your very much liked wrist watch. I liked it very, very much. It is so useful. Also, your box of candy and the tape recording. I played it on this recorder I borrowed, and you guys sound so nervous, ha ha! But it was so wonderful to hear you all. I am going to tape over it and send it back so you can hear me.

I am sure I can buy a car before I leave Viet Nam. I can save 7-8 hundred dollars and maybe another 7 percent discount later next year. Please let me know if you're getting all my letters. I know I wrote 4 in Dec. now, and one to Mike. And Mike is getting a little swift. Better cool his heels a little. No doubt you're getting my letters late because of all this Christmas mail.

Will

Joey Heatherton at the Bob Hope Show, source unknown

Photo of Royce Barrow in the Plainsville Tennessean

Dec-Jan 1966, LZ John near An Khe, Marvin Bierschbach with snake

Quinn returned from his R&R just after Christmas. Now that most of the work had been done, he found an unusually relaxed atmosphere about the new outpost manned by Will and their buddies in 4th Platoon. It was mostly boring on the outpost but relatively safe, and they would pass the time playing cards, clowning and taking pictures, and sometimes throwing around an old football. They normally didn't carry their air mattresses in the field. They were staying put for a while however, so Will and Quinn decided to bring them out for their stay at the outpost, LZ John. They even set up some empty ammo crates to make themselves makeshift beds. Patrillo's turn for R&R was coming up in about a week, and so Quinn lent him his camera to take on his own trip to Hong Kong.

During their Christmas "break" of sorts, other platoons in Alpha Company were assigned to guard duty in several of the towers surrounding An Khe. Meanwhile, Robert Matulac manned the radio in the rear battalion TOC (Tactical Operations Center). Here, he relates his own Christmas story:

Alpha Company had about five towers to man. One night, I got a call at the battalion TOC. One of the towers was asking if they could fire a few rounds toward the interior of the camp. "No!" I said. They radioed back and said that a tiger was circling around the base of their tower and was looking up at them. I attempted to get permission for them but was denied. So, I just told the tower to make sure they aimed straight downward at the tiger. Meanwhile, SFC Hall, the platoon sergeant in charge of 1st Platoon, was in his tent cleaning his M-16. It was in pieces when he was bumped by someone on the outside of his tent. Angry that this knucklehead, whoever he was, had made him drop the parts of his M-16, SFC Hall cussed and gave him a hard elbow jab. However, instead of getting an apology, he got a large growl from a tiger! Hall scrambled to get his weapon together and by the time he reassembled his rifle, the tiger had disappeared into the brush. So that ends our Christmas story.

On December 27th, the nightmare scenario everyone feared had befallen another company of the 1st Air Cavalry. At 1:00 AM, an artillery firebase in the Kim Son Valley had been attacked and nearly overrun by North Vietnamese regulars. Two batteries of artillerymen occupied the firebase known as LZ Bird at the time of the attack. Severely undermanned, infantrymen of Charlie Company, 1/12th Cav were providing security. They had just received many new replacements in their company, most of whom had not seen combat. Just under two hundred Americans occupied the firebase that night. In the darkness, a force of approximately seven hundred NVA troops had crept up to within fifteen feet of their perimeter. With supporting automatic weapons emplaced and in range, the enemy attacked en masse. Several howitzer positions were defended to their death by the artillerymen, only to be overrun by the swarming enemy troops. All communications were knocked out, and brutal hand to hand fighting ensued. Illumination rounds were fired from LZ Pony, a nearby firebase in the Kim Son Valley, bathing the combatants in an eerie light.

LZ Bird would have been completely obliterated if not for a young lieutenant and sergeant. Shouting at their own troops to get down, 1LT John Piper and SSG Robert Underwood managed to load and fire two 105mm Beehive rounds directly at the enemy troops engulfing the firebase. The Beehive is an artillery round that releases over eight thousand burning steel flechettes that fly like insects in all directions. It is specifically designed for stopping mass infantry attacks. In a *Soldier of Fortune* story written by Al Hemmingway, radio operator SP/4 Clint Houston was quoted, "It was so haunting. It screeched like a million bees. I saw a big hole in their ranks, and then I heard screaming. Those bodies were ripped to shreds. Then they fired again with the same results. The assault was stopped dead in its tracks."

With the assistance of ARA gunships, the enemy was beaten back after two hours of hellish combat. The rising sun revealed a grizzly scene as the bodies of nearly thirty Americans and over two hundred North Vietnamese lay strewn about the outpost. Sixty-seven Americans had been wounded. Charlie and Delta Companies of the 1/8th Cav were flown in to relieve the beleaguered defenders and pursue the fleeing enemy into the surrounding mountains.

Shortly thereafter, certain elements of the 5/7th Cav were flown in from An Khe to join the pursuit of the enemy. It is unclear exactly which elements were sent. Bravo Company's Robert Powers recalled having his Christmas "break" cut short when he and others were sent in, and Alpha Company's Robert Matulac recalls arriving at LZ Bird himself, as dusk set in on the evening after the attack:

When we got to the LZ it looked like a disaster area. The gun emplacements were still there, but of course, no guns or equipment. Just paper, scraps of cloth, some empty boxes, some barbed wire. A couple of us went down to the lower emplacements and we found flechettes scattered on the ground. There was an eerie atmosphere to imagine the battle that was fought there.

As he and the others milled about the abandoned outpost preparing to move out, Matulac noticed some small pieces of paper with handwriting on them. He bent down to pick one of them up and brushed off the dirt. Dated 27 December, it was a half-finished letter written by a soldier who was there, presumably on guard when the attack came. Minutes later, they marched out into the surrounding jungle in search of Charlie. Many soldiers of the 5/7th Cav had themselves pulled security at LZ Bird on several occasions, and each of them had patrolled through the surrounding Kim Son Valley in mid-October. The fear of a massive night attack was something that had lurked in the mind of many a young skytrooper. They now knew it could happen.

Aftermath of LZ Bird, photo by Robert Matulac

13
THE OUTPOST

No, I don't need a toothbrush, but tell Doc I have one and thanks anyway.

As December ended, work continued on LZ John, their new outpost near An Khe. Aside from heating C-Rations, C-4 was also used for blowing up trees. In order to make the C-4 explode rather than just burn, a remote detonator was required. The block-like charges of C-4 were strapped to the tree trunk with the detonator in place. An extra charge had been set on what was a particularly large stump, so Will decided to move back and take cover farther away. The charges went off before he could get back down, sending a rock into the upper part of his arm. It felt like he'd been hit in the arm by a hammer. Though not bleeding profusely, a significant amount of blood was running down his arm. Lodged deep inside his muscle, the rock was not coming out. He was taken back to An Khe for treatment. X-rays were taken to show where the rock was located. The doctor dug around in his arm for a while, but it could not be removed. The wound was disinfected and eventually sewn back up, leaving the rock inside. As a kid, I remember being able to feel the rock that was still stuck in my dad's arm. He would spend a week in the hospital and another week on light duty as his wound healed. The only action he would miss while recovering was clearing more trees and filling more sandbags.

30 Dec '66 – 28 weeks left

Dear Folks,

I lucked out again. I got a small stone in my upper right arm. So this means, I guess, about a two-week profile. You see, I just got back with my platoon yesterday and I was helping our sergeant blow this stump with C-4. We were using a large amount this time and I told my sergeant I was really going to split to the other end of our position. Well, he set it off before I got there and a rock hit me behind the bicep. It didn't hurt too bad, but the medic out there said I better go in and have it x-rayed. So I did, and they found a rock. Then they operated on my arm, but couldn't get the stone. Have to wait now, until it heals. It was really neat, worked two hours and bingo, back into camp again. Rod is still out there working on our position and he didn't like to see me go in. "Out here 2 hours and going back in again," he says, "he's just faking, sergeant." I told him I had to get another fifth of whiskey. He told me you wrote him a letter and he wanted me to tell you, to tell his folks, that he's still working his ass off at our position and hasn't had much time for writing.

There's something funny about this Army. In civilian life, the last thing you want is to get hurt. In the Army, you're always hoping to get hurt. I am in a building that looks like Louie Simon's shed, but it's only 15 feet high. On a nice bunk with a soft mattress and 2 clean white sheets. Breakfast and dinner served in bed. This is what I like, wow. I hope later I can get a pass for An Khe. Packers should be playing either today or tomorrow. Ought to be on the radio, for sure. Got some wild music on the radio now. It's almost 5 o'clock by your most splendid watch.

This is a news clipping of Bob Hope. He said in his show that Dean Martin would be elected to distribute liquor licenses and Mickey Rooney would distribute marriage licenses. He also said in Saigon, the best things in life are not free, but off limits, ha!

I know it isn't going to rain, now that I have a good roof over my head. And don't forget to tell Mrs. Henning that our platoon is putting Rod to work building bunkers and chopping logs in 6 inches of mud, ha! Poor guy. Oh well, today marks the end of another year, another letter. Doc says I'll be here a few more days. So wish the Green Bay Packers well and not me. I like it here too well, despite the needles.

So long, from a cool, clean, dry and comfortable son named,

Will

1 Jan '67 – 28 weeks left

Dear Folks,

Did we ever have a wild time last night, Kool-Aid and cookies. It's noon now and this very minute everyone back home is having a rip-roaring time. Doc said he was going to sew me up tomorrow. The Packers are going to play today. I'll hear it on the radio by tape tomorrow. I started on a good paperback book, "The Mob's Man". It's really interesting. Tells about his start into playing hooky and small robberies, and then into a big syndicate. All I've been doing is just reading, writing, and listening to the radio. The radio here plays 5 to 8-year-old rock and roll music as if it were on the top 50. Music, I know will be part of my life. I am even going to have a tape recorder in my car, and someday a stereo set. You know, music is so important to me, I think I'd rather have that than a new car, or tractor, or T.V. set. Makes you feel real good. Maybe because I'd been away from it for such a long time.

I wrote Rod a letter. Telling him how nice it is here and that the work best be done when I get out of the hospital. I can see old sergeant swearing a blue streak at me, ha!

Read that Larry Geissler got into a little wreck again. I got the newspaper you sent. Man, I was surprised to see the N.F.O. back in the show again. Hope I can make it home when the action begins. Dad, do you belong to it yet? If not, best get with the program.

Got some Vietnamese kids here and with New Year's noise makers. They're cute. Act like kids in the U.S. I'm still glad I'm here under a roof. It's been raining, raining, raining, raining, etc., etc. I doubt if the sun shined in the past 2 weeks.

Man, I tell you one thing that ain't going to bother me anymore, and that's work. I bet I could work 16 hours and stay up half of the night and it wouldn't be hard. Be my usual schedule. When I get back into The World again, I believe I'll work in Minneapolis as a machinist and do a little night school as a construction welder. I'm sure that's what I'd like to do. Farming for me, I guess, is too much to manage.

Seen a show last night that reminded me of Larry Geissler. It was about a guy on his first date. Was it ever funny. How about you guys going to learn taxidermy. Be a good hobby, you know.

Full of needle holes,

Will

8 Jan '67 – 27 weeks left

Dear Folks,

Great news, getting out of Viet Nam in 6 days. 6 more paydays that is. Ha Ha. Dirty trick, huh? Three years ago today I was in High School. Two years ago today I left for Chicago. The 12th will be one year that I graduated Basic Training. And today I sit with a sore arm in Viet Nam.

No I am not alive, just a ghost writing. Now the last time we had a battle where A-5-7 and I got a little scared was Thanksgiving Day. Now we probably will not see any action until March. Like Rod and D Company today are going on a little patrol. Nothing more dangerous than you crossing the highway to get the mail. So don't get worried.

Got out of the hospital yesterday, sorry to say. But, I've got up until 14 Jan. on light duty. I tried to hit the town today, but First Sergeant Potter says if you've got a profile, no pass. OK with me, but the minute I am put on detail, I'm heading toward town. Got a haircut today, been over two months I think. I wonder how long they would have let me go. The surprise of the year, the mess hall is having coffee breaks now. Twice a day, ha! I almost dropped my teeth. Had a few beers with Fred Brodosi at the Club last night. I talked with quite a few guys that got hit with this artillery unit the V.C.s attacked at LZ Bird. Heard a rumor that the 25th Infantry Division is going to Bong Son. Allen Simon belongs to the 25th. Fred said our chaplain is looking for an assistant. Man, if I could only get that job, my worries would be over. I'll have to look into this. Never wanted to be one before, but it's a different story now. Seen enough killing. Going to see about being a gunner on a chopper, too. It's a slim chance about getting out of the infantry. What do I got to lose?

I met up with Elmer yesterday and I asked him about the many word phrases I learned in "The Mob's Man" like a "heist job", "he has been burned", the "numbers racket" and "policy racket". You see, he lives in Harlem, the roughest section in New York. But Elmer is the finest guy I know from New York. He is going to get the pictures of the Bob Hope show, *a week or so from now and he'll give me some or all of the negatives, and I can send them to you.*

Say, I am quite sure now I am going to Hong Kong the middle of Feb. Just had to talk to the right guy.

Larry Schindler has $60 left to pay on my car yet, right? I only got one letter from him so far. So he's getting married in Feb. Oh boy!

I was looking over some old letters here and throwing them out to clean my old bag out. Ma was wondering if I kept all my letters. Well, how many will a steel helmet hold? Only a few. Been looking through these old pictures you sent long ago. They sure all look nice. My nights sure must be restful 'cause I never dreamt so much about home before, as I did the past week. Is it dry here, you asked. Are you kidding? I can't remember when it ever was dry. In the back of our mess hall it is 10 times worse than our pig pen. By the way, our mess hall is really beautiful. Tin roof, wooden walls, and cement floor and venial tables. Say, if you can get a small flag of Wisconsin, send it over. We'll hang it up in our mess hall, OK?

How you feeling Ma? Did you get an operation on your stomach? I hope it's OK. Yeah, I know we can eat meat on Friday. Besides, we're allowed to eat meat 'cause we're in the service. No, I don't need a toothbrush, but tell Doc I have one and thanks anyway. What do you mean you can't send food? Rained so much the ants and bugs all jumped in their boats and moved out.

I'll get a camera someday. Or say, if you want to see if you can buy me a 16mm pocket size camera, that is what you can send me for my birthday. Should clean my radio. Been almost a year now that I've had it, guard it with my life. No finer radio around. Guys here have great big radios and can only get one American station, ha! I listened to all of these football games too. Read that the Super Bowl ain't going to be so great. Nobody's going to see it 'cause it's being played neither in Green Bay nor Kansas stadiums. Biggest game of the year and nobody sees it, what a joke. Well, I am closing out. Supper time. Mike better get to writing!

Easy,

Will

14 Jan '67 – 27 Weeks Left

Dear Mike,

Got myself an office job. For tonight that is. CQ runner, and stay up all night long and don't do a darn thing. Man, this is the life of Riley. Ain't much for news 'cause I am getting over like a fat rat and clean as an onion, like the guys always say. I don't have anything to say really. Just finding out if I can still type. Only place I get my shoes dirty is from coming from the Mess Hall and into the bar to have a few beers. Only bar in the Division that doesn't have liquor. Oh well!

Sergeant Fulford is making coffee so we stay awake I guess. My faithful radio helps too. It's starting to go on the blink once in a while. Sergeant is all wrapped up in a sleeping bag to keep warm. You know how I was thinking about going on a hike when deer hunting comes this year? Take our sleeping bags and camp out until we get one.

Almost 1:30 a.m. and getting sleepy. Think of what I'll be doing a month from now on R&R.

Well, I found out about being a door-gunner on a chopper. You almost have to re-up in the Army to get that job. Guess I'll settle for being a ground-pounder.

Just heard that Queens N.Y. got a big fire going. Got a couple buddies from there.

All these cooks and office clerks have rain suits and buckle boots. Today is the first time in over 3 months that I wore underwear. It took too long for your clothes to dry if you had underwear on, so we threw them away.

How's the basketball going, win any games? Ma says you dig on art. Send me some of your work. Say, if I get to town I am going to buy you all a little present. I am sure I'll get there soon. I hope. I gotta close up. I just can't think of anything else to type about. And be sure you type back, I mean write back, Fuzzy Face.

White Collar Worker,

CAPTAIN: WILL E. BOWE

On January 15th, as the Green Bay Packers defeated the Kansas City Chiefs in the first Super Bowl in history, Will returned to LZ John where they would continue to improve fortifications and visibility for nearly another month. It was his twenty-second birthday. Patrillo had just returned from his R&R. Apparently, he'd had a great time and told them about a girl he met and stayed with in Hong Kong. While there, he had taken a photo of this girl and mailed it back to Quinn. He had forgotten to bring back Quinn's camera. "Don't worry," Patrillo said, "it's in my duffel bag. I'll get it for you next time we're in base camp."

During one afternoon of their stay at LZ John, a helicopter carrying a well-known celebrity landed at their outpost. The celebrity was a blonde bombshell, the stunning model and actress, Chris Noel. She could be heard regularly on the Armed Forces Network radio station playing songs and offering words of encouragement for the servicemen in Vietnam. She was the Allies' alternative to Hanoi Hannah, the North Vietnamese disc jockey who broadcast American rock and roll for the troops, accompanied by communist propaganda.

At this point, Noel had been in Vietnam longer than most of the soldiers. She would still be there, entertaining the troops for years to come. Unlike most celebrities who could only visit the most secure bases like An Khe or Cam Ranh, she would routinely visit these remote outposts all over

South Vietnam. The North Vietnamese had placed a ten thousand dollar bounty on her head. Over the course of her tours in Vietnam, she experienced mortar attacks, sniper fire, and her helicopter nearly crashed on more than one occasion. The following is an excerpt from her IMDb biography:

A tour of a VA hospital in 1965 altered her destiny, forever. Based on her minor pin-up celebrity, Chris impulsively auditioned for the Armed Forces Network (AFN) and started hosting her own radio show for the GIs in Vietnam, frequently flying to that war-torn country and visiting remote areas considered too risky for Bob Hope's USO shows. She became the GIs' favorite sexy radio and show personality while putting her own life on the line. As it turned out, Vietnam veterans would become her prime mission and life's work long after the war.

Will and his buddies gathered around to meet Chris. She would take photos with the boys, sign pictures, and joke around with them. Fifty years later, there's one thing my dad remembers most about this day. It was the first time he saw a girl in a mini skirt.

19 Jan '67 – 26 weeks left

Dear Folks,

Well, back to the grind. My arm feels fine. Had K.P. the first day off profile. So now I am back to filling sandbags. My dear radio went haywire, the speaker is loose. Am I ever lonely without it.

Suppose to have been out in the fields again, but I guess we ain't going until later. We might be attached to another unit to guard an R&R center in Viet Nam. Maybe, just a rumor. We're getting "bad news" Burtis back again. He was our old platoon sergeant that got shot 3 months ago. He came out the other day and showed us his wound and the bullet that hit him. Got shot twice. Actually, he and I get along pretty good. He put me in for E-4 last Oct, but when he got shot and Hayslip took over, well my name got wiped off the list and right now I'm again at the bottom. Bound to make it pretty soon.

Had about a dozen guys come by our position yesterday. Neatly dressed and clean, and we asked them how long they've been here and they said 6 days. What, 6 days? Ha ha ha! Man, did it make us feel good. They're 6 days and we're 6 months. Oh boy.

I sent a few negatives for Quinn to have developed, and so send back as soon as you get the pictures from them. These are color. These other guys want to have the negatives as soon as you send them back. This is the place we've been the last month and a half. We just got there and were still neat and clean. Our company commander, A.J. Wise, sitting on the sandbags with a rifle and a mean grin.

I got a letter from Joanne today, and Alice Yohnk and the Hennings, and your letter with those downright good pictures. Hey, why do you write the names on the back of them pictures? Don't you think I know who they are, gee! I hear it is very cold, like 30 below. I don't think I want to be home now, ha! Guess you were a little worried around Dec 12th.

Received your birthday cake the other day. Lit the candles and sang happy birthday. First time I can remember that happening. They kept asking, when are you going to open "our" package, sure glad we got "our" package today. So I opened our package and shared our cake. We all liked it, and it was in fine shape. Frosting was a little off, but still OK. Larry Geissler sent me a package, also on the same day. Yes, I got Mike's candy bars long ago. I think I told you I did. Yes, I have the raincoat still. The rainy season, I believe should soon end. No, Ricky Mitchell isn't stretching it when he said it reached 135 degrees. Especially down towards Saigon. It's about 110 in the sun today and it's January. Hasn't been this warm for a long time.

You know I could call home from base camp and it wouldn't cost anything. But I'd have to be in base camp, and would have to wait my turn. And when you talk you have to say "over," and then I would talk, and when I am through I'd say "over," and etc. I'll wait 'til I get to Hong Kong, but I hear it costs $50 for 3 minutes. I'll just reverse the charges, OK? Ha! …I just heard that a call home would only be about $9 for 3 minutes, that's just how fast rumors change. People here are like old women, gossiping.

I seen this guy about a new car. He says 20 percent off, but the only cars I can buy are Chrysler made cars. You can order a '68 also. I was looking at this Charger or maybe a GT.

So Charlie Rubenzer is re-enlisting. Wow, what a nut. Either that or he has a hell of a good job. Re-enlisting is worse than being shot at. If I don't get out of the Army when I leave here, I could bring natural death on basic trainees. Man, what a time that would be. It's 5 after 4 and you're not off the sack yet? Didn't shave, huh? Buckle not shiny, boots not polished? I can see it now. In fact, I hope I don't get discharged from over here. Got to get even for what they done to me and a little more. Give them a 10 min break, they expect 5, and you only give them 3. Inspecting rifles, dirty front sight, dirty rear sight, dirty bore. What you trying to do, grow a garden?

Mike done alright in the Klondike Race. He'd better write and tell me about it. What's Larry Schindler doing for work, still on the farm? That darn Dad must have folded this one letter 'cause I gave up trying to re-fold it. Ought to write a few more letters so he can get in practice. Well, ain't much else to say. I listened to the whole Packer game. Really whooped them.

Will

LZ John near An Khe, (left to right) Lussier, Fulford, Quinn, Anderson, Bierschbach, King, Bowe, sandbag bunker on far right

Martin Quinn (above) and A.J. Wise at LZ John, photos by Wilbur Bowe

(left to right) Will Bowe and Gerald Anderson

(left to right) Martin Quinn and Will Bowe

Photo of Chris Noel in the Cavalair

14

RUMORS
(Operation Pershing)

I will not use my grade or position to attain pleasure, profit, or personal safety.
-Creed of the Non-commissioned Officer

1 Feb '67 – 24 weeks left

Folks,

We're heading back into the fields this week. I don't know what they have in mind for us. So far, rumors have been good. Went rappelling out of a helicopter the other day. Jumping out as high as our big silo is back home. One guy nearly busted the rope. When I seen that messed up rope, well it didn't give me very much confidence.

Been getting "Boo-Coo" mail lately. That means a lot of mail. Got a birthday package from Mrs. Henning yesterday. Wow, it sure looks cold in them pictures you sent. Connie Geissler told me you got a little high at Ken Nelson's party, which you didn't mention at all. Ahem! Your camera you sent me is already here, but I have to get back to camp to get it. We'll be going in tomorrow, pretty sure we will. And then if Rod is back we'll try to soak up some beer. Even if he isn't there, I am still going to. I am dying for a dozen or two cans of beer. Can't hardly wait to get that camera. Thank you a whole lot.

Will

Alpha Company prepared for its next mission as February began. The company had changed dramatically due to both hostile casualties and sickness, as well as all the transfers. Many replacements had been assigned, and most had yet to see combat. Will's mortar crew was still together with Bierschbach, Bronson, and SGT Fulford leading their team. Also in early February, after spending nearly three months in the hospital recovering from being shot in the shoulder on November 19th, machine gunner Guy McNay (Juggy) returned to the field. Some strings had been pulled by a family member within the military to get him assigned to a duty station outside Vietnam. Instead, he requested to return to Alpha Company.

On February 3rd 1967, the 2/8th Cav took over the base defense mission from the 5/7th. Reconsolidating, the battalion prepared to rejoin Operation Thayer II, still in progress. Early the next morning, Alpha Company was flown in C-7A Caribou transport planes to LZ Two Bits, an established firebase west of Highway 1, just north of the Song Lai Giang River. From LZ Two Bits, both Alpha and Delta Companies would then be air assaulted to the peak of Nui Dat Set Mountain. At an elevation of over 1,500 feet, Nui Dat Set overlooked the An Lao Valley, and the village of Van Hoi where they had fought on Thanksgiving Day. The mountaintop was soon to become an established firebase, but for now it was undeveloped and densely forested, with no place for choppers to land. Therefore, at 10:06 AM Delta Company would rappel onto the new landing zone, dubbed LZ Hump, from Hueys that hovered above the treetops. Alpha Company would follow in Chinooks, descending onto the mountaintop using rope ladders. Martin Quinn was particularly aggravated by the time he got down the rope ladder as the guy above him was in a hurry and kept stepping on his hands. I've seen many photos of 1st Air Cavalry soldiers getting on and off Chinooks in this way. I have to say the whole thing seems like a really bad idea. With forty pounds of gear, climbing down a rope ladder attached to a helicopter hovering forty feet from the ground, it's hard not to imagine all the things that could go wrong. Apparently, CPT Wise felt the same way about this particular method of air assault. Actually, he said it was about the stupidest thing they were ever made to do. In rappelling, the soldiers could get to the ground fast, but climbing down on rope ladders was very slow and the Chinook presented a big target for the enemy. He felt his men were put in an unnecessarily vulnerable situation, and he expressed his concerns to the battalion. The soldiers under his command would never again make an air assault of this kind.

The troopers would spend the day clearing the mountaintop. Will would take several pictures here, as he had just received a new camera from home. He recalls a fellow named Royce Barrow teaching him how to best operate the new gadget. As soon as enough space had been cleared, a Sky Crane lowered a dozer to assist in their effort and a company of engineers was also flown in. As more area was cleared, Chinooks began lowering howitzers, along with their associated ammunition and artillerymen of the 1st Battalion, 19th Artillery. Like giant flying hippos, more Chinooks descended from the sky in a constant stream, dropping their loads onto the mountaintop and flying off again while the artillerymen began the herculean task of setting up the new firebase. Eventually the battalion forward command post would also be flown onto LZ Hump. From here, one company would guard the firebase as the others patrolled the surrounding mountains and valleys.

6 Feb '67 – 24 weeks left

Dear Folks,

Now we're on this high-ass hill for the next few weeks, LZ Hump. I got your camera. It's almost too good to have out here in the "boon-docks". I've taken quite a few pictures. I keep it in my ammo pouch and wrapped in plastic. So when I go on R&R, I'll send home the film. It's getting quite dark and I'll have to close. Working quite hard clearing the hill.

Will

7 Feb '67 – Morning now, log ship hasn't come in yet. Elmer gave me this picture he took of me Dec 26th. He and I on our way to the Hope show.

Soldiers rappelling from Huey, photo by Marvin Bierschbach

Vernon (Roy) Garrett after rappelling onto and cutting out a new LZ

AP Photo/Catherine Leroy - Helicopters, supposed to be able to land on a dime, found they couldn't touch down in narrow hilltops in the central Vietnam coastlands, Feb. 1967, but that didn't stop them from delivering right on the money. Engineers blasted drop areas clear and the giant Chinook choppers dropped their soldiers of the 5th Battalion, 7th Cavalry regiment to participate in operation Thayer II some 15 miles southwest of Bong Son, which is some 300 miles northeast of Saigon.

Alpha Company descending by ladder from Chinook, photo by Bill Purdy

Sling-loading supplies at LZ Hump, photo courtesy of 5/7th Cav Association

Sky Crane lowers dozer (top) and Chinook sling-loads howitzer and ammunition (bottom) at LZ Hump, photos by Wilbur Bowe

(top left to right) Patrillo, Quinn, Brodosi, (bottom) Patrillo wearing fedora, photos by Wilbur Bowe

(sitting left to right) Abegglen, Lussier, Hayslip, Patrillo (far back with hat)

LZ Hump, (left to right) Elmer, Lussier, Bowe, Patrillo

LZ Hump, soldiers stand in line for hot chow, photo by Wilbur Bowe

Alpha Company medic "Doc" resting in bomb crater, photo by Wilbur Bowe

(above) 1LT Leo Patrick, dozer clearing ground, (below) view from LZ Hump, photos by Wilbur Bowe

Soon it was back to search and destroy as Alpha Company and others moved down the mountain and into the An Lao Valley. Returning to their primary job of hunting the enemy in the wilderness, the soldiers had changed significantly since their first mission in the jungles along Highway 19 back in September. They had learned much since that time only five months ago when they were fresh off the boat and eager for action. They had learned the dark reality of this new war and how to, if not grieve, at least cope with the loss of their friends, how to put one foot in front of the other and endure. They had learned how to survive on C-Rations and cigarettes, and how to most efficiently heat instant coffee in the field. They had become familiar with the smell of death, learned that it was often random, and how dead bodies were heavy. They were hardened and savvy, their reflexes finely tuned. Like cats on the prowl, they now stepped through the depths of the deepest dark forest, quietly and stealthily. Their eyes darting back and forth, then up and down, in a pattern of sorts, scanning for trip wires, Bouncing Betties and mines, their ears strained to hear the slightest rustling of a nearby enemy. Well, this is how it started at least, whenever returning to the patrol after a break, or shortly after a firefight. But after a time, the hyper-alertness combined with the physical exertion and the extreme heat would become exhausting. Despite their best efforts, they would inevitably lose their edge and revert to clumsily plodding like mules. After descending the mountain, they returned to the village of Van Hoi where they would bivouac for the night. One Viet Cong would be killed by Alpha Company in the vicinity of the village. That same day, a Bravo Company soldier would be medevaced following a violent encounter with a water buffalo in the valley.

"The water buffalo didn't seem to like us," said Bill Purdy, recalling his own close encounter. While slogging through a flooded valley, one water buffalo in particular became agitated and started charging toward Purdy. It was a fight-or-flight situation and there was nowhere for him to go. He had a full clip of twenty rounds in his M-16, so he started firing his rifle at the beast. With his clip half empty, the buffalo was still charging hard. He may have been wondering just what kind of medal was awarded to soldiers wounded by angry water buffaloes. By now, nearly everyone in his 2nd Platoon was unloading on the animal. The buffalo eventually collapsed and splashed in the water only a few feet from where Purdy stood.

For the next week, each of the companies would continue patrols around LZ Hump, down in the An Lao Valley and its surrounding mountains. Each of the companies would make frequent contact with the enemy, taking sniper fire at times, but would not be attacked in force. It was readily apparent that there had been a lot of enemy activity in the area. Each day the companies of the 5/7th Cav would find abandoned bunkers, tunnels, hastily dug graves, punji stake pits, numerous caches with over three thousand pounds of rice, and a variety of booby-traps and weapons. Also found in an abandoned bunker complex, was a twenty-inch thick stack of enemy documents. Amidst these documents was found a photograph of a captured U.S. Navy pilot and a photocopy of his ID card. At 6:03 PM on February 7th, Delta Company would find a human skeleton amidst several half-dug foxholes on a jungle-covered mountainside. After days of searching and destroying in and around the An Lao Valley, on February 9th Alpha Company was lifted back up to LZ Hump to take its turn at guarding the outpost for the remainder of the operation. During their week spent operating out of LZ Hump, the battalion would count eleven enemy killed and three wounded, while capturing three prisoners. The week would also see nine of the battalion's men wounded in action, mostly from mines, punji stakes, and a few who were shot by snipers. There was but one fatality during this week, when a soldier from Delta Company was killed while searching a hut down in the village of Van Hoi on February 4th.

As his letters suggest, Will had become good friends with Rodney Henning, his hometown Army buddy that he'd met while reporting for induction in October of 1965. Their mothers also became friends with each other and were constantly exchanging information. They were always asking their sons where the other one was and what they were doing. No doubt they were both scared to death for them. Assigned to the 5/7th's Delta Company, Henning's platoon was designated a Long-Range Reconnaissance Patrol platoon, or LRRP. Now in the early months of 1967, they were led by the 5/7th Cav's former Intelligence Officer, the tall, good-looking and competent CPT Walt Swain. He had recently been transferred and put in command of Henning's Delta Company. Swain had long yearned for a company command, and would quickly earn his men's respect and admiration.

As LRRPs, Rodney Henning and his platoon were routinely sent on missions that required stealth, which prohibited air assaults directly onto their objectives. This required them to move farther and deeper into enemy territory by foot, enduring longer periods of time without helicopter support. The idea was for the LLRP to find the enemy units, allowing regular elements to fix and finish those units. It didn't always work out that way, and these patrols would often find themselves in dangerous situations. Henning would often lead his formation as point man, and later would be promoted to radio operator. Point men and radio operators were known for their short life expectancies, but Henning would survive his stints in both jobs.

Henning's platoon had an especially harrowing adventure, lost in elephant grass while attempting to follow a creek bed. Night was approaching, as were approximately seven hundred Viet Cong. Woefully outnumbered, the platoon was yet undetected. They crouched in the six-foot-high grass, turned off their radio and remained silent, hoping the enemy would pass. The men of Henning's platoon sat with their backs to each other, rifles clutched at the ready, waiting to be stumbled upon. The Viet Cong were close enough to be heard talking to each other throughout the night. As usual, it began raining. They were concerned that light would reflect off their helmets, so they covered them with camo. It was a long, wet, sleepless night. The slightest movement or sound would bring death upon the entire platoon. It was the essence of fear, a study in just how still, and just how silent, a human can be, and for how long, when it's a matter of survival. I have to believe this was the longest night of their lives. By some miracle, the enemy had left by daybreak, and the platoon moved on.

During their tour, Henning was promoted to Staff Sergeant and placed in charge of his platoon. Along with his frequent brushes with death, he also had an unfortunate brush with some nasty punji stakes that ran through both his legs, while being fired upon by an enemy sniper. At one point, Henning would reach the end of his rope, quite literally. Rappelling from a helicopter during a mission, his rope turned out to be far too short. Either that, or the helicopter was hovering too high. In any case, he survived, but hurt his neck in the fall. He would be awarded the Purple Heart and sent to the hospital. As soon as he had recovered, he would be sent back out to join Delta Company in the field. As the result of another episode, Henning and two of his friends would be recommended for and awarded the Bronze Star with "V" Device many decades later, in 2006.

August 15th, 2006

In early January, 1967, members of D Company, 5th Battalion, 7th Cavalry, 1st Cavalry Division, Reconnaissance Platoon had set up an L-shaped ambush on a road near Bong Son, South Vietnam. About dusk, a figure, which appeared to be a person, was approaching the ambush. At once, the figure disappeared. With no desire to kill a civilian, SSG Bealer Caudill and two volunteers, Rodney Henning and Jimmie Dir, were sent to investigate what was going on. When they approached the place where the image disappeared, they were close enough to see someone raising a rifle. At this time the NVA soldier, Caudill, Henning and Dir fired their weapons at approximately the same time. They had killed the NVA soldier, captured his AK-47, gas mask, and other important documents. For risking being fired on in the dark by their own fellow soldiers, I am recommending them for the Bronze Star with "V" Device. The reason this recommendation is so late is because I, the Platoon Leader, came down with an illness and was sent to the hospital, and the Platoon Sergeant was wounded in a firefight shortly thereafter and taken to the hospital.

James D. Watson
Major (Ret)

LZ English, (left to right) Wilson, Rodney Henning, photo by Wilbur Bowe

10 Feb '67 – 23 weeks left

Dear Folks,

Everything's going smoothly so far. Got a bad cold and sore tooth. It hasn't rained since we've been here, but man has it been hot and I got a real nice tan. We're back to building bunkers and filling sandbags like we've been doing the past two months. Every 4 to 5 days a company comes in for about a day. Food has been quite good. Ice cream and chicken once in a while. We've been getting beer or a Coke the past 3 nights. One thing the Army really surprised me with is no more steel pots, only soft caps. I almost dropped my teeth. Heard Rod hurt his neck pretty bad and got a punji stake a while back.

Yes, Joanne told me she was expecting in June. I'll be an uncle 8 times. No, I wouldn't like my bedroom colored pink. My goodness, of all colors. But so long as it isn't Army green, doesn't matter to me, any color is fine.

Will

After his death, Matulac had written to Donald Rankin's mother and at times, they would correspond. The following is one of those correspondence.

11 Feb 67

Dear Mrs. Rankin,

I am very glad that my letter answered your questions. In reference to your query, Thanksgiving Day over here was the day before Thanksgiving back home.

I also want to thank you for the invitation to stop by and visit. If I am around that part of the country I will be sure to stop by and pay my respects. I showed your letter to everyone in the section, and they were quite interested in the postcard, and also were happy to hear from you. Donald always talked about his family and the country where he had lived, so I feel that I almost know all of his friends and family personally. If I can be of any more assistance to you, don't hesitate to write.

Sincerely,

Roberto Matulac

P.S. – We are now operating in the same area where Donald was hit. I am hoping we can even the score.

On February 11th, the battalion commenced movement to their next area of operation. As they departed LZ Hump, so ended Operation Thayer II. It had been the longest sustained operation of the 1st Air Cavalry Division since its arrival in Vietnam. 1,757 NVA and Viet Cong had been killed, at a cost of 242 American lives.

Kicking off Operation Pershing, late that afternoon each company was airlifted in waves from LZ Hump to LZ Santana. Following the rest of the battalion, Alpha Company lifted off at 5:05 PM, touching down at 6:15 PM. Dark clouds had been gathering that afternoon, and as Alpha Company arrived at LZ Santana the skies turned angry. The downpour was such that the battalion command post would not be able to make the final lift of the day, following Alpha Company as planned. There would be no cutting and clearing necessary this time, as LZ Santana sat atop a very dry, sparsely vegetated rocky hill approximately seven kilometers from the sea. Instead, the companies were immediately sent eastward down the hill, into the northern Bong Son plain. The terrain here was much the same as in Phu My. Compared to the highland areas of An Lao and Kim Son, it was much more densely populated here and villages seemed to be everywhere.

Operation Pershing would not officially commence until 12:00 AM on the 13th, as a truce of sorts was being held through the 12th, in observance of Tet, the Vietnamese New Year. Despite the supposed truce, there was no shortage of enemy contact as they moved through the Bong Son plain in preparation for the new operation. Scout ships in the area were drawing small arms fire, and each of the companies took some kind of enemy contact. There was more activity, and more of the enemy here than there had been in their previous area in An Lao. Each company would take a handful of prisoners on this day. Alpha Company would bivouac near the base of the long-rising rocky hill, atop which sat LZ Santana.

This time however, they would not stay together as a company. Rather, the platoons would remain spread out over two kilometers of both rice paddies and sweet potato fields along the base of the hill. It was part of a new strategy favored by their new battalion commander. Aside from frequent hit-and-run sniping and mortar attacks, the Viet Cong were known to only attack in force when they significantly outnumbered the Americans. As Matulac explained, the purpose was to actually draw such an attack, then envelope the enemy with nearby platoons. In other words, they were VC bait. Another new tactic employed during this time was the use of five-man reconnaissance teams from within each of the companies, sent ahead during patrols to detect the enemy, and in ambush positions at night. Each reconnaissance team's call sign was a different number "Custer" (Custer 1, Custer 2, etc.) and there were approximately nine of these teams within the battalion. Matulac related a time when one of these teams encountered the enemy:

One of our reconnaissance teams with SSG Coit and SP/4 Hirschuber, spotted a large group of NVA approaching their position. They hid in some elephant grass hoping the enemy would pass. However, the NVA surrounded the recon team and settled down. When the team called in the position of the NVA, they were asked where was the NVA in relation to their position, and if they were close by. The answer received on the radio was a whisper. "If you want to talk to one of them, I could give the handset to the closest guy."

Regarding these terrifying moments in the elephant grass, Jim Hirschuber would recall how he had to keep a certain button on the radio pressed down to keep it silent. He swore that he could hear his own heartbeat while waiting for the enemy to pass.

This particular rice paddy, where they had bivouacked on the night of the 12th, was terraced, formed in what could be described as a series of steps leading up to the rocky hillside. As it was now the dry season, the water wasn't as deep as it would have been in October or November, but it was still wet. Each platoon would stake out its own area, forming a line of sorts along the base of the hill, some along the rice paddies, others amidst the mounds of sweet potatoes.

This was determined to be the night that both my dad and Marvin Bierschbach recall spending the night in a rice paddy. Along with that night spent trying to sleep in a small cement building on their first operation, and the night spent trying to sleep on the side of an exceedingly steep hill, this was one of the few nights in particular that the two of them both remembered vividly. In the area where Bierschbach and Will were to set up, foxholes could not be dug, and they attempted to sleep on their backs along a narrow dike, taking great care to not roll over into the muck on either side. The dikes themselves were saturated with the stuff and it would ooze out of the dirt under the weight of their bodies and pool around them. In the darkness, Will could hear hushed cursing and grumbling as the others settled in. With the back half of his body soaked and the front half merely damp, he stared at the stars above and thought about what Bronson had said about him months earlier, how he never complained. Their commander, A.J. Wise would recall that his command group had set up amidst some sweet potato fields, further up toward the hill along with 1st Platoon.

At this time, Kenneth Rathyen had replaced Donald Rankin as radio operator for the company net. Royce Barrow still manned the battalion net radio. As night fell, in the very center of the perimeter formed around 1st Platoon and the command group, they dug out a foxhole next to a clump of trees where they would monitor their radios. When setting up for the night, they would also replace the regular antennae on each radio with an extra-long one to improve communications. CPT Wise checked on his men, then went to sleep for the night. He was among the few who actually used the inflatable sleeping mat. Barrow and Rathyen would take turns between sleeping and monitoring both the company and battalion radios. As Barrow recalls, the moon was about half-full. At 11:23 PM, Kenneth Rathyen heard shots fired in the distance. A call from 3rd Platoon came in on the company net informing him that they had just shot and killed a prisoner trying to escape.

The company had still suffered no fatalities since Thanksgiving. Along with the ending of the Tet Truce, so too would end their good fortune. The following was recorded in the battalion's daily staff journal on February 13th:

3:00 AM – Custer 6 to TOC: 10 minutes ago rifle shots started down the valley from my location, 3 to 4 shots fired 4 different times; will keep you informed; no estimated distance; Custer 6 believes the sounds to be echoes of artillery rounds firing over the valley and the sounds are traveling back through the valley to us.

TOC, or Tactical Operations Center, was just another name for the battalion command post.

Barrow awoke to commence his turn manning the radios. At 4:00 AM all companies and recon teams within the battalion reported their status as "green" meaning "all clear". After reporting Alpha Company's status, Barrow lit a cigarette, cupping it with his hand so as not to be seen. As he did this, he heard the sound of branches cracking from beyond the perimeter. Then a trip flare went up. He thought it was probably an animal or something, as that's what it usually turned out to be.

4:14 AM – A Co to TOC: Some action on my perimeter, may be an animal. Am checking it out now.

A moment later, he heard a grenade explode. It was said that Rocco was on watch when the attack came that night, and that he had fallen asleep. In 1st Platoon, he and Joe Sanchez's friend from Philadelphia, Leonard Pelullo, had dug their foxhole just down from where the command group was set up with the radios. That first grenade exploded in their foxhole, killing Pelullo. Following the explosion, Barrow looked up to see brilliant streams of green tracers coming at them from multiple positions in the darkness just outside their perimeter. They were under attack from approximately twenty Viet Cong who had stumbled upon their position, and fire was coming in all over the place. Barrow shouted, "we're under attack!" as he hit CPT Wise on the boot.

Wise recalls his forward observer who had been with them since their first mission, 1LT James Ulrich saying, "I've been hit, sir". He asked him where, and he said, "in the neck." Those were his last words. From Brecksville, Ohio, he was twenty-five years old. The enemy was just outside their lines and within range of their own hand grenades. To avoid giving away their positions, many of the troopers along the perimeter threw grenades rather than opening up with their rifles. Amidst the gunfire, 1SG Potter leapt to his feet while Barrow yelled, "Top, get down!"

"That son of a bitch shot me in the leg," 1SG Potter was heard to say. He had taken a round in his knee but would survive. At one point, Barrow looked up to see sparks mysteriously raining down on him from above, and he wondered what could be causing them.

Two more would be killed in the darkness before the fighting ended approximately ten minutes later. Among them was 4th Platoon's PFC Donnie Ward. From Pollocksville, North Carolina, he was twenty years old. Also killed, was SP/4 Carl Mueller, age twenty-one, from Covington, Kentucky. The deaths were a reminder to the soldiers of Alpha Company; it would still be a long tough fight to make it home alive.

4:26 AM – A Co to TOC: Activity has stopped, probing throughout perimeter from the east at 1st Platoon and company command post location; negative contact; we are getting illumination at this time.

1LT Ulrich's radio operator, Danny Garrity, began calling in illumination rounds, but the enemy had already slipped away and was nowhere to be seen. The illumination rounds revealed an eerie scene of grim-faced men tending to the wounded and the dead as their shadows swayed back and forth. In the darkness and with an unknown number of enemy in the area, the medevac would not come in. The company stayed on one hundred percent alert, which is to say that no one slept, for the rest of the night. Barrow returned to monitoring the radios.

The *Philadelphia Daily News* ran this article about Leonard Pelullo sometime after his death:

Memory Honored in a Pizza Parlor

"Lenny" Pelullo carried an old-fashioned silver certificate dollar bill in his wallet for years, recalled Vincent Tacconelli, a neighbor who operates a pizza parlor a few doors from the Pelullo home. When the young man received orders for Vietnam, Tacconelli warned him about carrying the currency into the war zone. "He was such a nice guy. We wanted to kid him a little bit," Tacconelli said. "We told Lenny if he was captured with the silver certificate, the Viet Cong would think it was a map and try him as a spy." So before leaving for Vietnam, Pelullo turned the currency over to him for safekeeping. Hearing news of Pelullo's death, Tacconelli tried to return the dollar to Pelullo's parents. They told him he should keep it, and since that day it has hung in a frame on the wall of his pizza parlor.

Pelullo was an altar boy at Mother of Divine Grace Roman Catholic Church and a 1963 graduate of Northeast Catholic High School. He was active in Port Richmond baseball and basketball leagues and worked for a lumber company before entering the Army in October 1965. The 21-year-old Private First Class, a machine gunner, was assigned to Company A of the 5th Battalion, 7th Cavalry, 1st Cavalry Division (Airmobile). Pelullo was killed on February 13, 1967, during a Viet Cong assault on a 1st Air Calvary company command post north of Bong Son in Binh Dinh Province.

Terraced rice paddy in foreground, photo by Wilbur Bowe

Leonard Pelullo

Donnie Ward

Carl Mueller

1LT James Ulrich

At first light, Alpha Company's soldiers surveyed the destruction. Barrow noticed that his extra-long radio antennae had been shot to hell. It was bent over and in pieces, held together only by its inner nylon cord. It then dawned on him, this is what had caused all those sparks to fly over his head during the attack. He would also find two enemy bullets lodged in the extra battery pack for their radios, and CPT Wise's sleeping mat had gone flat as a result of two more bullets. Their four dead were wrapped in ponchos and laid out in a neat row, awaiting the dust-off along with several wounded who sat nearby, solemnly smoking cigarettes. They would find but one dead Viet Cong just outside their perimeter. As Barrow recalls, he had been blown to bits by a hand grenade.

The medevac chopper arrived to take out their dead and wounded. As it lifted off and disappeared into the sky, they marched out into the Northern Bong Son plain along with the rest of the battalion, searching villages and taking prisoners.

Just after 6:00 AM, Bravo Company came under sniper fire, killing one of their own. At 8:50 AM the same morning, Charlie Company would find a cache of rice and kill two Viet Cong. At 9:00 AM Charlie Company reported picking up a female nurse with a Red Cross card and medical supplies. At 9:15 AM Custer 9 reported two Viet Cong captured when they smoked them out of a cave. At 9:17 AM Delta Company found approximately nine hundred pounds of rice. At 9:18 AM Bravo Company found a pair of sandals near a blood trail and footprints leading north. At 9:30 AM Delta Company captured two Viet Cong prisoners in a hut. At 9:35 AM Charlie Company would report finding approximately two thousand pounds of rice in a storage bin. And on and on it went throughout the day. The constant action was in stark contrast to all those days spent in the highlands in October, when they would often search for days without seeing the enemy. Here the enemy seemed to be everywhere, and much more apt to fight than before. At 11:05 AM Bravo Company called in a medevac for a young girl in a village with a bleeding tumor, in desperate need of medical care. At 11:30 AM, Alpha Company would capture three more Viet Cong prisoners hiding in a hut within a village less than a kilometer east of where they had been attacked the night before. At 1:56 PM, Alpha Company would report three more enemy soldiers captured in a village another kilometer east, toward the sea. In another village along a small river, Alpha's 3rd Platoon would capture two more at 2:11 PM. At the same time, 2nd Platoon would remove another two Viet Cong from an underground bunker at gunpoint. At 4:15 PM, Bravo Company requested a medevac for a wounded civilian woman who had been shot in the hip the day before. At 4:36 PM, a Viet Cong prisoner claimed that Bravo Company soldiers had taken two thousand dong (Vietnamese currency) from him.

4:45 PM – B Co to TOC: Could you get a ship to come out to pick up the money that belongs to the POW? My 3rd Platoon has it. They said they found it in the bushes where they picked him up.

As the companies scoured the Bong Son plain below, finally the battalion forward command post arrived at LZ Santana. Shortly thereafter, Sky Cranes began lowering howitzers from the artillery unit, who were also transported that day from LZ Hump. By the end of the day, Alpha Company had returned to where they had started that morning, along the rice paddies and sweet potatoes at the base of the hill. Again, they would spend the night here. The first official day of Operation Pershing was an especially long and dangerous one for the men of the 5/7th Cav. The next day would bring another air assault for the battalion, followed by more searching of countless villages.

At 9:13 AM on February 14th, Alpha Company was flown approximately five kilometers north to LZ Cochise, air assaulting onto a plateau area of the mountains along the northern reaches of the Bong Son plain. Meanwhile, the other companies were flown to LZ Cherokee, on another mountain plateau approximately two kilometers southwest of LZ Cochise. From here each of the companies would move back down into the plains to conduct more searching of villages, while scout ships flew above in search of the enemy. At 6:05 PM Bravo Company's 2nd Platoon would become pinned down by approximately ten enemy snipers while crossing a rice paddy. In response, one of Alpha Company's platoons was picked up and assaulted onto the high ground from which the enemy fire came, but no further contact was made.

The men of the battalion trudged on through the next two days encountering much of the same action, until 4:51 PM on the 16th when Charlie Company's 2nd Platoon began taking machine gun fire from a nearby village approximately five kilometers east of LZ Santana. By 4:56 PM, the 2nd Platoon Leader was dead. By 5:04 PM the first wave of Delta Company troops were en route to assist from LZ Santana. In the command chopper, LTC Canham and one of his lieutenants arrived in the area just after Delta Company, at approximately 5:30 PM. Minutes later, attempting to make their way to Charlie Company, LTC Canham and several Delta Company soldiers were hit by an ARA strike from a friendly gunship. The commander's leg was badly wounded. Evacuation of the wounded was attempted using the command chopper, but they were shot down shortly after lift-off. As the fighting raged on into the night, many attempts were made to medevac the battalion commander and the nine other wounded men. They were to no avail however, as the enemy took the dust-offs under fire every time they got close. At 7:32 PM the wounded were finally airlifted out and flown to the field hospital at LZ English. At 7:55 PM, Bravo Company, 1/8th Cav was air assaulted into the area to further assist in the battle. They would have to move overland for a half-hour before linking up with Charlie Company. By the time it was over on the night of February 16th, four of Charlie Company's soldiers were dead and four were wounded. Delta Company would count nine of their own wounded, and one of their medics as missing. The next day, LTC Andrew J. Gatsis would replace LTC Canham as commander of the 5/7th Cav.

That night, many in Alpha Company went to sleep in utter exhaustion on LZ Santana while their buddies pulled guard duty. They would awaken at 1:45 AM to the explosions of grenades lobbed into their position by a small force of Viet Cong. Machine gun positions opened fire in all outward directions as flares were shot into the sky to illuminate the area. Those who had been sleeping scrambled out of their hooches, half-dazed, blinking and shooting into the dark. Another night attack, just up the hill from where the last one had claimed the lives of four on February 13th. No muzzle flashes or green tracer rounds could be seen, however, and soon the bleary-eyed troopers realized that no one was out there. They had simply thrown their grenades and disappeared. As they ceased their shooting, the cries of the wounded could now be heard emanating from various corners of their patrol base. One was from a machine gunner whose emplacement had been hit. Flashlights with red lenses moved about in the darkness and confusion as medics and others attempted to find and treat the wounded. The radio crackled as Matulac called for a dust-off. It was a confused mess of a situation, but they had been through it before and knew what to do. Soon the distant thumping could be heard, becoming louder and louder until the chopper landed to collect their four wounded. It thumped away back into the night, leaving them again in silence. The grenade that hit the machine gunner had also knocked the gun down the hill, and no one wanted to go down there in the dark to search for it. Upon searching the area below the emplacement at daybreak, it was apparent that the Viet Cong had made off with the machine gun.

17 Feb '67 – 22 weeks left

Dear Folks,

Been over a week since I've written I believe, so better write once again. Those steel pots, well we're wearing them again. We moved from our last hill, LZ Hump, to this rock and scrub brush hill, LZ Santana, only 5 miles from the sea. This area our battalion is operating in is nothing but bad news. I just talked with this guy last night at supper, and he got killed later last night. A good friend of Rod, too. I seen Rod for the first time in about 2 months. He might have gotten hurt for all I know. Don't tell Mrs. Henning about it. Our Colonel got shot in the leg. Probably heard about us by now on the news. I heard D Company made it back on the hill, and Quinn says he saw Rod. So I guess, I'll see what he has to say about the bad news. This should be, or is our last operation and I guess it'll last 'til June or July. I don't know and the Generals don't know. It depends on what we run into. Us guys here haven't been getting along too good with our new sergeant. I don't know what it really is.

Been taking a few pictures around here. One of myself with over a week's growth of beard. Some of the artillery guns and all of the fellows here. When I am in Hong Kong, I'll have them developed and send them home. Say, I got a Valentine and letter from Mrs. Henning. It was sweet smelling, too. Woo, woo!

Did Larry Schindler ever pay the $60 yet? Have to write to him and tease him about married life. Ron Bowe said his hands were ice cold when he congratulated him on his wedding.

So long,

Will

17 Feb '67 – 22 weeks left

Dear Hop-a-long,

Been an awful lot of action going on lately. B, D, and our company ran into a lot of shit last night and this morning. I took a few pictures of where we've been fighting. Less than a mile away from our big hill. Huey gunships, Chinook gunships, 2 jets, and 2 old-type fighter planes, plus artillery and us guys with our mortars. Leveling everything in sight. Last night, about 8:00 or so, seen some tracer rounds from a V.C. shooting at a gunship. Man, that chopper whipped around and shot at the V.C. Oh Lord have mercy, did he ever bring smoke on him, wow. He turned on that machine gun that looked like a red snake. Good gravy, that V.C. didn't shoot back anymore. I hate those choppers, too. Every time they blow our tent down, our gear flies away and our food gets dirt in it. After they did our V.C. in, I'm not even going to say a bad word against them. They just might hear me.

That's real good of you guys, winning a blue ribbon. The competition must have been real stiff. Yes, I remember old Paula Marie. Never had her for any subjects. Did you have Sister Jean d'Arc? I had her for biology. Do you like that subject? You're taking out Donna Bohl? My goodness, puppy love, ha ha! What do Ma and Dad think of this? That's worse than fighting a war sometimes! Tell me, what's it like? Do you walk around starry-eyed? I can see you two in school now, yeah, yeah!

Well, I'll let you go now, so I can write another letter to someone before chow gets here. Talk about food, last night we had all the hot dogs and sauerkraut, cake and ice cream, we can eat. Ain't that unbelievable news. Ok, lover boy. Next time I write, I'll just drop a line. Oh yes, return those negatives as soon as you get them developed. The one I just sent home, OK?

Camera Man,

Will

On February 18th, Bravo Company was ordered to conduct a recon-in-force operation in a large village where an enemy command post was suspected. In the preceding days of searches, much intelligence had been gathered from village chiefs, as well as from surrendering Chieu Hoi soldiers. They had reported that many enemy fighters had recently moved into the village known as Tuy An, from the mountains to the west. A battalion after action report described what happened that day:

Upon approaching the area at 4:01 PM, Company B came under intense small arms and automatic weapons fire from within the fortified hamlet. Company B established a base of fire with the platoon that was in contact, called for supporting fires, and attempted to maneuver other platoons to the flanks of the hamlet. The base of fire and company command post began receiving 82mm mortar fire until the position was detected and put out of action by a 90mm recoilless rifle round. Companies C and D were combat assaulted into the contact area along with Company D, 1st Battalion, 7th Cavalry in an effort to encircle the enemy force, estimated at 100 men, inside the well-fortified hamlet. Due to the intense enemy fire across the open paddy areas and the quickly arriving darkness a physical link-up between elements could not be effected. Artillery and ARA fires were employed all night within the hamlet.

As the sun set on the evening of the 18th, six of Bravo Company's soldiers lay dead, as well as one from Charlie and another from Delta. At 5:20 PM that night, Alpha Company's 4th Platoon would take sniper fire from the southeast while still guarding LZ Santana. Fire was returned, killing one Viet Cong.

At 9:08 AM the next morning, Alpha Company was air assaulted to the southwest side of the large, palm tree laden village of Tuy An, where Bravo Company and others had fought the day before. Hundreds of villagers had already evacuated the village at daybreak, and just minutes before Alpha Company's arrival, airstrikes had pummeled enemy positions throughout the village. Along with Charlie and Delta, Alpha Company would form a cordon around the village and sweep through, encountering sporadic resistance throughout the day. Many fighters were found dead in the village, and more were taken prisoner. A few however, chose to fight on, despite being trapped and outgunned. Various firefights erupted over the course of the battalion's search and clear operation. Four of Charlie Company's troopers would be wounded by a booby-trap, one of whom would die later. Later that afternoon, two soldiers of Delta Company would be hit by a grenade. After thoroughly searching and clearing every hut, bunker, tunnel and water well in the village, the troopers continued their mission in the areas surrounding Tuy An. The search and clear mission would continue for an additional two days until February 22nd, when the 5/7th Cav prepared for its next move.

SSG Matulac was responsible for calling and guiding in each of the helicopters that supported the company. His responsibilities involved giving the pilot the proper direction from which to approach the landing zone, as well as setting off smoke grenades to indicate their exact location once the pilot was in the area. As the chopper approached, he would guide the pilot in using hand signals. Once the nose of the chopper was nearly touching his chest, he would lower his arms to his sides, signaling the pilot to touch down. Matulac recalls what happened the morning of February

22nd as he was guiding in a log ship to the company's patrol base in the field:

One time I gave the pilot the azimuth (direction) to land and told him to ignore what appeared to be the proper approach. All of a sudden, the bird disappeared. Then I heard the chopper coming in behind me. As he attempted to land, his tail hit a hidden rock crop. The tail section was ripped off. When the team came out to assess the damage, I told the Major in charge, "I told him to come in on this azimuth and he decided I didn't know what I was doing, so he came in the wrong way." I was told it was pilot error. I was very relieved.

Barry Gallagher recalls how one of his soldiers, Rocco, began to fear becoming the target of "friendly fire". Many believed he had been sleeping while on guard before the night attack that had killed four on February 13th. Whether the threat was just perceived or real, he was beginning to crack under the strain, and they eventually pulled him from the field for his own safety.

Sent to Alpha Company to replace their forward observer, 1LT James Ulrich, who had been killed during February 13th's attack, was 2LT George Kalergis. He had only been in Vietnam about a month, but had already gained much combat experience calling in artillery strikes on the enemy. When he'd arrived in-country the month before, he was initially assigned to the 1/9th Cav. He recalled preparing for his first mission, "I knew I should have studied harder in college. It seemed like just yesterday I was opening the letter from Uncle Sam. The next thing I knew, I had volunteered for Officer Candidate School at Fort Sill, Oklahoma and after six grueling months, graduated as a Second Lieutenant, a commissioned officer in the field artillery. Now it's January 1967, the sun is setting and I'm sitting in a GP Medium tent at LZ Pony." Sweating in the heat and amidst the smell of hot canvas, he and other officers of the 1/9th, along with their pilots, awaited the arrival of their battalion commander. The newly-minted 2LT Kalergis was filled with both excitement and anxiety. Excitement, because this was his first real mission. Anxiety, because the only live artillery rounds he had called in before were at Fort Sill's training range, approximately three rounds in all, all while sitting comfortably on a folding chair perched atop a hill overlooking the fort's impact area.

Everyone rose to attention as the 1/9th's battalion commander entered the tent. "At ease men," he said as he picked up a pointer and motioned to a map of the An Lao Valley.

Kalergis would describe the commander as confident and fit, "If they made a Top Gun movie about helicopter gunship pilots, he would have been cast in the lead role."

"This is our new forward observer, Lieutenant Kalergis," the commander began. "Charlie Troop, he will be flying with you tomorrow and will take the place of a door gunner with one of your red teams. He will be available to call in artillery and request air strikes. Welcome to 'Nam,

Kalergis. Do you have your radio and maps ready for tomorrow?" Kalergis responded in the affirmative, and the commander continued his briefing for the next morning's mission. The 1/9th Cav aviators operated Red, White, and Blue teams. The White Team "scouts" flew in their lightly-armed, bubble-shaped H-13 scout ships, searching the jungle below for enemy movement. The Red Team "hunter-killers" did the same in their heavily-armed Huey gunships, attacking any enemy they found with mounted grenade launchers, rockets, and machine guns. Following the Red Team's aerial assault, the Blue Team Hueys would drop in and unload infantry soldiers of the 1/9th Cavalry to pursue and destroy whatever was left of the enemy. Primarily responsible for calling in artillery, Kalergis was also tasked on his first mission to take the place of one of the Red Team gunship's door gunners. He had never so much as fired an M-60 machine gun, much less from a flying aircraft, and so he was given a quick "crash-course" instruction by the crew's other door gunner just prior to take-off.

Kalergis would describe his first flight on the Red Team's gunship as a roller coaster ride on steroids, the chopper laboring upward over the mountain rises to the north of LZ Pony, then plunging wildly down the other side and into the An Lao Valley. "Holy shit," he thought with a sense of panic, "I've never been on a gunship before and here I am flying into combat on one... and manning a machine gun I have never fired." Despite the adrenaline induced by the gunship's wild maneuvers, they would not encounter the enemy for some time. For about an hour or so, the gunship continued to follow the scout ship through the valley, their new forward observer in tow. Before long, Kalergis became comfortable with the movement of the chopper. He started to enjoy the ride, and began to notice the breathtaking scenery of the An Lao. As he described it, the valley floor appeared as an emerald carpet that became terraced as it approached the surrounding mountains. The wide, clear Song An Lao River wound its way through the center of the valley. So clear was the water, and so low their flight, that he could see dozens of fish swimming just beneath the river's surface. He also noticed many burnt out villages here and there, and still others that remained unscathed but looked deserted.

Making a sharp turn at a curve in the valley, their gunship began following a ravine that ran up the side of a steep mountain. A small group of Viet Cong soldiers were running up a trail below them. Kalergis had just noticed them when he heard the pilot over the intercom, "Fighter Red, rolling in hot!" He felt the aircraft lurch upward briefly before nose-diving and firing a rapid stream of 40mm grenades at the fleeing Viet Cong. He watched the men fall violently, as if struck by some invisible force. Soon, he only saw patches of blood where the soldiers once stood. The other door gunner had opened fire. Kalergis followed suit, but was told to hold off as there were some friendlies in the area and he didn't have any experience with the weapon.

His heart was still pounding from the initial action when the gunship moved farther up the valley. Here they would spot a lone middle-aged man working in the field near what appeared to be an abandoned village. The entire area had supposedly been evacuated and was considered a "free-fire zone", but the man did not look to be a soldier. Another helicopter descended toward the nervous looking man as Kalergis and the gunship crew hovered above. The door gunner from the chopper below leapt into the dried up rice paddy with his .45 pistol, preparing to take the man in for interrogation. Kalergis suddenly noticed dirt seeming to erupt all around the chopper below and for a moment, he wondered what was going on. He couldn't hear the enemy machine guns beneath the deafening sound of his own chopper. As the door gunner fell face-first into the paddy, he realized they were being taken under fire from Viet Cong machine guns inside the village. The chopper below strained upward, leaving its door gunner to die alone in the paddy. In that same moment, the gunship carrying Kalergis lurched toward the village while unleashing a fierce volley of rockets on the enemy machine gunners. He would describe the rockets as giant Roman Candles as they launched from the sides of the gunship, engulfing him in a torrent of red sparks that swirled erratically through the chopper's open doors. The pilot yelled over the intercom, "Why aren't you shooting?"

"You just told me not to!" Kalergis yelled back.

"Just shoot, God damn it!" Now he was in the fight, unleashing a stream of hot lead at six hundred rounds per minute. The gunship banked to the left to make another rocket run. On their second run, a bullet tore through the floor of the chopper, right next to Kalergis's boot. It exited through the wall of the chopper near his head, leaving him momentarily dazed. After several more gun runs, the Blue Team chopper arrived to assault its payload of infantrymen into the paddy below. Kalergis would describe the sight of the troopers jumping from the chopper, "like popcorn jumping wildly from beneath the lid of a popcorn popper." He was relieved to see that the previous chopper's door gunner, who he had thought was dead, was still alive and now running toward the troopers. As the gunships ran low on ammunition the pilot directed Kalergis to, "put some artillery on the village." He got on his radio and called in two hundred rounds of 105mm high explosive shells on the edge of the village where the machine gun fire had come from.

Watching two hundred rounds of artillery rain down on that village seemed virtually unreal to Kalergis, the incandescent flashes, the billows of black smoke, the shock waves that followed, all forever etched in his memory. "It was more artillery than I had ever adjusted," he said, recalling his first combat mission, "hell, it was more than I'd ever seen."

The next day, Kalergis would go out on mission with the H-13 scout ship. He would call in even more rounds than he had the day before. In the middle of their attack, his pilot would be shot in the neck, but was able to continue the mission. Eventually, the pilot grew weak and they returned to LZ Pony.

Now in late February, Kalergis found himself on a log ship chopper full of mermite food containers and mail, en route to his new assignment with

Alpha Company, 5/7th Cav. Amidst the whirling dust storm of the chopper's down-draft, a squinting CPT Wise would greet him as he jumped off. He soon introduced Kalergis to his new radio operator, Danny Garrity. He liked his new commander and his new radio operator, and would get along well with both of them. And so began his life as a ground-pounder with Alpha Company.

For their next mission, the 5/7th Cav had been designated as the 1st Air Cavalry Division's reserve force (often called Ready Reaction Force or RRF) for the rest of the month. As such, the companies would be split up and sent to different LZs throughout the division's area of operations. When needed, the nearest company could be called in to assist a beleaguered unit in contact with enemy forces. The battalion command post would set up shop at LZ Two Bits along with Delta Company. Meanwhile, Alpha Company would be flown to LZ Pony, Bravo to LZ English, and Charlie to LZ Dog. Before flying to LZ Pony on February 22nd, Alpha Company would first be flown to LZ English where they would be afforded a rare opportunity to get cleaned up. Here Will would run into some of his buddies that had been transferred to the 1/7th Cav in December, and meet a little monkey who frequented the outpost looking for handouts. After their short visit, they were flown back to LZ Pony in the Kim Son Valley. This firebase was located on a short but wide hill mass, flanked by rice paddies, and surrounded by distant mountains. It was accessible by a dirt road that also led to a nearby hamlet. It was approximately eight kilometers east from where LZ Bird had been nearly overrun by seven hundred North Vietnamese on December 27th. A couple days later, 3rd Brigade commander Colonel (COL) Jonathan R. Burton would visit the firebase and present the men of Alpha Company with the Air Medals they had earned for performing over twenty-five air assaults.

Kim Son Valley, source unknown

LZ English, Will Bowe with monkey

Alpha Company flies the flag at LZ Pony, photo by Robert Matulac

Fire mission at LZ Pony, photo by Robert Matulac

Chinook delivers howitzer and ammo to LZ Pony, photo by Wilbur Bowe

24 Feb '67

Dear Folks,

Sorry about the dirty paper, but beggars can't be choosey. We left our hill, LZ Santana, and went to LZ English. We had a little time to spend, so we went to the village and had a beer, and a bunch of bananas. Met old Figueroa, Leona, and big King. Well, they're with the 1-7th. Later that day, we came to LZ Pony. It ain't too bad here, right next to the village. Taking all kinds of pictures, wish I had brought more film with me. When we first got here, Doc and I were standing around and a full Colonel came up to talk to us. We had a nice little chat. Gave us the scoop to what's happening. He whipped out his knife and made some sketches in the dirt. The 25th Div. is just a little ways from us. Rest of the stuff is pretty much confidential. You know how it is when important people discuss war tactics. Yeah, got to keep a tight lip. Well anyway, got a kick out of it. Everyone else was sitting down watching us. I had my shirt off, maybe he thought I was a lieutenant.

Getting our Air Medals. This is for making 25 Air Assaults. I am going to throw the medal, along with my C.I.B., if them damn cooks and clerks get one. I'll throw them away along with a dollar, and then I can say I threw something away.

All the guys in D Company say they really like their C.O., Captain Swain, they say they're in good hands. I hear we're going to lose our C.O., Capt. Wise. Hate to see him go.

Say, I am going on R&R the 21st of March. Closed up for now. Mosquitoes are getting so bad you need a blood transfusion every morning. And it's starting to get hot, hot, hot. And also getting dark.

So long,

Will

Bierschbach mentioned some scuttlebutt he had recently heard. Apparently, one of the Vietnamese barbers at An Khe had been giving information to the North Vietnamese. You could never be sure of who your friends were in this place. Also through the grapevine, he'd heard a rumor that someone in the battalion supply shop had been caught selling loads of their stuff to locals in An Khe. Although both his identity and fate were unknown, it would seem to explain the severe clothing shortages they had suffered earlier. Before this, Will had just assumed that going over two months without a change of clothing was just the way it was supposed to be in the field.

In Bernard Grady's book, *On The Tiger's Back*, he relates the entire tale of how he caught the soldier in charge of the 5/7th's supply shop in a scheme to line his pockets by selling poncho liners and other items to the locals. By this time, CPT Grady had been transferred from Charlie Company to the 5/7th's rear battalion headquarters where he would serve as Battalion Adjutant (S-1), in charge of administration for all battalion personnel.

The thing about poncho liners is that they were lightweight, semi-waterproof, and dried out quickly. They were a significant improvement on the old wool blankets that were heavier, readily soaked up water and never dried out, which made them heavier still. In the damp conditions these soldiers suffered in, the poncho liners were far superior in terms of dryness, comfort, warmth, and weight. As such, they were also prized by the Vietnamese who would actually sew them into jackets. There were plenty of old wool blankets laying around the 5/7th supply shop, but no poncho liners in sight. According to the guy in charge of the supply shop, there was a "severe shortage" of poncho liners throughout the division. This was the excuse he gave to the company commanders for why all of their replacement soldiers were showing up in the field with the old wool blankets. In reality, these new soldiers would unwittingly sign for the new poncho liners, and he would later write them off as "field losses" or lost in combat. He was also selling "surplus" Lifeline packs. It is not known for certain if he was also selling "surplus" uniforms, but it would explain why the soldiers went for months without any clean fatigues. It brings to mind that supply clerk, Gene Cross's grade school friend Donald Duncan, and that mysterious disagreement he had with his boss in the supply shop – the disagreement that led to his fateful joining of Alpha Company in the field, where he would die.

The soldier in charge of the battalion's supply was eventually caught red-handed by MPs who had been tipped off by CPT Grady. He was selling the supposedly non-existent poncho liners to a Vietnamese laundry in the town of An Khe. Apparently, he'd felt that he and CPT Grady were friends, and seemed genuinely surprised by the action taken against him. He asked Grady why he did it. In his book, Bernard Grady quotes his own response:

For the good of the men. For the guys out in the boonies with a wet blanket. You wouldn't know because you've been back here in relative comfort and safety. They're the reason. Good Lord, man, we've shipped fifty or sixty good soldiers home in boxes already. Don't you think they deserve some comfort before they're zipped into a body bag?

15
REST & RELAXATION

They all call me "Bow-E," ha! What a time we all have.

Finally, Will had something to look forward to later in the month of March as his turn for R&R was coming up. Like all soldiers, he had been looking forward to it since the beginning of his tour. They were offered a choice of destinations, including Tokyo, Taipei, Singapore, Kuala Lumpur, Bangkok, Manila, or Hong Kong. Just like his buddies Patrillo and Quinn before him, Will chose to go to Hong Kong on his well-earned week off.

Matulac would often take up mail call duty, and recalls SFC Thomas Meek often asking if there was a package for him. Every time a log ship would arrive with mail, Meek would be looking for his package. Sometime later, two bags of mail arrived. One was filled with letters, the other mostly empty, save for a crushed box at the bottom. The much-anticipated box was for Meek. "Sorry," Matulac said as he handed him the box with his crushed birthday cake. He was disappointed, but he took the box anyway, sat down and ate the crumbs.

On March 1st the battalion was released from its duties as the division's reserve force and sent back to the same area of the northern Bong Son plain where they had operated the week before. At 9:35 AM the first wave of Alpha Company choppers touched down at LZ Geronimo. Delta Company had preceded their arrival and secured the landing zone. The battalion forward command post would also set up shop here later in the day. Bravo and Charlie Companies were flown to different landing zones in the same area that morning. As the men of the battalion commenced their patrols, they quickly realized that nothing had changed in Bong Son. The villages and forests here were still rife with Viet Cong, twelve of which they captured on the first day of the mission. The next day, they would capture three and kill four.

4 Mar '67 – 21 weeks left

Dear Folks,

Best start this letter before it gets dark. We humped with the company the other day. Those rice paddies sure haven't changed much. We came to guard an artillery unit, but we're moving out tomorrow now. Now we're on this hill called Geronimo.

Well, happy birthday Ma. Wish I could send something, but the best I can do is my thoughts in a letter. I got a letter from the Simons the other day, and they said Allen's coming home the 12th of March. He said he has 2nd and 3rd degree burns. Say, I got Joanne's flag, also a letter, so I must thank her. I wanted to put it in the mess hall, but it's closed down. So I'll put it in the barracks when I leave for R&R. When I'm on R&R, I am going to send something home. It'll be a very pleasant surprise, and so I won't say what.

Will

After four days of patrolling around the area of LZ Geronimo, Alpha Company was lifted off and flown west on March 5th. Air assaulting into the mountains between An Lao Valley and the northern Bong Son plain at 9:21 AM that morning, they set out on their patrol to the south. The next evening, after bivouacking for the night, one of the company's ambushes would spot a group of Viet Cong moving in from high ground on the east. Artillery was called on their location. They would find three killed. Another had been wounded but escaped capture. Another stakeout team would also report movement near its area at 11:05 PM. Again, artillery rounds were called in. This time they found only packs and no bodies, though they did spot one man running away with a flashlight.

On March 7th, the men of Delta Company would discover a cave suspected of housing Viet Cong. Rather than simply throwing in heavy explosives to kill whoever may be inside, their commander, CPT Walt Swain, wanted to bring them out alive. A former intelligence officer, he valued information over dead bodies. So instead, in an effort to scare but not kill the enemy, he placed a grenade just outside the cave's small entrance and pulled the pin. Following the explosion, six Viet Cong fighters emerged through the smoke to surrender. Rather than sending in one of his troopers to search the tunnel as most officers would have done, he then stripped off his gear and crawled inside himself, armed only with his .45 pistol and flashlight. Minutes later, he emerged smiling with five enemy rifles.

That same day, on March 7th, Alpha Company was picked up and flown north to a small river valley in the mountains. Here in the valley, the company would report finding ten water buffalo in a pen. Battalion told them to move on and leave the water buffalo alone. In addition to the booby-traps, tunnels, and rice caches, each of the companies would also come across many hastily dug graves of enemy fighters. In fact, they would be found on a daily basis during this time. The troopers would have to dig up each of these graves as they found them, so as to inspect and search the decomposing bodies for papers, maps and other sorts of intelligence. Aside from these, they would just as often come across seemingly random dead bodies of both enemy and civilians. After bivouacking for the night of the 8th in another area of the small valley, Alpha Company was informed that they were being watched. At 8:35 PM a scout ship reported three individuals observing their movements from atop a hill to their south, on the other side of the valley.

After two more days of patrolling in and around the river valley, Alpha Company and the rest of the battalion would once again airlift to separate LZs for security missions. Tasked this time as the brigade reserve force, Alpha Company was lifted back to LZ Pony on March 10th along with the battalion command post. Bravo lifted to LZ Pistol, while Charlie Company was flown to a bridge that spanned the Song Lai Giang River near the town of Bong Son. Bridges were prime targets for enemy attacks, and a company was kept at the Bong Son Bridge for security at all times. Also on the 10th, at 12:05 PM Delta Company would report finding elephant tracks along with those of humans along a trail in the jungle. Elephants were known to be used at times by the enemy, as transport.

During their stay at LZ Pony, they had been given a little free time. Taking along his new camera, Will decided to visit the nearby village with Willie Harris and a few others, including Matulac's skiing buddy, Polish immigrant Kazimierz Slomiany. They visited with many of the villagers here and even learned some Vietnamese phrases. One of the villagers Will made friends with was a twelve-year-old boy named Ten Ninh, whose job it was to tend cows.

Ten Ninh standing in front of other children, photos by Wilbur Bowe

Village near LZ Pony in Kim Son Valley, Willie Harris and kids

Kazimierz Slomiany (middle) and buddies, photos by Wilbur Bowe

(left to right) unknown soldier, Willie Harris, Will Bowe

14 Mar '67 – 19 weeks left

Dear Folks,

I better start writing, for it's been awhile. We started to hump the hills, and wouldn't you know it, it rained from the very first day to the last. Well now we have been back here at LZ Pony a few days. Went to Mass last Sunday. Didn't know it was Passion Sunday already. Easter will be on my R&R. Lucky, only 3 more days and I'll be cutting out of the field. This is for certain, no more Army after the 1st of August. Hot dog. But have to be in Viet Nam at least 'til the 25th of July. So we signed papers for our release. Hard to believe.

I got a good Vietnamese friend, about, he says, 12 years old. He has 5 cows he tends to every day. His name is Ten Ninh. Nice little kid.

I have to order a car sometime between now and the end of April, if I want a car to drive home. It takes 3 months to order one.

Had a hard time staying up on guard

At 11:40 AM on March 14th, the battalion command post was notified that the brigade commander's helicopter had been shot down near the banks of the large Song Con River, approximately six kilometers into the mountains west of the Kim Son Valley. This was the same river valley that ran below LZ Venus, where SSG Burtis and two others had been shot by snipers in October. By 12:26 PM Alpha Company's troopers were descending into the valley to secure the chopper. By 2:00 PM a Chinook arrived to carry the command chopper away, and Alpha Company returned to LZ Pony.

The next day, Alpha Company's 1st and 3rd Platoons were again air assaulted into a smaller valley within the mountains that lay east of LZ Pony where enemy activity had been spotted. No contact was made, but the company kept patrolling in the area until the following day. On March 16th, 3rd Platoon would encounter three recently occupied enemy huts, finding bloody ID cards amongst other miscellaneous items. Later that afternoon, 2nd Platoon would come across the same on their patrol. After thorough searching, the huts were burned. They would return to LZ Pony before dusk.

16 March '67

Dear Folks,

I didn't sign my name on the last letter because we all were in a hurry to rescue a downed chopper, and had to pack and leave in a hurry. Yes, I got your package, but so small, my goodness. Send me a big box of those walnut cookies, and some seafood, and some instant cocoa, and some Kool-Aid. Cocoa goes good with guard duty, and Kool-Aid for this bad water. Yes, I know General Norton. Doc was going to take a picture of me yesterday while I shook his hand, but he never showed up.

Will

Early 17 March '67

Up and ready to take off. All excited. So I won't be writing too much for a while. Well, I best pack up. Don't want to miss the flight back to English, and then to An Khe, and from there to Cam Ranh Bay, and to Hong Kong. So be ready for a pleasant surprise in about 3 weeks, OK?

Rip-Roaring R&R,

Will

Will Bowe aboard Huey

On March 17th, Will hopped on the morning log ship and took a series of flights until arriving at Cam Ranh Bay. From here, he was flown straight to Hong Kong on a jetliner filled with servicemen from other units in Vietnam. For the first time since August 1966, he was not in a combat zone. He stayed in a hotel with some guys, tried some rather exotic food, and went out drinking every night. For fifty cents, rickshaws would take them wherever they wanted to go. He even attended church while there. After the service started however, he realized that he was in the wrong church, these were Presbyterians. As this was a regular destination for American servicemen during the war, many of the businesses catered to the military clientele. He visited many shops and purchased a Beatles album and a reel-to-reel recorder, as well as a silk jacket with an embroidered map of Vietnam on it. With the exception of the recorder, all of this he mailed home.

From its forward base at LZ Pony, the 5/7th Cav continued with its mission. The daily staff journal from February 17th contained the following notable entries:

10:06 AM – B Co to TOC: At 9:20 AM at BR 750-925 D Co Patrol #3 found decomposed body in a cave entrance, also found 2 empty NVA packs. They tried to remove the body but only removed portions of it.

12:30 PM – A Co to TOC: 3rd Platoon at BR 791-832 burning huts.

At 10:05 the next day, a medevac would be called in for a man who had shot himself in the hand with his pistol. An hour later, Alpha Company would be flown from LZ Pony to take over Charlie Company's security mission at Bong Son Bridge.

Staying awake on guard duty was always a major concern. On March 19th, the following entry was made in the battalion's daily staff journal:

SUBJECT – Inspection of Sector & Bunkers: Inspection was conducted at 4:50 AM by CPT Frey, S3 Air. Bunkers 8, 9, 10, 11, 12 were inspected with no discrepancies noted. Remarks: C Co commander has been notified of lack of Claymores and will adjust his platoon until others arrive. Bunker 12 was very alert and answered questions without hesitation.

Continuing their security mission at and around Bong Son Bridge, Alpha Company sent the following report on March 21st:

5:06 PM – A Co to TOC: ARVN unit advisor reports that at 4:30 PM a woman was killed by a mine at BR 808-961. This was reported by the village chief of Lang Quang. People will carry the body down to the river at BR 809-959 and will bury the body.

Civilians were everywhere as the soldiers guarded and patrolled the area around the Bong Son Bridge. Bill Purdy spoke of one rare occurrence when their 2nd Platoon Leader, 1LT James Harmon got really pissed. They were on a hilltop near the bridge. There usually wasn't much action here, but they had been taking sporadic fire from snipers. As this was going on, one of the "Coca-Cola girls" who made money by selling soda to the soldiers, was braving the bullets to make her way up the hill. The soldiers were thirsty, and some of them were holding out their money to her. 1LT Harmon was livid, and chewed them all out for risking the poor girl's life. The other time 1LT Harmon really got angry with them was when their platoon sergeant, SFC James Bonner, went around their perimeter to check on each of their guard positions one night in April. He found absolutely none of them awake. "1LT Harmon was really disappointed in us that night," Purdy recalled. No one meant to fall asleep on guard duty, but they were all extremely sleep-deprived and at a certain point, it was inevitable.

During this time, most of what was being patrolled by the 5/7th Cav were areas under evacuation orders, where no people were supposed to be unless they were engaged in the war. Civilians were routinely found however, and moved out to safe areas. Many were relocated to New Life hamlets, built and supported by the South Vietnamese government. As mentioned before, men of military age were of particular interest, and would always have to be brought in for interrogation. The following staff journal entries from March 21st through the 24th illustrate just how many civilians on the battlefield there were to deal with during this time.

21 March 67, 8:38 AM – Custer 1A to TOC: Have picked up 3 young kids ages around 12 years old, and 2 old ladies driving cattle. CO of D Co requested we pick them up. What should we do with them?

S2 to Custer 1A: Move them towards LZ Pistol then release them, just get them out of the area.

22 March 67, 7:22 AM – D Co to TOC: 3rd Platoon picked up 9 male Vietnamese in white uniforms at BR 771-908, ages 20 to 30 years old.

7:30 AM – D Co to TOC: We now have 50 detainees. There are ARVN forces at my 3rd Platoon location and they are protesting against my 3rd Platoon picking up these individuals of military age. A couple of ARVN men with BARs have gotten down into position and have made some threatening gestures.

8:30 AM – D Co to TOC: These individuals turned out to be farmers getting hay for their cattle.

11:13 AM – A Troop 1/9th Cav to TOC: I am going to insert my Blue Team at BR 855-852, will be searching villages in that area.

11:45 AM – A Troop 1/9th Cav to TOC: As soon as we started our prep it looked as though the whole valley started to move out. People started moving northwest carrying their belongings and herding their cattle.

12:45 PM – D Co to TOC: 3rd Platoon at BR 833-892 picked up 7 Viet Cong suspects, one dressed in gray garb, Buddhist type, herding cattle. He says he is a Buddhist yet he knows nothing of Buddhism. Found this out after interpreter questioned him, who also believes he is Viet Cong. Remainder of Viet Cong suspects 25-30 years old dressed in black pajama shorts.

2:50 PM – D Co to TOC: 3rd Platoon at BR 847-889 found some huts with writing of, "American GI go home." In Vietnamese writing says the people like the VC and the VC will win the war, etc.

2:50 PM – A Co to TOC: Some ARVNs came up to my 36 element and said that there were 4 Viet Cong moving east at BR 885-953. 36 element is going down to pursue them, also artillery was called in.

2:55 PM – S3 Air to Brigade: Request scout ship to check out area where ARVN spotted 4 Viet Cong.

Brigade to S3 Air: They will proceed as soon as artillery firing stops.

4:45 PM – A Co to TOC: Reference 4 Viet Cong spotted earlier by ARVN, while pursuing the Viet Cong A Co 36 element spotted 3 Viet Cong suspects get into a boat on the river at BR 889-958, scout bird called in, observed 3 Viet Cong suspects in the boat smiling and waving at the bird, no weapons sighted.

23 March, 11:38 AM – Scout ship to S3 Air: At BR 865-865 we have spotted several people, looks as though they are moving out, also several military age personnel working in rice paddies.

12:01 PM – D Co to TOC: Between 10:00 AM and 11:00 AM we picked up 25 Viet Cong suspects moving across rice paddies along the blue. Wearing assorted pajamas and straw hats. All males, are being returned to LZ Pistol.

12:06 PM – Scout ship to TOC: We haven't seen anything of significance in the area, except there are about 75-80% fewer people than when I got here.

4:41 PM – D Co to TOC: Request medevac for 4 wounded in action from a booby-trap at BR 785-885. Booby-trap made from butterfly bomblet. Point man tripped what appeared to be vines stretched across the trail. Blast covered about 60 meters.

5:06 PM – C Co to TOC: 36 element found 1 booby-trap at BR 784-868, was US hand grenade with pin pulled and safety pin inserted. We destroyed it.

6:36 PM – B Co to TOC: At 5:45 PM B Co 1st Platoon spotted 5 Viet Cong at BR 852-886, believed they had weapons. Fired over their heads and they fled. 1st Platoon pursued, pushing them into a blocking position set up by 3rd Platoon. Scout ships were called in.

6:37 PM – B Co to TOC: Reference to previous message, when 1st Platoon fired over the 5 Viet Cong, 1 individual was hit, result 1 woman killed in action. 3 individuals dressed in black pajamas. The woman killed had khaki shirt and black bottoms. 5th individual had light blue trousers and black shirt, also had weapon.

SUBJECT – Inspection of Sector & Bunkers: The barrier at LZ Pony was inspected at 10:00 PM, by CPT Frey. Comments: All personnel questioned were very alert and responsive. Mosquito nets have been ordered but have not yet arrived.

24 March 67, 10:25 AM – D Co to TOC: Reference booby-trap that went off last night, point man says it was a grenade inside of a coconut.

12:55 PM – A Co to TOC: At 12:10 PM 2nd Platoon while reconning, reported receiving 2 sniper rounds at BR 884-953. Also when on ground received 2 or 3 rounds. Spotted them in rice paddy. Unknown size force. Artillery and armed Chinooks were called in. The armed Chinooks did receive a couple of sniper rounds.

1:20 PM – Scout ship 3 to TOC: In restricted area out from LZ Pony, southwest side of river, there are a few people herding buffalo moving north, about 15 to 20 people, male children and females.

1:35 PM – A Co to TOC: Request medevac for 2 hit by booby-trap. 1 serious, 1 not serious, booby-trap believed to be a grenade with a trip wire. It was not on the trail but on their flank.

Vietnamese with wounded on stretcher, photo by Marvin Bierschbach

Vietnamese civilians, photo by Marvin Bierschbach

On March 26th, all companies of the 5/7th Cav were relieved in place by companies of both the 1/5th Cav and the 2/12th Cav. Delta Company remained at LZ Pistol while Bravo and Charlie Companies remained with the battalion command post at LZ Pony, and Alpha Company at Bong Son Bridge. They would now prepare for a contingency mission they were being sent on. The entire battalion would be sent back into the beautiful and deadly An Lao Valley. Lift-off for Alpha Company was set for 10:15 the next morning. Matulac described their previous eleven days at Bong Son Bridge:

A little break from combat and entertainment for the troops. We were assigned to provide security to the Bong Son Bridge area because the NVA attempted to destroy the bridge as it was the main thoroughfare for that area. All day long people would bring things to sell at the local markets. Animals, pigs, chicken, ducks, etc. All sorts of foodstuff from bread to vegetables, rice, and of course, even furniture. Also, we had Army vehicles using the bridge. It gave us a break and we washed our uniforms and bathed in the river. Guarding the bridge was boring. We had a check-point set up to ensure that VCs weren't attempting to infiltrate. When we had some patrols sent to different areas, the mortar platoon would provide mortar fire for support if requested.

One day the "Donut Dollies" who were Special Service volunteers came down to entertain us and of course to give donuts and candy. Well, they were accompanied by officers, some of whom (though we didn't know at the time) were from our battalion. Anyway, they decided to take a swim. Of course, the enlisted were not invited to the soiree. But while the officers and dollies were cavorting in the water, I noticed some "logs" floating in the water, coming from some houses further upstream. These were not wooden logs, but rather brown logs of defecation. When I pointed this out, the swimmers evacuated the river really fast! The speed with which the party broke up was enjoyed by the troops.

When we got our traveling orders, back to the An Lao Valley, the battalion priest came and gave mass. As the mass was taking place, the helicopters were landing on the pickup zone.

Aerial View of Bong Son Bridge, photo by Robert Matulac

Bong Son Bridge spanning the Song Lai Giang River in the town of Bong Son, photo by Robert Matulac

4th Platoon fires mortars near Bong Son Bridge, photo by Robert Matulac

4th Platoon soldiers near Bong Son Bridge, photo by Robert Matulac

Near Bong Son Bridge, (left to right) Patrillo, Doc, Quinn, Fulford, Bierschbach, Anderson, Lussier, photo courtesy of Marvin Bierschbach

Bill Purdy near Bong Son Bridge

On the banks of the Song Lai Giang River near the town of Bong Son, Father Tom Widdel conducts Mass, photo by Robert Matulac

Soldiers of Alpha Company pray before air assault into An Lao Valley, photo by Robert Matulac

SFC Bonner coordinates lift-off from Bong Son Bridge, photo by Robert Matulac

Aerial view of An Lao Valley, source unknown

Following Father Tom's sermon on the morning of March 27th, Alpha Company loaded its choppers on the banks of the Song Lai Giang River. They headed west over the mountains and into the northern An Lao Valley. At 10:38 AM Alpha Company would be air assaulted to LZ Beaver in the mountains on the west side of the valley. Charlie Company would be flown to LZ Buffalo, to their south, and Delta to LZ Bear, to their north, also on the west side of the valley. After their initial assaults, the companies would move through thick jungles and down extremely steep mountainsides to take up their blocking positions. Winding through the two to three-kilometer-wide valley was the Song An Lao River, along which were many large villages.

The mission was launched in conjunction with the Vietnamese Marine Corps (VNMC). Bravo Company secured the battalion command post on a high mountaintop to the northeast, overlooking the valley. Alpha, Charlie, and Delta Companies would block the enemy's escape to the west as VNMC forces moved through the valley. Throughout this mission, each of the companies would encounter several recently used enemy huts and burn them all. The heat was relentless and some soldiers would pass out from heat stroke. Delta Company would suffer one wounded on their initial assault, then four additional wounded from punji stakes that afternoon. A couple hours later, they would briefly make contact with three enemy snipers and survive unscathed. Charlie Company would suffer the worst of the enemy action on the first day, suffering two wounded on the initial assault. Three more would be wounded by punji stakes while hacking through the jungle, and a medevac chopper would be shot down attempting to extract them. At 2:12 PM snipers would kill one of Charlie Company's troopers and wound two more. At 5:00 PM two more would be wounded by an artillery round that fell short of its target. The dead and wounded of Charlie Company would have to wait until the next morning to be lifted out. Killed by the sniper fire was SFC Thomas Meek, the sergeant who Matulac had recalled eating his crushed birthday cake not long before. He had recently been transferred to Charlie Company from Alpha when he was killed. From Grand Rapids, Michigan, he was twenty-nine years old.

Thomas Meek

On the same day, Will was making his way back from his R&R. Stopping at An Khe along the way, he ran into his buddy Rod Henning and had a chance to catch up. He just happened to be leaving on his own R&R at the time. His next stop was LZ English, another major hub for aircraft of the 1st Air Cavalry. He decided to have one last beer and pen a letter home before his return to the field, and so he made his way to the clubhouse.

27 March '67 – 17 weeks left

Dear Folks,

Back at LZ English today. I am just hanging out in the E.M. Club and writing this letter. I hope you received the package I sent. It went Air Mail. I sent another by boat with my tailored sport jacket, pants and shirt, and 4 rolls of film. I can't wait 'til you see my first package. I know you guys will be so happy to get it.

I seen Rod today, just as I left An Khe. He came in to go on R&R in Taipei. I'd give $100 to be in his place. When I was at Cam Ranh Bay, a 1st Lieutenant offered me $50 to delay my R&R two days. I said, "Sorry about that."

How did the holding action turn out? I read in Stars & Stripes that it has made some progress. How many lbs of milk did you dump? Are the neighbors going along with it? Larry wrote a letter about it, saying that Frank Stoik is a fool. I'll have to write that Geissler kid a few cutting words.

Your son,

Will

    Will returned to Alpha Company's patrol base in An Lao on the log ship the next morning, March 28th. That afternoon, the company would report finding women and children washing rice along a stream near a cave, with one male of military age among them, approximately sixteen years of age. About a half-hour later, they would spot three Viet Cong with weapons moving along the same stream toward their positions in the mountains on the west side of the valley. Artillery strikes would be called in on the three.

    Meanwhile, Charlie Company would suffer six more wounded in action from punji stakes. One soldier would encounter a crossbow-type booby-trap, resulting in an arrow shot through his pack, but would not be injured. Extraction of their wounded continued to be problematic, and hoists would be used to sling-load their casualties out the next morning. Also the next morning, Alpha Company would move down into the valley, along the stream where the three Viet Cong had been spotted the day before. Meanwhile, South Vietnamese forces searched the villages throughout the valley.

    On March 30th Charlie Company was flown to LZ Sandra while Alpha and Delta were lifted and air assaulted to the very northern tip of the valley to continue patrols. Alpha Company would find signs of recent enemy activity in the area, including many more enemy huts to burn. At 2:36 PM they would receive more sniper fire, but the enemy still proved elusive. Late in the day, a fake extraction was performed to encourage the enemy to move into their area. On March 31st Alpha and Delta Companies continued their patrols in the mountains just north of the An Lao Valley, finding more huts, bunkers, and tunnels, all recently used. Another soldier would be evacuated with heat exhaustion, along with others suffering punji stake wounds.

That afternoon, Alpha Company's platoons were again split up and moving on their own. 1LT James Harmon's 2nd Platoon was searching along a small tributary stream of the Song An Lao River, where a narrow offshoot of the valley jutted north into the mountains. Bill Purdy was in 2nd Platoon with his buddies, John Kruetzkamp, also from Kentucky, and A.G. Hensley. Hensley was on point as Purdy followed, carrying his M-60 machine gun. Purdy related the following account of what happened next:

Following the stream, the going was tough in the thick of the jungle and we were moving slow. 1LT Harmon was on the radio with the battalion command chopper, as a result of the slow movement. Following a heated exchange with the command chopper, our platoon was ordered to cross the stream and move on to a parallel trail. Normally, we avoided trails whenever possible due to ambushes. Before moving out along the trail, we took a five-minute smoke break, where John Kruetzkamp, Ed Raciborski, and A.G. Hensley and I shared some C-Ration cheese crackers and a canteen of "iodine cool-aid".

I can still picture it in my mind as if it were yesterday. When we moved out along the trail, we started across a clearing. Hensley was carrying his M-79 grenade launcher and approximately ten feet in front of me. Immediately ambushed; upon entering the clearing, Hensley was shot and killed and another soldier was wounded. 1LT Harmon was instrumental in recovering Hensley's body while we returned fire on the enemy's suspected position. When it was over, Hensley's body and the wounded soldier were flown out to LZ English.

Purdy believes that if Hensley had just gotten down and waited a few seconds for the machine gun to be employed rather than immediately returning fire with his M-79, his life might have been spared. He spoke of how during the ensuing firefight, he just kept firing his machine gun while others were trying to get Hensley's body. He recalled how his assistant gunner, Ed Raciborski, kept loading the ammo chains, bringing up two more cans of ammunition as they ran low, then running down to the stream and filling his helmet with water to cool off the barrel. As he finally quit firing, the barrel was overheated and its rifling worn out, having caused his bullets to fly haphazardly all over the place. SP/4 A.G. Hensley was twenty-one years old, from Limestone, Tennessee.

A.G. Hensley

(left to right) John Kruetzkamp and 1LT James Harmon, photo by Bill Purdy

(left to right) Marty Scull, A.G. Hensley, Buford Bennett, photo by Bill Purdy

Alpha Company descends into a hot LZ, photo by Robert Matulac

Alpha Company patrols through pineapple plantation in An Lao Valley, photo by Robert Matulac

Another river crossing, photo by Robert Matulac

*Taking break after river crossing in An Lao Valley
photo by Robert Matulac*

3rd Platoon Leader, 1LT William Nelson, photo by Robert Matulac

Signaling log ship after river crossing in An Lao Valley, photo by Robert Matulac

Log ship arrives with replacements in An Lao Valley, photo by Robert Matulac

Soldiers waiting for pick-up in An Lao Valley, photo by Robert Matulac

Alpha Company picked up in An Lao Valley during change of mission, photo by Robert Matulac

On April 1st, Alpha Company's platoons would be lifted from separate pick-up zones and flown further into the mountains, just north of where 2nd Platoon had fought the day before. For the next two days, snipers would continue to follow and harass Alpha Company's platoons as they patrolled the mountains just north of An Lao. After receiving more sniper fire at 10:50 AM on April 2nd, ARA gunships would be called in.

12:20 PM – A Co to TOC: Letting gunships go, would like to get another one. We are checking the area with negative results. A Co C.O. believes it's the same two snipers that have been harassing us the past couple of days.

At 2:54 PM that same day, Alpha Company again lifted off, this time returning to the Kim Son Valley. Secured by Delta Company, the battalion command returned to LZ Pony. Bravo and Charlie Companies were left in An Lao to assist the 1/9th Cav who had recently made enemy contact, with Bravo securing the firebase at LZ Sandra. While 2nd and 4th Platoons secured an artillery firebase at the Hoai An District Headquarters, also in the Kim Son Valley, the rest of Alpha company would patrol from northeast to southwest, through the main trunk of the valley. They would pick up some civilians along the way and move them out of the area, but would not encounter the enemy.

6 April '67 – 15 weeks left

Dear Folks,

Me and Graham went to the town of Bong Son last week. People there you can tell are not as friendly as at An Khe. They even have a Shell station and a machine shop. But the place has such a bad odor. Right now we're taking it pretty easy, guarding an artillery battery. Guess we move out again in a few days. We're having a lot of fun with these people in the nearby village. I get along with them better than most guys 'cause I can talk their language a little bit. They are really dinky dau (crazy). I think the children are the most precious things in the world. They are so happy, innocent, and cute. I wish I could take some home. And talk about kids, there are so many of them, wow. This country is going to be in a bind 20 years from now. They are not really starving. I haven't ever seen a skinny one, but they're always asking, "Give baby son, chop, chop!" They all call me "Bow-E," ha! What a time we all have. About the only nice thing over here is the people. These other units, like the engineers and artillery, burn my ass when they try and show how bad they are by kicking these people around. Man, I hate them when they show off.

Artillery had a fire mission a little while ago. This is when some company or squad spotted some V.C. and they're blowing them up with six 105 guns. When they're not shooting at V.C.s, they're shooting at the hills for the hell of it. It really gets sickening to hear all that banging every day. Those crazy choppers flying around. I am really weary and fed up with this war. Been over here 8 months and still I don't know why I am here. If we'd fight this war with everything we got, OK let's fight. Yeah, if only I were President, I'd bring smoke.

You guys exaggerate too much. I meant it as a joke, saying the shorter my time gets, the deeper my foxhole. It's the same as saying the less time I have over here, the more scared I get. And we all feel more cautious and much more careful than when we first started. You mentioned before too, that I don't mention everything in my letters. Now I don't say any more to anyone else than I do to you. Of course, I'm not going to write the same type of letter to you as I would to the Schindlers or to the Geisslers. Once in a while we do have a little fight, but nothing to speak of. So cool your heels. You do more worrying than the whole company.

I hope you got my packages by now. Can't wait to know what you say about it. I received your package last week. The chocolate candy was melted. Can't expect it to hold up in 100 degree weather. I got an Easter package from Mrs. Henning. She's always thinking of me. I wrote her a letter today.

It's getting so hot over here now, I don't care too much about eating. When I went on R&R it was the first time in 8 months that I tasted some good whole milk. And then you guys are dumping the milk, good grief. I was reading about the N.F.O. and listening to it on the radio. I hope everything is OK and made some progress. You might have lost a lot of money dumping your milk Dad, but you gain a lot of respect and pride from me and I am sure from a lot of other people, too. You're not scared to make a mistake and also trying to make farming a bit easier for your sons and the next generation.

That Mike better be good in English in school. I wasn't and it sure shows in my letters, in spelling and vocabulary. I don't feel too bad 'cause a lot of guys are worse at it than I am. Yes, school is very important. I only wish I had made more use of it. So Mike, don't ever let sports deprive you of your education. So hop along when Ma says that most hateful "S-T-U-D-Y".

Right now I am in my bunker with a flashlight over my head and it's 12:30. Ten more minutes and I go off guard. It's pretty secure around here, so a light is OK. 3:20 AM now. An hour and 20 min of guard duty left, then I can go and sleep until 9. Three of us pulled from 10 to 6, 1 hour and 20 min twice. It starts to get light about 6.

You know that R&R is a funny thing. Sleeping in a nice soft clean big bed, watching T.V., walking the streets and drinking in the bars seems so natural, as though it were only yesterday I was doing the same thing. You just completely forget about the war. It was really so very wonderful. And then the day you come back to this ugly place and sergeants telling you to do this and that. What a rotten day that was. And for those people that re-up, for God's sake I don't know why. Sergeants that have been in the Army

10-15 years say they're fools. Yeah, that R&R was just a big tease. But it was something I looked forward to ever since I got over here. Rod is probably back from Taipei by now. He should have went to Hong Kong. It's morning now and I hope I get this letter off before the log ship gets in.

Em' a w on'

Will

30 March 1967, Shell station in the town of Bong Son, photo by Wilbur Bowe

30 March 1967, town of Bong Son, photos by Wilbur Bowe

As Alpha Company continued its patrol in the Kim Son Valley, the following message was relayed from 3rd Brigade:

8 April 67, 8:40 AM – Brigade to TOC: Brigade desires to have as many as possible individual pictures or negatives of dead Viet Cong or atrocities committed by Viet Cong taken by individuals while on search and destroy missions. Individual pictures or negatives should have date and location of picture if possible. This request is from division psychological warfare department and any film or negatives will be replaced.

On April 9th, with the exception of 1st Platoon, Alpha Company was lifted to LZ Pony, where they would replace Delta as the security force. 1st Platoon would be sent to replace 2nd Platoon as security for the other firebase at Hoai An District Headquarters, approximately four kilometers north of LZ Pony. The company would remain here until April 12th, when they would set out by foot from LZ Pony, crossing the Kim Son River and patrolling north through the valley, making virtually no enemy contact.

On the morning of the 14th they returned to be airlifted first to LZ English, then to the battalion's next area of operation. At 4:53 PM Alpha Company touched down at LZ Hatch, approximately thirteen kilometers north of An Khe, just south of the Song Ba River. This was the exact same area the men had patrolled during the first day of their first air assault mission in September, Operation Golden Bee. For the next six days they would patrol jungle and river areas, searching for Viet Cong. Although they found thousands of punji stakes, smoldering fires from enemy encampments, as well as dozens of huts, tunnels and bunkers, and even some elephant tracks, the enemy himself would prove elusive.

On April 19th the battalion was lifted back to An Khe for a three-day reprieve. On the morning of April 22nd, with all of its companies on stand-down at An Khe, the battalion would hold a ceremony to honor their fallen and present awards to the living.

The next day the battalion would return to the mountains near the southern An Lao Valley, setting up its command post at LZ Hump with Alpha Company air assaulting onto the same mountain ridge, just a kilometer to the northwest. The entire battalion would commence a sweep operation in the valley below and in the surrounding mountains over the next ten days. On the second day of the mission, the battalion command post would be flown north to LZ Laramie, on the west side of the central An Lao Valley. During this time Alpha Company would conduct several more air assaults. As both scout ships and gunships circled above, they would patrol the valley, finding enemy huts and bunkers to be burned, as well as rice caches, equipment, and many dead bodies left behind by the enemy. For the time, enemy contact was unusually light for An Lao, the only wounded to be medevaced being a heat stroke and a snake bite.

Despite the "light" level of contact, tragedy would strike Rodney Henning's Delta Company on April 26th when their dashing and charismatic commander, CPT Walt Swain met his fate. Delta Company was in a blocking position in the An Lao Valley while Charlie Company swept through a village from the opposite side. CPT Swain had taken off his helmet in the stifling heat. A round fired from one of the tanks supporting them had ricocheted off a tree. When it exploded, one of its shell fragments struck Swain in the head. Another fragment hit one of his troopers, and they were both critically wounded. In his book, *On The Tiger's Back*, Bernard Grady would recall finding his friend and fellow officer lying alone on a cot in one of the medical tents at LZ English, only minutes before he succumbed to his wounds. The docs had already given up on him, moving on to those in adjacent tents who they could actually save. The tent smelled like "hot canvas and antiseptic" and was eerily dark and quiet as he lamented, "They finally got Walt Swain."

On April 27th, Matulac would respond to another letter from Mrs. Rankin:

Dear Mrs. Rankin,

I received your letter this evening, and it was a very pleasant surprise. It's funny, I was thinking of you the other day. You see, I'm always catching myself thinking that Donald would have liked to have seen this or that. For Donald loved beautiful things. A beautiful flower, a beautiful baby, and scenery, etc.

I know it must be hard for you to lose such a loving son. He mentioned you often, and he spoke of his home all of the time. I hope you don't mind but, I showed your letter to some of the boys from Kentucky and to the boys in the section. As I said before, your loss is great, and it is the eternal cross that mothers everywhere must bear.

I guess, when you are doing your housework or have a free minute, you may come across some memento Donald may have left, or memories of his childhood may enter your thoughts. Those childhood days are the happy days of your helpless baby becoming strong and inquisitive. Strong enough to stand on his own two legs and finally totter around. Later, he grows more bold and sure of himself. He asks questions like 'why is there a moon, why is the grass green' or things like that. Later he grows up and starts school and still later he goes to college. And after a few years of manhood, he is struck down suddenly, and you ask yourself why. Why was it my son?

All of us here are living with death by our side every day. It is terrible, but we just go on doing our jobs, hoping the next one is not for us. Yesterday, a company commander was killed. Captain Swain, a man who was a dedicated soldier. We (the old-timers who knew him well) all felt bad, depressed. Not one of us can explain death, although we are familiar with it.

I guess people must die, but why is it always the good ones? I guess only God has the answer to this question. Whenever I think of Donald as that broken soldier lying in the rice paddy – I push these thoughts from my mind and think of the days when he was happy, smiling and worried about what he wanted to do in life. This helps me very much. And when I look at the men in my section, I tell myself it is my duty to bring them home safe, and I must try harder to keep them alive. It is very difficult for me to write to a mother and tell her of the death of her son. Before I wrote to you, I stared at the blank paper for three days, trying to think of what to say.

I have been in the Army for 14 years now, and I have seen my home in San Francisco very little. I guess you can say I'm the eternal traveler. Being the mother of servicemen, I guess you know how my mother feels about me being here in Viet Nam. It's ironic, but did you notice on the back of the clippings you sent to me, is the story of An Khe being attacked? Several men were killed in that action.

Right now, we are in the same area, not far from where Donald was killed. I keep hoping I meet the VC's that killed him, for I vowed to myself before, that I would kill 10 VC's for each man that is hurt in my section. I know it sounds cruel, but that is what I'm here for.

We have done a lot in the past 9 months. I just hope that in the next three months everyone will be able to make it home safe and sound. I will remain here, but not with the 1st Cavalry. I cannot stand to see any more boys hurt. I'll be going to Ving Tau where the transportation units are.

I hope that someday soon, we can both find peace.

Sincerely,

Roberto Matulac

Continuing the mission in An Lao, on April 30th Alpha Company would conduct a raid on Hung Long, a large village in the center of the valley, near the banks of the Song An Lao River. It was somewhere around this time that Bill Purdy recalls being picked up in a rice paddy along with John Kruetzkamp and others in 2nd Platoon. As the chopper hovered just a foot or so above the dikes, Purdy threw his M-60 and pack aboard and climbed on. As they lifted off, he saw that Kruetzkamp's legs were still stuck in the muck below and he was being left behind. After yelling at the crew chief, Purdy leapt from the chopper to help his buddy. In doing so, he had injured his knee. His knee would require surgery, and he would eventually end up at a hospital in Okinawa.

It was somewhere around this time that Quinn remembers a replacement soldier from New York named Kenny Jensen arriving in their company. "Jensen was from Jamaica Queens, he had a hard life," he recalled. Jensen had been initially assigned to 1LT James Harmon's 2nd Platoon but wanted to get in with the mortars in 4th Platoon, maybe because their was a large group of fellow New Yorkers in that platoon. Whatever the reason, he talked to their platoon sergeant, SSG Bobby Hayslip, and they managed to get him reassigned. Jensen had a girl back home named Dolly that wrote him letters. He showed his new platoonmates her picture, a real blonde bombshell is how Quinn described her. One day, Jensen received a letter from Dolly asking if he had any friends that her girlfriend Georgina could write to. He wrote Dolly back saying that his buddy Quinn could probably use a letter once in a while. After mail call one night, Jensen asked Quinn if he had gotten a letter. "Yeah," Quinn replied, "from some broad named Georgina."

"Well, you're welcome" Jensen said.

"Gee, thanks Jensen. Wait a minute, what does she look like?" She turned out to be an attractive Italian girl, and for the rest of his time in Vietnam, Quinn would have someone besides his mom to write home to. Jensen would soon become good buddies with Quinn, Will, and the rest of the original 4th Platoon soldiers, who were now increasingly referred to as "old timers".

Late in April, Will received a Red Cross message from home. His dad, Eddie, was undergoing surgery for complications resulting from an accident with a tractor. He was needed at home to tend the farm, and Millie had sent a request to bring him back for a few weeks. He was to stay on patrol with the company through the end of April and be sent home the first week in May.

Dear Folks,

I received your letter yesterday and Captain Grady is typing up papers for me to take back to An Khe. So it is up to them to let me go. I am with the company and tomorrow we hump the hills or paddies again. But at the end of this month, we should be going in for a while. The battalion, that is. Everything is looking good. It is still too hard for me to believe that I'll be home very shortly. It seems so unreal. Wish only that Rod was coming with me. This is all going too fast. It needs time to sink in. I really don't know how long it will take for them in An Khe to let me go. Maybe a few days or a few weeks. At least I'll be home soon.

In a daze,

Will

Moving upstream, searching for Charlie, photo by Robert Matulac

(left to right) Patrillo, Fulford, Evans investigate dead body on trail

Huey spraying Agent Orange in valley, photos by Marvin Bierschbach

Huey landing on hilltop, photo by Marvin Bierschbach

April 1966, An Lao Valley, Bobby Hansen, photo by Robert Matulac

(front to back) Knight, Spaur, Fox, Elmer, photo by Wilbur Bowe

Matulac marking position before airstrike

Will Bowe wades through elephant grass

16

THE CREW CHIEF

I thought for sure I would have gotten a medal for this...

For the daily danger they faced, the infantrymen had great respect for the pilots and flight crews that supported them in the field. One such crewmember was Dave Mason, who years later would become Will's brother-in-law. They did not know each other at the time, however. Assigned to the 196th ASHC, Dave was the crew chief of a Chinook, resupplying units of the 1st Air Cavalry and the ROK in the Central Highlands from February 1967 to February 1968. During their flights, he manned the M-60 machine gun on the right side of the aircraft. He recalls that many infantrymen were glad to see him and his crew when being evacuated from dangerous areas. He also recalls getting flipped off by some of them as their Chinook often blew down their tents and made a mess of their outposts.

While attempting to resupply a Special Forces unit north of Pleiades, in Pleiku Province near the Laotian border, his aircraft came under fire from enemy ground forces. A .30 caliber round smashed a heater transformer between him and the pilot. The pilot banked left and hauled ass down the mountain pass, and right into a torrential rainstorm, as pieces of the transformer and the spent round rolled about the floor of the aircraft. As they were coming out of the mountains, the heavy rain forced the crew to land in an open area, basically in the middle of nowhere. Upon inspection, they found two forward rotor blades had also been hit. One round had pierced the leading-edge spar of the blade, after which it had been flung to the end of the blade's tip cap where it remained lodged. The pilot and co-pilot kept the enemy rounds as souvenirs.

A far worse forced landing took place for Dave's crew while flying ROK troops who were dropping barrels of CS gas (tear gas) on a target area. The barrels were fitted with small TNT charges that would set off the gas, on a delay of approximately ten seconds from when the charge pins were pulled. The Korean soldiers would pull the pins, then push the giant barrels of tear gas out the back of the flying Chinook. With three barrels left, they had pulled the pins from one of the barrels, but during turbulence, the barrel had tipped over and rolled back toward the cockpit. Ten seconds was not enough time for them to get the barrel out of the aircraft. The barrel exploded inside the cabin, killing one of the Korean troops instantly. A scene of chaos and panic ensued, as tear gas filled the burning aircraft. Fortunately, the pilots had been wearing their gas masks, and were able to activate the aircraft's fire suppression and auto-rotation systems. Desperate for air, several troops used their heads to smash through the portal windows. Engulfed in flames, the Chinook was expertly landed on a

ROK outpost in the valley. Dave would forever remember this as his worst day at the office.

Dave also told the story of his most unusual load in his own words:

A Special Forces Major oversaw this loading. During loading the first cow, two Hmong Soldiers held the cow right and left with slings. Being a brave farm boy, I held the sling leading the cow onto the aircraft. About half-way up the ramp the cow went crazy! The Hmongs let go and that cow charged me full force! It knocked off my glasses as I grabbed on to its horns and it carried me all the way to the companion way of the cockpit!

I was really hot by this time, I could only hold on to those horns for dear life! I thought for sure that cow would put me through the ceiling before they pulled it back! The Hmongs returned to pull the cow away from me and tied it down in the cabin of the aircraft. I moved down the steps on the starboard side and cocked a round in my 45. The Special Forces Major noticed this and said, "What are you going to do?"

I replied, "I am going to shoot that son of a bitch if they let it go again!"

He replied to me, "That's right son, you shoot it!" It was then that I calmed down enough to realize that he thought I was about to shoot his Hmong troops. I do not know how many times that cow smashed me to the ceiling of the companion way, but it sure was plenty, she knocked the wind out of me! I thought for sure I would have gotten a medal for this, but I guess there are none issued to those attacked by mean cows? You will note the plastic put down (in the photo) to keep the cow shit off the floor. During the flight, I do not think any of these cows hit it once!

Joseph Galloway, co-author of *We Were Soldiers Once... And Young*, would remark about the aviation pilots and crews:

No matter how bad things were, if we called, you came. Down through the green tracers and other signs of a real bad day, off to a real bad start. To us you seemed to be beyond brave and fearless – that you would come to us in the middle of battle in those flimsy, thin-skinned crates. And in the storm of fire, you'd sit up there behind the thin plexi-glass, seeming so patient, and so calm, and so vulnerable. Waiting for the off-loading and the on-loading. We thought you were God's own lunatics and we loved you, still do.

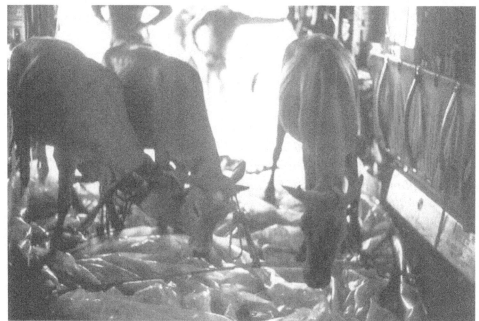
Hmong cows loaded for transport aboard Dave Mason's Chinook

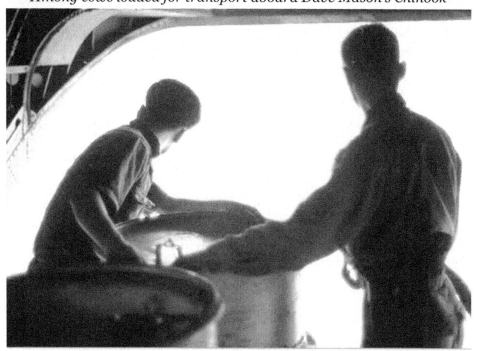
Korean soldiers drop barrels of tear gas from Dave Mason's Chinook

Korean soldiers boarding Chinook for air assault mission

Dave Mason (left) and crew

17
HEART OF DARKNESS

I take it no one told you yet.

In May, Will was sent home on emergency leave. Making several stops along the way, he would eventually find himself on a commercial jet bound for San Francisco, from where he would then fly to Minneapolis. While en route to his connecting flight at the San Francisco airport, he noticed throngs of journalists hurriedly passing by and gathering further up the concourse. Wondering who could be at the center of this mob, he made his way through the crowd. There in the middle of it all was Senator Robert F. Kennedy, holding a press conference. Although a little blurry, he managed to capture a picture of the senator as he spoke to the reporters.

Senator Robert Kennedy holding press conference at airport

Will was picked up by his family at the Minneapolis airport. As one would expect, Millie was overjoyed to see him. Returning to the farm was a strange experience after everything he'd been through, especially given the knowledge that he would soon return to Vietnam. Eddie's surgery went as planned and without incident. For the next few weeks, Will stayed on the farm and took care of the daily chores with his younger brother Mike, while their dad recovered in the hospital. Home cooked meals, a soft bed to sleep on, and an unlimited supply of clean, and more importantly, tasteless water. Life on the farm had never seemed so good. On a few occasions, friends would stop by to visit, including his best childhood friend from up the road, Larry Geissler. They sat in the kitchen while Millie cooked supper, recounting his recent adventures. As he fed and milked the cows each morning and night, he couldn't help but think about what could be happening eight thousand miles away.

Continuing the mission in An Lao, on May 2nd Alpha Company was lifted to LZ Sandra, a firebase in the mountains northwest of the An Lao Valley. They would pull security at the outpost for six days, and on the 7th would air assault back to LZ Hump to begin their patrols once again, moving northeast toward the valley floor. Although the enemy had largely disappeared at this point, refugees seemed to be everywhere. Many were headed through the valley toward resettlement camps with whatever they could carry.

8 May 1967, 11:42 AM – A Co to TOC: At BR 770-951 we picked up 14 refugees (13 women, 1 child), 5 Viet Cong suspects dressed in black pajamas; would like to get them picked up as soon as possible.

12:26 PM – A Co to TOC: At BR 770-951 have a total of 21 persons – 10 males, 11 females, 2 males are categorized as Viet Cong suspects, also have 8 male children.

1:11 PM – A Co to TOC: Request medevac for one Vietnamese child who is very sick at BR 775-960.

2:26 PM – A Co to TOC: Disregard the medevac for the sick child, he has died.

Early in the month, Bobby Hansen and his buddy Jim Hirschuber were transferred out of Alpha Company to other units. Hansen argued against his transfer, but to no avail. As he recalls, there were only three original members left in his squad when he was transferred, SSG Kenneth Gregory, Phil Jones, and Guy McNay.

As the operation progressed in May, enemy contact began to pick up. On May 11th, Guy McNay, the Kentucky soldier who'd insisted on returning to Alpha Company after recovering in the hospital, wrote to his sister, Annette Sebastian. She knew him simply as "Juggy". He remarked that he'd almost been shot again, but had been saved by his sergeant. He also mentioned that he was soon to be advanced to the rank of Specialist-Four.

On May 16th, Alpha Company would find itself deep in the mountains approximately three kilometers northeast of LZ Sandra. At 3:55 AM one of the company's ambush patrols would be overrun by Viet Cong. During the attack, communications were lost with the patrol. As 4th Platoon fired illumination rounds over the area, movement could be seen, but the company could not determine if they were seeing friendly or enemy movement. Another patrol was dispatched to locate the one in contact, but was unsuccessful in the darkness with communications lost. At 4:44 AM the main body of the company began receiving machine gun fire. Contact would not be made with the beleaguered patrol until 6:08 AM. They would find that five had been wounded and one had been killed, Corporal (CPL) James Ray from Spruce Pine, North Carolina. Twenty-five years old and married, CPL Ray had joined Alpha Company as a replacement in February.

James Ray

Bill Purdy's buddy in 2nd Platoon, John Kruetzkamp, recalled how one of his friends was in that ambush patrol that was overrun. His friend told him that he'd simply played dead while some of the Viet Cong came through to check bodies. He thought, perhaps, they could hear his heartbeat, probably the scariest moment of his life as they took his rifle, then took the boots right of off his feet before slipping back into the jungle. Kruetzkamp remembers how they all moved down off the hill they were on the next morning and patrolled through the valley, then returned to the same area that night. This time it was Kruetzkamp's turn to go out on ambush patrol with about five other guys. He was prepared for the worst, given what had just happened the night before. In the darkness, they spotted a group of enemy approaching. Kruetzkamp tried to radio back to the company but no one was answering. He figured the radio operator on the other end had fallen asleep. They felt outnumbered and wanted to get back to the company, but without radio contact they would risk being shot by their own men as they came in. They had no choice, however, so they set a trip wire on one of their Claymores and headed back. As they were running back in, Kruetzkamp wounded his leg on some bamboo that had been cut down for fields of fire just outside the company perimeter. As the medic was tending to his wounds that night, he asked who had been monitoring their radio, but no one would tell him.

Later in May, a chopper would deliver more fresh meat for the war, nineteen-year-old replacement soldier Caesar Pinto, a Portuguese fellow from New Bedford, Massachusetts. He was what might have been called a "change of life" baby in those days. His mother was deceased, and he had two sisters who were over twenty years older than himself. Pinto had struggled through basic training. His bunkmate, Paul Plaine, had taken Pinto under his wing and helped him along. After each day of training, they would go over what they had learned. Assigned to different units, the two would go their separate ways after their training. As they said their goodbyes at Penn Station, Paul reminded Pinto to pay close attention to his sergeants and to ask for help when he needed it, and most of all, to be careful. Paul had a foreboding feeling as he watched Pinto board his train.

Alpha Company's commander, A.J. Wise, had been replaced by a Cuban exile named Jose Dorta. He had been a Major in the pre-Castro Cuban Army. He was tall and tough, with white hair, and smoked a cigar most of the time. Of course, English was not his first language. He spoke very fast when he got excited, to the point where the platoon leaders couldn't understand a word he said. Fortunately, one of the new replacements spoke Spanish and would often serve as an interpreter of sorts for the new commander. Forward observer George Kalergis would recall how CPT Dorta showed up in the field with an excessive amount of gear. Bringing everything but the kitchen sink, Kalergis would have to help him carry it all as they set off on their first patrol together.

Now in the latter part of their tour, both drugs and desertion were becoming a problem for the company. Soldiers would be sent back to An Khe on occasion for medical treatment or R&R, and a handful of them would take the opportunity to disappear. Some had been influenced by the Black Power movement, which encouraged desertion of the "white man's" war. Matulac would find himself visiting virtually every field hospital in Vietnam in search of these lost sheep. He would inquire with each of the field hospitals to see when they were discharged, then begin his search of the surrounding camps. At one point, Matulac was searching for fourteen different soldiers who had managed to disappear from the company. As he asked around, he put the word out that they could be charged with desertion and sentenced to death under the UCMJ (Uniform Code of Military Justice). Unlikely a scenario as it was at the time, he wanted them to know he meant business. Eventually, he found a large group of these wayward troopers hanging out in the company area at An Khe. "We heard you were looking for us, sergeant," one said sheepishly. Matulac advised them that they would all need to get on the next chopper going out to the company. One of them refused, saying he was too scared to go back. Despite his refusals, Matulac managed to get him aboard the chopper eventually. He would be killed by a sniper the next morning.

Smoking pot was somewhat tolerated so long as it wasn't done while on patrol. A few troopers, however, insisted on smoking up during operations. One guy in 1st Platoon had brought a rather large amount of pot back with him from R&R. He was warned not to smoke it while on mission, but he wouldn't listen. Matulac heard a loud clang in the middle of the night, from the other side of the patrol base where 1st Platoon was bivouacked. Moving around at night was a good way to get shot, so he waited until the next morning to investigate. Apparently, this same guy with the stash of pot had gotten high and passed out while on guard duty, and his squad leader had knocked him over his helmet with an entrenching tool. Sometime later, as the company was setting up their patrol base for another night in the field, Matulac checked to confirm that each of the platoon sergeants had account of all their men. 1st Platoon was missing one man. The last time anyone remembered seeing him was during their last smoke break while on patrol. As it turned out, he had smoked some pot and fallen asleep, and they had inadvertently left him behind. It was getting dark as Matulac prepared to report the incident to battalion. Just then, a lone figure that looked to be a soldier came walking up the trail. His face was ashen, as if he'd seen a ghost. "I can't believe they left me," he said, "out there in Indian Country."

Assigned to Alpha Company during Operation Pershing was a female scout dog named Krim whose job it was to alert her handler for both booby-traps and enemy ambushes. The following is an article that was published in the *Cavalair* about the dog's actions on the 19th of May:

Sergeant Saved By Alert Dog
By SP/4 Marc Davies, staff writer

"I'd rather been shot than that dog. She saved my life twice that day," said Staff Sergeant Harry W. Coit, of the 1st Air Cav Division's 5th Battalion, 7th Cavalry. He made the statement with deep serenity about a scout dog named Krim. Coit, of Long Beach, Mississippi, had his doubts about the scout dog who was working with his platoon during Operation Pershing. He claimed it lacked drive and had passed several booby-traps without giving an alert. Coit was even thinking of having the dog sent back for further training. But SP/4 Michael Lister, the dog's handler, and Krim showed their value and left no doubt in Coit's mind that they were indeed a valuable team in search of the elusive enemy.

Alpha Company was moving cautiously along a trail deep in the jungle some 250 miles north of Saigon when Krim gave her first alert. Upon investigation, the troopers found fresh enemy positions. In the next thirty minutes, the dog and handler alerted the infantrymen eight more times. Then Krim gave two strong alerts and Lister pointed them out. Just then, the enemy opened fire from one position and hurled a grenade from the other. Lister saw the grenade coming through the air. He took the enemy under fire and killed him. The rest of the enemy withdrew.

After evacuating a wounded squad leader, Alpha Company went in pursuit. After chasing the enemy for about an hour, Krim gave another strong alert, but this time did not wait for her handler to inform the infantrymen. She jumped into a bush where three enemy soldiers were waiting in ambush and fought the enemy until one shot her. Medic PFC Gerald K. Robinson of Adams, Mass. came up and gave the dog first aid. Krim had been shot through the nose but calmly let Robinson administer to her wounds. Men of the company improvised a stretcher for the dog and gave her water out of their canteens. They knew that a lot of them were still alive because of the dog's alertness and courage.

Later, the men of the company drafted a letter to Mrs. Betty Rowe of 2110 Kentucky St., Midland, Mich. who donated Krim, and thanked her for sending the dog. Lister, of San Antonio, Tex. and Krim were both put in for Bronze stars with "V" device for valor in combat.

The *Cavalair* article did not mention what befell Alpha Company later that same day, May 19th.

Now the first week in June, Will found himself back in An Khe, checking in at the 5/7th's rear battalion headquarters where CPT Grady now held court as Battalion Adjutant. He remarked, "We need more guys like you out here, guys with experience." Will was then flown to LZ English, where he would await another chopper that would bring him back out to the field. Here he would run into Rod Henning, who happened to be there for some reason or another. They would find that LZ English had been attacked by enemy mortars the night before, some of which managed to hit the camp's large ammunition dump. The resulting fire and subsequent explosions lit up the sky and wreaked havoc at the camp throughout the night. Two soldiers were killed by falling debris, and nearly forty were wounded. Explosions were still going off with debris landing dangerously close to personnel as cooks prepared breakfast the next morning. The camp's medical tent and over sixty nearby civilian homes were destroyed in the resulting fires that also killed one child.

LZ English with ocean in background, photo by Dave Mason

LZ English, photo by Dave Mason

LZ English ammo dump, morning after explosion, photo by Wilbur Bowe

When it was time to depart from LZ English, Will rode in a Huey along with the company's dinner, looking down at the rivers and valleys he had become intimately familiar with. Like a seductive woman with a black heart, the landscape was serene and picturesque from above. He knew all too well its dark violent side, a testament to how men could turn even the most beautiful place on Earth into a living hell. This time, leaving the farm was much harder than it had been before. With each leg of his journey back from The World he felt a knot of anxiety and despair growing in the pit of his stomach. To assuage his gloom, he thought about how good it would be to finally catch up with the guys. He looked forward to telling them about his brief encounter with Senator Kennedy. Although he had been glad to be out of that place and by no means wanted to return, he missed his friends. They were closer to him now than any friends he had before his life in the Army. It's all downhill from here, he told himself. Just a couple more months to knock out, and then they could all get out of this place, together. Descending one last time into the heart of darkness, he envisioned the light at the end of the tunnel growing brighter.

    The company was operating down in the valley floor of An Lao and had set up its patrol base in the usual fashion. The sun was setting as soldiers milled about, some setting up hooches, others guarding the perimeter. He grabbed a bag of mail for the troopers and jumped off, while others swarmed the chopper to quickly unload the company's dinner. He needed to get his hooch set up and dig in before dark. He also wanted to throw down some chow as he was starving after a long day of traveling. But all that would have to wait, first he needed to find his buddies. The chopper was blowing clouds of dust in his face and coating his new fatigues in a film of red dirt as he looked around squinting, searching for the guys in 4th Platoon. There were so many new guys now, he barely recognized his own platoon. He saw Quinn smoking a cigarette by his hooch. He looked around for Sergeants Fulford and Hayslip, as he first needed to check in with his leaders. They were nowhere to be seen. He walked over to Quinn, anxious to catch up on what had been going on. Quinn had a grim look on his face, "I take it no one told you yet." He offered Will a cigarette, then delivered the news. Fulford and Patrillo were dead. So was Hayslip. They had been killed in a battle that claimed the lives of seven Alpha Company troopers on May 19th.

    The grief was crushing. Fulford and Patrillo were particularly close friends, two of only a handful left of their platoon's original troopers who had made the voyage with him on the Gaffey. And he hadn't been there with them on their last day, to help them or be with them when they died, to so much as cover their dead bodies. He wondered what their last moments were like. The "what if" questions filled him with heartache. He walked off by himself and sat down on a dead tree that was lying near the perimeter of their patrol base. He pictured Patrillo with his fedora, reading the comics and smoking his Pall Malls. Just moments before, he'd imagined that light at the end of the tunnel, and it was gone now. The next two months would be much the same as the previous nine, but perhaps a bit darker and a lot lonelier.

A few days earlier, Quinn had written a letter to tell Will about what happened, but he was already on his way back to Vietnam and never received it. Fifty years would pass before he found it mixed in with his own letters home that Millie had kept over the years. I wondered what must have gone through Millie's mind as she read this letter from Will's buddy as her boy returned to the war zone.

Sgt. Martin J. Quinn
A Co 5th Bn/7th Cav, 1st Cav Div.
San Francisco, Calif. 96490

May 29, 67

Hi Wilbur,

Sorry for not writing sooner but Will, it's been hellish here. I have some sad news to tell you. On May 19th we got into a terrible firefight and of course there were many fellows killed and wounded. From our platoon, Sgt. Hayslip, Fulford and Patrillo were killed. I tell you it was terrible. If I told you everything I would have to write at least 20 pages. But now everyone is working together. There have been many changes in the platoon. We now have Sgt. Lyons as platoon leader, Lussier as platoon sergeant, Elmer and me are Sgts. And we are squad leaders. Andy is section chief. As for everyone else, they have been transferred to other units. Bierschbach was transferred and Bronson was too. We all wish they were back. We have many new replacements in the company and platoon. Well, enough of the sadness.

How are the folks doing? Fine I hope. I am doing A-OK with 62 days to go. I hope all works out for us. Well I hope you don't come back here. We all want to see you, but not back here. Well you sure were my best buddy here and of course you still are. I hope to make it to the farm one of these days.

I bet you're boozing and flying every day and night. Knowing you, you're fat catting it, but you sure deserve it.

Right now we are at LZ Sandra, but tomorrow are making an Air Assault. I don't want to go, but that's the breaks.

Well Wilbur, I will write again and the guys are always thinking and talking about you. Regards to the family. Take care and keep out of trouble.

Sgt. Quinn
Ha! Ha!

The battle had taken place approximately six kilometers north of LZ Sandra, in the jungle-covered mountains of Quang Ngai Province. After finding nothing of the enemy the day before, aside from a bloody poncho left on a trail, Alpha Company had found a Viet Cong tunnel system and several bunkers that morning. What follows are some of the details the *Cavalair* article left out and what happened afterward, according to the recollections of both Kalergis and Quinn.

The company's forward observer, George Kalergis, who had joined Alpha Company in February, described their patrol that day. "Ninety men strung out single file for at least a hundred meters along the side of a steep jungle-covered mountain. The ground we walked was at such a steep incline, I felt that I was constantly leaning to the left and thought, *this is what it must feel like to wear one high-heeled shoe and one flat.* We could only see ten meters or so up the trail because the vegetation was so thick. The light was restricted, making for an eerie kind of semi-twilight. For some reason, the jungle noises were strangely subdued." His radio operator, Danny Garrity, had fallen ill with Malaria, and now a fellow named John Curtis walked beside him with his radio. At approximately 11:40 AM the lead platoon came upon their initial contact from approximately three Viet Cong. One of their squad leaders had been shot in the leg or the hip. A dust-off was called in but an adequate landing zone could not be cleared, so a hoist was dropped in from the chopper and they strapped him in. Kalergis recalls the sight of the wounded soldier spinning around in the hoist, and wailing in pain as he bounced off the many trunks and branches of the canopy that obstructed his ascent toward the hovering chopper.

Casualty sling-loaded on hoist, photo by Marvin Bierschbach

John Curtis (left) and George Kalergis (right), photo by Robert Matulac

In 4th Platoon, Quinn was now serving as SSG Bobby Hayslip's radio operator and was following him closely through jungle brush as they moved up the narrow trail. Patrillo was following close behind Quinn.

Initially, Kalergis and Curtis marched along as usual, next to their new commander, CPT Dorta and 4th Platoon's mortars in the middle of the company formation. However, they had lagged so far behind now that Kalergis feared the lead platoons were too far ahead of him. "Sir, I better move up front. The company is strung out so far around this mountain that if we get enemy contact, I won't be able to adjust the artillery for fear of hitting the lead platoon." CPT Dorta agreed, and so Kalergis and his new radio operator, John Curtis, started double-timing it to catch up with the lead platoon.

As Kalergis and Curtis reached the lead element, their German Shepard scout dog, Krim, was walking out in front of them. Kalergis recalled, "She was mangy and seemed rather docile. I wondered, *is she really cut out for this fighting stuff?* She earned her dog food that day, though. She suddenly runs and leaps with a fierce growl into the jungle to grab a Viet Cong with a machine gun who was about to fire on us. Curtis and I dive off the trail and a flurry of AK-47 and M-16 gunfire is exchanged. When the dust clears, several enemy soldiers are dragging one of their wounded companions down the trail. Man, I had sure misjudged that dog! She had taken a bullet to the nose to save several soldiers' lives, very possibly mine and that of Curtis." Kalergis radioed their situation back to CPT Dorta, who told them to pursue the fleeing Viet Cong. Kalergis pleaded with the commander to let them stop so he could call in artillery on the enemy ahead, but CPT Dorta insisted they continue their pursuit. As they ran to keep up with the lead platoon, Kalergis remarked to Curtis, "CPT Wise would have never had us running down this trail like this... We'll stay near the front, but not so close to the lead element. I'm pretty sure there are more Viet Cong up this trail and the company is in perfect position to be ambushed." With that, Kalergis and Curtis dropped back to the rear of the lead platoon. He recalls how the lead squad of the platoon was now about fifty meters up the trail from them, moving much too fast he thought, as he watched them disappear down into a deep ravine. At that moment, 3:58 PM according to the battalion's staff journal, a barrage of AK-47 gunfire was unleashed from above on the entire platoon and Kalergis would witness several of the soldiers immediately in front of him being cut down. Deep in the jungle, they had been led into a deadly trap by the wounded Viet Cong fighter. After jumping off the trail and taking cover behind a small tree, he grabbed the handset from Curtis and radioed for artillery fire.

By now the command group and 4th Platoon's mortars had lagged nearly two hundred meters behind the two lead platoons. Quinn recalled Patrillo, who was following close behind and in relatively good spirits, remarking just moments before the attack, "My brother's getting out of Korea today... and only seventy days left for us." Then bullets began cracking through the leaves and bouncing from trees about their heads. Quinn and most the others hit the ground where they couldn't see anything.

"It started out with just a few shots, then the jungle exploded and everyone went crazy," Quinn recalled. SSG Hayslip said the shots were coming from snipers up in the trees. "No, their coming from just over that ridge," Quinn yelled over the gunfire. SSG Hayslip was only a couple feet away when he started to get back up and was immediately struck in the head by an enemy's bullet. Just over that ridge near the top of the hill lay several fortified machine gun bunkers, and an estimated battalion-size force of Viet Cong. The bunkers were staggered approximately thirty meters apart, up and down the craggy hillside. Many soldiers were struck down in the initial blast of enemy gunfire, with helmets sent flying as the bunkers unleashed their machine guns on the company. According to the staff journal, the enemy was also firing from trees, spider holes, and caves. Quinn was now lying next to his dead platoon sergeant, convinced he would soon meet the same fate.

With the two lead platoons still pinned down and separated from the rest of the company, the soldiers of 4th Platoon were ordered to make their way farther up the hill in order to secure a landing zone at the top. Aside from Quinn, this included Will's team leader and friend, SGT John Fulford, their buddies Al Patrillo and Kurt Elmer, as well as Will's fellow mortar team members, John Bronson and Marvin Bierschbach. Following the command group, the mortar platoon was typically not in the middle of the action when this sort of thing happened. This time however, the Viet Cong had sent a wave of soldiers to attack the rear of the company. As a torrent of enemy fighters descended from the high ground above, Patrillo loaded his M-79 and began firing grenades. His aim was accurate, but the enemy was already within thirty meters, too close for his grenades' detonators to activate. Nonetheless, his unexploded rounds managed to knock down three or four of the enemy. Precisely what transpired after this is still a bit of a mystery. I've found that award citations rarely match up exactly with what fellow soldiers remember about a fallen friend's last moments. Nonetheless, his citation for the Silver Star provides some idea of what happened.

The President of the United States of America, authorized by Act of Congress July 9, 1918 (amended by an act of July 25, 1963), takes pride in presenting the Silver Star (Posthumously) to Specialist Four Albert John Patrillo, United States Army, for gallantry in action. Specialist Four Patrillo distinguished himself by exceptionally valorous action on 19 May 1967, while serving with Company A, 5th Battalion, 7th Cavalry during a search and destroy mission in Quang Ngai Province, Republic of Vietnam. Specialist Patrillo's company was following the trail of a wounded Viet Cong sniper when two platoons became pinned down by intense automatic weapons fire. Specialist Patrillo's platoon was sent up a hill with another element with instructions to secure a landing zone at the top. Upon approaching the summit, the platoon was fired upon by Viet Cong in treetops and camouflaged bunkers. Recognizing the danger to his comrades if the enemy proved successful in halting their advance, Specialist Patrillo left his cover and moved against a heavily fortified bunker complex. Firing his weapon continuously, Specialist Patrillo pressed his determined attack until he was struck and mortally wounded by hostile fire. His gallant action contributed to the ultimate success of the company in securing the landing zone and evacuating the wounded. Specialist Patrillo's display of personal bravery and devotion to duty was in keeping with the highest traditions of the military service, and reflects great credit upon himself, his unit, and the United States Army.

SGT Fulford was cut down shortly after Patrillo as they fought desperately to reach the top of the hill. In Quinn's mind, the fighting was just a blur of screaming and machine gun fire, but he vividly recalls one moment in particular. Taking cover on the ground in the middle of the firefight, he felt around his chest for his miraculous medal, but the Virgin Mary was gone now.

Another Silver Star was awarded to SGT Vernon Garrett, known to his buddies as "Roy", who served in one of Alpha Company's rifle platoons.

For Gallantry in Action: Sergeant Vernon Garrett distinguished himself by exceptionally valorous action on 19 May 1967, while serving as a squad leader with Company A, 5th Battalion, 7th Cavalry during a search and destroy mission in Quang Ngai Province, Republic of Vietnam. On this date, the company was pursuing a wounded enemy sniper when it came under intense hostile fire. Sergeant Garrett was directed to join his squad with a platoon and move up a hill to secure a hilltop landing zone. While advancing up the hill, both elements were taken under heavy automatic weapons fire from treetops, trenches, and fortified bunkers. Due to the intensity of the fire, Sergeant Garrett's squad was instructed to withdraw to the base of the hill, leaving behind the bodies of three mortally wounded members of the platoon, their weapons and equipment. Sergeant Garrett, with his squad covering him, moved up toward the bodies. Attacking two bunkers, he killed one enemy soldier and wounded another. With complete disregard for his own safety, Sergeant Garrett fought his way to the position and recovered the soldiers and their equipment. When he was sure that his mission had been successfully completed, he covered his squad's withdrawal to the base of the hill and finally withdrew himself. Sergeant Garrett's gallant action is in keeping with the highest traditions of the military service, and reflects great credit upon himself, his unit, and the United States Army.

Kalergis had been calling in artillery during the fighting, but his initial round had flown clear over the hill where the Viet Cong were dug in. He then radioed, "drop two hundred," to bring the fire closer. The second round landed behind him and the platoon he was with. Uncertain of his exact position in the jungle and unable to adjust the artillery fire accurately on the hilltop, he feared blowing up his own men. Kalergis yelled to his radio operator, "We have to get closer to the front, I can't see our soldiers or where the rounds are landing!"

"You gotta be shitting me, sir!" Curtis replied. Nonetheless, he dutifully followed Kalergis, running up the trail under fire for another thirty meters or so, to where several of their dead and wounded were lying.

"It was like a movie I was watching in slow-motion as we ran up the trail," Kalergis said, "I was scared much of the time moving through the jungle, but during the ambush I was almost emotionless, full of adrenaline and everything seemed crystal clear. I would later be scared shitless just thinking back on it."

Now even closer to the enemy bunkers at the hilltop, Kalergis managed to get some ARA gunships on station. He popped a red smoke grenade to signal their location to the pilots, but the smoke drifted and weaved under the jungle canopy, emerging from the treetops far away from their actual location. As a result, the initial rockets came in almost on top of them. "Check fire!" he radioed, fearing they would all be killed by their own gunships.

Kalergis spoke of a couple of visions that still haunt him to this day. "One of our dead soldiers being dragged back by his feet, his limp head bouncing on the ground every time he hits a bump in the trail. Another vision from that day... two young soldiers who were friends and had joined the company just a week before. One of them had been killed in the ambush and I see the other one curled up, moaning in the fetal position next to his dead friend."

Taking the hilltop and bunkers would prove impossible that night, but by approximately 6:30 PM they managed to break contact. Under sporadic fire, they pulled back and regrouped to an area near a crude dirt road farther down the hill. They had not been able to recover all of their dead. With darkness approaching, the enemy still dug in, and no landing zone, the medevac choppers could not make it in. Their seven wounded would have to wait along with their five dead.

As soon as they had put enough distance between themselves and the enemy bunkers, Kalergis would call in the airstrikes. The first was an AC-

130 Spooky gunship. The giant aircraft circled in the darkness above. Its guns made a low-toned foghorn-type sound as it sprayed the hilltop with a steady red-glowing stream of 20mm rounds. The Spooky gunship continued its lead saturation of the hilltop until it was forced to refuel. Next, just before daybreak, came the bombers. Quinn recalls the drone of their engines growing louder as they approached, then witnessing an apocalyptic scene as they dropped napalm all over the hilltop and enemy bunkers. They could feel the heat of the blasts and the earth shake beneath them with each bomb dropped. Walls of flame erupted from the hilltop. Everything before them was burning, engulfing them in a haze of black smoke and the smell of burnt rubber and gasoline.

The first rays of sunlight now filtered through the trees, revealing an other-worldly hellscape of sorts atop the hill. By this time, two more of the company's troopers had succumbed to their wounds, bringing the death toll to seven and making May 19th's battle the deadliest to date for Alpha Company. The exhausted soldiers advanced back up the hill. Most of them were covered in both dirt and blood, either their own or that of their friends. The enormous bunker complex was now a smoking black heap, completely obliterated, with a few bodies and parts scattered about. The only enemy left alive were those taking refuge in the caves and spider holes, though most had escaped before the airstrikes. The troopers made their way into those holes and caves to pull out many dead Viet Cong and prisoners. Most of them surrendered with little or no resistance. Awaiting them was a South Vietnamese interpreter who commenced intense interrogations as they were being tied up. Amongst the prisoners were a handful of women. Although they carried weapons, they were not primarily fighters but rather, propagandists. It was later determined that this area had been used as an ammunition depot, indoctrination center, and training camp. Once the area was deemed secure, the medevac choppers were finally called in to land on the hilltop.

Quinn found Patrillo. He could only identify him by his blonde hair. With the help of a few others, he carried him up the hill to the waiting chopper. He took one last look at his friend as they loaded him on the dust-off. He then turned to see four others carrying Guy McNay, the nice quiet guy he remembered from their time at Fort Carson. For a moment, he just stood and watched. As his body passed before him, McNay's eyes opened, staring him straight in the eye as if he had just woken up. Another one of those visions that stick in your mind.

A few days later on Sunday evening, Al Patrillo's childhood friend, Tom Ivey was working on a college lab report in his family's kitchen. The Patrillo's home was directly across the street. Sensing some movement along the sidewalk outside the kitchen window, he looked up from his report and noticed two soldiers in dress uniform ascending the steps to the Patrillo's front door, along with their priest. Realizing he would never see Al again, his heart sank. All the years of their shared childhood and misadventures flashed before him, from riding their tricycles together to Al buying his '57 Ford Fairlane convertible, and to their last conversation, the day before he left for Vietnam. Survived by his parents, Millie and Cy, and his two brothers, Tony and Vincent, Al was laid to rest with military honors in his hometown of Susquehanna, Pennsylvania on Memorial Day 1967. Virtually the entire town turned out to see him buried. His older brother, Vincent, had just been discharged from the military on the very day he was killed. His younger brother, Tony, would later volunteer for service in Vietnam.

Their new commander, CPT Dorta, was also said to have fought bravely during the battle of May 19th, even after being shot in the back. He would survive his wounds and be replaced by CPT C.W. Creech. A week later, one of Alpha Company's platoons would air assault onto a new landing zone, named "LZ Dorta" in his honor.

In addition to Guy McNay and the three from 4th Platoon, Patrillo, Fulford and Hayslip, among the dead were PFCs James Eldridge from Nickerson, Kansas and Juan Gonzalez from Uvalde, Texas, as well as SP/4 Anton Bornstein from Bellingham, Washington. Gonzalez was a replacement who'd been with Alpha Company for less than three weeks before he was killed. Anton Bornstein was twenty-one years old and had also just arrived in Vietnam, along with PFC Gonzalez. He was also awarded the Silver Star for his actions.

The President of the United States of America, authorized by Act of Congress July 9, 1918 (amended by an act of July 25, 1963), takes pride in presenting the Silver Star (Posthumously) to Specialist Four Anton Thomas Bornstein, United States Army, for gallantry in action. Specialist Bornstein distinguished himself by exceptionally valorous action on 19 May 1967, while serving with Company A, 5th Battalion, 7th Cavalry Regiment, 1st Cavalry Division (Airmobile), during a search and destroy mission in Quang Ngai Province, Republic of Vietnam. Specialist Bornstein's company was in pursuit of a Viet Cong sniper when two platoons became pinned down by heavy automatic weapons fire. The two remaining platoons were also taken under heavy enemy fire while attempting to secure a hilltop landing zone. Seeing a fellow soldier fall to the ground with wounds in both legs, Specialist Bornstein voluntarily left his position of cover and exposed himself to the enemy in order to pull the man to safety. After removing his comrade to a reasonably secure position, he called for medical aid, placing a suppressive fire on the enemy positions to enable the Aidman to reach his location. After killing two of the Viet Cong, Specialist Bornstein began seeking a better position, but he was mortally wounded before he could reach his objective. His courageous and aggressive action was in keeping with the highest traditions of military service and reflects great credit upon himself, his unit, and the United States Army.

Kim was a friend who knew Anton Bornstein as "Andy" and had graduated with him from Bellingham High School in June of 1965. She recalls working as a telephone operator at Pacific Northwestern Bell and hearing the toll of the nearby church bells during his funeral as she grieved quietly at her station.

On Sunday, May 21st, SGT Charles Thornell, Jr. stood in dress uniform at the doorstep of Annette Sebastian at 17 Division St. in Erlanger, Kentucky. In his hand he held a telegram. Its message was painfully brief, informing her that her brother "Juggy", Guy McNay, Jr. had been killed two days earlier. She had just received his letter written on the 11th, telling of how he would soon be promoted to Specialist-Four.

On that same day, May 21st, both Alpha and Charlie Companies found themselves searching through the area in which the battle had taken place two days before, on May 19th, as well as that of where their ambush patrol had been overrun in the wee morning hours of the 16th, when CPL James Ray was killed.

1:45 PM – C Co to TOC: At BS 803-248 found one more Viet Cong KIA, had his head completely blown off, unable to tell his age, was wearing khaki shirt and black pajama shorts. Also found 5 steel helmets, one set of field gear, 2 rucksacks with equipment, all of this equipment belonged to A Co 5/7th Cav. Found one M-79 grenade launcher SN 3627, possibly the one A Co lost about 4 days ago.

4:40 PM – A Co to TOC: Follow up on the area of contact 19 May 1967, after searching the area BS 801-248 found one Viet Cong body in a grave, shot in chest. Dressed in khaki pants which were rolled up and black pajama shirt. Also found 350 pounds of processed rice and 100 pounds of potatoes, both of which were destroyed. Found 17 natural rock formation bunkers which were well fortified. Area also had many natural caves and tunnel complexes. Area could accommodate up to 50 persons. There was a lot of bamboo scattered in this area. Also found one clip with 10 rounds of 7.62mm short ammo, 2 of these rounds were armor piercing. Also found 5 helmets, 4 of which belonged to A Co and were lost in the initial contact, the other helmet appeared to have been worn by a Viet Cong. Also found 2 packs which belong to A Co and were also lost in the initial contact. One M-79 grenade launcher was found, this was lost by A Co on the morning of 16 May 1967. This area was well worked over by ARA and artillery strikes. A lot of flesh, blood and hair found in the area. Appears there were many Viet Cong KIA and WIA, but were dragged away from area.

With sadness, Martin Quinn remarked about May 19th 1967, "It's sad. I think about it every day. Like certain things will cross my mind, and I think of how this guy or that guy isn't here, never had a chance to get married or have children. I think about how Bobby Hayslip had just gotten married before coming to Vietnam."

Funeral of Albert Patrillo, photo courtesy of the Patrillo family

Guy McNay (center) and friends writing letters

Anton Bornstein

Guy McNay

James Eldridge

Juan Gonzalez

John Fulford, photo by Robert Matulac

Photo by Robert Matulac

Albert Patrillo

CPT Jose Dorta, photo by Robert Matulac

18

AMONGST FRIENDS AND STRANGERS

Cav Records 10,000th Kill Since Arrival

In the period from May 1st to July 31st 1967, the 1st Air Cav's approximately 19,000 soldiers would suffer 160 killed in action, 885 wounded in action, 640 non-battle injuries, and 2,504 diseases of various type, including 412 cases of malaria. The division also accounted for twenty-nine cases of hookworm, thirty-two psychiatric cases, three cases of immersion foot, sixty-five cases of heat stroke, thirty-four animal bites, and one hundred punji stake wounds.

8 June '67 – 7 weeks left

Dear Folks,

Well I finally made it back into the field. Seen Rod today. He and I were going to do some serious drinking tonight at English, but the First Sergeant says, "Out in the field with you." Quinn says "hi" to you all. Made E-5 Sergeant, ha! I finally made E-4. Gee, am I excited. At least it's good to be back with the guys again. Only 4 of the old regulars left in my platoon. Just about all the old originals got transferred. The company is really up to strength now. So many new guys that don't know anything, makes it hard in a way. Have this one new guy. No matter what we say, he did or has something better. Oh boy. Well, I guess I'll go and set up for the night. Get Sergeant Quinn to dig my foxhole, ha! He's my squad leader now.

Will

On June 12th Alpha Company was picked up from the valley floor near the Song An Lao River and flown into the mountains approximately thirteen kilometers north, air assaulting into LZ Jay at 1:44 PM. This was the deepest they had ventured into the highlands thus far. From here, certain platoons were sent out to patrol the surrounding area, while others set to work preparing the new LZ to receive artillery and the battalion forward command post. Within two hours, they had encountered and killed the first of the enemy in their new area.

15 June '67 – 6 weeks left

Dear Folks,

We captured 5 V.C.s and some 8 tons of rice, and two weapons. Plus, no injuries. Right now we're at LZ Jay. A small place for a little rest. Bierschbach got transferred, so I'll probably see him once I get home. I know not if I asked before, but what is the name Joanne gave the baby?

Counting my days,

Will

Cav Records 10,000th Kill Since Arrival

The 1st Air Cavalry Division killed its 10,000th communist since its arrival in Vietnam in September, 1965.

Specialist Four Pascal Harrell of Dixon, Tennessee, a member of Company B, 2nd Battalion, 8th Cavalry, was credited with the kill when he shot a Viet Cong as he ran out of a tunnel during operation pershing on the Bong Son Plain.

Harrell had previously thrown a grenade in the tunnel when he saw movement inside, but it failed to kill the occupant. As Harrell approached the tunnel following the explosion, the Viet Cong hurled a grenade at him. The blast knocked him to the ground and injured his shoulder.

"I had picked up my M-16 rifle after I had thrown the grenade," said Harrell. "I figured he might come out of the tunnel. When he did I let him have it."

Harrell has been in Vietnam 10 months.

June had brought with it a severe heat wave, and on the 16th, one of Alpha Company's troopers would be medevaced with heatstroke. On the 18th, the battalion command was lifted from LZ Sandra to LZ Jay along with an artillery battery as Alpha Company provided security. At 8:30 the next morning, one of Alpha Company's platoons would conduct an air assault onto a nearby mountaintop dubbed LZ Fang. At 9:10 AM the same morning, a medevac would be called in for a trooper bitten by a bamboo viper.

19 June '67 – 6 weeks left

Dear Folks,

40 days left. Been at LZ Jay for a week straight and moving out today to do some humping. The guys have been telling me what a great C.O. they had when I was home. It was this Cuban who could hardly speak English. He would work right with us and wouldn't be afraid to speak against any officer higher ranking than he. He got himself seriously wounded during May and is in good shape now. Even then he wouldn't be evacuated until his company was in control and safe. He is being awarded with the Silver Star or even the Flying Cross for his valor. Everyone that I talked to that knew him says he was the best commander they'd ever had and wished he was back again. Guess I'd missed something good. We've got a lot of new guys in our platoon. In a way I hate to be close friends with any of them 'cause I'll be leaving soon and will leave them behind in such a horrible place. It sure is a good feeling when no one has less time left than you. When I got in the Army, some of the guys would razz us by saying they got 5 days left, or a week or two. Well now it's finally my turn, and man I am letting the guys here know how short I am, rubbing it in, too.

My turn,

Will

On June 19th, the following reports were sent to the battalion:

1:20 PM – A Co to TOC: 1st Platoon at 10:30 AM at BS 708-334 found 2 butchered cows, around which were found 3 sets of footprints which lead off to the south, approximately 3 days old. At 10:45 AM at BS 713-329 1st Platoon found and destroyed one hut. In the hut was a campfire approximately 3 days old. About 100 meters from the hut was a stream where it appeared someone had washed off some meat.

1:40 PM – A Co to TOC: Found 2 canteen covers, NVA type, pair of sandals, pair of Viet Cong jungle boots, 2 M-16 magazines (empty). This area had once been occupied by U.S. forces due to the fact there were beer cans and C-Ration cans on the ground.

Later that month, the soldiers would learn the fate of a good friend. He was the Polish immigrant who'd hoped to earn American citizenship for his Army service, Matulac's skiing buddy at Fort Carson, Kazimierz Slomiany. He had recently been transferred to Bravo Company, 2/5th Cav. He had only been with them a few days when on June 19th, while walking point he spotted a Chinese Claymore hanging on a palm tree. Sensing an ambush, he opened fire and was wounded in the resulting firefight that killed four others. Badly wounded, he was put on an armored personnel carrier to be evacuated. The APC hit a hole and threw Slomiany off, after which he was run over and crushed. He was twenty-two years old.

Kazimierz Slomiany

On June 20th, Alpha Company moved southwest from LZ Jay, making it about half-way down the mountainside toward the small valley below. Contact would be made with three Viet Cong during the night. Illumination rounds would be called in, but the enemy slipped away in the darkness.

On patrol the next morning, Alpha Company would send the following report:

7:05 AM – A Co to TOC: At BS 722-268 patrol 2 while returning found one Viet Cong body dressed in black pajamas, had been dead for approximately 10-15 days, also found one pair of black pajama pants and some baskets with C-Ration cans in them. Estimate 2-3 Viet Cong WIA. One cave with fresh straw inside, there were footprints all around this cave and also some blood. Prints heading south. Also found 35 hogs feeding off a dead water buffalo.

Medevac was called for another heat stroke at 9:28 AM. They moved down into the valley, then around the mountain they had just descended and back up a draw on the other side. At 10:43 AM, they would find a large abandoned encampment with over twenty huts, thirty bunkers, and over twenty spider holes dug into the earth. Everything would be destroyed before they moved out.

On June 22nd Alpha Company was picked up and assaulted onto another mountain three kilometers east, still south of LZ Jay. The soldiers continued hacking their way through the jungle until the 23rd, when another victim of the heat would be medevaced at 11:30 AM. About a half-hour later, the company was lifted back to the firebase at LZ Jay. With this particular mission over, the entire battalion was airlifted in Chinooks to LZ English in preparation for their next operation.

From their days at Fort Carson, through their miserable voyage on the Gaffey, and all those months spent in the field from August to December, Alpha Company had remained basically intact, a family of sorts. During that time, Will had known everyone in his platoon quite well, and even some in the rifle platoons. He had felt like he knew everyone in his company, at least in a way, because of what they had all been through together. Even those he never spoke to, he recognized, and they certainly weren't considered strangers. That was before, everything was different now. With so many either dead, wounded, sick, or transferred to other units, Alpha Company bore little resemblance to its former self. The company was now mostly composed of replacements. Many were brand-new troops fresh from the states who had received less training than the original group. Their original battalion commander, LTC Swett, had fallen ill in December. His replacement, LTC Canham, had lost his leg in battle alongside Delta Company in February and also had to be replaced. 1SG Potter was gone as well, shot in the leg during the night attack that killed four on February 13th, down the hill from LZ Santana. With CPT Dorta shot in the back on May 19th, they were now on their third company commander. Even within his own platoon, Will now felt he was largely amongst strangers. He didn't much feel like getting to know any of them either, not after losing two of his closest buddies. Soon enough, he knew these new guys would suffer their own losses and experience their own grief, and he would not be around to share it with them.

John Kruetzkamp recalled the day he returned to the company after recovering from his wounds inflicted while running over cut bamboo in May. He didn't recognize anyone at first and told the pilot, "This isn't my company, you're dropping me at the wrong place." He also remarked about the many new guys sent in as replacements, "After our patrol was done for the day, they weren't digging foxholes or clearing fields of fire like we'd been trained. They just wanted to eat their C-Rations and listen to their transistor radios."

As June of 1967 came to a close, only five of the original thirty-some soldiers remained in Will's mortar platoon, Bowe, Quinn, Elmer, Anderson, and Lussier. With Fulford dead, and Bronson and Bierschbach transferred, Will was the only one left from his original four-man mortar team. Thankfully, Quinn had been promoted and put in charge of their squad. "The only good thing about being a squad leader was that I didn't have to pull KP duty anymore when the food came in," he remarked. "The bad part was that I now had to be the first one to jump out of the helicopter whenever we flew into a landing zone. I was always afraid I was going to get shot by one of our own door gunners."

One day, a tall black guy was assigned to Quinn's squad as a replacement. "Sarge, whatever you want me to do, I'll do," he said.

Quinn replied, "I don't want you to do anything 'cause I'm not giving anyone any orders."

The remaining five "originals" of the platoon had all been drafted in 1965. They had been yelled at by their drill sergeants and endured many of their collective punishments together. They had trained together, gotten drunk together, and had broken the rules together. They had set out on their first patrol, made their first air assault, and experienced their first firefight together. They had suffered together, and they had grieved together. They had become men together. One month left in this purgatory of sorts. Of this they were pretty sure at least, even though they hadn't been promised a specific date. And thank God, Will thought, for the small handful of good friends that were still there with him. The five of them would rely on each other for whatever time they had left, in the hope that they could all leave this place together. The odds of this were uncertain at best, given the deadly region they were headed to, and the inexperience of the rest of the company.

Patrolling through jungle in Central Highlands, photo by Wilbur Bowe

Evacuating heat stroke casualty, photo by Wilbur Bowe

Looking westward across Central Highlands from helicopter, photo by Wilbur Bowe

Will Bowe carrying mortar tube

Soldiers of Alpha Company's mortar platoon (back, left to right) Williams, Billy Smith, P.J. Rainy, Wilkerson, unknown,(front, left to right) Bill Knight, unknown, photos by Wilbur Bowe

19
THE FINAL PATROL
(Operation Greeley)

It was really neat. Just like in the movies.

24 June '67 – 5 weeks left

Dear Folks,

I hear we are moving west of An Khe. Maybe it's cooler over there. Three guys had heat stroke the past three days. It sure is hot around here. My feet are cleared up from ringworm and athlete's foot. Elmer says he'll come home with me. Wants to know if there's any planes leaving Eau Claire to Chicago daily. No sweat I'll make it home, only 25 days left. If I get bumped off over here, or whether I am crossing the road to get the newspaper and get run over, doesn't make a difference. When your number is up, ain't much you can do.

Will

Late in the afternoon of June 24th, the battalion was flown far to the west in giant C-130 cargo planes. Alpha Company was the first to arrive at the Special Forces base near the city of Kon Tum, just after 6:00 PM. As the 1st Air Cav continued with Operation Pershing in the east, the 5/7th Cav, along with the entire 3rd Brigade, would be put under the operational control of the 4th Infantry Division. They had been sent to assist in Operation Greeley, in the bamboo-covered mountains of Kon Tum Province. These were, perhaps, the highest of the highlands, in the northwesternmost reaches of II Corps. They were moving close to the Laotian and Cambodian borders, where thousands of NVA soldiers were known to cross into South Vietnam each month. With virtually no rice paddies and little farmable land, it was sparsely populated, mainly by the indigenous tribesmen known as the Montagnards, the French term for "people of the mountain".

The Montagnards were a semi-nomadic people, hunter-gatherers who also practiced agriculture. They would clear small plots of land upon which they would grow corn, yams, and other crops until the soil was no longer farmable, then move on. Hundreds of years ago, they had been driven out of southern China, migrating to the coastal plains of Indochina, after which they were driven out and into the uninhabited highlands by the Vietnamese. Their lifestyle relatively unchanged since the Bronze Age, the Vietnamese considered these "hill people" savages, and generally treated them with contempt. As such, the Montagnards generally distrusted the South Vietnamese but hated the communists, and readily fought as mercenaries for both the French and the Americans. In the early years of

American involvement, in the era of advisors, Special Forces units had trained and armed hundreds of tough Montagnard fighters.

While preparing at the Kon Tum base, Will's mortar team received two new replacements. The other guy now on his four-man team had just arrived in May. The essence of "fresh meat", the pair looked like they belonged in high school rather than a war zone. They seemed rather out of place with their clean-shaven faces and new fatigues.

After a few days of preparation, Alpha Company would follow Bravo, air assaulting onto a mountain known as LZ Top at 4:09 PM on June 27th. As the battalion set up its command post and firebase here, Alpha Company and the others moved out. As they patrolled south through the mountains the next morning, scout dogs would pick up a trail, but could not find the enemy. The terrain was even more rugged here, the mountains higher, the jungle impenetrably clogged with bamboo, and at times it felt like they were lost. This would be the most physically punishing phase of their tour. With their new commander leading so many brand-new troops over the most treacherous terrain, Will felt like the company was in over its head, and it seemed only a matter of time until they ran into a force larger than their own. Gunships and artillery support would be problematic here, and such a scenario could mean certain death. And how would his new guys hold up in a firefight? He didn't want to find out.

Moving out at daybreak on the 29th, the command group and 4th Platoon's mortar teams followed two of the rifle platoons through the jungle with one rifle platoon trailing. They were moving in a line formation down a craggy mountainside in thick vegetation. The lead platoon had it worst, not just because of the added danger, but also because they bore the brunt of the hacking. Progress was halted several times that morning. Every so often, platoons would be rotated to the front in order to share the burden. The jungle was dark and each could only see as far as the next guy in front of him. Will checked back constantly to see the fresh teenage faces of the two new guys following him. He couldn't shake the thought that they just didn't belong here.

Still moving downhill, the first two platoons had already entered into an open area as 4th Platoon approached the same clearing. As they negotiated the steep downward slope, moving out into the light, they watched blood explode from the shoulder of one of the rifle platoon soldiers and a split-second later, heard the pounding of machine gun fire. Troopers were jumping down the slope, running for cover, hitting the ground and returning fire. Within seconds, they were engulfed in gun smoke. As soon as it became apparent that no one was shooting back, the commander shouted, "cease fire!" Everything was silent now except for the radio, crackling with beeps and voices from a distant outpost.

The attack had come from the tree line on the other side of the clearing, just far enough away that artillery could be called in. The ground beneath them shook as they watched the earth erupt and trees explode before them. Then the gunships descended to spray lead into the same area. Two of

Alpha Company's men now lay wounded, and their scout dog handler had fractured his leg while trying to negotiate the rocky slope as the firefight broke out. A dust-off was en route to pick up the wounded, along with the handler and his dog.

With caution, they moved across the clearing and into the forest to search for the enemy. They would find three of them, or parts of three of them, scattered about craters, amongst shattered stumps, bamboo and tree roots. The two new guys had just survived their first firefight. Covered in dirt and with ripped fatigues, they seemed to fit in now.

29 June '67 – 5 weeks left

Dear Folks,

The whole battalion is operating out of Kon Tum. Not too far away from the Cambodian border. Not near as many rice paddies here. I saw Rod yesterday. You know what? He applied for O.C.S. (Officer Candidate School). He thinks about re-enlisting, can you imagine that? Sending these pictures back. As you can see, they're a bit sticky. Sure are nice pictures Mike took of us. Showed them to the guys. Received those doughnuts, they were all moldy. Can't hardly see, too dark.

Will

The patrol continued through the next day, finally ending near a mountaintop over three thousand feet above sea-level. The company moved out again the next morning. After another day of humping the hills, late in the afternoon of July 1st, the troopers were flown back to pull security at LZ Top. Again, they would come under attack from snipers while guarding the firebase that evening.

The men were still on edge following the brief firefight as dusk fell. Silhouetted by the setting sun, three figures could be seen approaching the outpost. As the men on perimeter guard readied their weapons, they could see the figures waving their hands above their heads. Emerging from the wilderness was a small family of native Montagnards, a man, woman and child, trying to escape the bombardment of artillery in the hills.

2 July '67 – 4 weeks left

Dear Folks,

We got sniped at yesterday. All I remember is a few shots zipping over my head. Don't even remember running to the foxhole. Just like old times. No one got hurt too bad. I tore my hand a little bit while breaking some bamboo, that's why I can't write too well. I really got a kick out of these new guys after the little firefight. Big-eyed and thought it was really something. They're digging deeper next time, ha! Me too. We are today on LZ Top. Figure to stay here a while and maybe do some humping just once more before the 15th. 12 days left in the field I am fairly sure of, and they say on the 15th we go in. And I am shaking in my boots. So the gooks got one more chance to get me. It's really nerve-wracking. Rod and his company were on this hill until we came and kicked them off. Now they are out humping, ha! I got the guys to open my C-Ration for me 'cause of my sore hand, ha! Darn Chinook blew our tent down. Be so darn happy to get away from them.

12 ½ days and counting,

Will

After two days of rest, Delta Company arrived at LZ Top on the evening of July 3rd to take over the security mission. As the last of their Chinooks descended, again the outpost was taken under fire by snipers. Alpha Company was still at the firebase the next morning when more sniper fire was taken at 11:25 AM. They would respond with both machine gun and mortar fire, and they would call in the gunships. That afternoon, Alpha Company would be flown approximately thirteen kilometers north, to LZ Hasty near Dak To. As the first of Alpha Company's lifts departed, those left behind would continue to be shot at by the snipers surrounding the firebase at LZ Top. Shortly thereafter, airstrikes would be called in on the enemy that had been harassing the outpost. Secured by Alpha Company, both the battalion command post and the artillery battery would move from LZ Top to LZ Hasty later that evening.

4 July '67 – 4 weeks left

Dear Folks,

Got sniped at again on LZ Top. But the V.C. is sorry now 'cause we threw everything at him except the kitchen sink. One of our guys got shot in the neck by our own men. Guess he's OK. Going to LZ Hasty today. Tomorrow we make an air assault. You won't find any LZ's on the map 'cause they're tiny places and only temporary. Bad news again. Don't know when we're going in. Sometime in July, I suppose. General "what's his face" wants us back in the An Lao Valley 'cause all the V.C.s came back in and are partying it up. C.O. is trying to get us old-timers out of the field as soon as possible, but he knows darn well the Major or Colonel won't approve. A rumor came down yesterday saying all sergeants may be extended if necessary, ha ha! Quinn and Elmer are worried. I and a couple of guys had a moustache, but the C.O. made us shave it off. The Cuban C.O. we had before wanted everyone to have a moustache. That's all the news from the Peanut Gallery.

Will

Alpha Company set off by foot from LZ Hasty the next morning, July 5th. For those who had arrived in August the previous year, it marked the beginning of the end. This was to be their last patrol. It would be, however, a particularly long and grueling one, as they would spend the next two weeks climbing up and down mountains over extremely rugged terrain, while chopping their way through tangled vines and bamboo.

As the rain set in, the mountains they climbed became increasingly muddy and slippery. While hacking their way up their slopes, their feet would routinely give way, resulting in fatigues that were soaked in mud. All of this made their painfully slow advance through the bamboo forests even more frustrating and demoralizing. Only one thing could keep Will and his few remaining buddies going, and that was the promise of going home. As they counted down the days, nature would grow increasingly resolved to break their will, while for its part, the Army was determined to squeeze every last ounce of fight from their bodies before letting them go.

They made their way south down the mountain, into a narrow valley through which ran the Dak Akoi River. That night, Alpha Company's soldiers would find a hidden complex of twenty bunkers and caves that had recently been occupied, as well as an NVA helmet that had been left behind. They would set up camp in the area that night. The next morning the weather turned bad, and as the rain poured down they made their way northwest through the valley, following the river. As rain continued on the 7th, the troopers searched the draws leading up the hills on the east side of the river, finding more enemy huts, clothing, spider holes, and punji stakes. As they continued northwest through the valley that afternoon, movement was detected off to the right of the formation and artillery was called in on the suspected enemy. They would continue moving northwest the next morning, securing a river crossing for Charlie Company.

Charlie Company, 5/7th Cav in highlands, photo by John Goodpaster

On July 9th Alpha Company soldiers would find a hidden man trap – a pit filled with punji stakes, as well as a grenade-type booby-trap. The rain had subsided and only half-way through the morning, the heat was punishing. A medevac would be called in for a soldier with a temperature of 103 degrees who was heaving blood. Later in the afternoon, a long downpour began that would continue through the next day. On the night of the 10th, another soldier would suffer an epileptic seizure. He would be medevaced the next morning. Also the next morning, Alpha Company was alerted to prepare for lift-off to another area, but it was called off and they resumed their patrol.

10 July '67 – 3 weeks left

Dear Folks,

Only a short letter, getting dark and it's been raining and raining. Been humping the past 6 days. It's hard to say when I'll get home. At least I'm out of the field no later than the 24th of July. That's all I am worried about. I don't care if it takes 3 months after that. I doubt now if Elmer or Quinn will make it home the same time as I. No, I haven't heard from Don Mc Ilquham. Got a letter from Joanne, seems like a lot of rain back home.

So long,

Will

11 July '67 – 3 weeks left

Dear Darrell, Joanne and Gang,

I hope everyone is making out OK, especially the baby. Ma says he looks so much like Scotty. Just been humping our legs off and getting wet. I know it can't be raining more back home than it is here. Seen very little of the sun since we moved to the Cambodian border. I'll be as white as a sheet when I come back this time. It's all I ever think about, if I can make it just 13 more days, then I'll be out of the field. Guess I better dig a hole before it gets too dark. Can't afford not to. Getting too short, you know. Really get a kick out of these new guys. I remind them every morning of how short I am, ha ha! By the way, don't call me SP/4, "Mr." will be fine.

A short-timer,

Will

They continued moving south along the east side of the river on the 12th, crossing over to the west side around noon. The bamboo on this side of the river was virtually impenetrable. At 2:10 PM a medevac was called in for soldiers who had suffered severe lacerations from the jagged remnants of bamboo stalks and elephant grass that they were attempting to cut their way through. There were signs of his presence everywhere, but Charlie himself could not be found. For now, the land itself would seem to be their greatest adversary. The circumstances were much like they had been just two months prior, when the company encountered nothing but signs of the enemy for days until running into a battalion of dug-in Viet Cong that killed seven of Alpha Company's men on May 19th.

The next morning, they would cross back over the river and begin moving north along the east side. At 9:00 AM Alpha Company would report finding smoldering campfires near the river before crossing again back to the west. At 5:50 PM another medevac would be called in for a soldier who had accidentally shot himself in the foot with his M-79. The grenade did not explode, but the impact had badly fractured his foot. He would be lifted out of the jungle in a hoist.

On July 14th at 11:22 AM, Alpha Company would be air assaulted onto another mountaintop, two kilometers east of LZ Hasty. As they continued their patrol the next day, they would find another enemy encampment on a jungle-covered hillside. Instead of destroying it, their commander decided to leave a patrol as over-watch through the night, hoping to catch the enemy returning to their camp. The enemy did not return, however, and the huts would be burned at daybreak.

14 July '67 – 2 weeks left

Dear Folks,

It's been our 10th straight day of humping. Never humped so hard before. This C.O. sure doesn't know what he's doing. Just 10 more days at the very most. I bet it rains at least 2 inches every day now. Miserable, holy smoke. Itch, scratch, what a mess we're in.

A hobo,

Will

16 July '67 – 2 weeks left

Dear Folks,

Everything is going as usual. Nobody knows what they're doing. Right now we're on the highest hill in Viet Nam. These hills don't have a top to them. At least it is very cool. Rain, rain, that's all it's been doing. But yesterday and today we're getting a little sunshine. Just ate some C-Rations and we started to move out and a guy just stepped on a punji stake. So I thought I'd drop a few lines while waiting for the medevac chopper. What grabs me is that he just got here yesterday. Rod and D Company are back at LZ Hasty again. When, I wonder, are they going to take this fool company in. Well, I am hoping to get out of the field on 21 July. I hope the 24th for sure. Come hell or high water, I am going. Can't hack this humping much longer.

So Long,

Will

  The rain continued on July 17th as the soldiers made their way north, now traversing the mountains approximately three kilometers northeast of LZ Hasty. They hacked their way through their last patrol in the pouring rain, ankle-deep in mud, able to see only a few feet in front of them and hoping desperately to not encounter the enemy. It may have seemed amusing for Will to think back on the ambitions he and Rod had about going to Airborne school, and the excitement of belonging to this famous cavalry regiment with their Australian bush hats, spurs, and camouflage scarves around their necks. Esprit de corps. He remembered the anticipation of being sent to where the action was, and how anxious he had been to make his mom and dad proud of him. The thrill of it all was long gone, gone since November if not before. He had experienced the reality of this war, its unrelenting drudgery and brutality, its pain and its stench, its despair and misery. Even in victory, it offered little glory. In this war, victory meant dragging charred human remains out from tunnels, stacking up bodies after a hard-fought battle, and burning the villages of those who had cooperated with the enemy. Their commanders would speak of impressive kill ratios, ten or more enemy killed for every one of their friends. Even on their worst days, they had never so much as lost a battle. And yet they would always return to the same valleys and the same hills, only to find more Viet Cong to kill. They were told they were winning, but it was hard to tell. If any victory was to be achieved at this point, it would be a personal one, that of survival.

The sun had come out briefly as they ended the day's patrol near the top of another mountain that towered nearly four thousand feet above the valleys below. This would be the perfect time for a cigarette, but Will only had one left and decided to save it for his guard shift. He awoke in the middle of the night to someone nudging his shoulder. "Your turn, buddy," said Quinn. It had been raining again and had recently subsided. It was still dripping from the trees and off the edge of their ponchos that were buttoned together and stretched over their shared foxhole. Quinn laid down in the dampness while Will rose to a crouch and lit his last cigarette, keeping it just beneath the edge of the foxhole. Staring into the inky darkness, he commenced his watch. Against the chorus of jungle insects, he strained his ears for the sounds of foot soldiers shuffling through the brush, as well as that dreaded metallic "shunk" of enemy mortars in the distance. They'd been attacked at night before, and here they were waiting for it to happen again. With a small amount of moonlight shining through the parting clouds, he could discern the outline of some bushes and trees.

They seemed to come out of nowhere, with no rhyme or reason, random images that once again flashed through his mind. Unlike before, these mental snapshots were from a more recent time. The running man, running for his life through the valley - Tall Lee Roy, just standing there on the dike getting shot at, just standing there, looking around - their radio operator wrapped in a poncho flapping violently from the chopper's downdraft - a blonde Hollywood model hopping out of another chopper onto their outpost - Burtis standing there reading the paper, moments before being shot - the chopper disappearing into the sky - Vietnamese kids smiling and laughing - burnt bodies pulled from a tunnel - the last time he saw Patrillo - the letter sitting on the kitchen table.

It seemed like it had all been a dream, the weird part was that he was still dreaming it. He tried to concentrate on the shapes of the bushes and trees before him. It was hard to stay awake, real hard. The end was near, yet it seemed rather elusive, knowing not for sure just when he and Quinn and the others would be sent in from the field, the anticipated date forever changing. The whole fact of not knowing was messing with his mind, he could feel it. He checked the illumination dials on his wristwatch. It had been only twenty minutes.

Droplets on his poncho glistened as Will awoke the next morning to the familiar sounds of shuffling, clanking, muttering and cursing. As usual, his fatigues and the rest of his possessions were damp. His feet ached, and the first few steps in the morning were always the worst. He shook the water off his poncho, packed it up with the liner, and prepared to move out again. A dense fog lay in the valley below where they had just patrolled the day before. They would soon descend back into that fog. He considered brushing his teeth. Out of smokes, he bummed one from Quinn, who said they wouldn't be moving out just yet. Apparently, they were waiting for a chopper to come in or something. "You know Will, maybe I'll actually get a chance to meet this girl," Quinn said as he showed him a photo of Georgina, the Italian girl that Jensen had set him up with. As their cigarettes dwindled, the chopper's ever-familiar thumping could be heard growing louder as it neared their patrol base. With any luck, there would be hot breakfast on board for the weary skytroopers. Instead, leaping out of the chopper were soldiers of Bravo Company, as more choppers descended onto the landing zone. They had been sent to relieve them in place. It was over.

19 July '67 – 1 ½ weeks left

Dear Folks,

I am making this my last letter, 'cause by the time you receive this I should almost be on my way home. We finally got out of the field yesterday. We are pulling security on LZ Hasty. Tomorrow or the next day, we should be going in to An Khe, and go through processing, and should leave between the 28th and the 1st. I hope I leave on the 1st, 'cause I'll get 65 bucks more. The Colonel gave out awards today. It was really neat. Just like in the movies.

Got Mike's cookies today. I was wondering what happened to them chocolate covered cherries, and a box full of cookie crumbs instead? Ha! And Ma, you're telling me not to re-enlist. Ha ha ha! What a laugh. Good grief.

You know I can hardly believe it is really the end. No more Army or Viet Nam. Finally, I am finished. No other day can be finer than the day I leave the Army. I know that is a fact. Right now I have a hard time sleeping at night and I don't care much for eating. I am so happy, and so proud. What a feeling. I have just one deep sadness, and that is two of my buddies didn't make it. That's the worst experience you can have. Nothing more to write about. Every day gets more exciting. It's getting so that I forget to breathe. I can dangle my feet off the edge of this letter, I am so short. Well, this is it. The beginning of the end. I am finished, through, sitting in my bunker nervously smoking one cigarette after another. Walking in a daze. Telling everybody how short I am. Yeah, this is finally it. The living end. Think I am going to crack up.

Happy,

Will

18 July 1967, LZ Hasty, five "originals" of mortar platoon after final patrol, (front) Lussier, (left to right) Bowe, Anderson, Elmer, Quinn

20
FOR WHAT IT WAS

*All wars are fought twice, the first time on the battlefield,
the second time in memory.*
-Viet Thanh Nguyen

The overall war strategy was dramatically changed when General Creighton Abrams replaced General Westmoreland as commander of MACV in 1968. The goal of the search and destroy strategy had been to kill the communists at a faster rate than the North could replace them, a strategy of attrition. Upon taking command, Abrams shifted the focus from attrition and body count, to winning Vietnamese hearts and minds, protecting the population from guerrilla attacks, and rehabilitating the South Vietnamese military. The new approach was more effective, but far too late in coming as so many years and lives had been wasted on simply trying to kill as many communists as possible. When Abrams took command, public support for the war was already deeply eroded, as were the experienced ranks of the United States Army and its morale. It's impossible to know if this strategy could have won the war if adopted in the beginning, but it would have had a better chance of success, and at a far lower cost in American lives.

The agreement signed between the United States and North Vietnam in 1973 allowed our forces to leave with honor, our POWs to return home, and for our allies to be defeated in our absence. In 1975, with the Republic of Vietnam on the verge of collapse, President Gerald Ford pleaded in vain with Congress to continue our support of South Vietnam in money and weapons. I'd always believed that had Congress done so, the republic could have survived. For sure, they could have at least delayed the communist takeover, along with its predictable killing of dissidents, re-education camps, and the mass exodus of refugees. Whether or not the South's government, as inept and unpopular as it was, could have kept the country free with our material support is unclear. The North had many advantages, such as weapons supplied by the Chinese and Soviets. As a communist state, public support for their war was not an issue as they would simply kill those who refused to support them. Most importantly, they were deeply committed to their cause. Despite being outgunned and defeated in virtually every major battle, they were willing to die in far larger numbers than we were.

Despite all the unknowns, it can be said without hesitation that President Lyndon Johnson failed miserably in preparing the country for war. He made the case for keeping our commitments and defending our allies, while at the same time exempting large swaths of the able-bodied male population from service. I don't normally think of things in terms of class and privilege, but here it's painfully unavoidable. While many well-to-do young men actually volunteered to serve and did so bravely, the fact remains that if you were in college, had political connections, or were otherwise privileged, chances were that you could avoid serving your country. It's all very contrary to my own thoughts on how our country should deal with war. I've always believed that all men, both rich and poor, should be obliged to serve. Maybe that's an overly-romantic notion, and maybe that's never truly been the case throughout our history, but it is my sincere opinion on the matter.

The reason for the massive amounts of exemptions made available in the 1960s was simply that the administration did not want to antagonize those in the country with the most political clout. The President's unwillingness to level with the American people was also manifest in his shocking refusal to mobilize the National Guard and other reserve forces, which until then, had been called upon in virtually every other major conflict. Doing so would send the message that this was an actual war, and that was not the message the Administration wanted to send. Nothing could have done more to damage the reputation of the National Guard. That reputation would not be restored until the Global War on Terror, where at times approximately half of all deployed American ground forces would be from the National Guard and Reserves.

I attended a book signing event where Mark Bowden, the author of *Blackhawk Down*, and more recently, *Hue 1968*, was being interviewed and fielding questions at a Barnes & Noble bookstore in Edina, Minnesota. He noted how over most of this time since the war ended, there have been two well-defined and vehemently opposed sides on the subject of Vietnam. You were either pro-war or anti-war, and there was no significant middle-ground. He spoke further of how today, in contrast, even though there is no universally accepted point of view, a certain understanding seems to have grown on both sides - and everyone is allowed to hold their own truth on the matter. His words visibly resonated with the small crowd of sixty-five to seventy-five-year-olds, many of them veterans, as it did with me.

"...still the man, he hears what he wants to hear and disregards the rest." It has nothing to do with Vietnam, rather it is about poverty and loneliness, but that line from Simon & Garfunkel's *The Boxer* speaks to how we all tend to view things in a way that fits what we want to believe. Some would like to view the entire Vietnam project as corrupt and immoral, while the rest of us would prefer to see it as a heroic struggle in the cause of freedom for our fellow man. I've heard it said that while the South Vietnamese government was never worth saving, the people of South Vietnam were. I think it's important to at least try to remember Vietnam, not for what we want it to be, but rather for what it was, as imperfect as that may seem. My own truth is that it was a valiant effort for a noble cause that simply wasn't meant to be. It became a monumental tragedy that tore our country apart.

We may never agree on the worthiness of the cause that this war was fought for. I hope there is a basic understanding that we can agree on, however. The men who fought this war did not choose this war. They had no say in its conduct, or in its strategy of search and destroy and body count. In service to their country, they fought as bravely and admirably as any generation of servicemen throughout our history. Led by commanders who had triumphed in conventional wars, they were sent into the jungle to confront the unique brutality and frustration of guerrilla warfare against a vicious and competent enemy. Their morality and humanity would be challenged in ways that no man could be prepared for. Regardless of what we may think of the war, how it was conducted, or how it ended, they deserve our respect and gratitude.

21

HOMECOMING

Oh, where have you been, my blue-eyed son?

It was the first week in August 1967. Will stood in line once again, this time at the 5/7th Cav's rear battalion headquarters at An Khe with what was left of the original Alpha Company, each man clutching his precious discharge paperwork as if it were worth a million dollars. They were going home. Quinn recalled how the night before, after cleaning and turning in their weapons, they had all gone into town to get haircuts for a dollar, then came back and got stoned at the clubhouse on base. Many were hungover as they took their showers, packed their bags, and put on their dress uniforms in preparation for a long day of travel. Soon they were getting ready to board a military transport plane that would take them to the Pleiku Air Base, from where they were scheduled to depart Vietnam that day. As they waited, once again the band was playing *Garry Owen*, a little esprit de corps to send them home. Such a light-hearted Irish tune amidst such darkness and tragedy. Although left unspoken, the irony did not go unnoticed. Nonetheless, the music sounded better this time than it had a year ago. Amidst the heavy smell of engine fumes, Will took one last look around the place while boarding the plane. He recalled how he had first seen the words "An Khe" near a dot on a map of Vietnam during his time at Fort Carson, how obscure and far away it had seemed at the time. Since their arrival at An Khe in August of the previous year, thirty-one soldiers had given their lives while serving with Alpha Company. The database maintained by the National Archives accounts for only twenty-nine, but does not include their company medic, Bill Garcia, or their forward observer, James Ulrich, who were both attached to Alpha Company from other units when they were killed.

A torrential rain commenced as they landed in Pleiku. Their hearts immediately sank when they were told that because of the rain, they would not make it out that day. They were then sent to some makeshift barracks to await further instruction. Fortunately, someone was willing to brave the monsoon in order to go out and find beer. Waiting out the storm, they would spend one last night in Vietnam smoking, drinking, and playing cards. Eventually, they just fell asleep in their dress uniforms. Despite staying up late, everyone got up before dawn the next morning, too anxious to sleep in. As Martin Quinn recalls, when the sun finally rose it revealed a beautiful clear blue sky. Before long, they were all milling about near the airstrip, smoking and joking as soldiers do. They would swap a few war stories, but mostly talk about what they were going to do upon their return to The World. After what seemed an eternity, a behemoth C-5 transport plane known as the "freedom bird" taxied toward them along the runway.

A few cigarettes later, they were finally given the go-ahead and piled on. As Will felt the plane's wheels leave the ground, an incredible sense of relief washed over him. At first, the men sat relatively subdued, many contemplating what had just happened. Some cried. They were still young, and had just endured a lifetime of ordeals compressed into a single year. Minutes later, the pilot announced that they had just left Vietnamese airspace, and everyone cheered.

After stopping to refuel in the Philippines, they were flown straight to California for out-processing. Their Army careers ended much in the same way they had started, with endless lines and paperwork. That night, however, they were all treated to a steak dinner where Will and Quinn would enjoy one last meal together.

·········

Their year spent in Vietnam had changed them in many ways. The country they fought for had also changed since that day in August of 1966, when the kindhearted people of San Francisco had showered them with flowers as they sailed off to war beneath the Golden Gate Bridge. The anti-war movement had grown. Amidst the social upheaval, young men were burning their draft cards on the streets and major cities across the country were now burning in race riots, the worst of them having erupted in Detroit during the summer of 1967. Within a year of their return, both Rev. Martin Luther King, Jr. and Senator Robert F. Kennedy would be assassinated – and in the wake of the bloody Tet Offensive, President Lyndon Johnson would make the shocking announcement that he would not seek reelection. They returned to a country that seemed to be coming apart at the seams, that knew little of what they had been through, and seemed to care even less.

After out-processing in California, Quinn took a red-eye flight to New York, then boarded the subway, arriving at his parent's home in the predawn darkness. His arms and hands still carried the remnants of jungle rot, and his mother wanted to take him to see the doctor. Quinn told his mom that the Army had already given him medicine for it, but she didn't think the Army doctors knew what they were doing. A few days later, his dad asked him when he was going to get a job, so he went out and found one the next Wednesday. He never managed to catch up with Georgina, the girl with whom he'd been exchanging letters.

Martin Quinn never got around to visiting the farm, but he and Will exchanged Christmas cards each year for many decades. In 1993, Will visited him while on vacation in New York. After that, they lost touch for about twenty-seven years. Quinn had built a career working as a purchasing administrator for a large hospital downtown. He now recalls a beautiful September morning about seventeen years ago, when he was walking through a skyway between two of the hospital buildings. He noticed billows of black smoke rising from distant buildings. He stopped in his tracks as he realized the smoke was coming from one of the World Trade Center towers.

Others began to gather in the skyway, wondering what had just happened. Moments later, he watched in horror as a commercial jet slammed into the second tower. Minutes later, they would watch the first tower collapse. Many casualties were brought into the hospital that day, and everyone there worked through the night. One of only a few mementos he kept from his time in Vietnam, he still has his green patrol cap.

Marvin Bierschbach and the rest of those who had been transferred to the 1/7th Cav or other units would be getting out soon as well. Figueroa, who had been transferred to the 1/7th in December, had been shot in the stomach. He was said to have been quite happy, laughing in fact, while being loaded onto the dust-off, knowing that he would finally be going home.

Marvin never got his "Dear John" letter, and would marry Jane about a year after returning home. Marvin still resides with Jane in their home in the country, alongside a county road near Saint Cloud, Minnesota. He and Will have kept in touch over the years. While I was writing this book, he was kind enough to talk with my dad and me about their experience together, and to share some of his newspaper clippings and photographs. Now retired, Marvin raises chickens and makes spear-fishing lures that he sells on the internet to local sportsmen.

Jim Hirschuber would return in August to his bride, and his five-month-old daughter. He had come in through Fort Lewis, Washington, and recalls a crowd of protesters throwing stuff at their bus as they left the fort on their way to the airport. Taking a train from Minneapolis on the last leg of his journey home, Jim found himself riding along with a group of what appeared to be about a dozen brand-new soldiers. When the Staff Sergeant in charge of the young men climbed aboard, he made them all move up to the front of the car, admonishing them not to speak to the soldier who sat in his dress uniform in the rear. Shortly thereafter, he would return to his job at a screw factory in Rockford, Illinois. He had only worked there a short time before being drafted, and so he knew only one other guy who was working there when he returned. On his first day back, he was advised by the personnel department not to mention to any co-workers where he had been for the last two years.

Upon his own return to The World, Hirschuber's buddy, Bobby Hansen, would return to his job at a newspaper in New Jersey. He would also buy that '68 Plymouth with the Hemi engine he had talked about with Alan Weisman before he was killed.

Killed on Thanksgiving Day, CPT Wise's radio operator Donald Rankin had willed all his worldly possessions, including a substantial part of his life insurance benefit, to his church in rural Kentucky. The proceeds of over $2,500 were used to help build an addition to the Silas Baptist Church in 1967, which was dedicated in his memory. To send his family sixty dollars would seem a rather trite gesture, and so for decades, fellow Alpha Company radio operator Royce Barrow would struggle over how to repay the money he had borrowed from Rankin before he died. In 2010, he would donate $250 to Rankin's church, in his honor. He would also name his son Donald, after his friend.

A neighborhood friend of Leonard Pelullo, Lou Lupo had joined the Army in March of 1967, the month after Pelullo was killed. He was sent to Vietnam the following November. In their high school days, Lou pulled duty as a crossing guard in the mornings before school. Every day, Lenny would wave to him from atop the front steps of the Pelullos' home in the Port Richmond neighborhood of Philadelphia. He was a few years older than Lou, and he remembers looking up to him like an older brother of sorts. After coming home from the war, Lou recalls seeing Lenny's parents at various veterans memorial events throughout the years. He always wanted to say something to them, but never had the heart to. In 2015, he and some fellow veterans erected a memorial stone in a city park in their neighborhood. Underneath the stone, Lou placed a card from Lenny's funeral along with his photo. He was hoping to see Lenny's parents there at the memorial's dedication, but regretfully, he did not.

Alpha Company, along with the 5/7th Cav and the entire 1st Air Cavalry Division, would continue their mission in Vietnam for years to come. There were many troopers left behind to carry on that mission, including Caesar Pinto, the fellow who had struggled through basic training and come to Alpha Company as a replacement in May. Paul Plaine, the fellow soldier who had helped Pinto along during their training, always had a foreboding feeling about Pinto's fate since they said goodbye to each other at Penn Station, and often wondered if he'd survived. Decades later, he would make the journey to the Wall, hoping not to find his name there. It was, however, just as he'd feared. PFC Caesar A. Pinto, killed in action on August 9th 1967, the thirty-second soldier of Alpha Company to give his life. Paul cried for him. He would continue to return to the Wall on every tenth anniversary of Pinto's death.

Caesar Pinto

An Khe, newly constructed battalion headquarters for 5/7th Cavalry

New Alpha Company barracks, in the distance the 1st Cavalry patch can be seen at the very top of Hon Cong Mountain, photos by Wilbur Bowe

August 1967, new barracks at An Khe, Lussier (left), Elmer (right), photo by Wilbur Bowe

August 1967, An Khe, (left to right) Quinn, Burtis, Anderson, photo by Wilbur Bowe

August 1967, An Khe, remaining original Alpha Company soldiers with discharge papers, photo by Wilbur Bowe

August 1967, An Khe, band playing Garry Owen for departing soldiers, photo by Wilbur Bowe

Alpha Company's forward observer, Lieutenant George Kalergis, would remain in Vietnam for several more months. In October of 1967, he found himself assigned as Fire Direction Officer for Charlie Battery, 1/21st Field Artillery. They had recently moved north into I Corps, establishing a new firebase dubbed LZ Colt that would also serve as the 5/7th Cav's forward command post and as a firebase for Charlie Battery. Monsoon rains had hampered efforts to fortify the new firebase's defenses. They had run out of both trip flares and Claymore mines. They were supposed to receive more from the 3rd Brigade but poor flying conditions kept the supply ships grounded. They were also short on concertina wire, with only one roll surrounding their perimeter rather than the usual three. Severely undermanned and located in a poor defensive position, a small rise amidst vast fields of rice paddies and jungle, Kalergis felt they were vulnerable to attack. He voiced his concerns to the 5/7th's battalion commander, LTC John Wickham, warning that an attack was likely. Kalergis was simply told that there was nothing they could do before being summarily dismissed by the commander.

In the early morning darkness of October 10th 1967, Kalergis was lying on his cot in the FDC (Fire Direction Center) tent and listening to the World Series on the Armed Forces Network radio station. He was rooting for the Boston Red Sox, and Jim Lonborg was in the middle of pitching a no-hitter when he heard the explosions. Mortars were raining down on LZ Colt, one of them destroying part of the FDC tent he had been resting in. He ran out with his radio, trying to see just where the enemy mortars were being fired from. He soon spotted the flashes of enemy mortar tubes set on a small hill mass about seven hundred meters in the distance. His hands shaking with adrenaline, he plotted the enemy's position on his map and called in an adjusting round. An adjusting round is a single artillery round used to gauge and adjust onto the target before firing multiple rounds simultaneously. He watched the first round land just beyond the enemy mortars. Into the radio he yelled, "drop five-zero, fire for effect!" This told the artillery battery to bring their fire in fifty meters closer, and to fire all their guns at once. As he waited for his "fire for effect" rounds to impact, he could still hear the voice of the sports announcer emanating from his transistor radio. Kalergis was informed that their battalion commander had just called in artillery directly on their own position at LZ Colt, mistakenly believing that their entire firebase had already been overrun. "Hell no, don't fire on us - everything's under control!" Kalergis radioed back. As the announcer delivered his play-by-play of the World Series, Kalergis continued to call in artillery until the enemy mortars fell silent. "End mission," he radioed.

The enemy mortars had been destroyed, but Kalergis and the others would soon discover that many enemy fighters were already raising hell within their perimeter. Easily cutting through the single roll of concertina wire, three squads of sappers had infiltrated their undermanned lines. They had done so while the defenders' heads were down and taking cover during the initial mortar attack. The attackers had run straight to the battalion command post tent, throwing in grenades and killing everyone inside. A satchel charge had also been thrown into the nearby tent of the battalion commander, killing one of his officers and gravely wounding the commander. It was shortly thereafter when the commander had attempted to bring artillery on their own position, believing that they had been completely overrun.

The enemy's plan had been to ultimately overrun LZ Colt. However, the sapper squads were primarily concerned with destroying the command post. A larger force was positioned to attack from the surrounding jungle following the initial breach, but the continuous fire of over two thousand artillery shells called in by Kalergis kept them at bay. Meanwhile, the firebase's defenders eventually managed to kill or run off each of the sappers who had infiltrated their perimeter.

In the end, seven Americans died and many more were wounded. Kalergis and Wickham were among a small number of the battalion's officers to survive the attack on LZ Colt. In 1983, President Ronald Reagan would appoint John Wickham as Chief of Staff of the Army. In that same decade, George Kalergis would retire as a Lieutenant Colonel. Along with those visions of his dead fellow soldiers on May 19th and October 10th 1967, he would also remain haunted by those of the poor Vietnamese peasants. In his mind, he can still see their grim faces looking through him, carrying all their worldly possessions on their backs, forced to leave their homes because the government had declared their particular region an "evacuation area". He would remark how he could feel his humanity leaving him, "like the smoke rising from the villages we were burning."

In 1968, the 5/7th Cav would be sent in to help take back the city of Hue after it had fallen to the communists, taking part in what would become the deadliest of all battles during the Tet Offensive attacks. In 1970, President Nixon would send them deep into the jungles of Cambodia, where after weeks of bloody fighting against the NVA, they would uncover an enormous underground stockpile of weapons.

Rather than going home with the rest of the original soldiers of the 5/7th Cav, their chaplain, Father Tom Widdel, chose to stay. He would remain in Vietnam for another year, preaching to the living, comforting the wounded, and positively identifying the dead.

Dave Mason, the Chinook crew chief from Chapter 16, would still be in-country during the Tet Offensive that began on January 30th 1968. Virtually every major city and military base came under attack during the offensive. The NVA had taken part of the city of Qui Nhon, and Dave's crew would be sent to pick up Korean troops in full combat gear from a small island nearby that the ROK used for R&R. They would assault them into the airfield at Qui Nhon in an effort to take back the city. As attacks continued deep in the highlands on the base at Dak To, Mason and his crew would spend approximately twelve hours per day in flight, carrying supplies from Pleiku to Dak To, and returning with dozens of dead and wounded soldiers.

They ended their missions at dusk each night, but would still have to perform hours of maintenance on the aircraft, then have the chopper ready to go an hour before take-off at dawn. With only a few hours left for rest, Dave simply slept on the aircraft during this time. With his combat tour completed, Dave would find himself being flown into Fort Hood in the dead of night. He didn't know it at the time, but it had been planned this way to avoid dealing with protesters.

Robert Matulac would stay with Alpha Company until September, then extend for four additional tours in Vietnam. He said that he felt as though he belonged there. He also mentioned that each time he extended his combat tour, he was given a 45-day pass to spend anywhere in the world. He explained that it was his theory that if the Army thought you actually wanted to stay there, they would pull you out. His theory was eventually proven correct in 1971, when he was told that he could no longer extend his tour.

He would not remain in the infantry after his initial tour with Alpha Company. If he had, he says that he would not be around today. After returning to Vietnam from his 45-day pass in 1967, he was assigned as communications sergeant for an engineer unit operating in Pleiku Province. Their mission was to build a road from Pleiku to Laos. In January of 1968, he was ordered to go to Saigon to pick up some classified documents. Complaining that Matulac always got to go to places away from the unit, one of their sergeants asked if he could go instead. He had the proper security clearance, so Matulac said, "fine, you can go for me."

It was later that night, or the night after, when Matulac heard the explosions. They were not the usual distant thumping of artillery rounds. Instead, these were 122mm mortar rounds raining down on the base itself, and the nearby airfield. Seconds later, sirens sounded. It was the initial wave of the Tet Offensive. A handful of soldiers were huddled behind the door of his barracks, and Matulac ordered them to get to their bunkers outside, which offered better protection than that plywood door. In their effort to thwart the attack, his men could only identify their targets in the distance by their tracer rounds, and initially began firing at friendly units outside the perimeter of the base. Matulac had to explain that the enemy used green tracer rounds, and friendlies used red.

The attack was short-lived and would turn out to be a diversion from the main assault, but many Viet Cong and NVA had been killed. The big attack would actually be launched a few hours later on Saigon, Hue, and dozens of other major cities and bases throughout South Vietnam. While making his way to the PX for cigarettes the next morning, Matulac passed by a general talking to reporters about the recent action. Not far away was a pile of enemy dead. It looked to be about ten feet high, and they were still piling them up. He had seen a lot of dead bodies before, but this was far more than he'd ever witnessed.

A week or so had passed without any sign or word from the sergeant that Matulac had sent to Saigon to retrieve those classified documents.

When he finally walked into their company's barracks in Pleiku, he was unshaven and his fatigues were filthy and tattered. As he explained, he had been in bed with a girl in Saigon when the Tet attacks came. MPs came into his room and drug him out to an armored personnel carrier. He spent the next week gathering the dead and wounded from the streets of Saigon while the fighting continued. "Don't do me any more favors," he said to Matulac as he handed him the documents.

Finally back in the United States for good, Matulac was on the last leg of his journey home to his parents' house in California in 1971. Duffel bag in tow, he was sporting his dress uniform decorated with medals from five combat tours. He had heard some terrible stories from fellow soldiers who had been welcomed home with protest signs and eggs. His parents lived in the heart of hippie country, and he was expecting the worst. To his surprise, he encountered no protesters at the airport or the bus terminal, only a kind lady who offered him her seat on the bus. Embarrassed, he tried to decline her offer, but she insisted he take a seat. When he arrived at his parents' house, they were out and the door was locked, so he went around the corner to the neighborhood bar. He ordered a Bud, and soon thereafter, the bartender set down ten ice-cold Budweiser's on the counter in front of him. "Oh, I can't drink all these," he said, "I only ordered one."

"Well, you better get to drinking," the bartender replied, motioning to a group of guys in the back, "they're from those guys over there. This Bud's for you."

Sometime after returning to his stateside post, Matulac was visited by two agents from the Army's Criminal Investigation Department. The agents asked him if he knew anything about black marketeering activities in Vietnam by a certain warrant officer and his supply sergeant. He told them that he had no idea what was going on in the supply room as he was in the field the whole time. All he could tell them was that they never seemed to get the supplies they ordered.

After twenty-seven years of faithful service to the United States Army, Robert Matulac would retire as a Sergeant First Class. He had been offered a promotion to First Sergeant, but was to be sent to Korea had he accepted it. With a wife and two young daughters at home, he told the battalion commander to "keep the stripe." He would go on to work in admissions at Monterey Peninsula College for approximately ten years, after which he became a very successful track coach at the same college.

Shortly after returning home, both Will and Rodney Henning decided to use their GI Bill to attend the University of Wisconsin in Stevens Point, for one semester. They also traveled together to Washington State, where they worked a construction job for about a month, then returned home. Later, Will would again use his GI Bill, this time to attend Dunwoody Technical Institute in Minneapolis, Minnesota. He became a licensed electrician.

In the spring of 1971, Will found himself en route to a club known as the Belmont-A-Go-Go in Minneapolis. His friend Dan was meeting a girl there that he'd been dating named June, and needed a ride. Walking into the bar, there was another girl sitting next to June at the table. Her name was Carol, and Will was immediately struck by her dark, long-flowing hair and her smile. By the end of the night, she agreed to give him her number, and in October, they married. They would have two sons, me and my brother Nicholas. In 2011, after sufficient prodding from my wife and me, and armed with a week's supply of Dramamine, my dad finally agreed to embark on his second voyage on the high seas, this time on the Norwegian Epic. Fortunately, it was nothing like his first, and there were no typhoons. My dad still feels regret over the day Staff Sergeant Burtis was shot.

Tom Ivey still feels regret over not having written to his friend, Al Patrillo.

1st Platoon's leader, Barry Gallagher, is still married to his high school girlfriend, Margie, who he'd married during his basic training. Over the years, he has worked as a high school English teacher and Human Resources professional. He continues to be haunted by the ghosts of the many men he lost in Vietnam, including PFC Michael Stoflet and his medic, SP/4 Bill Garcia, who were both killed on November 1st 1966. He vividly remembers the bravery of their battalion commander, LTC Swett, and the love he had for his men, recalling how he had landed his command chopper under heavy fire while trying to save Garcia that day.

President Lyndon Johnson presenting LTC Trevor Swett with Silver Star

The 5/7th Cav's original battalion commander, Trevor Swett, would eventually be promoted to Colonel and would retire from the Army. Personally presented with the Silver Star for Gallantry in Action by the President of the United States, he accepted the award on behalf of his men. Decades later, in a documentary produced by CBS journalist Norman Lloyd called *Shakey's Hill*, about Bravo Company's 1970 incursion into Cambodia, he spoke of a time after he had returned home from the war. He was invited to speak at his son's graduation ceremony, at the same prep school from which he had graduated years before. After he was introduced and began to speak, a large number of those seated in the front two rows got up and left. Most were professors, some were students. "I realized just how unpopular the Vietnam War was when that happened," he said. He would remain haunted by the death of Alan Weisman, the young Jewish soldier whom he had persuaded to do his duty while at Fort Carson in 1966.

Alpha Company's original commander, A.J. Wise, was talking to Weisman on the radio at the moment he was shot in the head on November 19th 1966. He would return to Vietnam in 1972, serving as an advisor to ARVN regiments in the An Loc region of III Corps. He was sent there to replace an officer who had been killed in action the day before. While flying into An Loc, Wise's helicopter would be shot down. After twenty-four years of service, a veteran of both the Korean and Vietnam wars, he would retire as a Major in 1976. He would spend several years as a high school teacher, and after that, work on an offshore oil exploration rig until he fully retired to his hometown of Blountstown, Florida.

When I first received a phone call from MAJ A.J. Wise (Ret) shortly before finishing this book, I immediately sensed that I was speaking with a true southern gentleman. He expressed great admiration for each of the men he led. He was very proud of them for what they had accomplished and what they had endured during their time together. He mentioned how he felt that as Alpha Company's commander, he had been given the best group of non-commissioned officers he could have asked for. He also noted how so many of the company's draftees had gone on to become very successful in their lives and careers after leaving the Army, and how the 5/7th Cav's veterans association was founded not by officers and senior NCOs, but rather by a handful of their lower-enlisted men. "They were not your average group of Vietnam Veterans, if there is such a thing," he remarked, "I tried to bring them all back, but I couldn't."

1LT James Harmon was lying by Alan Weisman's side at the moment he was killed. After leaving the Army, he would become a prosecutor, and serve as Assistant District Attorney in New York City. He would also provide pro bono legal assistance to many of his fellow soldiers in obtaining credit and benefits for their service in Vietnam.

Years later, after recovering from the wounds he received when he was blown up by a grenade in January of 1967, but before he became a police officer, Joe Sanchez was working as a delivery driver in New York City. He was somewhere near Wall Street when he saw his old buddy Rocco crossing the street. He pulled over and called out to him, but he disappeared into the crowd. Years later, Sanchez would reach out to the parents of his buddy, Leonard Pelullo – and each Mother's Day thereafter, he would send flowers to Lenny's mother.

The USNS Gaffey continued to transport thousands of troops to Vietnam until she was put into reserve in 1968. In 1978, the aging rust bucket would remain docked, and be used by the Navy for several years as a barracks ship for the crews of vessels undergoing major overhaul. She was still afloat in 2000, when the Navy decided to put her out of her misery, using her as target practice during an international naval training event near the Hawaiian Islands, along with two other ships slated for sinking. Both Australian and United States Air Force jets hit the ships. This was followed by two days of bombardment by naval gunfire, after which the other two ships finally sank. The old Gaffey, who many young troopers feared would surely sink during their encounter with that typhoon en route to Vietnam, now refused to go down. Divers with explosives would eventually have to be sent down to put her to rest. Now lying nearly three thousand fathoms under the sea, the Gaffey remains a symbol of a great turning point in the lives of hundreds of once-young men throughout the country. Their voyage upon her in 1966, during the massive build-up of forces in Vietnam, would also symbolize a great turning point for the country itself. Although they spent only eighteen days on her decks, those days at sea still hold some of the most vivid memories of their time in service.

In *Better Times Than These*, author Winston Groom, also the author of *Forrest Gump*, tells the story of a fictional infantry company, Bravo Company, 4th Battalion, 7th Cavalry, that sails to Vietnam in the summer of 1966. A large portion of his story tells of their voyage aboard the USNS Gaffey, and was actually inspired by his real-life voyage aboard that very boat during that same summer. In his book, he relates many of the comical misdeeds, misfortunes, and incidents that occurred aboard the ship, including the life vest fiasco. During our brief correspondence he mentioned, "In the boxing matches, my cabinmate Phil Collins got his front teeth bashed in. The doc said that if he could stay in Okinawa for a week, he could wire him up and save them – but the asshole colonel said no, so they pulled them."

I found it worth noting that instead of writing a book based upon the experiences of a psychological operations officer in Vietnam, one of the guys who flew in planes to drop leaflets encouraging enemy soldiers to surrender and such, he chose to write about those of the infantrymen. You could say that while the infantrymen lived the hardest of lives, they would also be left with the most compelling stories to tell. Although fiction, I found in his story many unmistakable parallels to the real events, places, and men of the 5/7th Cav during this time.

On the inside cover of *Better Times Than These* is a hand-drawn map of the Central Highlands. There is "Monkey Mountain", the fictional version of An Khe, at least according to my own interpretation. There is a hill known as "The Tit" and the "Valley of The Tit" and the "Village of the Running Man". Also depicted on the map, is a place dubbed "Village of the Banana Cat". In the story, one of the soldiers buys a small animal to keep as a pet from one of the local villagers. They called it a banana cat, and it was described as something like a small monkey or related creature of some sort. While reading the book, I was curious to see what a banana cat actually looked like, so I googled it. I soon came across a photo of an American soldier in Vietnam, holding what looked more like a large snarling rodent than a cat or monkey. The photo, however, was on a website that belonged to Joe Sanchez, and this is how I found Joe.

For several years, Bill Boyce continued to make payments of exactly one dollar per month for the weapon he'd lost after being shot on November 19th 1966. Eventually, the Army just gave up on trying to collect the debt.

SP/4 Brutus T. Bear, the original battalion's beer-chugging mascot from Fort Carson, would eventually make her own journey to Vietnam, lumbering ashore from the Navy ship Albion in Da Nang Harbor with her fellow soldiers of the 1/11th Mechanized Infantry in September of 1968. She had put on some weight since the days of her youth, now tipping the scales at over three-hundred pounds. Although she never faced enemy fire, sadly, Brutus would not survive her tour of duty in Vietnam. She would succumb to natural causes, officially pneumonia. However, her steady diet of canned dog food, soda and beer may have been contributing factors.

Among those who were sent back early was Bill Purdy, who had injured his knee in April while jumping into a rice paddy from a helicopter to keep his friend, John Kruetzkamp, from being left behind. Upon their return to the states, those who had more than ninety days remaining were kept on duty for the duration of their two-year service term. And so, after recovering from his injury, Purdy was sent to Fort Knox to serve out his obligation. He was assigned to a platoon of those who had just returned from Vietnam and were also serving out their final months in the Army. Their job was to assist the drill sergeants in training new soldiers headed to Vietnam. He also recalls how at one point, some of the guys in his platoon were sent off to quell riots in Detroit.

Returning to his ironworkers job, Purdy was soon confronted by an older co-worker known as "Red" while on the job. "So what do you think about all that baby-killing going on over there – you were a part of all that, right Purdy?" He had made a point of asking his question in front of everyone gathered in the break room. Purdy told him he didn't know what he was talking about, and after that the man spit on him. Faced with the prospect of fighting an old man, Purdy just turned and walked away. When asked by his co-workers why he didn't take down the guy who had publicly insulted him, he would simply say that it wasn't worth losing his job over. I tend to believe that after everything he'd been through, he didn't feel the need to prove anything. Over the next few years, eight of his co-workers would themselves be drafted. Like many, he still has occasional nightmares from his time in Vietnam.

In 1992, Bill Purdy got together with fellow 5/7th Cav troopers from the other companies, including Jasper Catanzaro and Don Shipley. Together they formed the 5/7th Cav Association and held their first reunion that August. Since then, every two years the veterans would get together to remember their time together and their fallen friends – their only rule, that they leave their politics, religion, and rank at the door. Over the years, they've reunited countless brothers-in-arms.

Finishing this book that took a year and a half to complete, I asked dad if there was anything else he wanted to add. "Although our mortar platoon was often in mortal danger, it was minor compared to that of the rifle platoon soldiers who were the first to take a bullet and to be killed. They are the crazy brave soldiers that deserve all the credit."

I'd like to know what happened to Ten Ninh, Will's little friend who tended cows in the Kim Son Valley. As only a privileged few of his country's young men were able to avoid service in the war, he surely would have been forced to choose sides as he came of age. His fate would be uncertain at best, given that the war would rage on for another eight years, and all the brutal reprisals that followed the fall of Saigon. I'd like to think that he managed to survive all of this, and is still alive today. If so, he is now sixty-two years old. Who knows, just maybe he still remembers a young American soldier named "Bow-E" who showed him kindness.

In August of 2018, dad and I flew to Pittsburgh to attend his first 5/7th Cav reunion. I had just printed the first two hundred copies of this book, and many had already been delivered to former soldiers of Alpha Company. One was Joe Williams, who greeted us in the lobby and made us both feel very welcome. "It's sort of strange reading something that's written about yourself and your friends," he said. While there, we met many more fellow troopers from the company, including Gene Cross, the guy whose helmet my dad recalls with the hole shot in it. He told me of how he had been grade school friends with Donald Duncan, the Alpha Company supply clerk who'd volunteered to go to the field after getting into a disagreement with his boss, and who was killed on Thanksgiving Day 1966. He showed me the scar that was left on his scalp from being shot through the helmet on October 4th 1966.

During one evening of the event, a guy known as "Krazy" Karl Haartz, one of the organizers, was speaking to the group as we sat at tables in one of the hotel's large banquet rooms. I learned that Karl had earned his nickname by stealing the Charlie Company First Sergeant's car and taking it for a joy ride while at Fort Carson. At one point he mentioned how he had finally met once again, someone he remembered from their AIT mortar training at Fort Carson, a fellow named Wilbur Bowe. I looked over at my dad and he looked nervous. In fact, I could see the tiniest of sweat beads beginning to form on his forehead. Karl asked him to come up on stage, and when he did, Karl gave him a big hug and everyone applauded. Dad returned to our table and said, "Man, I was scared there for a minute." I asked why and he replied, "I was afraid he was going to ask me to speak!"

We were sitting around late one night in the hotel, and Bobby Hansen was recalling their first big battle in the mangrove swamps, trying to rescue that downed helicopter pilot and his gunner. In very animated fashion, he was demonstrating how one of their Korean War veteran platoon sergeants would run from one spider hole to the next, killing NVA troops with wild abandon. "I got the little bastard!" he exclaimed. Another Alpha Company trooper I had just recently met, Chester Millay, remarked how all he could remember about that day was a bunch of noise, screaming and chaos. He was perplexed at how Bobby could remember everything so vividly, "like it was yesterday," as he put it. As I listened to their conversation, what struck me is that despite their outward appearance, they weren't old men to me. To me, they were the same nineteen and twenty-year-old kids they were over fifty years ago. It is, perhaps, the most unexpected thing that I've gained from this whole experience – the ability to see past someone's age and appearance, to see them for who they've been their whole life.

A year later, dad and I attended a second reunion and mom decided to join us. This one was a smaller affair as it was just for Alpha Company's soldiers. It was hosted by Jack Fleming of Alpha Company's 1st Platoon in Albuquerque, New Mexico. While working on the book's original publication, dad and I had not had a chance to speak with Martin Quinn as they had lost touch since their last visit in 1993. A couple months before the reunion, he called my dad out of the blue and said that he would join us in Albuquerque. He had lost his wife the year before, and so his cousin Dennis and his wife Bobbie would accompany him on the trip. I was hopeful to finally meet this guy who was good friends with my dad in Vietnam, and we were disappointed when he didn't show up on the first night we were there.

We had gathered again the next night when Jack got a call from Martin Quinn saying they were almost there and were trying to find the place. Apparently, their flight from New York had been delayed and they'd just gotten into Albuquerque that day. When Quinn stepped out of the car, I was surprised at how tall he was. In the one photo I'd always seen of him, he was standing between Gerald Anderson and SSG Donald Burtis and they actually made him appear short in the picture. After a few hours of reminiscing, we pulled out a copy of the book. He turned to the page that featured the letter he had written to Will, telling of the deaths of their friends Al Patrillo, John Fulford, and Bobby Hayslip on May 19th 1967. My dad had never seen the letter until I found it mixed in with his own letters home while researching for the book. He had been en route back to Vietnam from his emergency leave at the end of May when the letter was sent. Of course, Quinn hadn't seen it since he wrote it in 1967. It was heartwarming to see two old friends reunited after twenty-seven years. Also at the second reunion in Albuquerque, we had a chance to meet dad's old commander, A.J. Wise - the first time for me, and the first in fifty-some years for my dad.

In speaking with these men who served with my dad, I've learned that those who have faced real combat rarely speak of their bravery as they are more likely to tell you about their own comical mishaps and misdeeds. When it comes to the battles and firefights, they are more likely to just tell you how scared they were, rather than speak of their own acts of courage. In fact, I never knew that A.J. Wise had been awarded a Silver Star for his actions during the rescue of that pilot and his gunner on October 4th 1966. He'd never mentioned it in our conversations. It was one of his former radio operators, Royce Barrow, who informed me of this. It was Vernon Garrett's wife who sent me a copy of his own Silver Star citation for his actions on

May 19th 1967, saying that he doesn't really like to speak of the award. To say the least, soldiers have mixed feelings when it comes to such awards, often feeling that many deserving friends of theirs who faced the same circumstances never received one. Whether or not a soldier received an award depended on many factors unrelated to his actual bravery, such as whether or not his platoon leader or sergeant actually took the time to write him up as well as his leader's ability to write, not to mention his own reputation as a soldier amongst "the brass", who would ultimately approve or disapprove such an award. To me, of course, these citations are all important pieces of history that help to illustrate what each of the men experienced during Alpha Company's most harrowing moments.

....

Today, many of those who opposed the war have come to realize how some of their movement's excesses served to denigrate the service of so many who fought in that war with the best of intentions. Some things were said and done that can never be reconciled. However, I have to believe most of those who in their self-righteous fervor, had blamed our servicemen for the war itself, recklessly accused them of atrocities, or openly sympathized with the totalitarian regime of the North, now regret the worst of what they said and did during their youth.

It would be an understatement to say that today's soldiers enjoy a much better public perception and treatment from society at large than those with whom my dad served. Public gratitude is so pervasive these days that it's hard perhaps, not to take it for granted. Though I've never returned from war myself, I've attended the homecomings of several deployed units of the Minnesota Army National Guard. Typically, they arrive at the armory or airfield in a caravan of buses amidst the roar of Harley engines, escorted by throngs of leather-clad men and women on motorcycles as families wait to be reunited with their soldiers. Most of these riders are twice the age of the soldiers they help to welcome home, and many are Vietnam Veterans. One such rider is Michael Handley, the Illinois farm boy who served as combat medic in Alpha Company's 3rd Platoon in 1966. Known as the Patriot Guard, they see to it that no soldier is made to feel the way they felt when they returned home from an unpopular war.

When I decided to enlist in the Army National Guard in July 2007, both my mom and dad were opposed, as would be expected. Not your typical recruit, I was thirty-three years old and married, with several children at home. My wife, Misty, wasn't thrilled with the idea by any means, but was very supportive anyway, if only because she felt like she had to be. My mom didn't think it was fair to my family, and of course, she was right about that. The unit I was joining was just then returning from a twenty-two-month mobilization, sixteen of which were spent in the most dangerous regions of Iraq. I figured that my dad would be against it, but was surprised at the fierceness of his opposition. At the time, I didn't understand why he was so adamant. I get it now.

While I was going through my enlistment at Fort Snelling, Misty had found out from my recruiter, who was also our next-door neighbor, that I had signed up to be an infantryman. I thought it offered the best chance for me to kick in some doors. Disturbed by what seemed a reckless decision on my part, she called my dad, who in turn dialed my cell phone. He very forcefully insisted that I choose something else. "My God, if there's one thing you don't want to be, it's in the infantry." I already felt bad about going against his wishes, so I relented and signed up to be an artillery forward observer instead.

In 2011, I was preparing for my first deployment. With approximately a month left before our departure, I was informed that I would not be allowed to deploy with my unit, as I had been diagnosed with a non-cancerous pituitary tumor that required continued medication. That particular medication was not allowed in-country by the Army. At the time, I regretted the missed opportunity. I don't anymore.

....

August 1967, Philippines, layover en route to United States, photo by Wilbur Bowe

On August 4th 1967, SP/4 Wilbur E. Bowe out-processed and was discharged from active duty in Oakland, California. He had earned the National Defense Service Medal, Vietnam Campaign Medal, Vietnam Service Medal, Air Medal, Bronze Star, Combat Infantryman Badge, and Expert Rifle Badge. From here he took his final flight to Minneapolis, where Millie and Eddie would meet him.

"Oh, where have you been, my blue-eyed son?" Whenever I hear that line from Bob Dylan's *A Hard Rain's A-Gonna Fall*, I try to imagine what my grandpa Eddie might have said to his own blue-eyed son when he returned home from the war. While his friend, Martin Quinn, returned home in a graffiti-covered subway car, Will made his way along a dusty county road to the farm where he grew up. Understandably, not much is remembered about my dad's homecoming. There were no parades or celebrations, but no protesters either. They stopped at the drug store to drop off his last roll of film. By all accounts, it was anticlimactic. The important thing was that he was alive and he was home, this time for good. Millie and Eddie's long nightmare was over.

It was hard to believe that only twenty-two months had passed since that night when he came home to find that letter sitting on the kitchen table. It seemed so long ago, and yet life had gone on without him and everything on the farm was the same as before. Despite the social upheaval engulfing the nation's major cities and broadcast on the nightly news, life in Tilden, Wisconsin remained completely unaffected. Now, what to do with the rest of his life. Before he could think about that however, he needed to do a little housekeeping. He went back to the drug store to pick up his photos. He looked at them for a while, especially the one of Patrillo. Then he boxed them up along with his medals, some newspaper clippings, discharge papers, and other memorabilia from his time in Vietnam. He put the box on the shelf in the back corner of his closet. He took one last look at his dress uniform before zipping the garment bag and hanging it up, never to wear it again.

Everyone has regrets. I certainly do, though I always try to keep in mind how some of my most monumental failures have led to some of the best things in my life. If there's one thing I could wish for my dad and his friends, it would be to let go of any lingering regrets from that terrible year spent in Vietnam. At an age when most young men would have been going to school, going to parties and chasing girls, you were instead sent to fight in the jungles of a foreign land. You witnessed and endured things that most of us could never comprehend. At a time when so many would turn their backs on their country, you showed up, did your duty, carried out your orders every day until the very last day, and somehow you survived. In this war, that's as good as it gets. There's nothing to regret. And by the way, welcome home.

Garry Owen

ACKNOWLEDGEMENTS

To all the kind people who have posted reviews and ratings on Amazon, Goodreads, and elsewhere, you have my eternal gratitude. These reviews have made *The Ground You Stand Upon* a popular choice amongst readers of Vietnam memoirs and biographies, and now thousands of people around the world have come to learn about the experience of my dad and the men he served with. The most heartwarming part of this endeavor has been reading the comments of those who have been touched by our story. If you enjoyed reading this book or learned something from it, please let me know by posting a review on Amazon. It means more to me than you can possibly know.

I would also like to sincerely thank the following individuals who helped in contributing to this book.

Kathleen Perez and Cynthia French
Both daughters of Sam Daily, for providing documentation and background regarding their father, photographs of their father and young family, as well as additional information about the battle where he gave his life on October 4th 1966.

Patty Perkins and Vivian Deaton
Both nieces of Charles Bradford, for providing background information, personal memories and a wedding photo of their uncle Charlie, who also gave his life on October 4th 1966.

Annette Sebastian
For sharing news clippings, personal memories and photographs of her younger brother, Guy McNay, Jr. (Juggy), who was killed in action on May 19th 1967.

Lea Ann Bird
A family member of Guy McNay who was too young to know him, for obtaining additional information from other family members, and for putting me in contact with his sister, Annette.

Paul Plaine
A fellow Army veteran, for sharing his memories of his time spent with Caesar Pinto, who was killed in action on August 9th 1967.

Lou Lupo
A fellow Vietnam Veteran, and hometown friend from Philadelphia, for sharing background information and his own personal memories of Leonard Pelullo, who was killed in action on February 13th 1967.

Wayne and Tony Rankin
Wayne is Donald Rankin's younger brother. His son, Tony, was born the year before Donald was sent to Vietnam. Thank you both for speaking with me at length about Donald and for providing some of his letters home, as well as the photograph of him carrying the Vietnamese child.

Mo Dhania
Joe Sanchez's friend, who helped to edit and proofread more than one version of this book.

Dave Mason
A fellow Vietnam Veteran, Chinook crew chief, and my uncle, for sharing his recollections of some of his most memorable missions, as well as several photographs from his time in Vietnam.

MAJ A.J. Wise (Ret)
Original commander of Alpha Company, 5/7th Cavalry, for speaking with me at length about his background and experience, as well as his memories of the men he led into battle.

Marvin Bierschbach
Fellow mortar team member in Alpha Company's 4th Platoon, for taking time to meet with my dad and me in June 2017 to share memories of their experience in Vietnam, and for sharing many excellent photographs taken during their time there.

Robert Wagner
Fellow Alpha Company soldier, for sharing his experiences and memories of friends, particularly those of November 19th and Thanksgiving Day 1966. Also for providing documentation of Purple Hearts awarded to several soldiers for their actions on October 4th 1966.

Nick Lian
Fellow Alpha Company soldier, for sharing his memories of Vietnam and of my dad during their time there.

Bobby Hansen
Fellow Alpha Company soldier, for sharing his recollections of October 4th, November 19th, and Thanksgiving Day 1966, as well as his memories of Donald Smith, who was killed on October 4th 1966.

Bill Purdy
Fellow Alpha Company soldier, for putting me in contact with Bobby Hansen, and for helping to keep the 5/7th Cavalry band of brothers together over so many years. Also, for sharing his photographs of many soldiers featured in this book, as well as memories of his last moments spent with A.G. Hensley, who was killed on March 31st 1967.

Jim Hirschuber
Fellow Alpha Company soldier, for sharing his own recollections of Alpha Company's time in Vietnam, their voyage upon the Gaffey, the battle of November 19th 1966, and of his own homecoming.

SFC Robert Matulac (Ret)
Fellow Alpha Company soldier, for speaking with me at length and in great detail about the many battles they were involved in, as well as providing a great deal of background information about several soldiers in Alpha Company, and for sharing many of his own photographs from Vietnam. Also, for putting me in contact with Bill Purdy and Jim Hirschuber.

Joe Sanchez
Fellow Alpha Company soldier, for writing about his Vietnam experiences in his own book, for sharing photographs and personal memories of Leonard Pelullo, who was killed in action on February 13th 1967, and Alan Weisman, who was killed in action on November 19th 1966. Also, for spending several hours on the phone with me talking about his friends in Alpha Company, and for putting me in contact with several other Alpha Company troopers, including Robert Matulac, Nick Lian, and Robert Wagner.

James Harmon
Fellow Alpha Company soldier, for suggesting the reading of *Better Times Than These*. Without reading that book, I never would have met Joe Sanchez.

Gene Cross
Fellow Alpha Company soldier, for sharing his memories of October 4th 1966 and his childhood friend, Donald Duncan, who was killed on Thanksgiving Day 1966.

Michael Handley
Fellow Alpha Company soldier and medic, for sharing his memories of tending to the wounded on October 4th 1966.

Martin Quinn
Fellow member of Alpha Company's 4th Platoon, for making the trip to meet us in Albuquerque, New Mexico in August 2019 at the Alpha Company reunion, and for sharing so many memories of his time with my dad and their friendship.

Dennis and Bobbie Sheppard
Martin Quinn's cousin and his wife, for encouraging Martin to attend the reunion, and for accompanying him on the trip from New York to Albuquerque.

John Kruetzkamp
Fellow Alpha Company soldier, for sharing memories of his friends in Vietnam, during some of their most harrowing, and most comical moments.

Chester Millay
Fellow Alpha Company soldier, for sharing his own memories of battle, and of training at Fort Carson.

Jack and Josephine Fleming
Fellow Alpha Company soldier and his wife, for hosting the Alpha Company reunion in August of 2019, which gave my dad the opportunity to reunite with his old friend, Martin Quinn, after twenty-seven years, and for me to learn much more about their time in Vietnam.

Royce Barrow
Fellow Alpha Company soldier, radio operator, and friend of Donald Rankin, for speaking at length with me and sharing his memories of several fellow soldiers, as well as the battles that took place on October 4th and Thanksgiving 1966, as well as February 13th 1967.

Barry Gallagher
Platoon Leader of Alpha Company's 1st Platoon, for sharing some of his most harrowing experiences during the battle of October 4th 1966.

LTC George Kalergis (Ret)
Alpha Company's forward observer from February to June 1967, for sharing detailed accounts of his first combat missions with the 1/9th Cavalry in January 1967, as well as his experience with Alpha Company, 5/7th Cavalry during what was their deadliest battle to date, on May 19th 1967.

John Goodpaster
Fellow 5/7th Cav soldier in Charlie Company, for sharing memories of their voyage aboard the USNS Gaffey, and a photograph of Charlie Company on patrol in the jungle.

Don Shipley
Fellow 5/7th Cav soldier in Charlie Company, for helping to reunite so many veterans of the battalion over the years, for putting me in contact with other veterans of Alpha Company, and for suggesting the book, *On The Tiger's Back*.

Tom Ivey
Childhood friend of Albert Patrillo, for speaking with me at length about his memories of Al when they were young, from their riding tricycles together to when he watched soldiers in dress uniform approaching the Patrillo's family home in May of 1967.

John Benson
Schoolteacher and resident of Albert Patrillo's hometown of Susquehanna, Pennsylvania. In 2017, John wrote an article about Albert Patrillo for their local paper, memorializing the 50th anniversary of his death. After the original publication of this book in 2018, John was contacted by a friend of his who happened to be reading it. When his friend came across the name of Al Patrillo, he recalled the article written by John and called to tell him about it. Shortly thereafter, I received a call from John and he sent me the article he had written about Al's life growing up in Susquehanna. He sent additional photos provided by Al's family and also put me in touch with Al's childhood friend, Tom Ivey.

Harald Hendrichsen
Fellow Vietnam Veteran of the 604th Transportation Company (Aircraft Direct Support). When this book was originally published in 2018, I had included an aerial photo of the Mang Yang Pass in Chapter 6, attributed as "source unknown", as I could not determine who had taken the photo. In 2019, Harald emailed me to let me know that he was the one who took that photo, at the age of nineteen in 1969. He also sent me a copy of that same photo with certain landmarks labeled, including the French cemetery, which has now been included in the book. Harald has dedicated much of his time to memorializing his own company's experience in Vietnam on his website: www.604th.com

The Staff of the National Archives in College Park, Maryland
The staff at the National Archives were immensely helpful in our search for records of the 5/7th Cavalry in Vietnam. One particularly helpful staff member was a fellow Vietnam Veteran named Stanley Fanaras. Without their assistance, this story would not be what it is today.

ABOUT THE AUTHORS

Joshua Bowe resides in Chaska, Minnesota along with his wife, Misty, and children. From 2007 to 2019, he served full-time in the Minnesota National Guard as a member of the 1st Battalion, 125th Field Artillery. He continues to work for the Minnesota National Guard as a civilian. He is a 1992 graduate of Cameron High School in northwest Wisconsin, and before joining the National Guard, he owned a commercial janitorial company. In 2018, he published *The Ground You Stand Upon: Life of a Skytrooper in Vietnam*, the true story of his father's war experience.

You can follow his blog and post reviews on both his Amazon and Goodreads author pages. You can also check out his YouTube channel to view a slideshow featuring photos taken by his dad and others in Alpha Company during their time in Vietnam, as well as several excerpts from the Audible audiobook version of this book.

Co-author Wilbur Bowe is the author's father and lives in Cameron, Wisconsin with his wife, Carol, where they raised their two sons, Joshua and Nicholas. He was born and raised on his family's dairy farm in Tilden, Wisconsin. Drafted in 1965, sent to Vietnam in 1966, he returned as a combat veteran in the rank of Specialist-Four in August of 1967. Since then, he has spent most of his life working as a maintenance electrician. Now retired, he spends much of his time fixing and building things for his friends, neighbors, and at his local Catholic church. Along with many other soldiers from his infantry company, he contributed much to the writing of *The Ground You Stand Upon*. Much of his contributions were written over fifty years ago, in the jungles of a foreign land.

Website: www.thegroundyoustandupon.org

Facebook: www.facebook.com/thegroundyoustandupon.org

Wilbur Bowe, Co-Author

Joshua Bowe, Author

BIBLIOGRAPHY

ON THE TIGER'S BACK
1994, by Bernard E. Grady - CPT Bernard E. Grady (Ret) served as both the Executive Officer of Bravo Company and Commander of Charlie Company, 5/7th Cav during the battalion's initial tour of duty from August 1966 to August 1967.

1966 THE YEAR OF THE HORSE
2009, by Robert K. Powers - Robert K. Powers was an Indirect Fire Infantryman assigned to the mortar platoon of Bravo Company, 5/7th Cav. He was drafted in January 1966 and sent to Vietnam as an early replacement in October of the same year. He was wounded in action on May 18th 1967.

TRUE BLUE, A Tale of the Enemy Within
2007, by Joe Sanchez - Joe Sanchez was an infantryman assigned to Alpha Company, 5/7th Cav. After being turned away from enlistment in nearly every branch of service, including the Army, he volunteered to be drafted in 1965. Although his book is primarily written about his experiences as a cop in New York City and the corruption within the department that he fought to expose, it also contains many of his memories of training with Alpha Company at Fort Carson and their deployment to Vietnam, where he would eventually be wounded in action.

BETTER TIMES THAN THESE
1978, by Winston Groom - A work of fiction by a fellow veteran of the Vietnam War who also wrote *Forrest Gump*. It was written about an infantry company, Bravo Company, 4th Battalion, 7th Cavalry, that traveled to Vietnam in August of 1966. A large portion of the story details their voyage aboard the USNS Gaffey and was actually inspired by that of the non-fictional 5th Battalion, 7th Cavalry.

THE 1ST CAV IN VIETNAM, Anatomy of a Division
1987, by Shelby L. Stanton - CPT Shelby L. Stanton (Ret) served in the 82nd Airborne Division in Southeast Asia and was wounded in action. The book covers the 1st Air Cavalry Division's development and implementation of the Airmobile concept in Vietnam.

THE RISE AND FALL OF AN AMERICAN ARMY, U.S. Ground Forces in Vietnam, 1965-1973
1985, by Shelby L. Stanton (see above) - A critical assessment of the toll that waging the war in Vietnam took on the United States Army and Marine Corps, as well as the government's refusal to mobilize the National Guard and other reserve forces in significant numbers.

DEAR AMERICA: Letters Home From Vietnam
1985, edited by Bernard Edelman - A collection of letters home from dozens of servicemen and women serving in Vietnam. The book was also made into an HBO documentary. Both the book and film include the letter written by Alpha Company's Richard Cantale about the death of his friend, Donald Rankin.

A WALK AMONG THE BRAVE
2011, by Tina Susedik - This book is a compilation of war experiences of veterans from Northwest Wisconsin. It features profiles of Rodney Henning, Wilbur Bowe, his brother, Darrell Bowe, and several other veterans from the Chippewa Falls area.

1ST CAVALRY DIVISION, Memoirs of the First Team, Vietnam August 1965 to December 1969
1970, edited by J.D. Coleman

WHERE WE WERE IN VIETNAM
2002, by Michael P. Kelley - A Comprehensive guide to the firebases, military installations and Naval vessels of the Vietnam War 1945-1975

BUYING TIME 1965-1966
2015, by Frank L. Jones

COMBAT OPERATIONS: Stemming The Tide, May 1965 to October 1966
2000, by John M. Carland

COMBAT OPERATIONS: Taking The Offensive, October 1966 to October 1967
1998, by George L. MacGarrigle

INTERIM REPORT OF OPERATIONS, 1st Cavalry Division, July 1965 to December 1966
Compiled by Charles S. Sykes, published by 1st Cavalry Division Association

OPERATIONAL REPORT - LESSONS LEARNED, 1st Cavalry Division (Airmobile), Period Ending 31 July 1967
1st Cavalry Division (Airmobile) Headquarters, Declassified 31 December 1973

AFTER ACTION REPORT (3 Sep 66 Attack on Camp Radcliff)
17 September 1966, 1st Cavalry Division (Airmobile) Headquarters, Declassified 17 September 1978

OPERATIONAL REPORT - LESSONS LEARNED January to June 1967
USARV

BATTALION DAILY SITUATION REPORTS, September 1st 1966 to March 12th 1967
5/7th Cavalry, 1st Cavalry Division (Airmobile), obtained from the National Archives in College Park, Maryland

BATTALION DAILY STAFF JOURNALS, January 1st to August 9th 1967
5/7th Cavalry, 1st Cavalry Division (Airmobile), obtained from the National Archives in College Park, Maryland

PRESIDENTIAL UNIT CITATION FOR PERIOD 30 SEP 1966 TO 30 MAR 1967, SUPPORTING DOCUMENTATION
5/7th Cavalry, 1st Cavalry Division (Airmobile), obtained from the National Archives in College Park, Maryland

TOPOGRAPHIC MILITARY MAPS OF VIETNAM
University of Texas Libraries website

THE VIETNAM VETERANS MEMORIAL FUND WALL OF FACES (The Virtual Wall)
Memorial website maintained by the VVMF, the same organization that built the Wall in Washington, DC. Many personal details, backgrounds, and photos of the fallen are posted here.

THE COFFELT DATABASE (National Archives Online)
This database lists all servicemen killed in action during the Vietnam War, along with official Department of Defense information regarding their date of birth, date of death, home of record, branch of service, rank, unit of assignment, MOS, and enlistment status.

SHAKEY'S HILL (Documentary)
2007, by Norman Lloyd – Norman Lloyd was a CBS journalist embedded with Bravo Company, 5/7th Cav during their incursion into Cambodia in May of 1970. His film features much of the footage taken as they fought the NVA there. The film is named for the young soldier, Chris Keffalos (nicknamed "Shakey") who was killed atop a hill, shortly after discovering what turned out to be an enormous underground stockpile of NVA weapons. While producing this film decades later, Lloyd reunited many Bravo Company soldiers who served during the Cambodian mission.

Glossary

Agent Orange: An herbicide and defoliant chemical sprayed in large quantities over jungle areas of South Vietnam in order to deny concealment to guerrilla forces

Ambush: Position taken to catch infiltrating enemy soldiers by surprise, typically consisting of a handful of soldiers, primarily used during hours of darkness, just outside the area of a company patrol base or outpost

ARA: Aerial Rocket Artillery, rockets fired from a helicopter gunship

Airborne: Soldiers who jump out of airplanes

Airmobile: Soldiers who jump out of helicopters

ARVN: Army of the Republic of Vietnam, main South Vietnamese forces

Base Camp: Large military installation with some permanent structures and airfields, surrounded by perimeter wire and guard towers

Bivouac: Small, improvised, temporary military encampment

Bouncing Betty: Small anti-personnel mine that, when activated by stepping on its prongs, was propelled upward three to four feet before exploding

Brass: Military slang for high-ranking officers and important people

Buck Sergeant: A junior NCO in the rank of Sergeant (SGT), E-5

C-130: Lockheed C-130 Hercules, large military transport airplane, a heavily-armed modified version was also used as a "Spooky" gunship

C-4: A plastic explosive material that can be used in varying quantities and molded into the desired shape, and which will only explode by the shock wave of a detonator or blasting cap. Used frequently in Vietnam for blowing up trees in order to quickly clear landing zones. Also used as a heating agent as small amounts will burn fiercely but not explode when ignited.

C-5: Lockheed C-5 Galaxy, one of the largest military transport planes in the world, some configurations used to transport troops, others to haul supplies and equipment, capable of carrying other aircraft and tanks within its airframe

Caribou: De Havilland C-7A and C-7B, large fixed-wing military transport aircraft

Chinook: Boeing CH-47, large twin-propeller helicopter used as troop transport, air assault, and supply

Claymore: Directional anti-personnel mine typically placed around patrol base or other defensive position, activated by operator using detonator attached by wire

Cobra: Bell AH-1, heavily armed attack helicopter

C-Rations: Canned military food rations distributed to soldiers in the field, most packaged during the Korean War

Deuce-and-a-half: Slang for 2 ½ ton truck often used to transport troops and supplies

Dust-off: Informal term for medevac helicopter

ETS: Expiration Term of Service, a soldier's last day in the Army

Fields of Fire: Areas beyond defensive positions, cleared out of vegetation and other obstructions in order to give defenders visibility over potential attackers avenues of approach

Firebase: Military outpost with artillery, located in range to support infantry operations in area

Forward Observer: An artillery soldier, typically attached to an infantry company, responsible for planning, coordinating, directing, and adjusting artillery fire onto enemy positions

Garry Owen: Derived from the Gaelic, *Eóin* (an Irish form of John) and the word for garden, *garrai*, meaning "John's Garden" in Gaelic. John's Garden was actually that of a church founded by the Knights Templar and dedicated to John the Baptist in the city of Limerick, Ireland. This garden, known as "Garry Owen" was the subject of a popular Irish drinking song in the late eighteenth century that was eventually adopted as the marching tune of the 5th Irish Royal Lancers. A century later, this song that was popular among the Irish immigrants of the U.S. 7th Cavalry was adopted as their marching tune as well.

Grenadier: Soldier whose primary weapon is an M-79 grenade launcher (thumper)

Gunship: Helicopter armed with machine guns and aerial rocket artillery (most often Cobra or Hueys, sometimes Chinooks)

Hamlet: Rural Vietnamese village

Howitzer: Modern artillery gun with rifled bore, capable of shooting explosive shells for several miles, depending on the size

Huey: Bell UH-1 Iroquois, helicopter used as troop transport, air assault, supply, and gunship

KP: Kitchen duty

Lifeline Packs: Boxed kits issued to soldiers in the field that included candy, gum, cigarettes, shaving kits, and letter writing materials

Listening Post: Small team of soldiers with radio, set out at a distance from the company patrol base or outpost, serving as early detection for infiltrating enemy soldiers, primarily used at night, also referred to as an ambush

Log Ship: Helicopter used primarily for unit resupply (ammunition, food, mail, etc), also carrying troops at times

LRRP: Long Range Reconnaissance Patrol, a small unit of infantry soldiers sent on extended missions to infiltrate suspected enemy territory and report enemy locations

LZ: Landing Zone, a place to land a helicopter and drop troops into combat, also used to refer to an outpost or firebase

M-16: Standard rifle issued to soldiers in Vietnam beginning in 1965, replacing the M-14

M-60: Machine gun most commonly used by infantry squads in Vietnam, also mounted on helicopters

M-72 LAW: Light Anti-tank Weapon, rocket launcher that functioned as a mini-bazooka, used to destroy tanks and dug-in enemy positions such as bunkers

M-79: Shotgun-style grenade launcher commonly carried by infantrymen designated as grenadiers

MACV: Military Assistance Command, Vietnam, highest level of command over all services in Vietnam, responsible for running the war

Minigun: Gatling gun-style weapon mounted to attack helicopters, capable of firing over six thousand 7.62mm rounds per minute

MP: Military Police

Mortar: Operated by a four-man crew, the 81mm mortar system consisted of a base plate, bipod and barrel, and was used to lob exploding projectile rounds at the enemy

NVA: North Vietnamese Army, main-force communist soldiers infiltrated from North Vietnam, typically wearing khaki uniforms and helmets

Patrol Base: Improvised temporary encampment or bivouac, usually refers to that of a company-sized unit or smaller

Poncho: Large plastic sheet issued to soldiers with hole and hood for head, could be used as a raincoat or buttoned together with another poncho to be used as shelter, or hooch

Poncho Liner: Improved, lightweight blanket issued to soldiers that resisted soaking and dried out more quickly than a standard wool blanket

PRC-25: Standard radio telephone used by units operating in the field that could be carried on radio operator's back

PX: Post Exchange, the military's version of a convenience store

PZ: Pick-up zone, any place suitable for a helicopter to pick up troops in the field, typically marked with smoke grenades

Rear Echelon: Refers to those working primarily in base camp or headquarters area

Recoilless Rifle: A large, yet man-portable anti-tank rifle that fired explosive shells, used for destroying bunkers, varying size and models

ROK: Allied Republic of Korea forces

Sappers: Soldiers trained to breach and sabotage established firebases and base camps, typically operating at night with the intent of destroying command posts, communications equipment, aircraft, and vehicles

Scout Ship: Small observation helicopter primarily used to spot enemy activity and positions (reconnaissance)

Sky Crane: Sikorsky CH-54 Tarhe, heavy-lift helicopter capable of hauling equipment, other aircraft, and tanks

Skytrooper: Informal term for airmobile infantrymen who jumped out of helicopters

Sorry About That: interj. sorry; whoops; a gross understatement, said more as a self-deprecating joke than as an apology; Most often an ironic understatement, as when one has been responsible for making a big mistake; popularized in the 1960s TV program *Get Smart*

Spooky Gunship: Douglas AC-47, large military airplane armed with three miniguns and other armaments, capable of dropping five-hundred-pound bombs, as well as illuminating vast areas of terrain, also known as "Puff the Magic Dragon" - In 1967, the Lockheed C-130 Hercules replaced the AC-47 in this role as a large fixed-wing gunship

The World: Informal military euphemism referring to anyplace that wasn't Vietnam

Top: Informal name for a company First Sergeant

Trip Flare: Illuminating flare activated and propelled into the sky when its attached trip wire was pulled, typically used around patrol base or other defensive position at night

VC: Viet Cong, communist guerrilla forces in South Vietnam, typically wearing black pajamas and without helmets

VNMC: Marine Corps of the Republic of Vietnam, South Vietnamese Marine Corps

ARMY RANKS

Enlisted Ranks

Private: PVT, Pay Grade E-1, entry-level enlisted soldier, no rank insignia

Private 2: PV2, Pay Grade E-2, entry-level enlisted soldier with one stripe

Private First Class: PFC, Pay Grade E-3, enlisted soldier with one stripe, one rocker, and some experience

Specialist (or Specialist-4): SPC or SP/4, Pay Grade E-4, enlisted soldier with more experience

Corporal: CPL, Pay Grade E-4, junior non-commissioned officer or NCO, typically in charge of team of 3 to 4 lower-enlisted (E-1 to E-4) soldiers

Sergeant (buck sergeant): SGT, Pay Grade E-5, junior NCO, typically in charge of team of 3 to 4 lower-enlisted soldiers

Staff Sergeant: SSG, Pay Grade E-6, NCO typically in charge of squad comprised of 2 teams (6 to 8 soldiers)

Sergeant First Class: SFC, Pay Grade E-7, senior NCO typically in charge of running a platoon comprised of 4 squads (24 to 32 soldiers)

Master Sergeant: MSG, Pay Grade E-8, senior NCO typically on battalion staff or if at company-level, acting First Sergeant

First Sergeant: 1SG, Pay Grade E-9, senior NCO typically in charge of running a company comprised of 4 platoons (90 to 175 soldiers)

Sergeant Major: SGM, Pay Grade E-9, senior NCO typically in charge of running a battalion comprised of 4 to 6 companies

Command Sergeant Major: CSM, Pay Grade E-9, senior NCO typically in charge of running a Brigade comprised of several battalions, or a division comprised of several brigades

Officer Ranks

Second Lieutenant: 2LT, Pay Grade O-1, junior officer, typically in command of a platoon

First Lieutenant: 1LT, Pay Grade O-2, junior officer with some experience, typically in command of a platoon, or battalion staff

Captain: CPT, Pay Grade O-3, officer with more experience, typically in command of company or battalion staff

Major: MAJ, Pay Grade O-4, field grade officer, typically battalion staff or in command of a battalion

Lieutenant Colonel (light colonel): LTC, Pay Grade O-5, field grade officer typically in command of a battalion

Colonel (full-bird): COL, Pay Grade O-6, field grade officer typically in command of a brigade

Brigadier General: BG, Pay Grade O-7, general officer, typically assistant division commander, one-star insignia

Major General: MG, Pay Grade O-8, general officer typically in command of division, two-star insignia

Lieutenant General: LTG, Pay Grade O-9, general officer typically in command of a field force (several divisions), 3-star insignia

General: GEN, Pay Grade O-10, general officer in command of MACV (Military Assistance Command, Vietnam), that is to say, the entire war, 4-star insignia

Warrant Officer: WO1 to CW5, Pay Grades W-1 to W-5, officers with highly-specialized skills, but who do not command large units of soldiers as commissioned officers do (most Army helicopter pilots are Warrant Officers)

1ST AIR CAVALRY DIVISION STRUCTURE

1st Cavalry Division (Airmobile)
(not a complete listing of all assigned units)

1st Brigade

1st Battalion (Airborne), 8th Cavalry
2nd Battalion (Airborne), 8th Cavalry
1st Battalion, 12th Cavalry

2nd Brigade

1st Battalion, 5th Cavalry
2nd Battalion, 5th Cavalry
2nd Battalion, 12th Cavalry

3rd Brigade (Garry Owen Brigade)

1st Battalion, 7th Cavalry
2nd Battalion, 7th Cavalry
5th Battalion, 7th Cavalry

Division Artillery

2nd Battalion, 19th Artillery
2nd Battalion, 20th Artillery (Aerial Rocket Artillery)
1st Battalion, 21st Artillery
1st Battalion, 30th Artillery
1st Battalion, 77th Artillery

Support Command

8th Engineer Battalion
13th Signal Battalion
15th Medical Battalion
15th Supply & Service Battalion
15th Transportation Battalion
27th Maintenance Battalion
15th Administrative Company
15th Supply & Service Battalion Aerial Equipment Support Company (Airborne)
545th Military Police Company
191st Military Intelligence Detachment
371st Army Security Agency Company

11th Aviation Group (Airmobile)

227th Assault Helicopter Battalion
228th Assault Support Helicopter Battalion
229th Assault Helicopter Battalion
1st Squadron, 9th Cavalry

Made in the USA
Las Vegas, NV
16 June 2021